INDIGENOUS PROSPERITY

AND AMERICAN CONQUEST

INDIGENOUS PROSPERITY AND AMERICAN CONQUEST

Indian Women of the Ohio River Valley, 1690–1792

SUSAN SLEEPER-SMITH

Published by the OMOHUNDRO INSTITUTE OF EARLY AMERICAN HISTORY AND CULTURE, *Williamsburg, Virginia,* and the UNIVERSITY OF NORTH CAROLINA PRESS, Chapel Hill

The Omohundro Institute of Early American History and Culture
is sponsored by the College of William and Mary. On November 15, 1996,
the Institute adopted the present name in honor of a bequest from
Malvern H. Omohundro, Jr.

© 2018 The Omohundro Institute of Early American History and Culture
All rights reserved

Table 1 previously appeared in Susan Sleeper-Smith, *Indian Women and French Men: Rethinking Cultural Encounter in the Western Great Lakes* (Amherst, Mass., 2001), 126.

Cover illustration: Watercolor by George Winter, courtesy of Tippecanoe County Historical Association, Lafayette, IN

Library of Congress Cataloging-in-Publication Data
Names: Sleeper-Smith, Susan, author.
Title: Indigenous prosperity and American conquest : Indian women of the Ohio River Valley, 1690–1792 / Susan Sleeper-Smith.
Description: Williamsburg, Virginia : Omohundro Institute of Early American History and Culture ; Chapel Hill : University of North Carolina Press, [2018] | Includes bibliographical references and index.
Identifiers: LCCN 2017059439 | ISBN 9781469640587 (cloth : alk. paper) | ISBN 9781469659169 (pbk. : alk. paper) | ISBN 9781469640594 (ebook)
Subjects: LCSH: Indians of North America—Ohio River Valley—Government relations. | Indians, Treatment of—Ohio River Valley—History. | Indian women—Ohio River Valley—History—18th century. | Indian women—Ohio River Valley—History—17th century. | Kidnapping—Ohio River Valley—History. | United States—History—1783–1815. | United States—History—1783–1865.
Classification: LCC E78.O4 S58 2018 | DDC 977.004/97—dc23
LC record available at https://lccn.loc.gov/2017059439

The University of North Carolina Press has been a member of the Green Press Initiative since 2003.

To the women who raised me:

My grandmother, Hansine

My mother, Nellie

My sisters, Dorothy and Helene

ACKNOWLEDGMENTS

When I began research on my first book, I happened onto a little-known archive in West Lafayette, Indiana: the Tippecanoe County Historical Society. Housed there is a remarkable body of work by an English artist who arrived in Logansport, Indiana, in the 1830s. His interest in Indian people led him to portray many Miami and Potawatomi people who lived in nearby villages along the Wabash River. His sketches and paintings reveal a prosperous world where Indian people wore colorful calicoes, fine-woven woolens, and elegant silks, their clothing and bodies richly ornamented with trade silver. I remember briefly discussing George Winter's portraits at my first job interview; most scholars were surprised by Indian dress and questioned his depictions of Indian houses. Several scholars insisted that this was ceremonial dress, certainly not daily dress. Many historians still resist the notion of prosperous Indian communities in the Ohio River valley. Most scholarly literature remains embedded in the vision of a region peopled with colonist settlers whose hardy natures, perseverance, and farming skills rapidly replaced nomadic Indians. It is my hope that this volume will bring greater attention to a region that has been long neglected and shifts our focus to the Indians who first settled and farmed the Ohio River valley.

I have accumulated many scholarly debts in writing *Indigenous Prosperity and American Conquest,* and I am grateful to everyone who contributed time to reading and commenting on papers at seminars and workshops where I presented much of this material. Their invaluable observations have shaped this book and provided crucial feedback. Those errors that remain are entirely my fault. I know there are people that I will forget to mention, and I hope they forgive me.

I owe a debt of gratitude to Dan Usner and the late Drew Cayton for reading several versions of this manuscript. Their insightful commentary, careful reviews, and excellent suggestions transformed my extensive research into a comprehensive and coherent manuscript. I owe an even greater thank-you to the diligent and careful review of every statement and word in this manuscript by Paul Mapp and M. Kathryn Burdette. I could not have asked for more generous and rigorous editors. Their dedicated reading helped sharpen the focus of this manuscript. The Omohundro workshop on Early American Women provided a forum for my research, and Karin Wulf encouraged me to publish with the Institute. She has provided the opportunity to work with truly gifted editors, and the instances of elegant prose in this manuscript reflects Paul and Kathryn's meticulous and thoughtful editing. The long process of helping to make this monograph a reality also owes a great deal to my department chairman, Walter Hawthorne. He has been an inspiration and a much needed ally. Walter expends incredible effort in locating the funds and creating the circumstances that make it possible for our faculty to be productive scholars. His enthusiasm and support have made it a real pleasure to work at Michigan State University.

My work owes a great deal to the Newberry Library, which has been my primary research home. President David Spadafora has fostered a congenial scholarly atmosphere; he sets the tone for his staff and contributes to many scholarly seminars. I am thankful for the privilege of working with Danny Greene, formerly the Vice-President for Research, whose insight and diligence transformed the Fellows Seminars into a crucial discussion forum. Brad Hunt has both advanced the Newberry's intellectual life and enthusiastically supported my research. No one could ask for a more supportive staff than the directors of the D'Arcy McNickle Center, Scott Manning Stevens and Patricia Marroquin Norby. The working seminars in Indian Studies, Women and Gender History, and the Fellows Seminars have transformed the direction of my research. A special thank-you to the many scholars who have read and commented on my work: Leon Fink, Roy Fogelson, Brenda Child, Jeani O'Brien, Jeff Ostler, Cary Miller, Ella Tandy Shermer, Barbara Hanawalt, Cathleen Cahill, Kathleen Washburn, Juliana Barr, Colin Calloway, Frances Hagemann, Christopher McKee, Peter Nekola, Elliott Gorn, Liesl Olson, Margaret Newell, Toby Higbie, Mary Bane Campbell, Christina Stanciu, Margaret Meserve, Michael Schreffler, Phil Round, Jacob Lee, Lisa Freeman, Stephen Foster, and Rowena McClinton. The Newberry has a vast range of supportive staff, and both John Powell and Catherine Gass have patiently guided me through the ins and outs of the Newberry's rich collection of archival images.

I have had the good fortune of being generously supported by an NEH grant from the Newberry Library, by the Filson Historical Society, and by the Michigan State University College of Social Science. Glenn Crothers and the staff of the Filson provided invaluable direction in navigating the archives. There are many smaller archives with very limited personnel that have been tremendously supportive: the Tippecanoe Historical Society, the Porter County Historical Society, the Michigan State Archives, and the Northern

Indiana Historical Society. The Indiana Historical Society, Burton Historical Collections in Detroit, the Wisconsin Historical Society, Minnesota Historical Society, the Chicago Historical Society, Special Collections at the University of Kentucky, the Missouri Historical Collections, Historic New Orleans Collection, Library and Archives Canada in Ottawa, and the British Library have been crucial to my research. A very special thank-you to Special Collections at Michigan State University. I am always thankful when I have the opportunity to work with Peter I. Berg, who is our head of Special Collections. He has transformed a once small collection into an outstanding resource for scholars of early history, creating a strong collection that has drawn people to the library. In *Indigenous Prosperity and American Conquest,* there is an equally important archive that can be found in the campus landscape. We have an amazing Department of Plant Biology at Michigan State, where Professor Frank Telewski has created an amazing Native garden in the Beal Garden, an important inspiration for my work. Frank Telewski provided extensive information about an incredible range of natural plants harvested by Native people. I also want to thank the history faculty at Western Michigan University for allowing me to present my research on agrarian landscapes at their faculty seminar and to José António Brandão and Michael Nassaney for their insightful comments on my project.

We have had an amazingly supportive group of deans at Michigan State; their support of scholarship in American Indian Studies has made this research possible. Thank you, Karen Klomparens and my former college dean, Marietta Baba.

Above all, I want to thank several people who helped this book come to fruition. They have been there for me throughout this project. I would like to especially thank Nancy Shoemaker and Sarah Pearsall, who provided excellent commentary and ongoing support and encouragement. Jacob Jurss and Aaron Luedke were diligent and cheerful research assistants and library moles. Dawn Martin worked tirelessly to secure illustrations and permissions. Hers was an incredibly difficult task, since many of the illustrations in this text have disappeared from museum inventories in the United States, vanishing from public sight. Only Dawn, the best and most persistent archival detective, located those obscure images. Ellen White, my superb cartographer, has endured my endless revisions with incredible good humor. Jackie Hawthorne rescued me from the depths of photographic despair. The Director of the Cranbrook Science Center, Cameron Wood, enthusiastically shared the rich array of Indian artifacts in the Cranbrook collections with me, and his assistance has visually transformed this volume. He cheerfully supplied multiple images, offering me a rich menu of visual choices and encouraging me to look at, feel, and examine the variety of textiles in the collection. Finally, the Humanities and Art Research Program at Michigan State University provided funding to make possible the publication of the color plates in the cloth and digital editions.

No one has given me more support than my husband, Robert C. Smith. His love, unwavering support, ongoing encouragement, and unconditional, positive regard have helped make this book a reality.

CONTENTS

Acknowledgments / vii

List of Illustrations / xiii

Introduction / 1

1 The Agrarian Village World of the Ohio Valley Indians / 13

2 The Evolution of the Indian Fur Trade:
   From Green Bay to the Wabash River Valley / 67

3 Reopening the Western Trade / 105

4 Webs of Community:
   "The Gris and Turtle Came to Us and Breakfasted
   with Us as Usual" / 129

5 Picturing Prosperity / 162

6 Plunder and Massacre / 210

7 Capturing Indian Women / 243

8 Aftermath:
   "I Foresaw, That if I Parted with My Land, I Should
   Reduce the Women and Children to Weeping" / 285

   Index / 321

ILLUSTRATIONS

MAPS

1 "River of Ohio," 1766 / 18
2 Ohio River system / 21
3 "A Plan of the Rapids, in the River Ohio" / 23
4 *Carte de la découverte faite l'an 1673 dans l'Amerique septentrionale* / 78
5 French explorers and the early exploration of New France / 80
6 Great Black Swamp / 93
7 Early French forts, 1720 / 110
8 French forts, 1634–1763 / 111
9 The portage of the Maumee and Wabash Rivers / 115
10 *Carte de la Nouvelle France ou se voit le cours de Grandes Rivieres de S. Laurens et de Mississipi* / 116
11 Villages along the Wabash River valley / 135
12 Fort Stanwix treaty line / 212
13 Tribal locations north of the Ohio River valley, 1779–1794 / 225
14 Land divisions in Ohio, by approximate date of first settlement / 226
15 "View of the Maumee Towns Destroyed by General Harmar, October, 1790" / 238
16 Map of Harmar's defeat by the Indians at Fort Wayne, Indiana / 240

FIGURES

1 "Alligator Gar" / 25
2 "Oróntium aquaticum" (tuckahoe, or golden club) / 38
3 "Jack-in-the-Pulpit" *(Arisaema triphyllum)* / 40
4 *"Batschia canescens"* (puccoon) / 45
5 "Building of the *Griffin*" / 79
6 "Nan-Matches-Sin-A-Wa, 1839, Chief Godfroy's Home" / 145
7 "Pecan, a Native American Chief of the Miami Tribe" / 161
8 Linen shirt with pierced brooches / 177
9 Woman's blouse with silver brooches, Miami / 178
10 Woman's blouse, Potawatomi / 179
11 Shawnee coat / 180
12 Miami skirt / 182
13 Wearing blanket, Potawatomi culture / 183
14 Chippewa leggings / 184
15 Chippewa hood / 185
16 Miami moccasins / 186
17 Cutwork moccasins / 187
18 "Wewissa," or Wesaw / 189
19 "Ca-Ta-He-Cas-Sa — Black Hoof, Principal Chief of the Shawanoes" / 191
20 "Thayeadanega, Joseph Brant, the Mohawk Chief" / 192
21 Indian women on hilltop / 194
22 "Indian Burial, Kee-Waw-Nay Village" / 195
23 "Saga Yeath Qua Pieth Tow, King of the Maguas" / 196
24 Trade silver eagle brooch / 199

25 Pierced brooches / 200

26 Native American earrings / 201

27 "Tens-Kwau-Ta-Waw, the Prophet" / 204

28 "The Son, a Miami Chief" / 205

29 "Nicholas Vincent Tsawanhonhi, Principal Christian Chief, and Captain of the Huron Indians" / 206

30 Cherokee portrait / 207

31 "Mas-saw in Fulton County" / 208

32 *The Columbian Tragedy,* broadside / 278

TABLES

1 European trade goods in the western Great Lakes, 1715–1760 / 172

2 Trade silver shipped to George Morgan / 197

3 Trade silver values at Albany / 203

4 List of Indian prisoners, 1791 / 268

INDIGENOUS PROSPERITY

AND AMERICAN CONQUEST

INTRODUCTION

With the president's approval, Secretary of War Henry Knox ordered the Kentucky militia in 1791 "to proceed to the Wea, or Ouiatenon towns of Indians, there to assault the said towns, and the Indians therein, either by surprise, or otherwise, as the nature of the circumstances may admit — sparing all who may cease to resist, and capturing as many as possible, particularly women and children." By ordering the militia to demonstrate that Indians were "within our reach, and lying at our mercy," President Washington sought to "impress the Indians with a strong conviction of the power of the United States." General Charles C. Scott, who led the militia forces, was assured that his vigorous efforts "were not bound by any moral codes of army behavior," and he was encouraged to "inflict that degree of punishment that justice may require." Scott was "to combat the Indians according to your own modes of warfare," and he recruited "men of reputation in Indian affairs" — experienced fighters who had no sympathy for Indians.[1]

Knox reinforced the president's directives by authorizing the Kentucky Board of War to send a second or even a third militia force against the Indian villages. Knox called for "five hundred picked men, mounted on good horses," and the *Kentucky Gazette* urged its readers to support the call to arms; 750 men volunteered within two weeks, well over the president's quota. Scott's men marched across the Ohio River and north into Indian Country, where they enthusiastically leveled all the villages surrounding Ouiatenon, torched the adjacent cornfields, uprooted vegetable gardens, chopped down apple orchards, reduced every house to ash, killed the Indians who attempted to escape, and captured and forcibly transported fifty women and children to Fort Steuben at the Falls of the Ohio. A second militia assault, launched a short time later, demolished Kenapakomoko (Kenapacomaqua), the peace village of

---

1. H[enry] Knox, "Instructions to Brigadier General Charles Scott," Mar. 9, 1791, in United States Congress, *American State Papers: Documents, Legislative and Executive, of the Congress of the United States...*, 38 vols. (Washington, D.C., 1832), Class II, *Indian Affairs*, 2 vols., ed. Walter Lowrie et al., I, 129–130 (hereafter cited as *ASPIA*).

Little Turtle's brother, captured another fifty women and children, and incarcerated the victims at Fort Washington.[2]

Most of the militia were backcountry men from Virginia who had fought with George Rogers Clark when he captured Vincennes during the Revolutionary War. Many of them remained in the west, often squatting on lands in Virginia's Kentucky District and settling just south of the Wabash. They frequently supplemented their scarce resources by plundering prosperous Indian villages along the lower Wabash. The wealthy villages surrounding Ouiatenon were a desirable but unattainable goal; small forces of 50 or 60 were easily defeated by Indian warriors. Now, under Washington's orders, 750 of these men were recruited into the militia, provided with guns and ammunition, and paid to plunder the villages at Ouiatenon.

Charles C. Scott was motivated by an intense hatred for Indians. They had killed two of his sons, one while fishing and the other on the battlefield of Harmar's Defeat. Scott had served as an officer in the Revolutionary War; Washington had known him since Edward Braddock's ill-fated British campaign of 1755 against Fort Duquesne. In 1785, Scott moved from Virginia to the District of Kentucky, where he established a reputation as a rough-and-tumble Indian fighter. Unfortunately, he displayed the type of emotional volatility and lack of self-control that Washington abhorred. An early history of Kentucky described him as "a man of strong natural power, but somewhat illiterate and rough in his manners." The church in Woodford County, where Scott first settled, asked him to leave the neighborhood and accused him of "corrupting the morals of our youth." William McClelland, who lived in Scott's house for several months in 1796, described him as "one of the wickedest men I ever saw."[3]

---

2. Knox, "Instructions to Scott," Mar. 9, 1791, *ASPIA*, I, 129; *Kentucky Gazette* (Lexington), May 7, 1791. Levi Todd, grandfather of Mary Todd Lincoln, provided a list of the militia recruits to Scott on July 5, 1791 (Levi Todd letter, MS 104, folder 2011, Margaret I. King Library, Special Collections, University of Kentucky, Lexington). See also James Ripley Jacobs, *Tarnished Warrior: Major-General James Wilkinson* (New York, 1938), 112; Harvey Lewis Carter, *The Life and Times of Little Turtle: First Sagamore of the Wabash* (Urbana, Ill., 1987), 100; Temple Bodley, *History of Kentucky*, 4 vols., I, *Before the Louisiana Purchase in 1803* (Chicago, 1928), I, 465. The Miami were politically organized into civil chiefs and war chiefs. Civil chiefs held greater power and authority, and the villages that civil chiefs headed were often referred to as peace villages. Civil chiefs did not join war parties; they were responsible for administration of the villages and central to peace negotiations. See Stewart Rafert, *The Miami Indians of Indiana: A Persistent People, 1654–1994* (Indianapolis, 1996), 21.

3. Charles Scott was born in Cumberland County, Virginia, in 1740. He settled in Woodford County, on the Kentucky River, and built his cabin and a fort at what was later known as Scott's Landing, not far from Mortonsville. He was governor of Kentucky from 1808

Scott depended on both the raw emotionalism of Indian hating and the promise of plunder as incentives for militia enlistments. His strategy was a far cry from the highly rational General Washington, who refused to allow his troops to engage in looting and believed "discipline is the soul of an army." As a young Virginia colonel, Washington had scorned the unruly backcountry militia; they were frequent deserters whom Washington clapped in irons, imprisoned in dark rooms, and liberally flogged. When these harsh measures proved less than successful, Washington erected a gibbet forty feet high, from which he hanged those who attempted to escape his control. Washington was likewise appalled by the backcountry militia's lack of self-control and unbridled emotionalism. Even the leveling spirit of the rebellious colonists had left Washington railing against the turbulent democratic ideals that had spread throughout New England; but, in the Ohio Valley, Washington would rely on the types of men he despised.[4]

What led George Washington to order a militia, recruited from Kentucky's disorderly poorer classes and led by an equally abhorrent militia general, to invade, ransack, and raze prosperous villages along the Wabash? To capture women and children and imprison them in a military fort for nearly a year? Washington's order to invade the Wabash Indian villages and kidnap Indian women has long escaped significant historical attention, but it merits consideration as an example of the Early Republic's horrific violence against Indigenous people.

One explanation historians have suggested for Washington's scorched-earth tactics is that he was retaliating against Indians for the defeat of the U.S. Army under Josiah Harmar in the fall of 1790. But this was a minor battle, and Washington had suffered far more humiliating losses during the Revolutionary War. He rarely reacted so emotionally to small setbacks, this one trivial enough that it has often been ignored by scholars.

What frustrated Washington was his ongoing failure to induce Indians

---

to 1812 and died in 1820. It is unclear whether his wife moved with him or whether she remained in Virginia. See Lindsey Apple, Frederick A. Johnston, and Ann Bolton Bevins, eds., *Scott County, Kentucky: A History* (Georgetown, Ky., 1993), 45; W[illia]m E. Railey, *History of Woodford County* (1938; rpt. Baltimore, 1975), 8, 110–111, 276–277; Jacobs, *Tarnished Warrior*, 71–73; J. W. Whickcar [Whicker], "General Charles Scott and His March to Ouiatenon," *Indiana Magazine of History*, XXI (1925), 98; Thomas Marshall Green, *The Spanish Conspiracy: A Review of Early Spanish Movements in the South-West* (Cincinnati, Oh., 1891), 134.

4. John C. Fitzpatrick, *George Washington Himself: A Common-Sense Biography Written from His Manuscripts* (Indianapolis, 1933), 102, quoted in David Hackett Fischer, *Washington's Crossing* (Oxford, 2004), 15.

north of the Ohio to cede their lands. The newly formed federal government had proposed to finance the national debt by selling Indian lands in the trans-Appalachian west. Indians insisted that the Ohio was the dividing line between the United States and Indian Country. The newly drafted constitution also stipulated that Indian lands be secured through treaty negotiations and that land cessions were voluntary, not forced. Washington had sought to pacify the Indians by abandoning the doctrine of discovery and reimbursing them for their lands. But they continued to refuse to come to the treaty table, condemned further land cessions north of the Ohio, and formed the first northwestern Indian confederacy to oppose intrusion on their homelands. When threatened by Harmar's forces, they vanquished the general. Washington had to find other means to undercut Indian resistance.

Those means involved razing villages, destroying the crops, and taking hostage the women and children the warriors were trying to protect. Under the guise of retaliation for Harmar's Defeat, Washington ordered the Kentucky militia to cut a wide swath of terror though agrarian communities clustered along the Wabash. Those villages, primarily populated by women, served as the breadbasket for Indian forces. Washington believed that the destruction of these communities and the kidnapping of their women and children would force those warriors to return to their villages and abandon their resistance to Washington's forces. He had done it successfully to the Seneca during the Revolutionary War, and he planned to do it again.

The violence of kidnapping can obscure the motives behind it; but Washington's use of it as a tactic suggests that he was conscious of the role that women played in creating and maintaining agrarian village life in this region. Washington's exploratory trips along the Ohio in the 1760s, as a land speculator, had given him an understanding of this agrarian village landscape. So precise was his knowledge that he was able to instruct the Kentucky militia on which villages along the Wabash to attack. Indian women had created a village world where cultivating the rich soil and harvesting wetlands plants allowed them to feed generously their highly populated villages and supply the warriors who opposed U.S. Army intrusion.

Washington's awareness of Indian women's agricultural role set him apart from the scholars who came after him. Many early historians of the Ohio River valley, exhibiting tendencies rooted in early modern prejudices and evident in classic sources, disregarded the agricultural activities of Indian women. Often, Indian women's agrarian work was dismissed as horticulture, which implied that they tended small plots of land adjacent to their homes. But along the tributary rivers of the Ohio, Indian women created fields that stretched for miles along the river bottoms. At Ouiatenon, their fields easily fed the five to ten thousand residents who lived in the adjacent villages. As early as 1718, women's cornfields stretched so far along the Wabash that Jacques-Charles de Sabrevois, an especially observant French commandant at Detroit, traveled on horseback for more than an hour before finally reaching the end of their fields. His journey could have equated with three thousand to five thousand acres of corn. Sabrevois's praise of Indian women's work was effusive, and he considered their "very industrious" nature as crucial in transforming the Wabash landscape into an agrarian Eden. Almost seventy years later, Anthony Wayne described leveling cornfields along the nearby Auglaize and Maumee Rivers as equally extensive and claimed that he had never seen "such immense fields of corn in any part of America from Canada to Florida." A more attentive reading of sources like Sabrevois, Wayne, and others — one sensitive to gendered roles and expectations — enables us to see the magnitude of Indian women's agricultural achievement.[5]

This agrarian world was threatened by the westward push of the new republic. When Washington ordered the Kentucky militia to attack Ouiatenon, he was targeting the women who had shaped this Indigenous landscape, securing these fertile Indian lands for American farmers, and, not coincidentally, profiting from his own land speculation. It was the villages along the Ohio's northern tributary rivers that would lead the sustained resistance to American intrusion. American conquest and Washington's Indian Wars in the 1790s destroyed the evidence of this prosperous Indian Country in the Ohio River valley, making it difficult for scholars to appreciate the world that was lost.

Fortunately, recent work in environmental history allows us to reimagine this landscape and to see what two centuries of environmental degradation has obscured: the Ohio River valley was a kind of paradise. It is not surprising that French writers referred to the Ohio as "la belle rivière." The rivers north of the Ohio served as the drainage basin for the Great Lakes. Melting snows carried rich soils south down the riverways, replenished cornfields, and sustained a wide-ranging network of wetlands. Since the Ohio River flooded unpredictably following winter snow melts, Indian villages were located along the tributary rivers, where a complex ecosystem encouraged settlement in dis-

---

5. [Jacques-Charles de Sabrevois de Bleury], "1718: Memoir on the Savages of Canada as Far as the Mississippi River, Describing Their Customs and Trade," in Reuben Gold Thwaites, ed., *The French Regime in Wisconsin,* part 1, *1634–1727,* State Historical Society of Wisconsin, *Collections,* XVI (Madison, Wis., 1902), 363–376; "Copy of a Letter from Major General Wayne to the Secretary of War," Aug. 14, 1794, *ASPIA,* I, 490.

tinctive landscape niches. Indian women developed a system to preserve the land's natural resources. In the extensive fields that lined the river bottoms, Indian women cultivated corn, beans, and squash; near the nexus of streams, they planted apple orchards; from adjacent wetlands, they harvested nutritious plants; and in the nearby forests, they gathered fruits and nuts. This research primarily focuses on the fertile crescent of agrarian villages located along the banks of the Wabash River, which extended across to the Maumee, Miami, and Sandusky River valleys. In each of the numerous villages lining the river banks, women's labor was complemented by male hunters. Men provided fresh meat from the nearby forests and caught or trapped fish from adjacent rivers and ponds, contributing the animal protein that was essential to healthy diets. In the hands of Indian women, the land produced extensive and almost unlimited food resources. Even small, isolated patches produced sufficient food to sustain large, well-fed villages. Women's work additionally fostered a sedentary lifestyle; Indians in the Ohio River valley were far from nomadic.

The failure to comprehend the extent of women's involvement in agriculture has masked the role that women played both in feeding heavily populated villages and in creating a prosperous Indian world that resisted U.S. intrusion. Descriptions of the lushness and fertility of the trans-Appalachian landscape have often been seen as ploys to lure Europeans across the Atlantic, but, in fact, much of the Ohio River valley landscape was quite verdant. Firmly established women's history, supplemented by an emerging environmental history, has led to new ways of understanding how Indian women both shaped and enriched the lands surrounding their villages.

This highly productive agrarian society was further enhanced by women's involvement in an Atlantic-based fur trade. North of the Ohio, extensive wetlands, including the Great Black Swamp, provided a rich source of furs. These areas supplied vast quantities of small peltry, which trimmed the robes of civil and religious officials throughout Europe. The late-seventeenth-century French ban on the western trade enabled Indians to take control of the Ohio River valley fur trade. Indian women processed peltry, and an increase in the number of matrifocal households enhanced female control over the exchange process. Women's influence transformed the fur trade into the cloth trade; Indian women secured well over half of all European trade goods shipped into the region. They fashioned European cloth into new and elaborate clothing styles, passing down from one generation to the next the skills required to cut, sew, embroider, and embellish clothing with beads, porcupine quills, and silk ribbons. Dress became the spectacular evidence of a prosperous Indian world. Prized clothing emerged as social capital and was instrumental in reinforcing the kinship networks that affirmed the alliances linking the agrarian villages of the Ohio River valley.[6]

Archaeological work allows us to go beyond the written sources to demonstrate the physical transformation of this world, where Indian women altered the agrarian as well as the architectural landscape. They replaced longhouses and bark cabins with log cabins. Inside women's houses was extensive evidence of European trade goods—iron pots and utensils, pewterware, silver spoons, and china teapots. Even in patrilineal societies, Indian women owned the houses and their contents. Kethtippecanuck, close to Ouiatenon, was physically destroyed by Scott's forces in 1791, but early-twenty-first-century excavations reveal startling evidence that allows us to mentally reconstruct a village where Spanish, French, and British traders lived side by side with Indians in more than one hundred well-made *poteaux-en-terre* houses and log cabins. The unusually large number of commingled artifacts confirms the joint residency patterns of European and Native families in a village archaeologists have described as a "thriving, substantial, multiethnic settlement with agricultural fields, livestock at pasture, and a number and variety of permanent structures."[7]

While adapting to an ever-changing world, Indian women incorporated newcomers into village life. French, English, and Spanish fur traders assimilated into the villages and contributed to this thriving Indigenous economy. Indians approached involvement in the fur trade from a position of strength: they resisted the imperial intrusion of both the French and English, scarcely supporting the French during the Seven Years' War and using Pontiac's Rebellion to teach the English a bitter lesson about who controlled Indian lands. For almost one hundred years, Indians lived in a world where foreigners adjusted to their norms, where Frenchmen and Englishmen found it wise to be more like Indians rather than be suspiciously regarded as outsiders. Social borders were porous, and Indians absorbed and welcomed fur traders, sharing their lands and resources. The Miami proved especially adept at establishing alliances with foreigners and using trade to enhance their political power. Having initially dominated lands west of the Miami River and along the Wabash, the Miami attracted refugee Indians and established a heterogeneous village land-

---

6. See Raymond Smith, "The Matrifocal Family," in Jack Goody, ed., *The Character of Kinship* (New York, 1973), 124–125. See also Karen Fog Olwig, "Women, 'Matrifocality,' and Systems of Exchange: An Ethnohistorical Study of the Afro-American Family on St. John, Danish West Indies," *Ethnohistory*, XXVIII (1981), 59–78.

7. Michael Strezewski et al., *Report of the 2006 Archaeological Investigations at Kethtippecanunk (12–T–59), Tippecanoe County, Indiana* (Fort Wayne, Ind., 2007), 133.

scape. Small groups, as well as large nations like the Shawnee and Delaware, lived adjacent to, as well as in, the Miami villages.

The Ohio River valley emerged as a prosperous, Indian-controlled land in the eighteenth century, with the peltry harvest often surpassing that of territories to the north. The valley was simultaneously a regional Indian world with multidirectional waves of Indian people continually moving through and often settling in it. In this zone of constant motion, agrarian villages created by women brought stability. A rich tapestry of change was woven into the fabric of Indian society before European arrival, creating an adaptable, accommodating world. For too long, the image characterizing the Ohio River valley has been the larger-than-life model of the Indian warrior and the pioneer settler. The "warrior" remains a durable stereotype of Indians, whereas incoming Americans are viewed as the settlers who transformed the forests into farmlands and brought peace and stability to the Ohio River valley. But the valley was an established agrarian landscape long before Anglo-American settler colonists arrived in the early nineteenth century and destroyed the crucial evidence of Indian women's agricultural activities. In an American world, farming was a male occupation, and the agrarian skills of Indian women proved invisible to incoming farmers, with generations of U.S. historians recounting this saga of western expansion.

This book explores the Indigenous settlement process in the Ohio River valley in two major sections. The first explores the rise of an Indian agricultural world, and the second explores the disruption of that prosperous Indian world. The initial chapters explore the environmental factors that influenced the river valley's evolution into an agrarian region, examine the organization and structure of village communities, and show how women constructed kin networks of social relations that transformed this village world into an interrelated trading network. Despite an increasingly diverse population, Indians created a shared landscape that was drawn together by a similarity in cultural practices: most inhabitants were Algonquian-speaking and followed a similar ritual calendar. Exchange patterns in the fur trade emerged as the glue of social formation and incorporated Europeans into an Indian world. The second set of chapters focuses on the attempt by the United States government to create mayhem in the villages of this river valley and to interrupt its ability to function as a coherent region. Rather than build on existing societal formations and recognize the legitimacy of Indian claims to lands north of the Ohio, the nation's first leaders, especially George Washington, deliberately disrupted the social networks and shared attitudes that were linked to the economic structure of this area. What had taken more than a hundred years to create was destroyed, and within a generation, most Indians were removed from the river valley.

The Ohio River valley has generally been viewed as a socially disordered landscape from the late seventeenth century to the early nineteenth century. Blame has focused on the seventeenth-century fur trade wars, when, historians contend, Iroquois onslaughts pushed Algonquian-speaking peoples from the Ohio River valley and forced them to flee to refugee villages along the western shore of Lake Michigan. When the wars ended with the Great Peace of Montreal in 1701, Algonquians returned to their homelands and were then inundated by refugee Indians fleeing settler appropriation of the Atlantic coastal region. Displaced Delaware, Seneca, Cherokee, and Shawnee flooded in and were believed to incite intermittent warfare and an ongoing contestation over land. French, British, and colonial traders from backcountry Virginia and Pennsylvania competed for control over the region before the Seven Years' War. Historians describe a fur trade fraught with conflict and write of how, in the aftermath of the American Revolution, Indians were driven off their homelands, which were claimed as part of an internal United States empire.[8]

Environmental history provides new options for reevaluating the purportedly chaotic nature of this region. In particular, a close look at the lands of the river valley, with their multiplicity of ecological niches, shows that Indians were capable of accommodating an expansive, mixed population. To see how environmental history is enabling us to take our arguments forward, it may be useful to step historiographically back. When Richard White wrote *The Middle Ground,* he suggested that patterns of intermittent warfare fashioned a unique blending of new peoples in the Great Lakes region. White's revisionist perspective argued for a social landscape that intertwined the lives of Indians, fur traders, habitants, and the military. This type of human blending was especially descriptive of Indians in the Ohio River valley, with its diverse, interethnic villages. Indian homelands were not territorially distinct, because this rich environment made possible a landscape of highly populated villages with porous borders, inhabited by diverse people. At places like Ouiatenon, Miamitown, and the Glaize along the Upper Maumee, there were Miami, Delaware, Shawnee, Wea, Kickapoo, Seneca, Mascouten, and multiple smaller groups living side by side. Fertile landscape niches along the Ohio's tributary rivers sustained a large, diverse population and encouraged compromise, rather than warfare, to define daily interactions.

8. Eric Hinderaker, *Elusive Empires: Constructing Colonialism in the Ohio Valley, 1673–1800* (New York, 1997).

An alternative vision of the Great Lakes sees it, not as a middle ground, but as an Indigenous-dominated landscape where the French were a minor political force, and northern Indian groups, like the Odawa, were a formidable but elusive empire. Farther south, the Illinois Confederacy dominated the nexus of lands adjoining the Mississippi and Missouri, and historians writing of the Arkansas River valley sometimes speak of a "native ground" rather than a middle ground.[9]

The Ohio River valley evolved into an integrated village world without a paramount Indian empire or people. In nineteenth-century treaty negotiations with the United States, the Miami claimed sovereignty over the vast expanse of western lands bordering the Wabash and Miami River valleys. Close study suggests that the Miami world was inclusive and readily incorporated strangers and newcomers, which secured and enhanced Miami authority and power. Although the Ohio River valley was linked by trade to various northern villages in the Great Lakes, the region's primary trading center was Detroit, with additional furs traded at Albany or shipped south to New Orleans. Environmentally different from the lands of the northern Great Lakes, the Ohio River valley had a longer growing season, where sedentary, agrarian villages secured peltry from the Black Swamp as well as from the numerous wetlands that bordered the villages. The research underlying this book offers a counter to the view of an Indigenous world torn asunder by ongoing eighteenth-century warfare. The fur trade created a prosperous Indian world and encouraged diverse people to band together and form the first Northwestern Indian confederacy that resisted intrusion on their lands. Together, they twice defeated the U.S. Army, first led by Josiah Harmar, then by Arthur St. Clair. The power of that confederacy led President Washington to fear that the region would remain in Indian hands.[10]

Indigenous people along the Ohio River created a functioning society that responded to their needs and was shaped by their cultural traditions. Indians engaged in rational and deliberate social action before contact with Europeans; when the fur trade brought about European interaction and the economic structure of the river valley changed, it was shaped by Indigenous cultural traditions. Involvement in the fur trade led to prosperity rather than

---

9. Michael McDonnell, *Masters of Empire: Great Lakes Indians and the Making of America* (New York, 2015); Kathleen DuVal, *The Native Ground: Indians and Colonists in the Heart of the Continent* (Philadelphia, 2006).

10. Sami Lakomäki, "'Our Line': The Shawnees, the United States, and Competing Borders on the Great Lakes 'Borderlands,' 1795–1832," *Journal of the Early Republic*, XXXIV (2014), 597–624.

decline. People responded to economic change within established social contexts, and, when necessary, they evolved new forms of social organization. This complex landscape—created in great part by Indian women—was not determined by outsiders.

A viable fur trade depended on villages that were part of a larger, stable social system. That is, the people themselves had to share attitudes about an exchange process, one that required devoting sufficient hours to hunting and processing furs to create a sufficient supply for trading. In great part, this work suggests that it was the development of a surplus food supply coupled with demographically stable villages that made it possible to link the fur-trade economy of the Ohio River valley to the market-based economy of the Atlantic world.

The sustainability of this village world was severely threatened in the 1780s and 1790s, when the terrorizing and plundering of Indian villages disrupted agrarianism and, subsequently, the fur trade. The successive waves of violence that spread over the Ohio River valley were the handiwork of the Kentucky militia, encouraged by a president who provided the funding, resources, and public credibility to wage war on Indians. Federal support for frontier violence ultimately destroyed the evidence of Indian women's extensive agrarian behavior: entire Indian villages were plundered and destroyed, cornfields and homes burned. This destruction drove Indians off their lands, lined the pockets of land speculators, and through public land sales financed the national debt. Engrossing, surveying, and selling Indian lands became a federal project, with eager American participants, that established the pathway for westward expansion.

Washington's imprisonment of Indian women and children at Fort Washington served as a rallying cry for Indian resistance. Little Turtle and Blue Jacket fueled Indian fears about U.S. intrusion throughout the Great Lakes and urged their allies to fight as part of the Northwest Confederation. The confederacy then dealt Arthur St. Clair's forces one of the worst defeats that the U.S. Army would ever face.[11]

St. Clair's failure endangered Washington's project of westward expansion, and the success of Indian resistance gave the president a reason to overcome public resistance against the creation of a large standing army (the army numbered fewer than seven hundred soldiers following the Revolutionary War). Washington called on Congress to fund a dramatically expanded army that

---

11. Colin G. Calloway, *The Victory with No Name: The Native American Defeat of the First American Army* (New York, 2016), 127–128; Wiley Sword, *President Washington's Indian War: The Struggle for the Old Northwest, 1790–1795* (Norman, Okla., 1985), 195.

could punish Indians and force them off their lands. Washington's Army of the Empire in the Ohio River valley led to creation of the Army of the West in the trans-Mississippi. Rather than allow Indians and settlers to work out their differences in frontier areas, the army intervened and removed Indians from the contest. Washington's reliance on the army in the Ohio River valley set a precedent: the army became an extension of executive authority and determined that Indians and whites would not live together.[12]

Washington's forces did not face an Indian world on the precipice of demise but sought to conquer a prosperous Indian world where the inhabitants were well fed and unwilling to cede their lands, and their sustained interaction in the fur trade encouraged them to secure support from the British to fund their resistance efforts. America's democratic experiment rested on westward expansion into this Indian world. The appropriation of Indian lands like those of the Ohio River valley became the foundation for a white settler polity stretching from the Atlantic to the Pacific. By restoring the Indians of the Ohio River valley to their proper role in that history, we can see that Indians were more than minor obstacles to western expansion. They constituted a viable alternative to it—an alternative lost for centuries under the ashes of burnt crops, charred villages, and the masculine monuments of a destiny made manifest only by amnesia and self-interest.

12. Patrick Griffin, "Reconsidering the Ideological Origins of Indian Removal: The Case of the Big Bottom 'Massacre,'" in Andrew R. L. Cayton and Stuart D. Hobbs, eds., *The Center of a Great Empire: The Ohio Country in the Early Republic* (Athens, Oh., 2005), 11–35. Indian resistance in the Ohio River valley influenced the shape of early federal governance, as St. Clair's defeat transformed Indians into significant actors in the history of the Early Republic. Both the legislative and executive branches were shaped by the events that unfolded in the Ohio River valley. Congress questioned Washington's leadership, and the first congressional investigation committee was formed. The president, displeased by the committee's request for massive amounts of correspondence, established executive privilege as a justifiable reason for withholding materials.

1

THE AGRARIAN VILLAGE WORLD
OF THE OHIO VALLEY INDIANS

The miamis are Sixty leagues from Lake Esrié. They number 400 men.... They have an abundance of women. They are very industrious, and raise a Kind of indian corn which is unlike that of our tribes at Destroit. Their corn Is white, of the Same size as the other, with much finer husks and much whiter flour.... From this Village of the miamis there is a portage of three Leagues to a very Narrow little River and that river, after following it 20 Leagues, falls into the oyo River, or beautiful River; the latter empties into the ouabache, another fine river.... It is on this ouabache River that the ouyatanons are Settled.... They have more than two Leagues of fields, where they raise Their Indian corn, pumpkins, and melons; and from that Elevation one sees nothing but prairies, stretching farther than the eye can reach, and abounding in buffalo.
—Jacques-Charles de Sabrevois de Bleury

The agrarian nature of the Ohio River valley was obvious to French observers by the early eighteenth century. Jacques-Charles de Sabrevois, commandant at Detroit from 1715 to 1717, described Miami women as "very industrious." He also praised Indian women's agricultural transformation of Grand Island, one of four islands at the entrance to Detroit. They had planted an apple orchard that covered almost the entire seven leagues of the island: "Those who have seen The apples on the ground say that they lie more than a half a foot thick." The apples were "as large as small sweet apples [*pommes d'api,* 'bee-apples']."[1]

---

1. [Jacques-Charles de Sabrevois de Bleury], "1718: Memoir on the Savages of Canada as Far as the Mississippi River, Describing Their Customs and Their Trade," in Reuben Gold Thwaites, ed., *The French Regime in Wisconsin,* part 1, *1634–1727,* State Historical Society of Wisconsin, *Collections,* XVI (Madison, Wis., 1902), 363–376, esp. 375–376. Sabrevois probably arrived in New France in 1685 and was appointed commandant at Detroit in 1712.

The Grand Island orchard was probably seeded by women from the Huron refugee villages along Lake Erie's shoreline. In 1675 and 1676, Jesuit father Henry Nouvel, a missionary priest at Michilimackinac, traveled south to visit the Lake Erie Huron, or Wendat, who were later known as the Wyandot. Like the Huron at his St. Ignace mission, the Wendat had been driven out of Georgian Bay by the Iroquois. The refugee Huron who had relocated to Lake Erie encountered a mild climate similar to their homeland and planted apple trees, perhaps with seeds brought from Huronia. Nouvel and his Jesuit companion journeyed a short distance from Lake Erie and described the "fine apple trees" that lined the riverways. These lands had "great Tracts covered with wild apple-trees," which offered Indians "ample" supplies of fresh fruit. The trees were planted at the confluence of rivers and streams, where the soil was fertile and the water supply plentiful. Allowed to grow wild, the trees flourished and produced a reliable food source in the late summer and fall. The Jesuits believed that the Wendat introduced apple cultivation into the region, but other Indian villages were just as likely to plant fruit trees, since the Ohio was a major east-west Native trade route where pits from fruit trees were frequently exchanged. When Jesuits finally ventured along the Ohio River in the mid-eighteenth century, apple and peach trees were a common feature of the landscape.[2]

Vaudreuil recalled him from the post; he returned to France, then took over in 1720 as commandant at Fort Chambly. He died in Montreal on January 19, 1727. See Nive Voisine, "Sabrevois, Jacques-Charles De," *Dictionary of Canadian Biography,* II, University of Toronto/Université Laval, 2003–, http://www.biographi.ca/en/bio/sabrevois_jacques_charles_de_2E.html. Sabrevois was also referred to as Jacques-Charles de Sabrevois de Bleury in early French documents, perhaps to distinguish him from his son Jacques-Charles (see [Sabrevois], "1718," in Thwaites, ed., *French Regime in Wisconsin,* part 1, 366).

2. Henry Nouvel, "Journal of the Last Winter Mission of Father Henry Nouvel, Superior of the Missions of the Outawacs," in Reuben Gold Thwaites, ed., *Jesuit Relations and Allied Documents: Travels and Explorations of the Jesuit Missionaries in New France, 1610–1791,* 73 vols. (Cleveland, 1896–1901), LX, 217, 221 (hereafter cited as *JR*). Helen Hornbeck Tanner details the scattering of Huron refugees and contends that some took shelter among the neighboring Tionontati, Neutral, and Erie living south of Lake Erie. See Tanner, ed., *Atlas of Great Lakes Indian History* (Norman, Okla., 1987), 30–34; Terry G. Jordan and Matti Kaups, *The American Backwoods Frontier: An Ethnic and Ecological Interpretation* (Baltimore, 1989). For early settlements along the Lake Erie shoreline, see also David S. Brose, "Late Prehistory of the Upper Great Lakes Area," in Bruce G. Trigger, ed., *Handbook of North American Indians,* XV, *Northeast* (Washington, D.C., 1978), 569–582. The Jesuits believed that it was refugee Huron who first introduced apple cultivation into this region, although other Indian villages were just as likely to plant fruit trees. The Jesuits never established a mission site in the Ohio River valley, and occasional missionary exploits left most

Indian women planted and cultivated European fruit trees before the first Europeans set foot on Ohio Valley lands. Florida Indians secured peach pits from sixteenth-century Spanish priests and traded them to northern villages. Lenni-Lenape, or Delaware, women planted the first peach trees in the Delaware region; early Swedish travelers commented on the wild peaches they found growing in abundance along the Delaware River valley. Peach pits were then traded along the Ohio River, where, like apple trees, they grew profusely in this region. Because peaches, unlike apples, take several years before they produce a harvest, these orchards required a sedentary lifestyle and horticultural expertise, suggesting that precontact arboriculture was practiced, perhaps using nut trees and persimmons. Indigenous fruits, such as persimmons and grapes, when located at the edges of fields and fallow lands, were likely managed to increase harvests. Following contact, apple trees located in villages were probably grafted and pruned to produce consistently reliable fruit. Eventually, the pits from these trees were traded west to the Mississippi and into the Great Lakes. This established practice moved fruit pits and seeds lengthy distances along Indigenous trade networks. Indians traded pits from trees indigenous to the Ohio River valley region, such as plum trees, and spread fruit cultivation well beyond its natural range.³

Indian women's agrarian skills went far beyond the cultivation of corn, the crop most associated with them. In the fertile Ohio River valley, Indian women's labor was extensive and diverse. By the time of French contact, Indigenous women cultivated cornfields that stretched for miles along the riverways, and they later incorporated familiar European crops, such as wheat. They also raised domesticated animals before the arrival of the French. In

---

missionary priests relatively unfamiliar with the region. By the mid-eighteenth century, apple and peach trees were a common landscape feature of the Ohio region, suggesting that they came from multiple sources, not just the Huron. See William Kerrigan, "Apples on the Border: Orchards and the Contest for the Great Lakes," *Michigan Historical Review,* XXXIV (2008), 32–33.

3. Everett E. Edwards, *Agriculture of the American Indians: A Classified List of Annotated Historical References with an Introduction* (Washington, D.C., 1933); R. Douglas Hurt, *Indian Agriculture in America: Prehistory to the Present* (Lawrence, Kans., 1987), 41; Carl Ortwin Sauer, *Sixteenth Century North America: The Land and the People as Seen by the Europeans* (Berkeley, Calif., 1971), 225, 289; Stanley Pargellis, ed., "An Account of the Indians in Virginia," *William and Mary Quarterly,* XVI (1959), 230; Paul D. Welch and C. Margaret Scarry, "Status-Related Variation in Foodways in the Moundville Chiefdom," *American Antiquity,* LX (1995), 397–419; Bruce G. Trigger, *The Huron Farmers of the North* (New York, 1969), 27–28. Michael Pollan contends that "anyone who wants edible apples plants grafted trees." Apples grown from seed often produce bitter, inedible apples (Pollan, *The Botany of Desire: A Plant's Eye-View of the World* [New York, 2001], 9).

many Indian villages, especially those in the lower Mississippi Valley, Indian women acquired hogs, chickens, and European fruit trees so early that explorers often reported them as indigenous. Indian women also secured pigs while men bred the small-hoofed horses that carried trade goods along the Ohio's tributary river pathways.

In short, connected to and influenced by developments across eastern North America, an array of Indian women's agrarian activities transformed the Ohio River valley. Because most seventeenth-century French and British accounts focus on the two nations that controlled the river's western and eastern gateways — the Illinois and the Iroquois — knowledge about this middle section of the almost 1,000-mile-long river remained minimal. The writings of Jacques-Charles de Sabrevois provided an extensive description of the area sometime between 1714 and 1718. His comprehensive overview of the Ohio River valley was sent to Versailles in the belief that France would establish firm control over the region and move French habitants into it. His vivid description of the river valley's fertility provides an environmental parallel to the eastern coastal region as well as a remarkable parallel to women's labors across other temperate zones with fertile soils.[4]

ENVIRONMENTAL LANDSCAPE OF THE OHIO RIVER VALLEY

In order for us to appreciate fully Sabrevois's particular account of the Ohio Valley and its human geography during the early eighteenth century, a general description drawn from a range of sources, scholars, and natural histories will prove helpful in understanding the environmental nature of this region. The Ohio River extends west across the continent and carries the largest volume of water of any of the Mississippi's tributaries. The massive drainage area of the Ohio extends from the Allegheny River west to the Father of

---

4. In 1680, René-Robert Cavelier, sieur de La Salle, and Henri de Tonti (aka Tonty), constructed the first fort on the east bank of the Illinois River and named it Fort Crèvecoeur. Eleven years later, in 1691, another fort was built by de Tonti and his cousin François Dauphin de la Forêst, which they called Fort St. Louis II. It was commonly referred to as Fort Pimiteoui. Although La Salle claimed that he navigated the Ohio in the 1670s, he went no farther east than the Wabash River and the Kankakee swamp. La Salle focused on building French forts in present-day Michigan, at the mouth of the Miami River (later the St. Joseph River) and at Starved Rock in Illinois Country. La Salle's primary interest was finding a warm-water port where furs could be shipped across the Atlantic to France. See Michael McCafferty, *Native American Place-Names of Indiana* (Urbana, Ill., 2008), 40–41; Sami Lakomäki, *Gathering Together: The Shawnee People through Diaspora and Nationhood, 1600–1970* (New Haven, Conn., 2014).

Waters, covers 189,422 square miles, and has almost two dozen major intersecting tributaries. Not surprisingly, diverse landscapes bordered each of these tributary rivers. From where the Little Miami intersects the Ohio to where the Allegheny intersects the Monongahela, at Fort Pitt, was a hilly region with steep ravines, forestlands, and oak openings. South along the Cumberland and Kentucky River valleys were expansive grasslands. The Appalachian foothills, with their red and white oak forests, dominated the eastern landscape of the Ohio. Under the canopies of ancient oaks that were more than six feet in diameter and fifty to sixty feet high were sugar maple, hickory, black walnut, sycamore, hemlock, cedar, beech, and buckeye trees. Smaller trees blanketed the steep hills and narrow ravines of the eastern Ohio; beech, maple, oak, ash, hickory, tulip, poplar, locust, cedar, sassafras, elm, chestnut, cottonwood, buckeye, and juniper lined the shores of the river. Dogwood, redbud, and magnolia bloomed profusely in the spring.[5]

Indeed, the Ohio River valley was distinguished by the some of the world's finest broadleaf forests. Robert Ridgway, an early-nineteenth-century naturalist who had traveled widely in South America, turned his attention to the forests of the lower Wabash River valley. He described "an exceedingly heavy virgin forest, some of the heaviest hardwood forest I have ever seen as I have twice visited the Tropics (Central America) — covering almost the entire floodplain on the Indian side." He measured sycamores that were twenty-five to thirty feet in circumference, with heights of 160 to almost 200 feet, and tulip trees 25 feet in girth, 91 feet to the first limb, and 190 feet in height. Two majestic sycamores that survived the onslaught of Anglo-American settlement grew to 42 feet 3 inches in circumference by 1915, and were then felled and had portions of their trunks preserved. Sycamores of gigantic girth had hollow trunks large enough to shelter people on horseback. It is hardly surprising that one night, in 1749, a party of Frenchmen dined in the hollow of a cotton tree, or that twenty-nine men gathered side by side in the hollow of an American sycamore. These trees preferred marsh and swampy ground and grew prolifically along the banks of the Ohio and in the adjacent wetlands.[6]

Enormous Ohio buckeyes thrived in these old-growth forests, and when,

5. George W. Knepper, *Ohio and Its People* (Kent, Oh., 2003), 8; "Account of the Voyage on the Beautiful River Made in 1749, under the Direction of Monsieur de Celoron by Father Bonnecamps," in *JR*, LXIX, 169.

6. Knepper, *Ohio and Its People,* 8–10; "Account of the Voyage," in *JR*, LXIX, 169; Marion T. Jackson, ed., *The Natural Heritage of Indiana* (Bloomington, Ind., 1997), xx; Robert Ridgway, "Additional Notes on the Native Trees of the Lower Wabash Valley," *Proceedings of the United States National Museum*, XVII (1894), 409–421. Ridgway measured trees that had been felled, so we are sure of his figures.

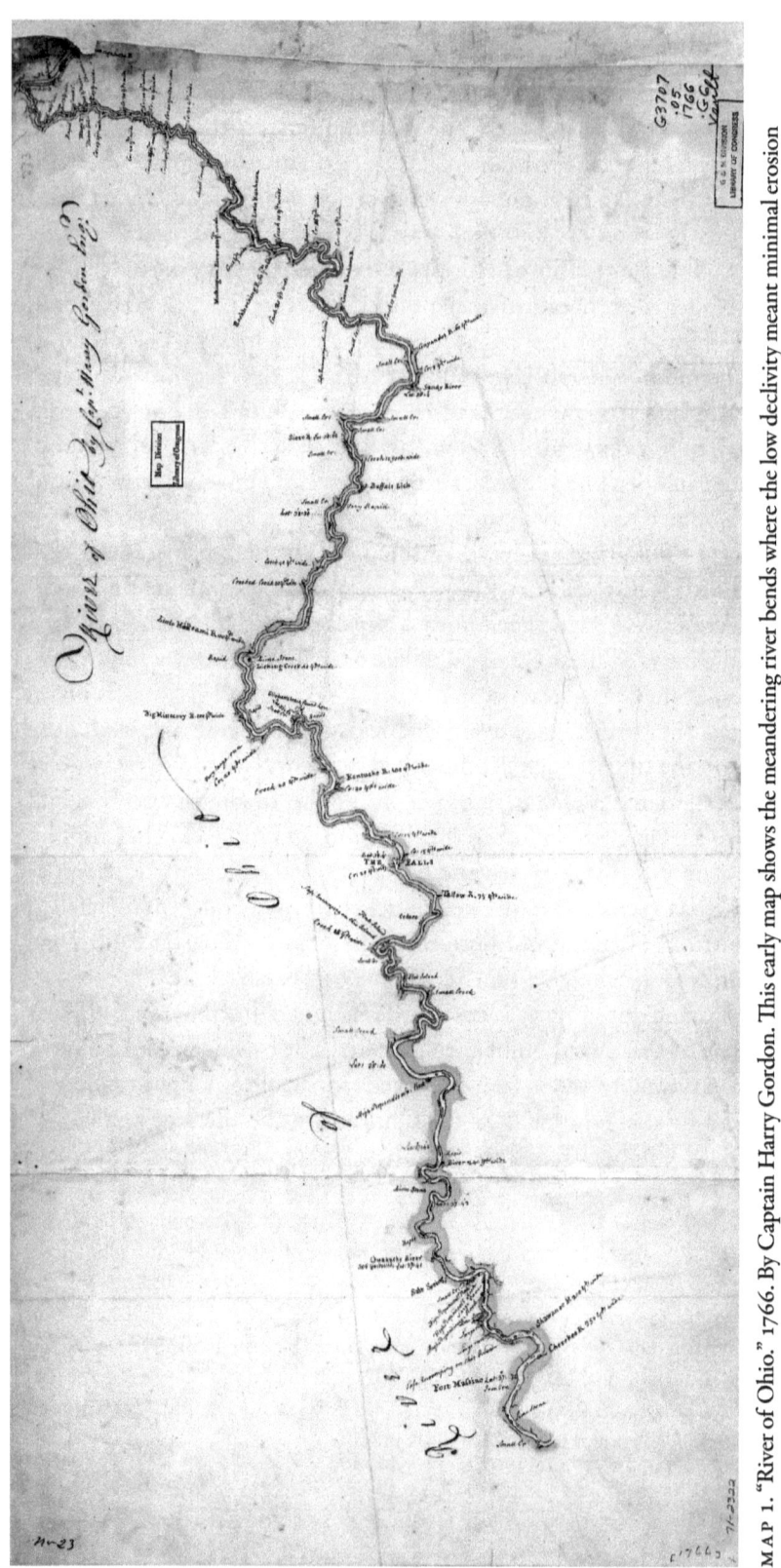

MAP 1. "River of Ohio." 1766. By Captain Harry Gordon. This early map shows the meandering river bends where the low declivity meant minimal erosion and the presence of tall, old-growth forests along the riverbanks. Numerals indicate latitude readings while names identify the tributary rivers and islands. Library of Congress, Geography and Map Division, G3707.O51753.P3

in 1840, William Henry Harrison had one chopped down to craft the celebrated buckeye canoe of his 1840 presidential campaign, it was almost 28 feet in diameter and 90 feet to the first limb. Indiana, like its adjoining neighbors, consumed 20 million acres of forestland before 1870 with only axes, grubbing hoes, horses, and oxen. Men carried the fallen trees on handspikes or rolled them into heaps in ravines, where they were set ablaze. In the first decades of the nineteenth century, thousands of fires burned night and day for months on end, turning the skies sallow. Before the conflagration, these forests had provided an unsurpassed hunting area that had drawn the Iroquois south and eastern villagers like the Delaware and Abenaki west to the Ohio River valley. The original 20 million acres of primeval forest that once covered Indiana was nearly enough to encircle the globe one and a quarter times in a mile-wide band. Today, scarcely enough old-growth forest remains to cover the Indianapolis Motor Speedway at the same one-mile width. Early Anglo-Americans did to this region what is presently occurring in the tropical forests of Brazil, Borneo, Sumatra, New Guinea, and the Democratic Republic of the Congo.[7]

Just to the west of the Appalachian foothills were the "glaciated till plains," bordered by forests of beech, elm, cherry, and ash. From present-day Ohio west to the Mississippi, natural meadows bordered the river bottoms, and indigenous grasses fed herds of deer, elk, and bison. These open plains, despite being some of the finest agricultural soil in the world, were not considered the river valley's most desirable lands. Early settlers believed "land that would not grow trees" was inferior for cropland. West of the Muskingum River were the Lake Plains, with extensive prairies that allowed the bluegrasses to grow as high as a horse's back and where small ponds and lakes teemed with flocks of waterfowl. The grasslands surrounding the Kanawha River produced an animal bounty that drew the Cherokee from the far south as well as Indians throughout the Great Lakes region. In 1770, when Washington went west to search for land, he described this as a "Country [that] abounds in buffaloes and wild game, of all kinds, as also in all kinds of wild fowl, there being in the bottoms a great many small, grassy ponds, or lakes, which are full of swans, geese and ducks of different kinds." Prolific game remained characteristic of this region until the mid-nineteenth century.[8]

7. Harrison's "huge canoe was pulled about the Midwest by six white horses bearing the banner 'Tippecanoe and Tyler Too.'" See Jackson, ed., *Natural Heritage of Indiana,* xx–xxiii; Ridgway, "Additional Notes," *Proceedings of the United States National Museum,* XVII (1894), 409–421; Charles C. Deam and Thomas Shaw, *Trees of Indiana* (Indianapolis, 1953).

8. When settler colonists stripped the forests, the corn belt moved to the western edge of these open plains. See R. Douglas Hurt, *The Ohio Frontier: Crucible of the Old Northwest,*

The most formidable environmental obstacle in the Ohio River valley, the Great Black Swamp, was north of the river, extending from the western shore of Lake Erie south to the St. Mary's River and bordered by the Sandusky on the east and the Maumee on the west. This nearly impenetrable area of thick trees was created by retreating glaciers that left murky, often chest-high waters. The swamp was more than 40 miles wide and created a dauntinge barrier that stretched south for 120 miles along the southern shore of Lake Erie. The Great Black Swamp was one of the richest sources of fur-bearing animals in this region, supplying much of the peltry for the eighteenth-century fur trade. Beaver, otter, mink, and muskrat, as well as vast flocks of waterfowl, including crane, heron, rail, plover, sandpiper, snipe, and bittern inhabited the swamps, bogs, and fens along the Ohio's northern shore. Furs were transported along the tributary rivers that provided pathways in and out of the swamplands, an area controlled primarily by the Miami and Wyandot with Wea, Piankeshaw, Kickapoo, Delaware, Shawnee, and Seneca wintering camps as well as other small Indian villages settled along the Wabash, Maumee, Miami, Little Miami, and Sandusky Rivers. The peltry-rich swamp and navigable river network encouraged the expansion of the fur trade and facilitated the transportation of peltry from the north bank swamplands of the Ohio to the Great Lakes and north to Montreal. A multiplicity of rivers connected the Ohio River valley to Lake Erie and the Great Lakes–St. Lawrence River system: the Miami, Auglaize, Maumee, Scioto, Sandusky, Muskingum, Wabash, Tippecanoe, Kankakee, and St. Joseph. Those lying south of the Ohio—the Monongahela, Kanawha, Licking, Kentucky, Green, and Cumberland—led into the mountains and linked the extensive grasslands south of the Ohio to the backcountry trading posts of Virginia and the Carolinas. These grasslands, populated by herds of deer, elk, and bison, were a lucrative zone of the southern fur trade.[9]

No other North American riverway resembled the Ohio: it was long, wide, and, for most of the year, flowed leisurely from east to west. Except for the

---

1720–1830 (Bloomington, Ind., 1996), 4–5; Archer Butler Hubert, "Washington's Tour to the Ohio," articles of "The Mississippi Company," *Ohio Archaeological and Historical Quarterly*, XXVII (1908), 431–488. Pioneer sketches of this region published in early historical society journals describe repeated slaughter of animals—it became commonplace for one settler to kill three or four deer, a half dozen to a dozen turkeys, and fifteen to twenty pheasants in a single day. See Robert R. Duncan, "Old Settlers' Paper No. 2," Indiana Historical Society, *Publications*, II, no. 10 (1894), 388; "Washington's Tour to the Ohio in 1770," *Olden Time*, I (1846), 416, 427–428; Jackson, ed., *Natural Heritage of Indiana*, xxiii.

9. Hurt, *Ohio Frontier*, 4–6, esp. 5.

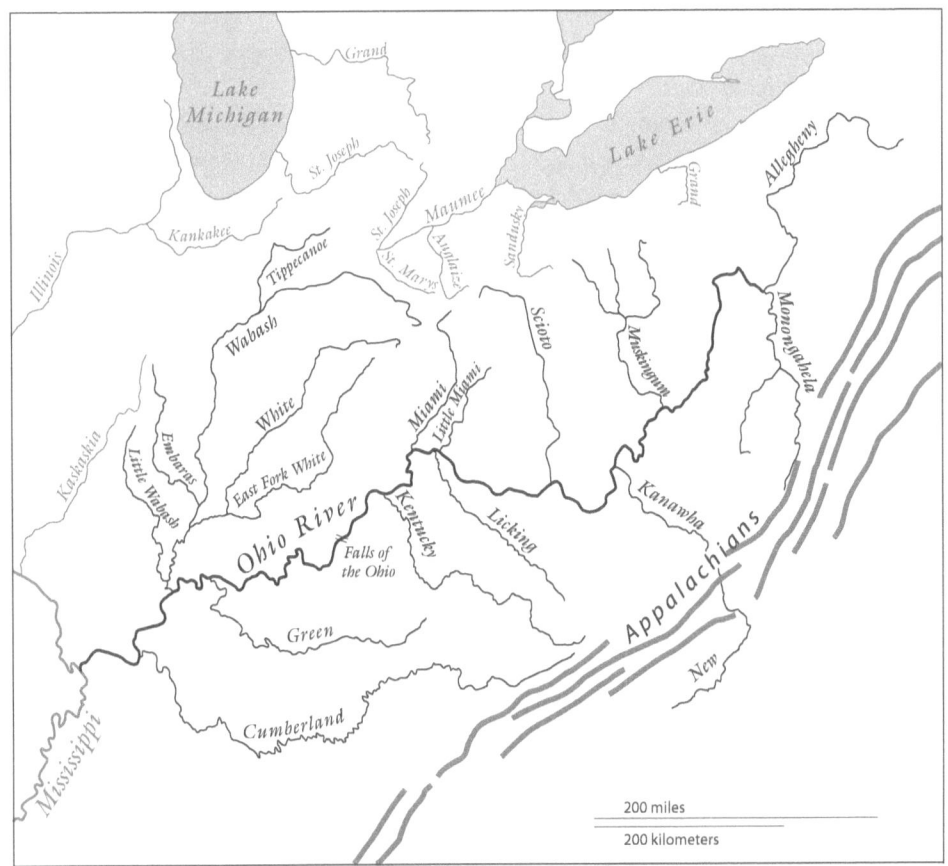

MAP 2. Ohio River system. Drawn by Ellen White

Falls of the Ohio, it was an almost uninterrupted highway that rose at the convergence of the Allegheny and the Monongahela and entered the Mississippi at present-day Cairo, Illinois, nearly doubling the Mississippi's volume of water. It might have been a perfect east-west highway except that it had an average of fewer than six inches a mile in its downward slope, and this gentleness of declivity resulted in a want of velocity. Worse, the Ohio had stretches so shallow as to render navigation often impossible. During the summer and winter months, when the water was low, there were sections where a child could wade across it. Continuous passage was possible only at two times of the year: when winter snows melted and when the autumn rains fell. Unfortunately, the same melting snow and falling rain that made it navigable also made it prone to flooding. The Ohio was a river of bounty and frustration, too cold, too high, too low, and then too high again. One disgruntled but insightful Virginian referred to it as "frozen one half of the year, and dried up during the remainder."[10]

It was not the Ohio River but, rather, its waters that shaped the settlement patterns of Indian villages. The tributary rivers that flowed south of Lake Erie to the Ohio created a vast drainage basin of rivers and streams adjoined by lands that were among the most fertile in North America. This large wetland region was dominated by the Great Black Swamp, and along the region's many rivers such as the Wabash, Great and Little Miami, Maumee, Sandusky, and Scioto were wetlands with a tremendous variety of edible plants that women harvested to feed their households. Streams that flowed from the rivers were often the boundary lines for cornfields in adjacent villages. They also provided a continuous supply of fresh water. Cornfields planted along the bottomlands of streams and rivers were annually replenished by winter snow melts. Along the Wabash River bottomlands, cornfields stretched for miles, with the fields of one household bordering those of its neighbors. This dual agrarian landscape of wet- and drylands yielded bountiful harvests that supported a dynamic population in the Ohio River valley.

Indians named the land after its distinctive natural features; consequently, these names can tell us much about the Ohio Valley landscape. Indians referred to the Ohio as the <8AB8SKIG8>, which can be roughly translated as either "white drum" or "white pots" in the Miami-Illinois language. The color white probably referred to the Ohio's most distinctive geological feature, the white limestone rock that formed the Falls of the Ohio. It is likely that the "white pots" referred to the pot-shaped white limestone holes caused by the descending, swirling waters. The falls were part of an ancient, fossilized reef of Silurian and Devonian limestone that formed an underground island across the width of the river and divided this river valley. The limestone ridge along the riverbed created the falls and transformed this section of the river into a prime fishing spot and popular ford. The Falls of the Ohio were a distinctive marker of this long, flat, meandering highway. Their churning waters

10. Flood season was the best time to descend the Ohio, but it was also dangerous. In the nineteenth century, inexperienced travelers were encouraged to lash their boats together and to remain in the main current of the river on a continuous journey that, at times of high flood, required fifteen hair-raising days to journey from Pittsburgh to the mouth of the river. A constant watch was required to ensure that boats were not ensnared by "planters" (trees rooted to the bottom of the river) or by "sawyers" (trees less firmly rooted that rose and fell with the water level). Landing on the riverbanks was discouraged because of the Indians, who took the opportunity to attack inexperienced travelers (James Hall, *The West: Its Commerce and Navigation* [1848; rpt. New York, 1970], 53).

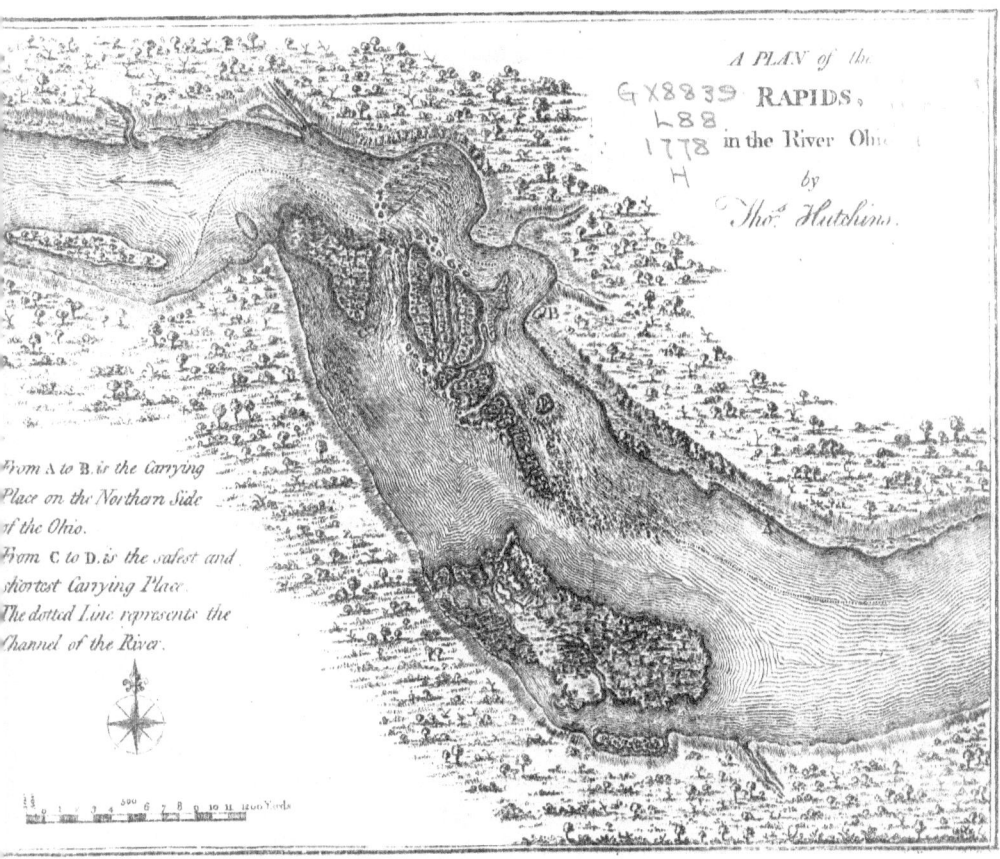

MAP 3. "A Plan of the Rapids, in the River Ohio." 1778. By Tho[mas] Hutchins. Hutchins created this as part of a British expedition down the Ohio in 1766. Wisconsin Historical Society, WHS-104834

were made more complex by the rock faces that were exposed at low water and by the islands that were located up- and downstream. Travelers navigating the falls during low water portaged along the southern shore of the river, but when spring floodwaters dramatically raised the water level, boats followed one of the three pathways through the rapids. Anglo-Americans identified this as shooting the rapids through either the Indiana, Kentucky, or Middle Chute. The Indiana Chute was the favored passageway, and its breadth governed the width of the flatboats that Americans later constructed to navigate the river. The falls created a region to the north linked to the Detroit fur trade while the Ohio's southern tributary rivers flowed from the Appalachian Mountains toward the Mississippi River, encouraging Indian engagement in the deerskin trade that attracted furs to the posts at Charleston and New

Orleans. The struggle that eventually ensued between Americans and Indians had much to do with who lived north and who lived south of this river. The north bank was referred to as the *Indian* shore; the south bank, the *Virginia* shore. At the end of the eighteenth century, Indians fought vigorously to confine Americans to the lands south of the Ohio. The falls also divided the Ohio River into two disparate east-west sections — the eastern portion, where colonial British influence was significant, and the western portion, where the French prevailed. The falls spanned two and a half miles of the Ohio, forming a barrier, which was the only permanent obstacle to water travel along the entire length of the river.[11]

The Ohio River created two environmentally distinct regions in another sense: the wetlands north of the Ohio and the better-drained, grassy plains south of the river. Most of the lands south of the falls later became famous for Kentucky bluegrass. Before the Americans arrived, these plains fed the bison herds that migrated across the shallow river during the summer months. Other than the ridgeline at the falls, prominent physical features were not readily apparent along the Ohio. But below the surface, unique geological features made it far more complex. The river formed during the last stages of the Ice Age, which marked it with deep, underwater recesses that became natural fish hatcheries. The slow, steady current of the Ohio's main channel and the slower, deeper pools provided the ideal habitat for an incredible volume and variety of fish. Species that were already rare at the time of contact could be found swimming in the Ohio. Many were quite large, survivors of the precontact landscape. Among the largest were the shovelnose sturgeon, which probably originated around AD 600, as well as paddlefish, lake sturgeon, spotted skipjack herring, blue sucker, and alligator gar (longnose and shortnose). Fossil records date the alligator gar back more than 3.5 million years. Various types of gar inhabited the rivers, lakes, and swamps north of the Ohio; their distinctive lung structure enabled them to thrive in the brackish waters of swamplands. Although the eggs of the female were toxic, the flesh of the adults was often smoked and eaten.[12]

Other unusual inhabitants of the Ohio included two equally ancient specimens: the alligator snapping turtle and the hellbender, a giant-sized salaman-

---

11. R. E. Banta, *The Ohio* (1949; rpt. Lexington, Ky., 1998), 12. The falls were located between Jeffersonville, Indiana, and Louisville, Kentucky. Bison crossed at the falls and followed the Buffalo Trace to reach the salt licks south of the river. John James Audubon created drawings of hundreds of birds that nested nearby (Jackson, ed., *Natural Heritage of Indiana*, 221).

12. James R. Gammon, *The Wabash River Ecosystem* (Plainfield, Ind., 1998), 105–114.

FIGURE 1. "Alligator Gar." Moon Lake, Mississippi, March 1910. Alligator gar are an endangered species in Arkansas, Kentucky, Tennessee, and Illinois; they have been reintroduced because they reduce the invasive species who endanger the ecological balance of the rivers. This fish was about ten feet long, belonging to one species of the genus *Aractosteus spatula*. Photograph by D. Franklin. AMNH 117075, American Museum of Natural History Library

der that grew to eighteen inches in length. The alligator snapping turtle was one of the Midwest's largest reptiles, more than two feet in length and weighing up to 160 pounds. In the 1800s, more than a hundred species of fish lived in the Ohio, including white and black bass, crappie, sturgeon, sunfish, rockfish, mullet, perch, carp, and several varieties of catfish—mudcats, channel cats, and Mississippi blues. Paddlefish, whose fossil record dates back more than 300 million years, and bigmouth buffalo fish inhabited the drainage areas from lakes and ponds that entered the river, positioning themselves in the incoming stream of waters with their mouths open to filter out the zooplankton. The American eel lived in the Ohio's freshwater tributaries and swam down the Mississippi to the Atlantic Ocean and the Sargasso Sea to spawn and die. When the young eels reentered the Mississippi and returned to the Ohio, they metamorphosed into yellow eels and then into adult American eels. Most reentered and matured in the tributary rivers. Seasonally harvested in small numbers, most of these fish survived and reached astonishing length. Even allowing for the proverbial exaggeration of fish stories, the sizes of some catches were astounding. John James Audubon, who lived at the Falls of the Ohio, landed a catfish that weighed 100 pounds. One early ethnologist, C. C. Trowbridge, described fish as a dietary staple of the Ohio's Indian villages and said, "Every kind of fish caught in the neighbouring lakes and rivers is eaten by them as also is the turtle, which is esteemed a delicacy."[13]

The Ohio's tributaries also provided an important habitat for freshwater mussels. Still found in the vicinity of the Wabash and the Ohio are shell middens, or shell mounds, that were the residue of mussels extracted from the rivers by Indians. There were about 250 species of mussel that grew in the Ohio, lower Wabash, and White Rivers. More than 40 percent of those once living in the Ohio River valley have been eliminated from its waters, and more than 10 percent are extinct. Several species were distinctive to this region, including the fat pocketbook, white cat's paw, tubercled-blossom, pink mucket, and Wabash riffleshell.[14]

There is abundant evidence of environmental diversity in the Ohio River valley region, and, despite this variability—indeed, paradoxically, because of it—similar systems of agrarian activity characterized the valley's entire length. Indian women located their fields and villages along the river bottoms, whereas wintering camps were located along the streams of the Black Swamp and in the eastern hills or in the forestlands north of the Ohio. In each village, cornfields produced sufficient foodstuffs to feed entire households and to store surpluses that fed the elderly, who remained in the villages during the winter months. An extended growing season of 120 to 200 days allowed Indian women to plant and harvest one, two, or even three crops annually and even replant entire fields destroyed by enemy invasions. The different rivers in the Ohio system shared similar environmental features: fertile soils, sufficient rainfall, and a long growing season that enabled Indian women's agrarian activity to become both large-scale and permanent.[15]

---

13. Jackson, ed., *Natural Heritage of Indiana,* 217–220; C. C. Trowbridge, *Meearmeear Traditions,* ed. Vernon Kinietz (Ann Arbor, Mich., 1938), 64; Gammon, *Wabash River Ecosystem,* 131–133.

14. Cheryl Claassen, "Washboards, Pigtoes, and Muckets: Historic Musseling in the Mississippi Watershed," *Historical Archaeology,* XXVIII, no. 2 (1994), 9.

15. Knepper, *Ohio and Its People,* 17–19; Michael Paul Gonella, "*Myaamia* Ethnobotany" (Ph.D. diss., Miami University, 2007).

WOMEN'S AGRARIAN PRACTICES

It is difficult to identify specific dates or even the events that triggered the cultivation of corn by Indian women, but archaeological evidence suggests that it began at least five millennia before the birth of Christ. Women's initial agrarian efforts started with wild cultigens, when they planted sunflowers, goosefoot, and sump weed. Scientific work in the 1980s revealed that corn first arrived in the Eastern Woodlands about AD 200. By AD 1100, maize constituted more than half of the population's annual caloric intake. Indian women also raised a variety of other plants for multiple purposes. By 1200, women had evolved a complex agriculture based on three major crops—corn, beans, and squash—with the harvesting of wild plants remaining an important food source that supplemented and enriched household diets. Wild plants produced medicines, fibers, wood for tools, housing, fuel, and dyes for cloth. Fish, fowl, and mammals were crucial sources of protein, supplied through the fishing and hunting skills of Indian men. Generally, women were not involved in the deaths of animals, since the shedding of blood negated their primary, life-giving function.[16]

Corn thus evolved as a staple crop of Indian villages in the Ohio River valley long before European arrival—and long before written sources existed to tell us about the process. This raises the question, How we can know about the pre-European world of the Ohio River valley? For one, by combining the earliest descriptions of French and English observers to arrive at an understanding greater than they, themselves, could have possessed. Although docu-

---

16. Bruce D. Smith, *Rivers of Change: Essays on Early Agriculture in Eastern North America* (Washington, D.C., 1992), 9–10. Numerous varieties of beans and squash were cultivated as food plants along with fleshy forms of *Cucurbita pepo*, green-striped cushaw, and the pale-seeded amaranth. See "Prehistoric Plant Husbandry in Eastern North America," ibid., 294–295; Hurt, *Indian Agriculture in America*, 11. For additional information, see Richard I. Ford, "The Processes of Plant Food Production in Prehistoric America," in Ford, ed., *Prehistoric Food Production in North America*, Anthropological Papers, no. 75 (Ann Arbor, Mich., 1985), 1–18; R. S. MacNeish, "The Origins of American Agriculture," *Antiquity*, XXXIX (1965), 88. For a discussion of gender roles in Indian societies, see Theda Perdue, *Cherokee Women: Gender and Culture Change, 1700–1835* (Lincoln, Neb., 1998), 1–40; Helen C. Rountree, *The Powhatan Indians of Virginia: Their Traditional Culture* (Norman, Okla., 1944), 32–57; Anthony F. C. Wallace, *The Death and Rebirth of the Seneca* (New York, 1969); Patricia Albers and Beatrice Medicine, *The Hidden Half: Studies of Plains Indian Women* (Washington, D.C., 1983); Nancy Shoemaker, ed., *Negotiators of Change: Historical Perspectives on Native American Women* (New York, 1995); Janet Spector, *What This Awl Means: Feminist Archaeology at a Wahpeton Dakota Village* (St. Paul, Minn., 1993); Gunlög Maria Fur, *A Nation of Women: Gender and Colonial Encounters among the Delaware Indians* (Philadelphia, 2009).

ments written in 1650 or 1750 can't tell us as much as we'd like about 1450, they can at least give us one basis for projecting our minds back into the past. The seventeenth and eighteenth centuries differed from the epochs that preceded them, but they exhibited traces of those earlier years. Later evidence can, at least, help us to raise and evaluate hypotheses. Additionally, changing emphases in recent scholarship may enable us to see what early observers and historians missed. Many authors, blinded by the gendered assumptions of their times, underestimated the importance of women's activities. Reading against the grain of old documents allows us to recover a fuller and richer picture. Moreover, we have much more than written sources: archaeological study enables us to go beyond the knowledge of these early-seventeenth- and eighteenth-century observers. Extensive field research by land grant universities, for instance, has generated remarkable information about the crop yields of these early Indian fields. We may never know as much as we'd like about the lost women's world of the Ohio Valley—but we can know more than we used to.

To take one example, for too long we have imagined that Indians relocated their villages when their fields became fallow, but recent research suggests the contrary. The geographer William Doolittle has analyzed the ethnographic, historic, and archaeological evidence about early maize cultivation and contends that Indian women developed agrarian practices that depended on continuous cropping. Jane Mt. Pleasant's agricultural field research has demonstrated that Indian fields produced higher crop yields than those of their European and Euro-American contemporaries. Seventeenth- and eighteenth-century Indian women developed a stable, continuous cropping system that maintained the organic matter in their soils by not plowing. We now refer to those practices as no-till, or conservation tillage; they provided sufficient nitrogen to produce forty to seventy-five bushels per acre of grain. Indigenous cropping systems had seed yield ratios of 154 to 320, compared to 4 to 21 for European wheat. When Americans acquired Indian lands, they relied on plows to grow maize. In fewer than fifty years, according to the agricultural data collected as part of the federal census, crop yields from these same lands decreased to fewer than thirty bushels per acre. American farmers continuously plowed their fields, oxidizing the soil's organic matter and reducing crop yields. Paucity followed the plow.[17]

17. William E. Doolittle, *Cultivated Landscapes of Native North America* (New York, 2000), 190; Jane Mt. Pleasant, "The Paradox of Plows and Productivity: An Agronomic Comparison of Cereal Grain Production under Iroquois Hoe Culture and European Plow

Indian women produced greater maize yields per acre than their Anglo-American successors, and this allowed them to feed more people with far less effort. Their knowledge about the cultivation of corn was orally transmitted over hundreds of years, which enabled women east of the Mississippi to eventually raise five distinct types of corn: dent, flint, flour, sweet, and popcorn. These were usually grown in the same fields, side by side. In those villages where maize culture took place, women perfected specific types of corn. The Miami were known for growing white seed corn. They separated corn into seed types, distinguishing seed corn from white seed corn. Indian women taught William Wood, an early and astute observer of agrarian practices, "to cull out the finest seede." Seeds were selected according to their length of maturity, and Indian women recognized that the length of different growing seasons required different types of seeds. When a trait was deemed desirable, agricultural scholars have inferred, Indians preserved and stabilized the seeds of that plant. Indians adapted corn to highly different climatic conditions: in the upper Missouri, Native women like the Hidatsa, collected seeds that required a short growing season, whereas, in the Southwest, corn plants were developed with long-growing roots that could reach the moisture below dry, parched fields. Several centuries were required to produce new varieties of corn because the gradual acclimatization of the corn plant took place farther and farther away from the original Mesoamerican site where corn was first introduced. The time required to stabilize these different varieties of corn and the subsequent and precise application of agrarian skills required to preserve the genetic integrity of the corn plant has been regarded as "'one of the most impressive facts' in the history of corn."[18]

Color selection was apparently of particular importance and might have been determined by religious and cultural concerns. The color of each kernel

---

Culture in the Seventeenth and Eighteenth Centuries," *Agricultural History,* LXXXV (2011), 487–488.

18. Hurt, *Indian Agriculture,* 11 (for additional information, see Ford, "Processes of Plant Food Production," in Ford, ed., *Anthropological Papers,* LXXV, 1–18; MacNeish, "Origins of American Agriculture," *Antiquity,* XXXIX [1965], 88); Roger Williams, *A Key into the Language of America; or, An Help to the Language of the Natives in That Part of America, Called New-England* (1743; rpt. Providence, R.I., 1936), 98; William Wood, *Wood's New England Prospect: A True, Lively, and Experamentall Description of That Part of America, Commonly Called New England . . .* (London, 1634), 70; Edwards, *Agriculture of the American Indians,* ix, 13; Everett E. Edwards and Wayne D. Rasmussen, *A Bibliography on the Agriculture of the American Indians* (Washington, D.C., 1942), 2; Clark Wissler, *The American Indian: An Introduction to the Anthropology of the New World* (New York, 1922).

is genetically determined by its different parts and depends on the fusion of a male and female parent. Ears of pure color were carefully maintained by unmixed stocks; in the Ohio River valley and along the River of the Miamis, the women raised "a Kind of indian corn which is unlike that of . . . [other] tribes. . . . Their corn Is white, of the Same size as the other, with much finer husks and much whiter flour." Miami women probably acquired white seed corn from the nearby Iroquois, who had long grown white corn, which is 50 percent higher in protein than most other field corns. In New England, the Pilgrims reported finding "a little old basket full of faire *Indian* Corne, and digged further and found a fine great new Basket full of very faire corne of this yeare, with some 36 goodly eares of corne, some yellow, and some red, and other mixt with blew, which was a very goodly sight: the Basket was round, and narrow at the top, it held about three or four Bushels, which was as much as two of us could lift up from the ground, and was very handsomely and cunningly made." These observations were confirmed in 1672 by John Josselyn, who described Indian corn as Indian wheat and noted that the ears were "yellow, red, and blew."[19]

The eastern half of the present-day United States, especially the lands between the Mississippi River and the Atlantic Ocean, offered an unusually lush environment that was conducive to corn cultivation. The resource-rich floodplains of the Ohio's tributary rivers were annually replenished by floodwaters, easily tilled, and highly prized for growing corn. These floodplains had attracted hunter-gatherer groups long before plant husbandry played even a minor role in subsistence patterns. One of the most important aspects of this region was the dependable aquatic protein sources of wetland and swampland foods that were found adjacent to the natural levee soils. These tributary systems were extensively settled and brought under cultivation during the Late Precontact period. Early European travelers provided accounts of riding for days along such natural levee ridge systems, through a landscape of planted fields with adjacent "infield gardens" dispersed widely within larger and more extensive "outfield" systems. Indian women gathered resources from a variety

---

19. Carl L. Johannessen, Michael R. Wilson, and William A. Davenport, "The Domestication of Maize: Process or Event?" *Geographical Review*, XL (1970), 409 (see also Johannessen and John L. Sorenson, *World Trade and Biological Exchanges before 1492*, rev. ed. [Eugene, Ore., 2013]); [Sabrevois], "1718," in Thwaites, ed., *French Regime in Wisconsin*, part 1, 375; Linda Murray Berzok, *American Indian Food* (Westport, Conn., 2005), 45; William Bradford, *Relation or Journall of the Beginning and Proceedings of the English Plantation Setled at Plimoth in New England, by Certaine English Adventurers Both Merchants and Others . . .* (London, 1622), 6–7; John Josselyn, *New-Englands Rarities Discovered* (1672; rpt. Boston, 1972), 52.

of environmental zones, supplementing corn crops with edible plants harvested from the marshes, swamps, and wetlands. Indian villages, located in environmentally diverse landscapes with wetlands next to fertile dry lands, were avoided by Euro-Americans, who favored dry land with waterways deep enough to transport large river craft. Deep water held little interest for Indian women because they retrieved an ongoing supply of plants with edible roots from shallow, fresh water. Euro-Americans with limited interest in swamps eventually drained and transformed them into dry land, stripping the Ohio River valley of its natural fertility.[20]

Ethnologists contend that Indian women learned to cultivate plants because domestic responsibilities kept them closer to home. Women identified the varieties of crops that grew best on the lands surrounding their villages and, because they tilled the soils, one can reasonably assume that they also created a demand for agricultural tools, especially for digging tools with metal tips, such as the awl. They progressed from using their hands to using digging sticks made from shoulder bones, antlers, or clamshells. When European traders arrived, women likely demanded the incorporation of iron tools and cooking utensils into the exchange process.[21]

Acreages remained in continuous production because Indian women used neither domesticated animals nor iron plows to cultivate their fields. They grew cereal grain maize, which was far more productive than wheat farming. Maize was uniquely suited to no-plow conditions because corn seed is much larger than that of cereal grains. It does not require a finely prepared seed bed of plowed soils and thrives in no-till conditions. No-plow agriculture enabled Indian women to intercrop maize with beans and squash, which returned nitrogen to the soil and enabled long-term, continuous cropping systems. Extensive field research on Iroquoian cornfields has conclusively shown that women's cornfields generated higher crop yields than Anglo-American wheat fields.[22]

---

20. "Prehistoric Plant Husbandry in Eastern North America," in Smith, *Rivers of Change*, 295; Helen C. Rountree and Thomas E. Davidson, *Eastern Shore Indians of Virginia and Maryland* (Charlottesville, Va., 1997), 13; Ford, "Processes of Plant Food Production," in Ford, ed., *Anthropological Papers*, LXXV, 1–18; MacNeish, "Origins of American Agriculture," *Antiquity*, XXXIX (1965), 88; Doolittle, *Cultivated Landscapes*, 414; M. J. Morgan, *Land of Big Rivers: French and Indian Illinois, 1699–1778* (Carbondale, Ill., 2010), 5–8.

21. Spector, *What This Awl Means*, 30; Hurt, *Indian Agriculture*, 11; Paul C. Manglesdorf, Richard S. MacNeish, and Gordon R. Willey, "Origins of Agriculture in Middle America," in Stuart Struever, ed., *Prehistoric Agriculture* (Garden City, N.J., 1971), 291.

22. Tillage refers to preparing the soil for planting by mechanically turning it over, either with a plow pulled by a tractor or, formerly, with a plow pulled by horses or oxen. When a

When European explorers first appeared, Indians on both the North and South American continents had well-developed agricultural economies. Pillaging Indian villages enabled European explorers to survive because of the ongoing labor of women, who generally stored two to three years' worth of grain as a guard against crop failure. Hernando de Soto's journals of his expedition through the Southeast contain the echo of voracious European appetites, devouring not only the crops that Indian women planted and harvested but the surplus they stored. Soto often wrote about the land through the language of food, identifying villages by the quantity and quality of their harvests. He memorialized Ocala (in present-day Florida) as a bountiful landscape because his men carted away enough corn to supply their army for three months. Soto meticulously recorded the names and details of specific villages with large grain reserves. Many of the explorer's journals were probably intended as a literary roadmap for future expeditions. Soto often identified noteworthy villages by the size of the fields and by the variety of vegetables that women harvested. For instance, he describes present-day Tallahassee as having "fields of corn, beans, pumpkins," as well as enough "other vegetables" to serve as "sufficient for the supply of a large army." As they marched along Florida's northern peninsula, "near Ibitachuco and Ucahile, De Soto's army passed through cultivated fields, presumably of corn, which ... extend as many as twelve miles."[23]

---

field is plowed, as much as a foot deep of soil is overturned, which leads to a 90 percent loss of the crop residue (the decomposing plant from the previous year) from the topsoil. The benefit of this high turnover is a disruption of the life cycle of any existing weeds and pests. Tillage is labor intensive, and often a plot of land needs to be tilled several times before planting commences. This practice damages soil and leaves it exposed to erosion, particularly by wind and water. No-till agriculture plants crops without disturbing the soil through tillage. No-till is also referred to as zero tillage or direct drilling. See Mt. Pleasant, "Paradox of Plows and Productivity," *Agricultural History*, LXXXV (2011), 460–492, esp. 462, 479–480; E. Cecil Curwen and Gudmund Hatt, *Plough and Pasture: The Early History of Farming* (1953; rpt. New York, 1961), 72; G. E. Fussell, "Ploughs and Ploughing before 1800," *Agricultural History*, XL (1966), 177; R. Douglas Hurt, *American Farm Tools: From Hand-Power to Steam-Power* (Manhattan, Kans., 1982), 7; Peter D. McClelland, *Sowing Modernity: America's First Agricultural Revolution* (Ithaca, N.Y., 1977), 16.

23. Hurt, *Indian Agriculture*, 27; Carl Ortwin Sauer, *Sixteenth Century North America* (Berkeley, Calif., 1971), 180; Lewis H. Larson, *Aboriginal Subsistence Technology on the Southeastern Coastal Plain during the Late Prehistoric Period* (Gainesville, Fl., 1980), 212, 214, 217, 219; Charles W. Spellman, "The Agriculture of the Early North Florida Indians," *Florida Anthropologist*, I (1948), 37, 41–42; John R. Swanton, *The Indians of the Southwestern United States*, Smithsonian Institution Bureau of American Ethnology Bulletin no. 137 (Washington, D.C., 1946), 308; Richard Hakluyt, *Discovery and Conquest of Terra Florida by Don Ferdinando de Soto and Six Hundred Spaniards His Followers, Written by a Gentleman of*

In northern regions, as well, explorers told of Indian cornfields and made particular note of where and how Indian women stored their harvests. Jacques Cartier's 1535 description of the "large cornfields" surrounding Montreal's Indian villages stated that women "stored [corn] under the roofs of their houses." A century later, Samuel de Champlain also described significant reserves of corn in the Indian villages near "Lake Erie and Ontario [where they] grew corn for their chief food as well as for trade with the hunting tribes." As he journeyed along the New England coast, Champlain described the deep holes that women dug in the sand dunes, where they placed maize in grass bags, then covered the holes with several feet of sand. The Pilgrims also found newly heaped sand hills full of stored maize, both shelled and on the ear. They survived by ransacking these grain stores, believing that this was the providential hand of God ensuring their survival. Throughout the Woodlands region, Indian women produced sufficient yields to provide food through the long winter months. Fields were so large that visitors often lost their way. As he traveled from one village to another, Father Gabriel Sagard would "lose my way usually in these corn-fields more than in the meadows and forests."[24]

As European fur traders took up residence among Native people, they developed a more nuanced understanding of what they were seeing, noticing that agriculture was women's work and remarking on the agricultural skill and proficiency of Indian women. Nicolas Perrot, a servant, or engagé, of the Jesuits, spent almost forty years living among Indians in the western Great Lakes and traveled continually across the region from 1680 to 1718. He described Indians as "naturally very industrious" and repeatedly claimed that every village "devote themselves to the cultivation of the soil." Perrot considered corn, beans, and squash such common and plentiful Indian crops that, "If they are without these, they think that they are fasting, no matter what abundance of meat and fish they may have in their stores, the Indian corn being to them what bread is to Frenchmen."[25]

Around 1699, one explorer identified a Quapaw village along the Illinois River where the people lived "on nothing scarcely but Indian corn," which

---

Elvas, Employed in All the Action, and Translated out of Portuguese, ed. William B. Rye, Works Issued by the Hakluyt Society, no. 9 (1851; rpt. New York, 2010).

24. Samuel de Champlain, *Les Voyages du Sieur Champlain,* March of America, no. 20 (1613; rpt. Ann Arbor, Mich., 1966), 124–125; Bradford, *Relation or Journall,* 7–12; Gabriel Sagard, *The Long Journey to the Country of the Hurons,* ed. George M. Wrong, trans. H. H. Langton (Toronto, Ont., 1939), 104.

25. Nicolas Perrot, *Memoir on the Manners, Customs, and Religion of the Savages of North America* (1864), rpt. in Emma Helen Blair, ed. and trans., *The Indian Tribes of the Upper Mississippi Valley and Region of the Great Lakes . . .* (1911; rpt. Lincoln, Neb., 1996), I, 102, 113.

grew from twelve to twenty feet high. Corn cultivation was equally important to the Sauk, who lived along the north side of the Rock River where it emptied into the Mississippi. One hundred twenty years later, the Sauk leader Blackhawk described the extensive cornfields cultivated by Indian women and maintained that their fields paralleled the Mississippi for two miles. Women cleared these fields, planted corn, and built and repaired fences around their fields. Blackhawk described his own village as having "about eight hundred acres in cultivation, including what we had on the islands of Rock river. The land around our village, uncultivated, was covered with blue-grass, which made excellent pasture for our horses. . . . The land, being good, never failed to produce good crops of corn, beans, pumpkins, and squashes. We always had plenty — our children never cried with hunger, nor our people were never in want."[26]

For the seventeenth-century Illinois, who lived along the Mississippi and its tributary rivers, corn was the primary village crop. In the Illinois Country, Indian women planted two varieties of corn; both ripened in late August, but they were preserved differently. For one variety, the ears were roasted on large griddles, then carefully watched and periodically turned to prevent the kernels from burning. Once fully roasted, the kernels were scraped from the cobs. The second variety was husked and the ears spread on mats. In the evening, women gathered the ears into a heap, covered them, and the next day, they were again spread on mats in the sun. After a week, the women threshed the corn with six- or seven-foot-long sticks, relying on mats to keep the flying kernels from being lost. Illinois women also raised a large number of other vegetables, especially pumpkins and melons. They dried and stored the pumpkins, preserving them so they could be used to flavor stews and soups throughout the winter months. Women hollowed out the pumpkins, cut them into slices, and hung them on racks to dry. After several days, they were removed and then cut into chunks. Later, they were boiled in pots of meat and corn, adding flavor and nutrition. This type of harvesting and preservation took place throughout the southern Great Lakes, so that households were well fed, even during the long winter months.[27]

---

26. Indian corn is not hybridized like present-day corn and grew to greater heights. Indian fields were seen from a long distance away, and platforms were often erected in cornfields, which women used to scare away birds but also to harvest the ears. See John Gilmary Shea, ed., *Early Voyages up and down the Mississippi by Cavelier, St. Cosme, Le Sueur, Gravier, and Guignas* (Albany, N.Y., 1861), 77; Donald Jackson, ed., *Black Hawk: An Autobiography* (Urbana, Ill., 1990), 88–89.

27. "Memoire concernant le paye Illinois," MS, Memoranda on French Colonies in

Corn was also a staple along the northern shores of Lakes Huron and Ontario. French travelers frequently commented on the large grain stores retained by Huron women, who relied on a two- to four-year surplus as a guard against crop failure and to provide an adequate commodity to trade. These Huron villages were often five to six times larger than others in the southern Great Lakes, and, because they accommodated a thousand people, had sizable storage facilities. Huron villages generally planted at least 360 acres of corn, which resulted in an average harvest of 390,000 bushels. Before the Iroquois onslaught, women of the Huron Confederacy probably cultivated close to 23,300 acres and harvested almost 17 bushels per acre. One anthropologist has suggested that Huron woman produced 1.3 pounds of corn for each family member's daily allotment, an amount that comprised about 65 percent of their diet.[28]

From Georgian Bay to southern Appalachia and west to the Mississippi, Indian women planted seed corn in the late spring in fields along the river bottoms and followed various techniques to secure higher crop yields. Often, they selected the best seeds and soaked them for several days in water before planting to speed the germination process. Women planted corn in holes about a step apart and then hoed up the soil around the stalks to prevent erosion. After the corn had sprouted a few inches, beans were planted in the same

---

America, Including Canada, Louisiana, and the Caribbean, [1702–1750], Special Collections Manuscripts, Newberry Library, Chicago, Ill. This manuscript was mistakenly identified as the De Gannes Memoir because this name appeared at the end of the document. It is more probable that these observations were recorded by Pierre-Charles Deliette, who arrived in Illinois Country at Fort Saint-Louis Le Rocher (Starved Rock) in 1687 to work with his uncle, Henri de Tonti. Deliette's "Memoir concerning Illinois Country" was part of a collection of documents purchased by Edward Ayers from a Paris bookseller, Charles Chadenat, in 1899. This three-volume series of hand-transcribed documents focused on exploration and trade were part of the library of a Swiss gentleman in the second third of the eighteenth century. This document was translated into English, archived as the "DeGannes Memoir" at the Newberry Library, and printed as the "De Gannes Memoir" in the *Collections of the Illinois State Historical Library*. Today, the Newberry holds the only known copy of this document. "Memoir of De Gannes concerning the Illinois Country" can be found in Theodore Calvin Pease and Raymond C. Werner, eds., *The French Foundations, 1680–1693*, vol. XXIII of Illinois State Library, *Collections*, 38 vols. (Springfield, Ill., 1903–1978), 343–344.

28. The evidence used to support these conclusions is drawn from Roger Williams's observations that Indian women in New England raised as much as 45 bushels of corn annually for each family member. See Hurt, *Indian Agriculture*, 34; W. Vernon Kinietz, *The Indians of the Western Great Lakes, 1615–1760* (1940; rpt. Ann Arbor, Mich., 1965), 16–19; Bruce G. Trigger, *The Children of Aataentsic: A History of the Huron People to 1660* (1976; rpt. Montreal, Que., 1987), 34, 40.

hills with the cornstalks, which provided support for the vines. Once ripe, the dried and shelled corn was stored in underground pits. Northern communities, like the Huron and Tobacco Huron, depended on agriculture for almost 75 percent of their nutritional needs.[29]

Vast stretches of Huronia were productive, but less so than the fertile Ohio River valley and other regions east of the Mississippi. The lower Potomac River valley and the Ohio River valley had comparable environmental and climatic conditions. Both were woodland regions at the same latitude, with similar soils, comparable growing seasons, and adjacent wetlands. Villages in both river valleys were interconnected by a maze of pathways, with waterways linking the smaller and larger villages. Trade provided a stable food supply and facilitated communication between villages. Intermarriage solidified these trading relationships and enabled diplomatic cooperation. Both regions possessed a growing season long enough for Indian women to plant agricultural fields containing multiple types of corn and a similar variety of vegetables. The agrarian labors of Indian women, the fertility of the soils, and the harvesting of adjacent natural resources ensured well-fed village populations.

England's settler colonists were usually focused on the fecundity of the landscape, and, for Virginia, they penned extensive firsthand accounts of Indian villages surrounded by widespread tracts of fertile agrarian land. Indian houses were "in the midst of their fields or gardens; which are small plots of ground, some 20 [acres], some 40, some 100. some 200. some more, some lesse. Some times from 2 to 100 of these houses [are] togither, or but a little separated by groves of trees." To create these fields, Indian men cleared large tracts of land. At Kecoughtan, Indian women planted large fields of maize on three thousand acres of cleared land along the riverways, whereas smaller, hundred-foot fields were located in the villages. Village crops such as macock gourds (or muskmelons), pumpkins, and tobacco required closer attention. These fruits ripened from July to September. Women also planted field apples, which were a wild fruit like pomegranates. Near the Falls of Powhatan were a series of vast fields planted with maize, beans, pumpkins, gourds, hemp, and flax that stretched to Powhatan's longhouse. Nearby, "the queen of Appomattox, who resided near the stream of that name, also had many fields in the same grain, one of these fields, in which these vegetables and tobacco were also planted, spreading over an area of one hundred acres." There were numerous adjacent fields that belonged to other werowances, and Powhatan's brother, Opechancanough, had a field that covered an equal area of land. The

---

29. Hurt, *Indian Agriculture*, 33, 34, 37; Trigger, *Huron Farmers of the North*, 26–27, 37, 34.

most striking evidence for the agrarian fertility of these landscapes were the great feasts that Indians prepared to welcome newcomers.[30]

To Virginia's Englishmen, the Indian lands were "an ample and faire Country . . . comparatively high, wholsome and fruictfull," with extensive cleared fields where food could be easily grown. Indian women were "better husbands [farmers] then in any parte ells," who produced surpluses sufficient to feed the English. Despite the English appropriation of their lands, Indian women continued to produce a sizable surplus.[31]

Corn was central to the Indian diet but part of a more complex and varied food supply. In both the Potomac and Ohio River valley regions, villages adjacent to wetlands harvested edible plants that supplemented and enriched household diets. Both regions were filled with wetlands created by the multiple rivers and numerous streams. In these marshes, Indian women harvested many varieties of wild plants. In both the Potomac and Ohio River valleys, tuckahoe was "so abundant that it was said that one individual could gather in a day sufficient quantity to furnish him subsistence for a week." Indian women harvested tuckahoe by digging up the starchy tubers that grew on the roots of large trees, which was difficult and time-consuming. The tubers were often as large as a man's thigh and could weigh up to forty pounds. Most stems and leaves were removed so that the tubers could be gathered into large bunches. Then they laid the tuckahoe on the ground and covered it with leaves and ferns and, finally, dirt. On each side of the mound, the women kindled a fire, which burned for twenty-four hours. When roasted in this manner, the plant became palatable and nourishing and often was eaten immediately. Alternatively, once the plant had been roasted, it was sliced and then dried in the sun. It was also mixed with meal and sorrel to enhance its flavor. After being cooked, it was so tender that it was ground into meal for making bread. Large numbers of Indian villages along the Atlantic harvested tuckahoe. The word *tuckahoe* can be found among Mohegan speakers *(tquogh)* and among the Shawnee, who also lived in the Ohio River Valley *(tukwhah)*. The word is

---

30. "Relatyon of the Discovery of Our River," "On the Naturall Inhabitants of Virginia," both in Edward Arber, ed., *Capt. John Smith, of Willoughby by Alford, Lincolnshire; President of Virginia, and Admiral of New England, Works, 1608–1631* (Birmingham, U.K., 1884), xlii–xliii, 1, li, 67; William Strachey, *The Historie of Travaile into Virginia Britannia; Expressing the Cosmographie and Comodities of the Country, Togither with the Manners and Customes of the People . . .* , ed. R. H. Major, Works Issued by the Hakluyt Society, no. 6 (London, 1849), 72.

31. William Strachey, *The Historie of Travell into Virginia Britania,* ed. Louis B. Wright and Virginia Freund, Works Issued by the Hakluyt Society, no. 103 (London, 1953), 67–68; Arber, ed., *Works of Capt. John Smith,* 158.

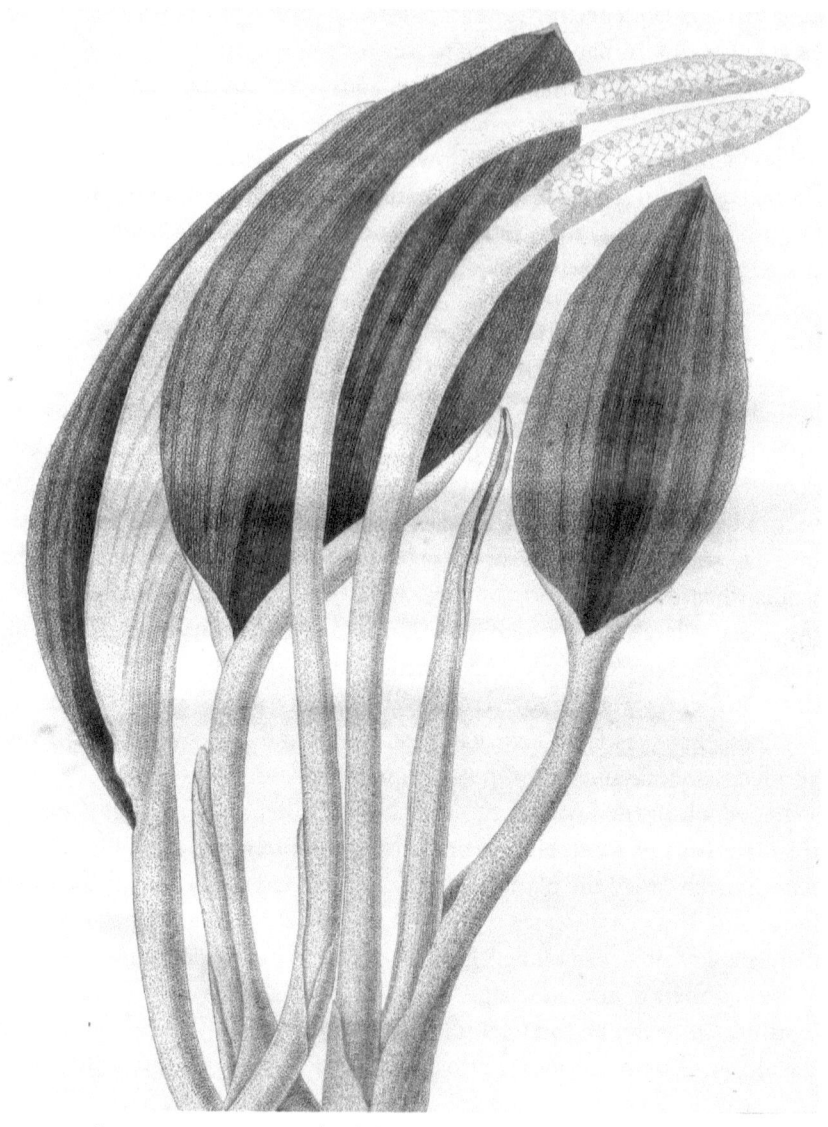

FIGURE 2. "Oróntium aquaticum" (tuckahoe, or golden club). In William P. C. Barton, *A Flora of North America: Illustrated by Coloured Figures, Drawn from Nature,* 3 vols. (Philadelphia, 1821–1823), II, table 37. Michigan State University Libraries, Special Collections, East Lansing, Mich.

perhaps also related to the Cree (Algonquian) word *pitikwaw,* meaning "made round."[32]

Recent archaeological excavations throughout the Ohio River valley have provided an extensive view of the types of plants that were harvested, and the seeds from these plants have been recovered and replanted in the Beal Horticultural Gardens of Michigan State University. Many of these plants are familiar to us, but we are rarely conscious of their nutritional value. We recognize ferns in wooded areas, or milkweed growing along a dusty road, or even the colorful jack-in-the pulpit spread along the floor of early spring forestlands. Each of these plants had nutritional value for Indian households. Fiddlehead ferns were a rich source of carbohydrates and were boiled in water and eaten like spinach. The immature pods of the milkweed were cooked and tasted much like okra, whereas the jack-in-the-pulpit, which we now refer to as Indian or wild turnip, was roasted in a pit for three days to produce a salt that seasoned foods.[33]

Wetlands proved such an important source of food to Native people that these marshes can be seen as breadbaskets. In addition to tuckahoe, Indian women harvested the roots of spatterdock, a yellow pond lily, and, south of the Ohio, the seeds of other marsh plants such as pickerelweed and wild rice. Indian women also made use of other natural products that required no tillage. They made bread from the seeds of the sunflower and the mattoon, which was eaten with deer suet. They gathered acorns of the white oak and ground the kernels into meal, which was then made into bread. The women also gathered large numbers of hickory nuts, which they ground in mortars and mixed with water to form a milky liquor known as pohickory. This could be drunk, used as a sauce for boiled beans, peas, maize, and pumpkins, or even served as a type of liquor. Colonel Norwood, who wrote *A Voyage to Virginia,* described his detention among the Indians and relished his memory of this dish in great detail:

---

32. Philip Alexander Bruce, *Economic History of Virginia in the Seventeenth Century: An Inquiry into the Material Condition of the People, Based upon Original and Contemporaneous Records,* 2 vols. (New York, 1896), I, 166; Berzok, *American Indian Food,* 63; Rountree, *Powhatan Indians of Virginia,* 44–54. John Smith was aware of the value of tuckahoe as a food, and he claimed, "In one day a *Savage* will gather sufficient for a weeke" (*Works of Capt. John Smith,* 58). Tuckahoe is also called Indian bread and is the edible, underground sclerotium of the fungus *Poria cocos,* found on the roots of trees in the southern United States.

33. Berzok, *American Indian Food,* 177–178; Charlotte Erichsen-Brown, *Use of Plants for the Past 500 Years* (Aurora, Ont., 1979), 234–235.

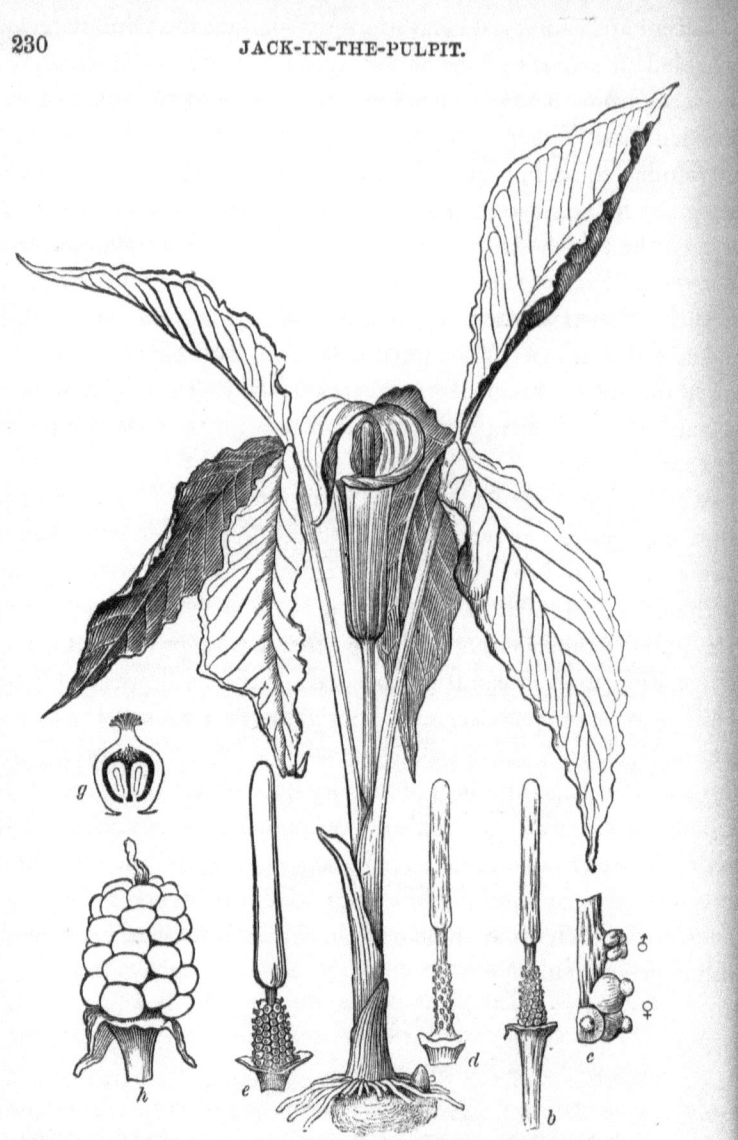

FIGURE 3. "Jack-in-the-Pulpit" *(Arisaema triphyllum)*. In Alphonso Wood and Joel Dorman Steele, *Fourteen Weeks in Botany: Being an Illustrated Flora* (New York, 1879), plate LX, 230. Michigan State University Libraries, Special Collections, East Lansing, Mich.

It was a Sort of Spoon Meat, in Colour and Taste not unlike Almond Milk temper'd and mix'd with boiled Rice. The Ground still was *Indian* Corn boiled to a Pap, which they call Homini, but the Ingredient which perform'd the milky Part, was nothing but dry pokickery Nuts, beaten Shells and all to Powder, and they are like our Walnuts, but thicker shell'd, and the Kernel sweeter; but being beaten in a Mortar and put into a Tray, hollow'd in the Middle to make Place for fair Water, no sooner is the Water poured into the Powder, but rises again white and creamish; and after a little Ferment it rises again white and creamish; and after a little ferment it does partake so much of the delicate Taste of the Kernel of that Nut, that it becomes a Rarity. Major Morison, who had been almost at Death's Door, found himself abundantly refreshed and comforted with this Delicacy.[34]

In the Ohio River valley, wetlands were far more extensive and contained larger numbers and greater varieties of wild plants. No plant fascinated more outside observers than macopin, which was even larger than tuckahoe, and more difficult to harvest and prepare, but which provided greater nutritional benefit. Pierre Deliette, who lived among the Illinois in the seventeenth century, described the harvesting and preparation of macopin:

> I have seen the women pull the roots up from the ground at the bottom of the water into which they wade sometimes up to their waist. . . . There are some as big as one's leg. . . . The women have peculiar difficulty in cook-

---

34. Bruce, *History of Virginia*, 165–167; see also *The History and Present State of Virginia by Robert Beverley: A New Edition with an Introduction by Susan Scott Parrish* (Chapel Hill, N.C., 2013), 99–101; Arber, ed., *Works of Capt. John Smith*, 57–58. In the Ohio River valley, the large oak trees provided substantial numbers of acorns, which were eaten raw or roasted like popcorn. Bread was also made from raw ground or parched acorns, and the flour mixed with water and baked in ashes. The bread resembles coarse black clay that has been sunbaked. See Charles Christopher Parry, "Food Products of the North American Indians," *Report of the Commissioner of Agriculture for the Year 1870* (Washington, D.C., 1871), 409–410. For details of how nuts were harvested, see Beverley's *History of Virginia*, 100, 142; "Of Such Things Which Are Natural in Virginia and How They Use Them," in Arber, ed., *Works of Capt. John Smith*, 56, 58; Bruce, *Economic History*, I, 167; Strachey, *Historie of Travaile into Virginia*, ed. Major, 121; [Henry] Norwood, *A Voyage to Virginia* (1732), rpt. in Peter Force, coll., *Tracts and Other Papers Relating Principally to the Origin, Settlement, and Progress of the Colonies in North America from the Discovery of the Country to the Year 1776*, 4 vols. (Washington, D.C., 1836–1846), III, 37; Rountree, *Powhatan Indians of Virginia*, 44–54; Rountree, *Pocahontas's People: The Powhatan Indians of Virginia through Four Centuries* (Norman, Okla., 1990). See also James S. Olson and Heather Olson Beal, *The Ethnic Dimension in American History* (Chichester, U.K., 2010), 19. The authors describe the tribes living south of the Ohio as gathering seeds, nuts, and wild rice.

ing them. Sometimes three or four cabins combine and dig a hole in the ground five or six feet deep and ten or twelve square. They throw a great deal of wood into it . . . and when it is aflame they throw in a number of rocks, which they take care to turn over with big levers until they are all red; then they go in quest of a large quantity of grass which they get at the bottom of the water and which they spread as well as they can over these rocks to the thickness of about a foot, after which they throw on many buckets of water, and then as fast as they can each cabin puts its roots in its own place, covering them over with a dry grass and bark and finally earth. They leave them thus for three days.[35]

Although Deliette often failed to record the names of the plants, he did provide extensive details about women's preparation of these wild plants. "Other roots . . . are as big as one's arm and . . . are full of holes. These give them no trouble to prepare; they merely cut them into pieces half as thick as one's waist, string them, and hang them to dry in the sun or in the smoke. . . . They also store up onions, as big as Jerusalem artichokes, which they find in prairies, and which I find better than all the other roots. They are sugary and pleasing to the palate. They are all cooked like macopines." These preparations insured the winter's food supply and were kept in underground storage pits, four to five feet deep, lined with tree bark. These were effective in protecting crops from the frost and could be used to store not only maize but onions and other vegetables, fruits, and pumpkins.[36]

Even small wetland patches produced high yields of food resources. Plants such as Solomon's seal, which was harvested for its roots and tubers, much like potatoes, also grew along the riverbanks and in the moist soils surrounding the wetlands. Indians boiled them and they were eaten in much the same way as potatoes, as an accompaniment to meat. Other plants were harvested and eaten without any elaborate preparation, such as the nodding onion, which

35. "Memoire concernant le paye Illinois," III, 310-311.
36. The frequent gathering of macopin was also confirmed by the explorer La Salle and by later observers, like the English painter George Winter and C. C. Trowbridge, who was an early ethnologist and an astute observer of Indian lifeways. Trowbridge described macopin as the root of the pond lily and confirmed Deliette's description of the harvesting and the difficulty of its preparation. Trowbridge proved adept at recording the harvesting of various plants and described the incorporation of Poakshikwileearkee, Keeshikeehaukee, Waukeepaaneekee, and Waukpeeseepina into the Miami diet. See George Winter, "Cedar Lake and Lindsay's Cabin, 1844," in Sarah E. Cooke and Rachel B. Ramadhyani, eds., *Indians and a Changing Frontier: The Art of George Winter* (Indianapolis, 1993), 187; Trowbridge, *Meearmeear Traditions*, ed. Kinietz, 65; "Memoire concernant le paye Illinois," III, 311-312; Berzok, *American Indian Food*, 122-123.

tastes like a scallion and comes from the same plant family. Indians ate them raw, but women also used them to flavor soup. Many plants grew side by side in the deciduous forests that lined the Ohio River valley, such as the broad-leaved waterleaf and Indian salad. Both were edible and used much like lettuce leaves. Many plants had multiple uses and were both edible and medicinal. The broad-leaved waterleaf, when combined with other roots, served as an antidote to poisons, whereas the fiber of the common milkweed acted as a wart remover. Early French observers like Pierre Deliette were confident that this multiplicity of plants was proof of "the abundance of all things in their country."[37]

Indian women used plants, their roots, and the bark of trees to create the dyes to color porcupine quills, the white hair of deer tails, and trade cloth. Women transmitted knowledge about the creation of dyes orally, from generation to generation. Making and using them required the skill to recognize and harvest these plants as well as the ability to combine them with other materials to ensure that dyes set and remained vivid. Indian women created a rainbow of colors from the world in which they lived. The root of the puccoon (poccoon; *Batschia canescens*) created the color orange, American yellow root produced a bright yellow, green was extracted from boiling the smooth bark of the hickory tree, and sumac flowers yielded black dyes, as did the bark of the white walnut. Red was the most popular color and was extracted from the slender root of a wetlands plant the Shawnees called "haut a the caugh," commonly known as madder red. These dyes were used to color processed skins, the porcupine quills used in decoration, or even embroidery thread. But, more important, these dyes were used to color the body and especially the face. Captain John Smith mentioned that the Virginia Indians used the puccoon root mixed with oil to "preserve them from the heat, and in winter from the cold." The Jesuit Bressani confirmed this observation: "This painting serves them in winter as a mask against the cold and the ice; in war, it prevents their countenances from betraying them by revealing inward fear, makes them more terrible to the enemy, and conceals extremes of youth or age, which might inspire strength and courage in the adversary."[38]

Indian women's knowledge about these naturally occurring dyes was directly related to prospective business ventures in the Early Republic. In a

---

37. Erichsen-Brown, *Use of Plants*, 340; Frances Densmore, *How Indians Use Wild Plants for Food, Medicine, and Crafts* (New York, 1974), 319–321.

38. Erichsen-Brown, *Use of Plants*, 457; John Smith, *A Map of Virginia: With a Description of the Countrey, the Commodities, People, Government, and Religion . . .* (Oxford, 1612), 93; *JR*, XXXVIII, 253.

paper presented at the American Philosophical Society in 1782, Hugh Martin first described madder red, a dye crucial to the cloth industry. Like his fellow naturalists, Martin frequently drew attention to Indian usage of roots, flowers, and bark as dyes—practices that could easily be transferred to the nation's fledgling cloth industry. Martin's paper explained the process by which Indians created the color red because, until 1868, natural rose madder supplied half the world with that color, and the plant lent itself to transplanting and cultivation. Unfortunately, Martin's paper identified this process merely as an "Indian" method rather than as Indian women's work, his lack of direct observation leaving him uninformed about the gendered division of labor. Countless first-person descriptions, in contrast, cast the dyeing of cloth and the manufacture of clothing as women's work. Despite its limitations, Martin's detailed paper provides a unique insight into the skill required to process plants into dyes and offers new perspectives on women's agrarian activity in the Ohio River valley. Martin, who had experimented with the processing of dyes, described the plants' habitat, the identifying marks for recognition, and the process for turning them into dyes. Madder grew prolifically in the Ohio River's low-lying wetlands and spread along the ground near the surface. The plant's orange and yellow roots were the source of the dye. Women dried these roots and, when they became brown, pounded them in a mortar; the women then added juice from apples, and when thoroughly blended, the mixture went into a kettle of water, along with the material to be dyed. The kettle was placed over a gentle fire until the desired color was fixed. Red was a symbolic color for many Indian communities and was especially prominent in dress in the Ohio River valley. French fur trade records identify madder red as Turkey Red, and records indicate that it was women who exchanged these dried plant roots as part of the fur trade.[39]

The vegetation that bordered the Ohio and its tributary rivers allowed women to secure the variety of materials necessary to produce the various dye colors. Dyes were extracted from the bark of trees, and in this virgin forest landscape, the incredible variety of trees defied imagination: hickory, beech, ash, chestnut, tulip, maple elm, and walnut were all common. Beneath the canopy of these dense forests, women harvested a variety of fruits indigenous

---

39. Hugh Martin, "An Account of the Principal Dies Employed by the North-American Indians," American Philosophical Society, *Transactions*, III (1793), 222–225. The use of dye had a long history that stretched back to the early Egyptian period, but its use ended in 1866, when the alizarin component from the plant was extracted and red became the first natural dye to be processed synthetically. For a detailed discussion of the process of using vegetable substances to secure a color and a mineral substance to set the color, see Densmore, *How Indians Use Wild Plants*, 369–374.

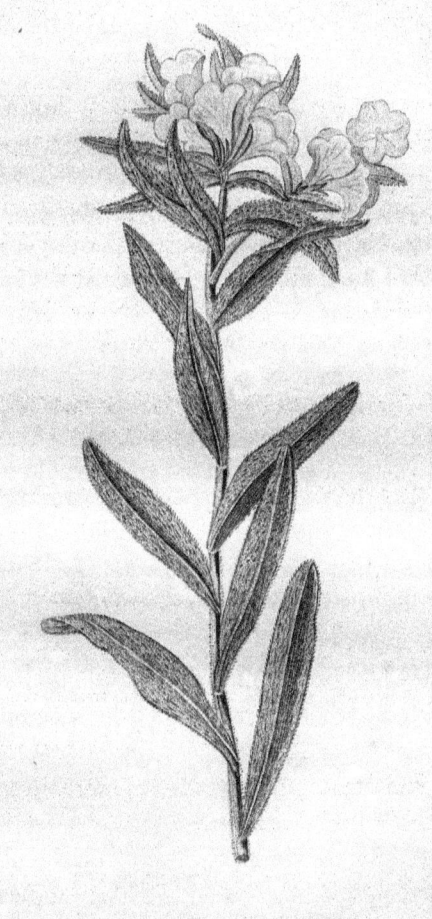

FIGURE 4. *"Batschia canescens"* (puccoon). In William P. C. Barton, *A Flora of North America: Illustrated by Coloured Figures, Drawn from Nature,* 3 vols. (Philadelphia, 1821–1823), II, table 58. Michigan State University Libraries, Special Collections, East Lansing, Mich.

to the Ohio River valley. Wild red currant and skunk currant were gathered from vines lying on the forest floor, and red currants were picked from upright bushes. Bittersweet was collected from the vines that twined along tree trunks and used to treat disorders of the skin and rheumatism. "Grapevines, heavy with fruit in season, laced tree to tree along the banks, and mistletoe clotted the branches. Sometimes a tree chopped through at the base would be held upright by the entangling vines." There were numerous indigenous fruit trees — persimmon, mulberry, thornapple, chokeberry, and pawpaw. These were eaten raw or dried for winter use. One of the delicacies for Indians came from the assimine tree, which produced an oval-shaped fruit that was "a little larger than a bustard's egg; its substance is white and spongy, and becomes yellow when the fruit is ripe. It contains two or three kernels, large and flat like the garden bean. They have a special cell. The fruits grow ordinarily in pairs, and are suspended on the same stalk." Throughout the valley region, there were numerous berries, such as persimmons, juneberries, mulberries, strawberries, and blueberries that women dried and used much as cranberries and dates are used today. In the fall, Indian women and their children gathered fruits, dried them, and then added them to foods during the winter months, giving more flavor to the dishes. Indians also collected a berry that reminded the English of capers, which was dried in the sun and then boiled in hot water for a prolonged period to remove the acidic flavor.[40]

Soil fertility and an abundant food supply characterized Indian villages in the Ohio River valley. East of the Appalachians, the fall line dispersed the winter snow melts and spared most river villages from springtime floods, allowing Indians to locate their villages along major riverways. On the western side of the Appalachians, winter snow flowed into the Ohio River, causing the river to overflow its banks. Villages were rarely located along the Ohio River itself, most being situated along the rivers that flowed on the adjoining lands to the north and south, where flooding was far less likely and dangerous. The Ohio flooded rapidly, often in unexpected and uncontrollable ways, and settlements along its banks had a precarious existence.[41]

40. Densmore, *How Indians Use Wild Plants*, 321–322; Erichsen-Brown, *Use of Plants*, 109–139; Scott Russell Sanders, "The Force of Moving Water," in Robert L. Reid, *Always a River: The Ohio River and the American Experience* (Bloomington, Ind., 1991), 14; "Account of the Voyage," in *JR*, LXIX, 173; Bruce, *Economic History*, I, 166.

41. Sanders, "Force of Moving Water," in Reid, *Always a River*, 20–21; Hall, *The West*, 54–55. In December 1847, the river at Cincinnati was high, but tolerably so and navigable. It rose fourteen feet in twenty-four hours, then another two feet per day for a full week. When it reached its uncontrollable maximum height of 62.5 feet, even that was still lower than the high-water mark set in the Great Flood of 1832.

Seventeenth- and eighteenth-century Ohio River valley Indians probably enjoyed healthier circumstances than their counterparts on the eastern seaboard. When Englishmen arrived on the Atlantic coast, they were incapable of feeding themselves, and the agrarian surpluses of Indian villages saved them from starvation. But repeated European raids on Indian food supplies reduced Indians to minimal subsistence levels, and disease microbes frequently depopulated these more vulnerable Indian populations. English traders did not move into the Ohio River valley until the early to mid-eighteenth century, when disease microbes encountered an Indian population with increased immunity levels, who lived in well-supplied villages where a food surplus amply fed visiting European traders. Indian villages along the Ohio also harvested a larger and more extensive variety of foods: plants from wetlands, abundant quantities of corn, beans, and squash planted along the riverways, fruits and nuts from forest lands, and large numbers of fish and animals that provided important sources of protein. Especially common along the numerous lakes and ponds in the lands north of the Ohio were enormous flocks of waterfowl. They were so plentiful, Europeans found that their presence hindered canoe travel. European arrival proved far less deadly in the Ohio River valley, offering dramatically different mortality rates from the Atlantic coastal region.[42]

Along the entrance to the Maumee River, Jacques-Charles de Sabrevois described wetlands so crowded with wildlife that "there is at all seasons game without end, especially in autumn and in spring; so that one cannot sleep on account of the noise made by the cries of the swans, bustards geese, ducks, cranes, and other birds." Similar conditions prevailed in the far western reaches of the Ohio River valley. When river levels in the marshes were low, the waterfowl moved to the lakes and rivers where "there is such a number of them in the river, and especially in the lake . . . on account of the abundance of roots in it, [that] when . . . this game remained on the water, one could not get through in a canoe without pushing them aside with the paddle, and yet the lake is seven leagues long and more than a quarter of a league wide in the broadest part."[43]

The southern banks of the Ohio River were bordered by extensive grasslands that teemed with animal life; it was these lands that served as the winter hunting ground for Indian villages in the valley and drew more distant northern and eastern Indians, such as the Iroquois, Potawatomi, Delaware, Abenaki, Cherokee, and Creek. Shawnee villages were initially located along rivers

---

42. David S. Jones, "Virgin Soils Revisited," *WMQ*, 3d Ser., XL (2003), 742.

43. [Sabrevois], "1718," in Thwaites, ed., *French Regime in Wisconsin*, part 1, 374; "Memoire concernant le paye Illinois," III, 265.

south of the Ohio, and although most Shawnee moved east in the 1690s, they returned to hunt in these vast grasslands. Men pursued deer, elk, bear, and turkey. In the fifteenth century, bison were introduced into daily diets. They appeared in the prairies of Illinois Country around 1400, and by 1500, they had moved into the Indiana prairies. Robert La Salle estimated the herds at between two and four hundred, and Sebastian Rasles described bison herds in the thousands: huge, lumbering animals that spread out "as far as the eye could reach." They hardened the ground to create the Great Buffalo Trace (the Shawnee called it Alanantowamiowee), which was twelve to twenty feet in width and led south from the prairies in present-day Indiana and Illinois. Bison crossed the Wabash River at Vincennes, followed the Buffalo Trace to the Falls of the Ohio, and then descended on Big Bone Lick and the barrens of Kentucky. The herds extended into the interior lands north of the Ohio River and stretched as far as the St. Joseph and Maumee Rivers. Thirty leagues from the mouth of the Maumee was the Glaize, where bison ate clay and then wallowed in it. In villages at Ouiatenon, the Wea commanded a hilltop view that afforded them an early glimpse of the approaching herds. From the summit of a hill near Ouiatenon, one French observer reported, "Nothing is visible to the eye but prairies full of buffalo."[44]

44. Kenneth B. Tankersley, "Bison and Subsistence Change: The Protohistoric Ohio Valley and Illinois Valley Connection," in Dale R. Croes, Rebecca A. Hawkins, and Barry L. Isaac, eds., *Research in Economic Anthropology: Long-Term Subsistence Change in Prehistoric North America*, Supplement 6 (Greenwich, Conn., 1992), 103–130; Robert La Salle, *Relation of the Discoveries and Voyages of Cavelier De La Salle from 1679 to 1681, the Official Narrative*, trans. Melville B. Anderson (Chicago, 1901), 81–82; *JR*, LXVII, 167; Jackson, *Natural Heritage of Indiana*, xix; McCafferty, *Native American Place-Names of Indiana*, 172–173; John D. Barnhart and Dorothy L. Riker, *Indiana to 1816: The Colonial Period* (Indianapolis, 1971), 67, 363; Morgan, *Land of Big Rivers*, 10–42; Lakomäki, *Gathering Together*, 30–31; Craig Thompson Friend, *Kentucke's Frontiers* (Bloomington, Ind., 2010), 99. Father Sebastian Rasles was a missionary priest among the Illinois and lived at Kaskaskia in 1692. For descriptions of Rasles, see Donald B. Ricky, *Indians of Missouri: Past and Present* (St. Clair Shores, Mich., 1999), 154; Gilbert J. Garraghan, *The Jesuits of the Middle United States* (New York, 1938), I, 4. The Great Buffalo Trace is discussed in George R. Wilson, *Trails and Surveys* (Indianapolis, 1919) as well as Gayle Thornbrough and George R. Wilson, "The Buffalo Trace," Indiana Historical Society, *Publications*, XV, no. 1 (1936), 192. John Heckewelder, who traveled west to the Wabash, described the salt licks, which attracted the bison herds. See "Narrative of John Heckewelder's Journey to the Wabash in 1792," *Pennsylvania Magazine of History and Biography*, XII (1888), 34–54, 165–184; Helen Hornbeck Tanner, "The Glaize in 1792: A Composite Indian Community," *Ethnohistory*, XXV (1978), 15–39. For a description of the way in which bison facilitated a woodlands-prairie transition among the Illinois, see Robert Michael Morrissey, "The Power of the Ecotone: Bison, Slavery, and

Organized bison hunts took place during the late spring and early summer months, providing crucial sustenance after the corn was planted and until it ripened. On the plains north of the Ohio, bison fed on the prairie grasses of the plains openings interspersed along the tributary rivers. Bison hunts required the labor of both men and women. Sieur Deliette, who lived among the Illinois, described the sequential relationship of hunting and planting: once women planted their cornfields, most of the villages left for the buffalo hunt.

> At the end of March, or at the beginning of April, they busy themselves gathering wood so as to be able to do their planting at the beginning of May. . . . When they wish to finish their sowing early, they offer a feast of flat sides of beef with mixed corn inside of it, and invite as many women as they need to spade up their fields. These do not refuse such invitations, and . . . at the beginning of June they hill up their corn, and after that the village sets out on the buffalo hunt.[45]

After the planting, a small group of women and children were left to tend and weed the corn while most of the other residents moved to summer villages for one to two months. Their first camp was only two leagues from the village, where women and young girls built temporary structures along the prairie's edge. They cut down trees and shaved bark from the trunks to build the residences and create tripods for cooking pots. They gathered wood for the fire, and, when the hunters returned, boiling water stood ready to cook the meat. Deliette noted that the party's first meal was venison, although they had come to hunt buffalo. The next day, when the bison herd appeared, everyone's attention shifted to the elders, who initiated the hunt. The elders harangued the young hunters, urging them to kill all of the bison herd. While one small group of young men stampeded the animals, a second group of the most agile and enduring hunters ran alongside the bison. Deliette remained among the elder hunters who guarded the camp, but, despite their protection, he found the bison so intimidating that he fled and took refuge in his quarters. His description, written from the safety of his hut, provides insight into the dangers involved and the careful organization required for a successful hunt:

> They started out in two bands, running always at a trot. When they were about a quarter of a league from the animals, they all ran at full speed, and when within gunshot they fired several volleys and shot off an extraor-

---

the Rise and Fall of the Grand Village of the Kaskaskia," *Journal of American History,* CII (2015), 667–692.

45. "Memoire concernant le paye Illinois," III, 303–304.

dinary number of arrows. A great number of buffalos remained on the ground, and they pursued the rest in such a manner that they were driven toward us. Our old men butchered these. As for me, I did not shoot. Their appearance filled me with terror.... The cows are as big as the big oxen here. They have a hump about eight inches high which extends from their shoulders to the middle of their backs. They have their whole heads covered with fine hair so that their eyes can hardly be seen....

They killed 120 buffalos from which they brought back a hundred tongues. The people from my cabin smoked these and distributed them among themselves.... We remained a week in this place in order to dry all this meat. They make for this purpose a kind of cradle ten feet long, three feet wide, and four feet high, which they call *gris,* upon which they spread out their meat after preparing it. Under this they kindle a little fire. They are at it for a day, when they wish to dry a flat side. There are two of these in a buffalo. They take it from the shoulder clear to the thigh and from the hump to the middle of the belly, after which they spread it out as thin as they can, making it usually four feet square.

The drying of this meat by the women and girls does not prevent the young men from going to the chase every day.

Deliette described multiple hunts during the summer months, which required tremendous stamina from both men and women. He described Illinois women as "very industrious, rarely idle, especially when they are married." Women built the lodgings, collected the firewood, cooked the meals, prepared the feasts, and smoked the meats that fed their families. They often sent smoked meat back to those women who remained in the villages to tend the corn. Larger villages engaged in several buffalo hunts; the rich bounty of the bison herd provided a necessary food supply for highly populated villages.[46]

The bison were a long-established food source that supplemented household diets, and women often transformed the bones of the bison into necessary tools, such as bone beamers, that were used to scrape hides in either a pushing or pulling motion. Bison robes were worn during the winter months, used for bedding, and exchanged as part of the fur trade. At early precontact sites, such as the Madisonville site near present-day Cincinnati, stone and bone hiding tools were found in abundance, as was red ochre, which was also used in hide preparation. In the late seventeenth century, hunting bison provided the greatest amount of flesh in return for the least energy expenditure. Bison meat was preserved as jerky and pemmican, a high-energy foodstuff

46. Ibid., 274–277.

containing the same nourishment in one pound as in five pounds of undried meat.[47]

Fur traders were understandably awed by the size of the bison, but we should not let their heart-thumping description of the beasts obscure the amazement they expressed about the general abundance of mammalian and avian life massed along the riverways. French and British traders journeying along the Ohio marveled at the bounty of the natural landscape. There were prodigious flocks of bald eagles, whooping cranes by the thousands, and ducks, geese, partridges, and pheasants by the millions. In 1765, George Croghan, an English trader, noted, "The country hereabouts abounds with buffalo, bears, deer and all sorts of wild game, in such plenty, that we killed out of our boats as much as we wanted." By the late eighteenth century, descriptions of the river became promotional, as when Thomas Hutchins, the first official U.S. geographer, praised the lands adjoining the Ohio River for their "healthfulness, fertility of soil, and variety of productions." He claimed that the bountiful animal herds were unsurpassed "by any on the habitable globe." Audubon related, "The margins of the shores and of the river were ... amply supplied with game. A Wild Turkey, a Grouse, or a Blue-winged Teal, could be procured in a few moments." Audubon, who lived at the Falls of the Ohio for several years, claimed that one neighbor had wantonly killed two hundred deer and eighty bears in one season.[48]

During the precontact and early contact periods, situating villages in ecologically distinctive landscape niches increased the sedentism and size of many Indian villages. Archaeologists contend that this resulted from access to sufficient environmental resources rather than from maize cultivation. Women focused their foraging activities in a prescribed area because of the fertile and

47. Penelope B. Drooker and C. Wesley Cowan, "Transformation of the Fort Ancient Cultures of the Central Ohio Valley," in David S. Brose, Cowan, and Robert C. Mainfort, Jr., eds., *Societies in Eclipse: Archaeology of the Eastern Woodlands Indians, A.D. 1400–1700* (Tuscaloosa, Ala., 2001), 90.

48. Berzok, *American Indian Food*, 78–80; Sanders, "Force of Moving Water," in Reid, *Always a River*, 13–14; "A Selection of George Croghan's Letters and Journals Relating to Tours into the Western Country—November 16, 1750–November 1765," in Conrad Weiser, *Early Western Travels, 1748–1846: A Series of Annotated Reprints of Some of the Best and Rarest Contemporary Volumes of Travel ...*, ed. Reuben Gold Thwaites, 32 vols. (Cleveland, 1904–1907), I, 131–132; Thomas Hutchins, *A Topographical Description of Virginia, Pennsylvania, Maryland, and North Carolina, Comprehending the Rivers Ohio, Kenhawa, Sioto, Cherokee, Wabash, Illinois, Mississippi, Etc.: The Climate, Soil and Produce, whether Animal, Vegetable, or Mineral...* (London, 1778); John James Audubon, "The Ohio," in Maria Audubon, ed., *Audubon and His Journal* (New York, 1897), II, 205–206.

abundant landscape of the Ohio River valley. They determined the timing and frequency of village moves, generally when cornfields decreased in harvest yields, but village movement dramatically declined in the Ohio River valley because of the multiplicity of natural, renewable resources incorporated into household diets from adjacent wetlands. Archaeologists working in New England claim that access to shellfish, an adequate supply of meat, and wampum production increased sedentism along the coast. The Ohio River valley offered parallel circumstances for women's household production: women's prolific cornfields were renewed each spring, and they supplemented household diets with a rich, diverse supply of indigenous plants from marshes and shellfish and fish from rivers. New England Indians had access to wampum as a trade item, but in the Ohio River valley, furs from the Great Black Swamp transformed the Indians into prosperous traders. Village sites became permanent because of their access to forest and prairie lands, where animals, fruits, and berries were plentiful. Skilled hunters provided reliable sources of protein. Indian women's cultivation of corn, their aptitude in harvesting natural resources, and plentiful numbers of deer, bear, and wild turkeys led to multiple villages' being located in proximity to each other.[49]

SABREVOIS'S 1718 OVERVIEW OF THE OHIO RIVER VALLEY

Before committing either financial resources or military detachments to a region, French policymakers at Versailles considered reports from an extensive network of travelers and informants. Jacques-Charles de Sabrevois was the first Frenchman to travel along the Ohio's numerous tributary rivers and to send a detailed overview of the region to the ministry of marine. A portion of his narrative was probably recorded when he initially journeyed from Fort Niagara in 1714; it evinces a sense of wonder characteristic of travelers coming upon this unexpectedly lush landscape. During Sabrevois's command at Detroit, French interests in the Illinois Country solidified with the construction of Fort de Chartres in 1718. Simultaneously, French attention shifted dramatically to the midsection of the Ohio River valley, where Sabrevois located the large Miami populations at the Maumee-Wabash River portage and the multiethnic villages of the Wabash River valley. French control over this short portage assured fur traders an almost uninterrupted journey

---

49. Mary Beth Williams and Jeffrey Bendremer, "The Archaeology of Maize, Pots, and Seashells: Gender Dynamic in Late Woodland and Contact-Period New England," in Cheryl Classen and Rosemary A. Joyce, eds., *Women in Prehistory: North America and Mesoamerica* (Philadelphia, 1997), 136–149.

from Montreal to Detroit, the Illinois Country, and the increasingly significant port of New Orleans. Sabrevois's identification of populous agrarian villages encouraged Versailles to assign small military units to the region and establish French trading sites adjacent to Indian settlements along the riverways. In addition, Sabrevois's portrait of the southern Great Lakes confirms the agrarian character of the Ohio River valley suggested by environmental analysis of the region.[50]

Sabrevois's account began with his initial journey from Fort Niagara, where he was stationed as an officer. Knowing of the French imperial interest in the creation of an infrastructure that could carry information to and from the continental interior, Sabrevois related his journey from Fort Niagara to Lake Erie. He traveled on horseback along a wide Indian path that linked the two regions. Long before military officers carved out a route linking the Great Lakes route at Presque Island (near Erie, Pennsylvania) to the upper reaches of the Ohio River, Sabrevois described the pathway that Indians followed from Fort Niagara to Lake Erie, which then carried them south along the Sandusky to the Ohio. This was much wider than the trails that Indians carved through forestlands. Sabrevois commented on the ease of travel, making it apparent that this was a well-established Indian road rather than a foot pathway. His procession along Lake Erie led him to remark on the lushness of the landscape; he found the southern shoreline far more "attractive than . . . the Northern side." Near Lake Erie, he had caught sight of his first bison, "which are not found on the Northern side." Bison were an ongoing part of the fur trade, but only travelers who ventured into the Ohio River valley set eyes on these huge animals.[51]

Sabrevois described the eastern entrance to the Sandusky River from Lake Erie, which allowed fur traders to bypass the fort at Detroit. This well-traveled path was wide and clearly marked and led to the Black Swamp and Scioto River. Sabrevois and his men rode along the Sandusky River trail for two to three days. Following a short portage of four miles, they traveled "over a fine

---

50. Kenneth J. Banks, *Chasing Empire across the Sea: Communications and the State in the French Atlantic, 1713–1763* (Montreal, Que., 2002), introduction, esp. 8–13. Transatlantic communications were directed to the marine, which was based in Paris but attached to whatever palace the court occupied and functioned similarly to the Spanish Council of the Indies.

51. One of La Salle's most glaring mistakes was his description of the Ohio as the Ouabanchi (Wabash), which he mistakenly identified as the long river that ran from Lake Erie to the Mississippi. LaSalle's interpretation transformed the Ohio into the Wabash. Subsequent French travelers then continued to misidentify the Ohio as the Wabash, including Sabrevois. See Michael McCafferty, *Native American Place-Names of Indiana* (Urbana, Ill., 2007), 28–29; Banks, *Chasing Empire,* 87–88.

road" for another quarter of a league and then stopped to camp. They spent several days constructing elm bark canoes, but during that time they were comfortable and remarkably well fed. Sabrevois's journal revealed both the ease of travel and the adequate food supply available to travelers:

> Any one wishing easily to reach the misyspy would only need to follow This river or the Sandosquet, and would run no risk of going hungry, for all those who have traveled over this route have often assured me that there was all Along that beautiful River so vast a number of buffalo and all other wild animals that they Were Often obliged to discharge their guns in order to clear a passage.

Sabrevois's men canoed on the Scioto River until they reached the Ohio, which he pronounced to be "beautiful indeed, for it is nearly a quarter of a League wide, and has a fine current without rapids, except a Single cascade which is only half an arpent long."[52]

Sabrevois's canoe trip north from the mouth of the Sandusky River to Detroit also demonstrated the potentially hazardous nature of travel in the Great Lakes. He had stopped briefly at the mouth of the Sandusky River, where a bay was then in the process of formation. But, in 1718, the area was a large marsh with little or no protection for boats. Lake Erie, the shallowest of the Great Lakes with a maximum depth of 210 feet, was periodically swept by fierce winds that created enormous waves and made canoe travel hazardous. In 1753, when the French priest Jacques-François Forget Duverger journeyed to the Illinois Country from Lachine, Montreal's embarkation point, the harsh lake winds and waves of Lake Erie daily threatened to capsize his canoe. He left Sandusky Bay on July 17 but did not arrive in Detroit until August 6. Likewise, Sabrevois, forced to wait for the winds to subside, headed off on his ninety-mile journey to Detroit, but his journey proved far less arduous and comparatively shorter than that of Father Duverger. Sabrevois relied on knowledgeable Indian guides to lead him across the lake in Indian fashion, a procession-like voyage that both guaranteed his safe arrival and assured him access to an abundant food supply. To counteract the winds, Indians traveled from island to island, where their knowledge of the flora and fauna ensured an abundance of food resources. The first stopping point was the island of Point Pelee, where Indians caught and feasted on "all sorts of fish, especially . . . enormous sturgeon, three, four, or five feet in Length." Their next island stop was overrun with raccoons. There were so many that "in a very short time [hunters] killed as many as 900." From there, Sabrevois entered the straits of

---

52. [Sabrevois], "1718," in Thwaites, ed., *French Regime in Wisconsin,* part 1, 364–365.

the Detroit River, which led to the fort. There were a large number of islands, probably thirty or more, and Sabrevois noted that the four largest islands were closest to the French settlement. He identified the four islands at the entrance to Detroit harbor: "L'île au bois blanc (Whitewood Island); The next, L'île aux poux (Louse Island); Another, L'île aux Esclaves (Slave Island), and The fourth, Grande Isle." But it was Belle Isle that was "very beautiful, fertile, and large," in which Indian women had planted "an extraordinary number of apple-trees." There was a "very fine meadowland" where, when the apples fell to the ground, they were more than "a half a foot thick, and the apple-trees are planted as if it had been done on purpose." From Whitewood Island, it was six or seven leagues to the fort and the French settlement; both sides of the river at Detroit were lined with "the most beautiful meadows and the best soil ever seen." Two leagues from Detroit, they passed L'île aux dindes, or Turkey Island, which was "always full of Turkeys." Turkeys multiplied profusely in these rich meadowlands, and with no forests, there were few natural predators. From Sabrevois's perspective, this was a landscape far more fertile and luxuriant than French lands along the St. Lawrence.[53]

At Detroit, Sabrevois described in great detail the Indian villages that bordered the fort. Rather than decry the warlike nature of Indians, he focused on their agrarian activities. His portrayal was colored by the extent to which he believed that these Indians had adopted French behaviors, but it is clear from his account that each one of these villages had large cornfields and vegetable gardens. The first village he entered was Potawatomi. Its distinctive houses were made from reeds that women wove into mats, or *apaquois,* and fastened to wooden frames. At each of the villages he visited, he noted that "[a]ll this work [was] . . . done by the women." Women "work in the fields, raising very fine indian corn, beans, peas, squashes, and melons" while the men hunted and supplied the game. Sabrevois was especially pleased with the Potawatomis' appearance. He thought them "well clothed, like our savages resident

53. E. L. Moseley, "Formation of Sandusky Bay and Cedar Point," *Twelfth Annual Report of the Ohio State Academy of Science, 1903,* Ohio Academy of Science, *Proceedings,* IV, part 1 (Columbus, Oh., 1904), esp. 179, rpt. as *Lake Erie Floods, Lake Levels, Northeast Storms* (Columbus, Oh., 1973); François Forget Duverger, "Relation d'un voyage," MG14, J 14, National Archives of Canada, Ottawa, Ont. Many of the islands have been destroyed by erosion or by channel dredging, and many of those that remain still reflect the former animals that could be found there. Those controlled by the Americans include Belle Isle, and the islands of Calf, Celeron, Edmond, Elba, Elizabeth, Fox, Grassy, Grosse, Humbug, Hickory, Horse, Mamaiuda, Meso, Mud, Powder, Round, Stony, Sturgeons, Sugar, and Swan. On the Canadian side are Bois Blanc, Crystal, Fighting, Grass, Peche, and Turkey Island. See [Sabrevois], "1718," in Thwaites, ed., *French Regime in Wisconsin,* part 1, 366–367.

at Montreal.... They use many buffalo-Robes, highly ornamented, to cover themselves in winter; and in summer they wear Red or blue cloth."[54]

Sabrevois's repeated observations of women as responsible for manual and agrarian labor led him, like his fellow French officers, to assume that Potawatomi men had two narrow pursuits: hunting and gaming. Lacrosse was the most popular pursuit, and Sabrevois remarked that the men were so competitive that the prizes amounted "to more than 800 Livres." Although Sabrevois frequently described women's "work in the fields," he also observed that when their work ended, they came together in the evenings to dance:

> They adorn themselves liberally, grease their hair, put on white chemises, and paint their Faces with vermillion, also putting on all the porcelain beads they possess, so that after their fashion they look very well dressed. They dance to the Sound of the drum and of the *sisyquoy* [rattle], which Is a sort of gourd with pellets of lead inside. There are four or five Young men who sing, and keep time by beating the drum and the *sysyquoy*, while the women dance to the rhythm and do not miss a step. This Is a very pretty sight, And it lasts almost all night.[55]

After visiting the Potawatomi, Sabrevois walked to the Huron villages, which received his highest praise. The Huron lived in proximity to the French fort, and he was quick to point out that "they hardly dance at all, and work continually raising a very large amount of indian corn, peas, beans, and sometimes French wheat." Women's agricultural skills impressed him, and he praised both their housing styles and their manner of dress. Huron women built elongated cabins of bark with round roofs and compartmentalized interior sleeping rooms. Inside the cabins, he observed, they kept each room very neat. Sabrevois was pleased that the Huron dressed in the French fashion, donning both jerkins and cloaks. Consequently, he considered the Huron "very clever" and "the Nation most loyal to French." The Huron raised both French and traditional Indian crops, followed seasonal hunting rituals, and during the winter months maintained a sizable population in their village to "guard it." This meant additional protection for the fort when most Indians were at their hunting camps.[56]

The Odawa (Ottawa) lived on the other side of the French fort inside a palisaded fort that resembled a French stockade. Their bark cabins resembled those of the Huron, but Sabrevois criticized these for being "not so neat

---

54. [Sabrevois], "1718," in Thwaites, ed., *French Regime in Wisconsin*, part 1, 366.
55. Ibid., 367.
56. Ibid., 368.

or so well made." Like the Huron and the Potawatomi, he also considered them "very clever and very industrious, both in hunting and agriculture." He deemed the Odawa similar to the Fox and found them overly fond of games, such as lacrosse, and gambling, favoring the game of dish, which was popular among many villages in the region. To play dish, one placed six black and white stones in a bowl and shook it; if all the stones landed with the same color, then a player received six points; five stones of one color and one of a different color yielded one point; other outcomes received no points. Sabrevois uniformly described Indian men as idle and more interested in gaming than hard work, perhaps a result of gender divisions that the new commandant misunderstood.[57]

Next, Sabrevois journeyed from Detroit to Miamitown, which was located at the Maumee-Wabash portage. The Miami were crucial French allies because this portage was the shortest route for French traders traveling from Montreal to New Orleans. Recently, a group of Miami had moved from Detroit to Miamitown, citing a scarce food supply and vulnerability to attack. Miamitown was protected by natural barriers: to the east and south was the impenetrable Great Black Swamp; to the north, the Maumee entranceway from Lake Erie was obscured by ten miles of continuous marshlands. It was difficult to negotiate the marshes and reach the village without an experienced guide. Miamitown had a bountiful and convenient food source in the adjacent marshlands and wetlands. The wetlands were populated "at all seasons" with an endless supply of game and, at the nearby Glaize, the buffalo wallow gave the Miami ready access to bison. Miamitown was then one of the largest and most prosperous villages in the region, with about four thousand men, and Sabrevois noted that "they have abundance of women." Although Sabrevois considered Miamitown men barely dressed, he did notice that they were well tattooed and that the women were fully clothed in elaborate deerskins. Sabrevois judged these Miami women "very industrious" and praised them for raising a distinctive white corn. When it was ground, it resembled white flour; perhaps for Sabrevois, this signified a French lifestyle.[58]

Miamitown was also accessible to the villages clustered along the Wabash. Just south of the Maumee-Wabash portage was another Miami village, Kenapakomoko, primarily populated by women. Nearby and a little farther south was Ouiatenon, one of the largest multiethnic villages in the Ohio River valley. Its physical appearance was noticeably different from the region's other Indian communities. Here the Indians had constructed a fort, with a clus-

57. Ibid., 369; Trigger, *Children of Aataentsic*, 40.
58. [Sabrevois], "1718," in Thwaites, ed., *French Regime in Wisconsin*, part 1, 376.

ter of diverse villages surrounding the perimeter. Men had built the fort, but women scrupulously maintained it. Women from the five adjacent villages had probably collected sand from the banks of the Wabash, spreading it to cover the ground inside the fort. Women kept the fort "very clean. They do not allow any grass to grow there, and the whole fort is strewn with Sand, like the Thyleris [Tuileries]; and, if a dog drops any excrements about the fort, The women pick Them up and carry Them outside." Sabrevois viewed the fort as a defensive structure; it was also a gathering place for nearby village residents. Perhaps this fort had been an earlier earthwork structure; earthworks had characterized much of the Ohio River valley's precontact landscape. Archaeologists have suggested that most precontact villages were organized around a central plaza, the focal point for communal activities. A large structure located adjacent to the plaza often served as a public building.[59]

Sabrevois painted a remarkable portrait of the large and diverse Indian villages bordering the Ouiatenon fort and used the term "Ouyataonons" to collectively describe all five of the separate villages. The "five villages, all built close together," consisted of distinctive communities. "One is called ouyatanons, another peangnichias [Piankeshaw], another Petitcotias [Pepicokes], another Les gros; as for the last, I do not remember its name. But they are all ouyatanons." He considered these people closely aligned to the Miami because "they speak like the miamis [on the Maumee River], and are their brothers; and indeed all the miamis have the same customs and style of dress." Sabrevois believed that the Ouiatenon community could raise approximately 1,000 to 1,200 warriors, and in his journal he noted that there were "one thousand or twelve hundred men [4,000–4,800 souls in all] . . . [that] live here in these villages."[60]

59. Ibid., 370, 376; Drooker and Cowan, "Transformation of the Fort Ancient Cultures," in Brose, Cowan, and Mainfort, Jr., eds., *Societies in Eclipse,* 91–92. Stewart Rafert contends that the Miami political system was more centralized than those of other villages: "Civil chiefs were paired with war chiefs. Civil chiefs were concerned with regulation of the village and negotiations for peace, while the war chiefs sent out war parties, planned strategy, and managed ritual aspects of warfare" (Rafert, *The Miami Indians of Indiana: A Persistent People, 1654–1994* [Indianapolis, 1996], 21). Shawnee clans had headmen who functioned in a similar way, with each clan having a *hokima,* "a male civil or peace chief," and a male war leader, or *neenawtooma* (Lakomäki, *Gathering Together,* 18).

60. [Sabrevois], "1718," in Thwaites, ed., *French Regime in Wisconsin,* part 1, 376. The number of warriors in a village is generally multiplied by 3.5 to obtain an estimate of the larger village population. Historians have used this to estimate Miami population levels in the Ohio River valley. See Rafert, *Miami Indians,* 8. This type of estimate was originally used by Emma Helen Blair in *Indian Tribes of the Upper Mississippi Valley and Region of the Great Lakes.*

In the eighteenth century, Ouiatenon was one of three large villages in the Wabash River valley. Sustaining these large village populations required that Indian women cultivate a substantial acreage in maize. At Ouiatenon, Sabrevois described "two Leagues of fields, where they raise their Indian corn, pumpkins, and melons." As a comparison, most early Huron villages were also large, and they were characterized by extensive cornfields. Most Huron communities included 1,000 inhabitants and generally had 360 acres of corn under cultivation. The size of the villages at Ouiatenon would have required four to five times that amount of land, or approximately 1,500 cultivated acres of fields, in order to sustain a population level of 4,000 to 4,800 people. It took Sabrevois more than two hours to reach the end of the village cornfields, a distance that could easily have equaled 1,500 acres. It is probable that the large, communal fields were subdivided into individual household fields, with the women in the village agreeing on the boundaries between the contiguous plots.[61]

Sabrevois's description of the Ouiatenon villages reflected the multiplicity of resources that surrounded villages located along the Ohio's tributary rivers. "It was situated near the mouth of the Wea River, a place where fish of many kinds were very plentiful. Nearby was to be found a fertile soil, easy of cultivation and well adapted to the simple agricultural methods of the times. Within easy reach were to be found extensive prairies and thickly wooded forests each supplying its own particular kinds of game. . . . While easy of access yet within signaling distance were elevations that commanded a view of the country in all directions." Indian villages at Ouiatenon were surrounded by an environmental patchwork quilt of rich soils, rivers, and streams that provided a continuous supply of fish and freshwater mussels, nearby forestlands that supplied game, and prairies where bison grazed in the early summer. The elevated Wea village appeared the most prominent because it was adjacent to the prairie lands and provided a view of the distant landscape. Food was scarce until the corn ripened in late summer, and the death of one well-fed

---

61. Conrad Heidenreich, *Huronia: A History and Geography of the Huron Indians, 1600–1650* (Toronto, Ont., 1971), 213; Hurt, *Indian Agriculture*. The Huron were primarily agricultural and grew sufficient maize to ensure a two- to three-year supply. The Huron cornfields were so large that at least one Frenchman got lost traveling from one village to the next. Cornfields located along river bottomlands were later described by Maxidiac (Buffalo Bird Woman), who grew up and tended those fields in the mid- to late 1800s along the upper Missouri River drainage. See Gayle J. Fritz, "Levels of Native Biodiversity in Eastern North America," in Paul E. Minnis and Wayne J. Elisens, eds., *Biodiversity and Native America* (Norman, Okla., 2000), 237; Gilbert L. Wilson, *Buffalo Bird Woman's Garden: Agriculture of the Hidatsa Indians* (Saint Paul, Minn., 1917).

bison supplied a large quantity of meat. These prairies were "fine ranges for immense herds of cattle."[62]

The villages clustered at Ouiatenon were also adjacent to wetlands where women harvested edible and medicinal plants. The numerous rivers and streams that branched off the Wabash created the wetlands that were crucial to this village landscape. On the west side were the Little Wabash, Vermilion, and Tippecanoe, whereas on the east side were the Patoka, White, Sugar, Raccoon Creek, Wild Cat Creek, Pipe Creek, Mississinewa, and Salamonie Rivers. The gathering of wild plants was essential to subsistence, and the nutrient content of wild plant foods is especially high, considering the ratio of nutrients to calories. Gathering was generally an arduous task, but at Ouiatenon the food supply was close at hand. Indian women often walked for miles, dug for hours, and returned to their villages carrying bundles of plants that weighed twenty to forty pounds. Adjacent wetlands minimized the time and energy women spent collecting these foods and maximized the amount of calories acquired from harvesting wild plants.

Sabrevois's report contrasted with many of the descriptions that the ministry of marine received from military commanders and envoys in the Great Lakes. He described neither a landscape disrupted by warfare nor internecine warfare between Indian villages. Sabrevois hoped to attract French settlers to the Ohio River valley, and he highlighted the attributes of this fruitful river region as well as the people who lived there. Other military commanders were invested in portraying a disrupted landscape, one that required an increased military presence and larger amounts of trade goods. Sabrevois, on the other hand, had traveled throughout the region with a small group of men, not an army. What he so vividly described in the years from 1714 to 1718 was the result of a well-established land management system: Indian women drew on the natural resources of a landscape where they planted and harvested crops that ensured that villages and households were well fed, and a surplus was available to feed French fur traders.

Sabrevois's remarkable glimpse and sweeping overview of the Ohio River valley and his description of the various village landscapes in this region attest to the lush environment of this geographically complex region. Its dramatic degradation by Americans in the nineteenth and twentieth centuries makes it

---

62. Oscar J. Craig, *Ouiatanon: A Study in Indiana History*, Indiana Historical Society, *Publications*, II, no. 8 (Indianapolis, 1893), 328; [Sabrevois], "1718," in Thwaites, ed., *French Regime in Wisconsin*, part 1, 376; Berzok, *American Indian Food*, 175–176; John Scott, *The Indiana Gazetteer; or, Topographical Dictionary*, Indiana Historical Society, *Publications*, XVIII, no. 1 (1826; rpt. Indianapolis, 1954), 119.

difficult now to understand how this river valley had so successfully supported a large Indian population and a multiplicity of Indian villages. The Ohio River valley was one of the most fertile landscapes in North America. Plow agriculture, filling in wetlands, damming rivers, and overhunting animals destroyed this ecosystem. These drastic changes were masked by the frontier myth of a rigorous pioneer past where farmers transformed the wilderness into farmlands and brought civilization to the region. Myth masked the destruction wrought by Americans moving west, who then peopled this landscape with imagined folk heroes in perfect harmony with nature. In the Ohio River valley, one mythical hero emerged, erasing from public memory the work of Indian women who had created this prosperous agrarian village world and the harsh ways in which Indians were forced off their lands.

From *Harper's Magazine* in the nineteenth century to present-day Disney movies, the mythological story of Johnny Appleseed masked the reality of frontier life in the Ohio River valley. Like many of the first Americans who arrived in the Old Northwest, Johnny Appleseed lacked the financial resources to purchase land, and he intruded on Indian lands as a squatter. The real man behind the myth, John Chapman, came from an impoverished New England family, and for several years he wandered the Pennsylvania frontier. Eventually, he stumbled on the idea of planting apple seeds, which, once mature, he then sold or bartered to incoming farmers so he could secure the necessary capital to buy lands.[63]

Apple trees were essential to frontier life. Those that Johnny Appleseed planted by seed generated a variety of apples. The most edible were harvested in the early fall and stored in root cellars. Farm women also dried apples, which they used to flavor winter sauces. Others were cooked in large kettles and transformed into apple butter. The remnants of the fall apple harvest, which were neither fit for storage nor drying, were hauled to the cider presses. Apple juice acquired an effervescent sparkle during the winter months, was transformed into applejack and apple brandy, and became the alcoholic staple of adult male diets. For women, boiled apple cider and vinegar were the crucial ingredients in preserving pickles, preserves, and mincemeats.

Chapman arrived just north of Pittsburgh in 1792, when the western

---

63. Chapman arrived through the back door of Pennsylvania's land rush and was part of the first arriving group of squatters who lacked the capital to purchase lands. He first settled on the Upper Allegheny frontier, and from 1794 to 1798, he repeatedly traveled up and down the Allegheny in an ongoing search for unoccupied land. Only on lands where there were no claimants could he establish squatters' rights. He first appeared on the 1801 census and lived alone (Robert Price, *Johnny Appleseed: Man and Myth* [Bloomington, Ind., 1954], 23–27).

movement was blocked by a hostile Indian presence. Anthony Wayne's victory at Fallen Timbers in 1794 partially opened the lands north of the Ohio to settlers. For the next six to seven years, Chapman headed into the Ohio River valley and planted apple trees at the nexus of tributary rivers that flowed into the Ohio. He arrived before the surveyors and planted his trees on Indian lands, anticipating the migratory routes of incoming settlers. Chapman's apple trees soon generated sufficient capital for his land purchases. But his orchards required no capital investment: he gathered the seeds from apple mills, transported them west, and planted them two to three years in advance of settlement. This plan eliminated the need for settlers to transport seeds from the cider presses, often a precarious task with little guarantee of success. Chapman provided newcomers with trees that were ready to produce fruit during the very first year of farming. With each successive wave of incoming farmers, he ventured farther west and planted trees that were in bloom and ready to transplant.

The Appleseed myth ignored or glossed over his skill as a businessman as well as his speculative real estate transactions. By the end of his life, John Chapman had gone from penniless squatter to affluent landowner. During the last six years of his life, he owned a significant quantity of land: a town lot in Mount Vernon, Ohio; seven parcels of farmland in Ohio and Indiana that totaled more than 350 acres; one ninety-nine-year lease on land in Richland County, Ohio; and at least four other Ohio land leases. He held three tracts of land along the Maumee River and had a nursery of 15,000 trees growing in 1845 at the time of his death.[64] The Johnny Appleseed myth rooted his desire to plant apple trees in a love of the land while the real John Chapman sold apple trees and raised capital to acquire more than 1,200 acres of land. Chapman's landholdings were considerably larger than those of the average settler in the Midwest. He cultivated an eccentricity that masked his acquisitive behaviors; his secondhand dress and the wearing of a mush pan on his head generated the impression that he cared little for worldly goods. But a close examination of his land transactions in the Old Northwest easily shatters that impression.

The folklore that surrounds Johnny Appleseed ignores Indian women's horticultural labor in the Ohio River valley. Along the Ohio and its tributaries, Indian women planted and cultivated fruit trees, long before Chapman journeyed along the Ohio. When he arrived in the Ohio River valley, the land was already covered by a tremendous variety of fruit trees. It is highly probable

---

64. Steven Fortriede, *Johnny Appleseed: The Man behind the Myth* (Fort Wayne, Ind., 1978), 21.

that Indian women planted many of the apple trees that Chapman claimed as part of his own handiwork.[65]

Fruit trees at the confluence of rivers and streams created numerous wild orchards while, in villages, Indian women cultivated fruit trees, grafting and pruning them to ensure a uniform and abundant harvest. Along the Allegheny River, at the entrance to the Ohio, were the remnants of extensive apple orchards that belonged to Seneca women. In 1791, when white settlers flooded into the region, these orchards continued to bear fruit, despite the damage inflicted on them during the Revolutionary War by the Sullivan Expedition. One observer noted, "Many of the trees are girdled, and marked by the destructive axes of the soldiery." Soldiers had nevertheless left tree trunks, from which new branches emerged. Indian women's work was then erased by the settlers who took possession of their lands and appropriated the remaining trees for themselves. Despite dispossession, Iroquois women continued to grow fruit. In an 1845 census, on the nine Iroquois reservations that remained in New York, Indian women had planted close to seven thousand trees that bore fruit.[66]

Before the arrival of Johnny Appleseed, there were numerous eighteenth-century travelers who described the horticultural lushness of the Ohio River valley. When official U.S. geographer Thomas Hutchins traveled the length of the Ohio River valley, he described a large number of existing fruit orchards. "All European fruits:—Apples, Peaches, Pears, Cherrys, Currants, Gooseberrys, Melons, and thrive well here." In 1792, when General Anthony Wayne directed Major William McMahon to scout the lands north of the Ohio River, he traveled along the Tuscarawas River. McMahon described extensive peach orchards at three abandoned Moravian Indian villages: Gnadenhütten,

---

65. Price contends that uncritical sentimentalism invented Chapman as the person who brought the first fruit into the Middle West. David H. Diamond sees Johnny Appleseed as a persistent national farming myth and believes that "Chapman's interaction with plants, as hired forest clearer and tree faller and as apple seed planter, were seldom nurturing, failing utterly to reach levels of horticultural artisanship exhibited by true craft nurserymen in the same region at the same time." See Price, *Johnny Appleseed*, 37–38; Diamond, "Origins of Pioneer Apple Orchards in the American West: Random Seeding versus Artisan Horticulture," *Agricultural History Society*, LXXXIV (2010), 424.

66. M. A. Leeson, *History of Seneca County Ohio: Containing a History of the Country, Its Townships, Towns, Villages* . . . (Chicago, 1886); Winslow C. Watson, ed., *Men and Times of the Revolution; or, Memoirs of Elkanah Watson Including His Journals of Travels in Europe and America* . . . (New York, 1856), 308; Henry Rowe Schoolcraft, *Notes on the Iroquois; or, Contributions to American History, Antiquities, and General Ethnology* (1847; rpt. East Lansing, Mich., 2002), 92–96.

Sale, and Schoenbrunn. There was an abundance of peaches, but nearly all the "branches had been broken by bears." At Gnadenhütten, Major McMahon discovered "the best apples he had ever tasted." Two years later and just one week before the Battle of Fallen Timbers, when General Wayne assembled his troops at the intersection of the Maumee and Auglaize Rivers, his journal contained a description of vast apple and peach orchards near the site of an abandoned Wyandot village. Following Wayne's victory, large numbers of Americans entered the lands north of the Ohio River and claimed the fruit trees and orchards of Indian women.[67]

Despite extensive cornfields, bountiful vegetable gardens, and fruit orchards, Indian women's labor generally went unrecognized by many incoming Europeans. Even when early accounts kept by explorers and settler colonists were later published in nineteenth-century historical society journals, those reprinted documents were often edited to minimize Indian agriculture. Nineteenth-century translations of early French journals for an American audience distorted the references to Indian agriculture as women's work. The early French texts relied on *ils* to refer to men's work and *elles* to refer to women's work, but American writers relied on the gender neutral term "they" to describe agrarian work. This compounded the mistakes of early French observers who failed to understand that women's agricultural labor went beyond the growing of corn. Since Indians were regarded as nomadic, references to Indian agrarianism were frequently reduced to descriptions of inconsequential vegetable gardens.[68]

Jefferson's *Notes on the State of Virginia* popularized the notion that the Indian's natural life was spent in the woods, wandering through forests in pursuit of game. Emphasizing the importance of the hunt to daily survival reinforced the concept of Indians as nomads and, in addition, imagined women as the drudges of society who performed the menial functions that kept ordinary existence intact. Indian women's agrarian work was reduced to a secondary role, as that of part-time horticulturalists who tended small vegetable gardens and grew patches of corn to compensate for sparse returns from the hunt. In the Ohio River valley, cornfields, vegetable gardens, and the

67. Thomas Hutchins, "A Topographical Description of Virginia, Pennsylvania, and North Carolina," in Harlow Lindley, ed., *Indiana as Seen by Early Travelers,* Indiana Historical Collections, III (Indianapolis, 1916), 8; Edward Rondthaler, *Life of John Heckewelder* (Philadelphia, 1847), 125; Paul A. W. Wallace, ed., *Thirty Thousand Miles with John Heckewelder* (Pittsburgh, 1958), 261; Henry Howe, *Historical Collections of Ohio* (Norwalk, Oh., 1896), II, 545.

68. Gabriel Sagard, *Le Grand voyage du pays des Hurons, situé en l'Amerique vers la Mer douce, ez derniers confins de la nouvelle France, dite Canada . . . .* (Paris, 1632), 133–135.

gathering of wild plants were far more important than hunting. Meat provided protein, but the starches, vitamins, and minerals that were essential to a healthy diet came from cultivating corn, squash, and beans and harvesting edible wild plants. Women were highly productive farmers who also learned to gather plants from the natural landscape, and although men did not farm, they helped to clear new fields. The invisibility of women's labor fostered the mistaken impressions that Indians were hunter societies.[69]

In the last half of the nineteenth century, when Indian women were increasingly confined to the home, their centuries of agrarian expertise was further masked by the cloak of domesticity. Nineteenth-century white farmers used the land to amass individual wealth rather than as a means of ensuring the welfare of the larger community. When agricultural inefficiency became problematic, land grant universities were founded to teach "scientific farming methods"; Indian women's agrarian expertise was completely ignored. Food production was linked to fertilization and higher crop yields. Eventually, food production was controlled by geneticists, who were primarily male, and research focused on scientifically controlled methods of crop production. Only recently have we begun to reassess the residual damage of environmental change fostered by western farming practices and to appreciate Indian women's agricultural production, as well as their ethnobotanical knowledge. The emergence of environmental history and women's history has led to new ways of understanding our lands and the role that Indian women played in shaping and enriching the lands where their villages were located.

This chapter makes clear the extent of women's involvement in environmentally shaping an agrarian landscape in the Ohio River valley. Neither "vacant-quarter" hypotheses nor "virgin land" characterizations should be applied to this region. By combining the evidence from archaeological and historical analyses, we can see how Indian women shaped these lands to produce sufficient food to feed their village households. Indian women and their precontact predecessors strategically reshaped the fertile lands along the river-

---

69. Thomas Jefferson, *Notes on the State of Virginia,* ed. William Peden (1954; rpt. Chapel Hill, N.C., 1995), 92–93; Bernard W. Sheehan, *Seeds of Extinction: Jeffersonian Philanthropy and the American Indian* (Chapel Hill, N.C., 1973), 165; Kelly Kindscher, *Edible Wild Plants of the Prairie: An Ethnobotanical Guide* (Lawrence, Kans., 1987), 4–5; Sagard, *Le Grand voyage du pays des Hurons,* 133–135; David D. Smits, "The 'Squaw Drudge': A Prime Index of Savagism," *Ethnohistory,* XXIX (1982), 281–306. Theda Perdue, a prominent historian of Cherokee women, discussed the invisibility of women's agricultural labors in "Women, Men, and American Indian Policy: The Cherokee Response to 'Civilization,'" in Nancy Shoemaker, ed., *Negotiators of Change: Historical Perspectives on Native American Women* (New York, 1995), 90–114.

ways, creating a landscape that was far from static. These women produced a surplus food supply that led to involvement in trade with other Indian nations and, subsequently, with the French. The next chapter explores the reasons why Indian villages often moved from the Ohio River valley to the Green Bay region. Indian women were actively involved in that decision-making; they controlled the goods of their households and the location of their houses, and they produced the surpluses necessary for trade. Increasingly, as the fur trade moved from foodstuffs to furs, women processed peltry, which led to their centrality in the exchange process. Although some Indian villages, like those of the Potawatomi, sought refuge in the lands west of Lake Michigan, not all were driven west by the "wrath" of the Iroquois. Indian women and men in many Ohio River valley villages were drawn west by the French traders who moved into the Green Bay region as they sought access to European goods.

2

THE EVOLUTION OF THE INDIAN FUR TRADE
From Green Bay to the Wabash River Valley

> There are brills of monstrous size. I have seen one whose two eyes were sixteen inches apart and whose body was as big as the biggest man. The late Monsieur de Tonti assured me that he had seen one with an interval of eighteen inches. I do not doubt that there are some even bigger, for one day a soldier of the garrison at that time among the Illinois, having gone fishing one night in a canoe, and having put out a big rock to anchor it, one of these brills, finding itself caught on the hook, made such powerful efforts that it carried away the canoe, the rock, and the man. The soldier, seeing this, exerted all his strength and was pulling it toward him when, unhappily, the line broke. It was of whitewood bark, twisted thicker than one's thumb.
> —[Pierre-Charles Deliette?]

The brill that pulled the French soldier across the lake was not a tall tale. This fish was probably a lake sturgeon; when fully grown, they were six feet long and weighed nearly two hundred pounds. Lake sturgeon had lived in North American waters since the Upper Cretaceous period (136 million years ago), when dinosaurs were at the height of development. As mentioned in the previous chapter, by the early seventeenth century, an abundance of huge fish inhabited the lakes and rivers that stretched west from the Ohio River valley to Illinois, across the Mississippi, and into northern Wisconsin. These early descriptions were not fanciful exaggerations but reflected the environmental sensitivity of an Indigenous presence before European arrival.[1]

---

1. "Memoir of De Gannes concerning the Illinois Country," in Theodore Calvin Pease and Raymond C. Werner, eds., *The French Foundations: 1680–1693,* vol. XXIII of Illinois State Historical Library, *Collections,* 38 vols. (Springfield, Ill., 1903–1978), 350–351. As mentioned

A rich swath of lands extended from the Ohio River valley to the southern tier of Wisconsin and into Iowa. Green Bay was a trading center, surrounded by extensive fishing sites in the heart of a fertile peninsula. It was lush, like the Ohio River valley. Indians gathered here to fish and trade during the precontact era, creating a world in continuous motion before European contact. The arrival of French traders in the 1660s and the large number of traders dispatched by Governor Frontenac in the 1690s drew Indians to Green Bay. Environmentally diverse resources supported increased Indian population levels. As one French observer, Bacqueville de la Potherie, put it in 1753,

> All these tribes at the bay are most favorably situated; the country is a beautiful one, and they have fertile fields planted with Indian corn. Game is abundant at all seasons, and in winter they hunt bears and beavers; they hunt deer at all times, and they even fish for wildlife . . . in autumn there is a prodigious abundance of ducks, both black and white, of excellent flavor, and savages stretch nets in certain places where these fowl alight to feed upon the wild rice. . . . All the year round they fish for sturgeon, and for herring in the autumn; and in winter they have fruits. . . . The fishery suffices to maintain large villages; they also gather wild rice and acorns; accordingly, the peoples of the bay can live in the utmost comfort.[2]

---

in Chapter 1, this has been erroneously identified and cited as the "De Gannes Memoir" rather than the "Deliette Memoir."

On sturgeon, see Brian G. Gardiner, "Sturgeons as Living Fossils," in Niles Elredge and Steven M. Stanley, eds., *Living Fossils* (New York, 1984), 148–152. Lake sturgeon inhabit large river and lake systems primarily in the Mississippi River, Hudson Bay, and Great Lakes basins. Their range spans areas that were once linked by the large lakes that formed as the glaciers retreated from North America at the end of the last ice age. Sturgeon inhabit the Great Lakes and the St. Lawrence River to the limits of freshwater and swim as far as Alabama and Mississippi. In the west, they reach as far north as Lake Winnipeg and the North and South Saskatchewan Rivers and are found in the Hudson Bay lowland. Environmental historian William Cronon viewed New England Indians as seasonally moving across the land to harvest the resources: "Indians held their demands on the ecosystem to a minimum by moving their settlements from habitat to habitat." As Indians moved into the Green Bay region, there was an increase in seasonal migratory behavior. Villages planted corn but also moved across longer distances to harvest wild plants. See William Cronon, *Changes in the Land: Indians, Colonists, and the Ecology of New England* (New York, 1983), 53.

2. Ronald J. Mason, *Great Lakes Archaeology* (New York, 1981), 20–21, 398; Mark Wyman, *The Wisconsin Frontier* (Bloomington, Ind., 1998), 28–29, 32–33, 36; Mason, "Two Stratified Sites on the Door Peninsula of Wisconsin," *Anthropological Papers, Museum of Anthropology, University of Michigan*, XXVI (Ann Arbor, Mich., 1966); W. J. Eccles, *Frontenac: The Courtier Governor* (Toronto, Ont., 1959), 275–278; Bacqueville De La Potherie, *Histoire de l'Amerique septentrionale,* in Emma Helen Blair, ed., *The Indian Tribes of the Upper Mississippi Val-*

Indian populations drawn to the Green Bay region in the mid-seventeenth century came from the southern Great Lakes, where villages along the Ohio's tributary rivers spun off households and clans. Larger nations, like the Miami, created a chain of villages that stretched west to Green Bay from the Ohio River valley. They established villages along the Fox River, near present-day Chicago, and among the Illinois, first at Fort Crèvecoeur and later at Lake Pimiteoui. The Miami joined the Mascouten, Wea, Kickapoo, Illinois, and Potawatomi, whose villages encircled Green Bay and lined the adjoining rivers. Green Bay was a precontact Indian world enriched by numerous Indian migrations. Villages were frequently multiethnic and relied on trade and intermarriage to incorporate newcomers. Rather than a shattered world of refugees, as it appeared in Richard White's famous formulation in *The Middle Ground*, this chapter envisions Green Bay as diverse villages drawn together by trade and exchange.[3]

Green Bay's access to prime coat beaver drew fur traders from Montreal and Quebec in the 1660s. At the time of French arrival, there were already large numbers of Indians living at and trading at *le Baye*. Indians inhabited the area well before the outbreak of the Beaver Wars, when the competition for furs motivated Iroquois attacks on villages involved in the Montreal trade. Many chose to avoid conflict and resettled among their allies at Green Bay, further increasing population levels. Ongoing encounters among Indigenous villages and Frenchmen taught diverse peoples much about each other, and

---

ley and the Region of the Great Lakes (1911; rpt. Lincoln, Neb., 1996), II, 304–306. This was first published in Paris in 1753.

3. For an in-depth examination of trade and its relationship to diplomacy, see Richard White, *The Middle Ground: Indians, Empires, and Republics in the Great Lakes Region, 1650–1815* (New York, 1991), 94–141; Michael Witgen, *An Infinity of Nations: How the Native New World Shaped Early North America* (Philadelphia, 2012), 29–115; Catherine M. Desbarats, "The Cost of Early Canada's Native Alliances: Reality of Scarcity's Rhetoric," *William and Mary Quarterly*, 3d Ser., LII (1995), 609–630; Giles Havard, *The Great Peace of Montreal of 1701: French-Native Diplomacy in the Seventeenth Century*, trans. Phyllis Aronoff and Howard Scott (Montreal, Que., 2001), 15–57. See also W. Vernon Kinietz, *The Indians of the Western Great Lakes* (Ann Arbor, Mich., 1965), 161–167; Stewart Rafert, *The Miami Indians of Indiana: A Persistent People, 1654–1994* (Indianapolis, 1996), 1–11; Bert Anson, *The Miami Indians* (Norman, Okla., 1970). White's *Middle Ground* provides an influential model for rethinking the Great Lakes as an identifiable colonial region that influenced the contest for empire between England and France. Unfortunately, the Franco-Indian creation of a middle ground ranging across a vast geographic region inhabited by diverse people assumes a monolithic Indian response to the French. This is a problematic model for explaining events in the Ohio River valley because the large, diverse population responded to the French in various ways.

many communities welcomed French traders as honored visitors, intimate strangers, and, sometimes, even as adoptees. Frenchmen were incorporated into an Indian world. Although the pathways of interaction could be tenuous at first, they began to stabilize by the last decade of the seventeenth century and first decade of the eighteenth.

Indian women were not at the forefront of the seventeenth-century fur trade, as they often were in the eighteenth century, but they did play a role in facilitating this early exchange process. They participated in the calumet ceremony, processed furs, manufactured products for the trade, and supplied food to fur traders. By the eighteenth century, as the trade shifted to the Ohio River valley and village life stabilized, the evolution of matrifocal households gave women greater power over the processing of furs and the exchange process.[4]

When New France closed the western trade in 1696 and access to French goods declined at Green Bay, the fur trade moved into the Ohio River valley. This brought the Miami, who controlled the Maumee-Wabash passage and access to the Wabash and Ohio Rivers, to the forefront of the eighteenth-century trade. Miami involvement in the Green Bay trade was crucial to their growing influence. With the closure of the western trade, Miami access to goods increasingly depended on access to English traders and goods at Albany. Working through the Iroquois facilitated the Miamis' return from Green Bay. The Miami became middlemen, indirectly supplying Albany with furs. They encouraged large numbers of smaller nations, such as the Wea and Kickapoo, to settle in nearby villages along the Wabash and become their suppliers.[5]

---

4. In a matrifocal household, the woman evolved as the center of economic and decision-making coalitions with her children, despite the presence of a husband-father. The woman is the focus of the relationship but is not the head of the household. See Raymond Smith, "The Matrifocal Family," in Jack Goody, ed., *The Character of Kinship* (New York, 1973), 124–125. See also Karen Fog Olwig, "Women, 'Matrifocality,' and Systems of Exchange: An Ethnohistorical Study of the Afro-American Family on St. Johns, Danish West Indies," *Ethnohistory*, XXVIII (1981), 48.

5. "Beaver Wars," or "Fur Trade Wars," is the term generally applied to the conflict between Iroquois and the French-backed, Algonquian-speaking tribes of the Great Lakes region. It purportedly began in the 1660s, when the Iroquois sought a greater share of the fur trade and were armed by both the Dutch and English. It was thought to have ended because of French intervention, the French allegedly providing the imperial glue used to reconstruct the Indians' shattered world. The idea of the Beaver Wars was central to White's conception of the western Great Lakes as a refuge for "shattered peoples" (*Middle Ground,* 23–40).

Recent criticisms of the *pays d'en haut* (Upper Country) as a shattered world are found in Michael A. McDonnell, "Rethinking the Middle Ground: French Colonialism and Indigenous Identities in the *Pays d'en Haut*," in Gregory D. Smithers and Brooke N. Newman,

THE IROQUOIS AND TRADE

Classic accounts of the Algonquian communities around Green Bay portray them as refugees from Iroquois assaults, and the depiction of the Iroquois as violent aggressors who were intransigent "in the face of European notions of civilization" rests on a lengthy historiographic tradition, which was heavily influenced by seventeenth-century Jesuit writings. The Jesuits accompanied Samuel de Champlain to Canada in 1633 and published annually their famous *Relations,* which contained accounts from the missionary priests who lived and worked among the Indians. Although, in their letters, the Jesuits appear relatively receptive to Native people, their narratives were nonetheless skewed by an imperialist agenda that was vehemently anti-Iroquois. The Jesuit accounts of life in the western missions were published by Sébastien Cramoisy, one of France's most powerful publishers, and were enthusiastically received by French government officials, wealthy nobles, and merchants. The Jesuits sought to expand the French imperial state, and their writings influenced French attitudes toward missionized Native Americans. The *Jesuit Relations* propagandized on behalf of royal power and appealed to wealthy, educated elites interested in expanding France's network of overseas possessions. The Jesuits assiduously campaigned for a war of conquest against the Five Nations and favored violence and coercion to achieve their vision of French hegemony in North America. Their vehement anti-Iroquois bias was intensified by the martyrdom of eight Jesuits in the 1640s. In waging literary war against the Iroquois, the Jesuits described them as a belligerent nation that had the power "to subject all our settlements to fire and massacre whenever they chose." The Jesuits believed that Iroquois defeat required a crusading army sent across the Atlantic by the French king; they continually pushed for a military commitment rivaling that of the Roman Catholic Church during the Crusades.[6]

---

eds., *Native Diasporas: Indigenous Identities and Settler Colonialism in the Americas* (Lincoln, Neb., 2014), 79–108; William James Newbigging, "The History of the French-Odawa Alliance: 1613–1763" (Ph.D. diss., University of Toronto, 1995); Heidi Bohaker, "*Nindoodemag:* The Significance of Algonquian Kinship Networks in the Eastern Great Lakes Region, 1600–1701," *WMQ,* LXIII (2006), 23–52.

6. Scott Manning Stevens, "The Historiography of New France and the Legacy of Iroquois Internationalism," *Comparative American Studies,* XI (2013), 148–149. Many historians blame the Jesuits for spreading negative views of the Iroquois, but Stevens believes that early historians of New France fully established this concept of Iroquois aggression in the subsequent historical literature (ibid.). See also Bronwen Catherine McShea, "Cultivating Empire through Print: The Jesuit Strategy for New France and the Parisian 'Relations' of 1632 to 1673" (Ph.D. diss., Yale University, 2011). The Jesuit martyrs were canonized in 1930

Close readings of the *Jesuit Relations* have led to reassessments of their depictions of the Iroquois as overpowering aggressors; new interpretations suggest that the Jesuits exaggerated their destructive power. These reassessments have been accompanied by an emerging French Atlantic world historiography, which has focused greater attention on the French Empire and the role that imperial policy played in furthering discord and warfare in the western Great Lakes. Openly antagonistic policies by governors of New France alienated the Iroquois and English and heightened their hostility toward the Indian allies of the French. Between 1666 and 1701, the French built almost thirty forts and fortified posts in the St. Lawrence–Great Lakes Basin. They erected several forts on Iroquois homelands without Iroquois permission. The French hold over the western fur trade routes was secured by constructing forts at seven locations around Lakes Ontario and Erie, on lands that the Iroquois used for hunting. The conflict intensified when New France attempted to exclude both the Iroquois and English from any share of the beaver trade.[7]

Reevaluations of Iroquois hostility have led to a more nuanced emphasis on the role that trade and diplomacy played in their extensive travels. Iroquois trade routes stretched from Powhatan lands in the Chesapeake westward to the eastern Ohio River valley, then north along the Hudson River

---

by Pope Pius XI: St. Jean de Brébeuf (1649), St. Noël Chabanel (1649), St. Antoine Daniel (1648), St. Charles Garnier (1649), St. René Goupil (1642), St. Isaac Jogues (1646), St. Jean de Lalande (1646), and St. Gabriel Lalemant (1649). See Jon Parmenter, *The Edge of the Woods: Iroquoia, 1534–1701* (East Lansing, Mich., 2010), 111.

7. Kenneth J. Banks, *Chasing Empire across the Sea: Communications and the State in the French Atlantic, 1713–1763* (Montreal, Que., 2006); James Pritchard, *In Search of Empire: The French in the Americas, 1670–1730* (New York, 2004); Robert Englebert and Guillaume Teasdale, eds., *French and Indians in the Heart of North America, 1630–1815* (East Lansing, Mich., 2013); Claiborne A. Skinner, *The Upper Country: French Enterprise in the Colonial Great Lakes* (Baltimore, 2008); Havard, *Great Peace of Montreal of 1701,* trans. Phyllis Aronoff and Howard Scott; Christian Ayne Crouch, *Nobility Lost: French and Canadian Martial Cultures, Indians, and the End of New France* (Ithaca, N.Y., 2014); Brett Rushforth, *Bonds of Alliance: Indigenous and Atlantic Slaveries in New France* (Chapel Hill, N.C., 2012). José António Brandão's comprehensive analysis of all Iroquois raids up to 1701 "reveals that raids for the purpose of economic gain (or theft raids) did not take place in significant numbers. The Iroquois were involved in 465 recorded hostile encounters before 1701; they initiated 354. In these attacks against Natives, Europeans, men, women, traders, hunters, warriors, soldiers, farmers, and fisherman, theft of goods or furs was reported in only 20 of them." Because this represents less than 6 percent of the known Iroquois-initiated raids, they appear to be "hardly a significant feature of Iroquois warfare" (Brandão, *"Your Fyre Shall Burn No More": Iroquois Policy toward New France and Its Native Allies to 1701* [Lincoln, Neb., 1997], 119).

valley to Lake Champlain and east along the St. Lawrence River to the Atlantic. These pathways were central to diplomatic, political, and economic initiatives and crucial in attempts to counter European colonialism. The Iroquois were able to link dispersed communities and created a wide-ranging, flexible notion of themselves as an interconnected Indigenous polity. The Mohawk were indicative of those Iroquois who traveled vast distances to pursue diplomatic goals, exercising what Scott Manning Stevens has called "Iroquois Internationalism."[8]

Migratory behaviors in the seventeenth-century western Great Lakes were similar to fifteenth- and sixteenth-century Iroquois movements along the Atlantic coastal region. Long-distance trade motivated the Iroquois to leave their homelands for the precontact trading center of Tadoussac, in St. Lawrence Bay, while Great Lakes and Ohio River valley Indians moved to Green Bay for similar reasons. As a precontact trading center, Green Bay was familiar; the subsequent arrival of large quantities of European trade goods drew increased numbers of Indian people to the area, where explorer Jean Nicolet saw them assembled "as if at a fair, buying and selling, in numbers so great that they could not be counted." In this ethnically diverse landscape, Winnebago, Menominee, Assiniboine, Illinois, Miami, Wea, Kickapoo, Mascouten, Nipissing, Ojibwe, and Odawa were among the first to be drawn from their homelands; they arrived at Green Bay before European contact. Those northern villages located along the southern edge of the Canadian Shield had poor soils, interspersed with exposed bedrock. Farming these marginal lands was far from productive, and only when frosts were late was there a chance of a harvest. But this thinly occupied region offered exceptional fishing and hunting, and a mutually beneficial trade was established with southern Algonquian-speaking Indians at Green Bay. Corn, tobacco, hemp, woven fishing nets, and even clay pipes went north in return for dried meat and fish, skins, and furs.[9]

Throughout the seventeenth century, as Europeans headed west, they left vivid descriptions of the western Great Lakes and the substantial Indian populations to be found at Green Bay. Frenchmen traveled long distances

---

8. Parmenter, *Edge of the Woods*, 13, xi; Stevens, "Historiography of New France," *Comparative American Studies*, XI (2013), 148–149.

9. Paul le Jeune, "Of the Hope We Have for the Conversion of Many Savages," in Reuben Gold Thwaites, ed., *The Jesuit Relations and Allied Documents: Travels and Explorations of the Jesuit Missionaries in New France, 1610–1791*, 73 vols. (Cleveland, 1896–1901), XVIII, 231–233, 233n (hereafter cited as *JR*); Ronald J. Mason, *Rock Island: Historical Indian Archaeology in the Northern Lake Michigan Basin*, MCJA Special Paper, no. 6 (Kent, Oh., 1986), 15; George Irving Quimby, *Indian Life in the Upper Great Lakes: 11,000 B. C. to A. D. 1800* (Chicago, 1960), 123; Mason, *Great Lakes Archaeology*, 297.

into unfamiliar Indian lands over extended periods of time. From 1615 to the end of the seventeenth century, a handful of explorers and then hundreds of traders traveled throughout the Great Lakes. Although Frenchmen feared the Iroquois, there were comparatively few recorded attacks on French travelers.

French voyages began as early as 1615, when Champlain sent Etienne Brulé west to live among Algonquian-speaking villages. He remained for the better part of the next decade but left no written records of his travels. He was followed by one of the most flamboyant French explorers, Jean Nicolet. An employee of the Hundred Associates, New France's fur company, Nicolet had been sent to live in fur trade villages to learn Native languages. For several years, Nicolet inhabited an Algonquian-speaking village along the Odawa River fur trade route. In 1620, he moved to the Lake Nipissing region, where he remained for nine years. Nicolet journeyed into the western Great Lakes on a Huron fur-trading expedition, explored and named Lake Michigan in 1634, and then headed south to *la baye des Puans* (Green Bay).

In 1634, women and children watched Nicolet enter Green Bay. Nicolet was surrounded by men; there were no women in his party. Women signaled peaceful intentions, whereas groups of male strangers were assumed to be war parties. Nicolet was strangely dressed, in an elaborate woman's garment, "a grand robe of China damask," hand-embroidered with large, colorful flowers. Rather than sitting in the canoe, he stood, holding aloft two pistols, one in each hand. Women and children knew nothing of guns, or perhaps had heard rumors of the danger and noise of these weapons. When the stranger fired his pistols, this unusually loud noise elicited a human uproar as several hundred women fled into the woods, screaming and wailing. Nicolet later wrote that these Indians considered the pistols as the work of "a man who carried thunder in both hands, — for thus they called the two pistols that he held." For people living close to Lake Michigan, thunder signaled the arrival of the supernatural thunderbird and the onset of fierce storms, and Nicolet's booming entrance signaled immediate danger. Within minutes, four to five thousand warriors emerged from the nearby villages. This massive assemblage, already aware of Nicolet's journey along the coastline, stood ready to defend their women, children, and villages.[10]

Nicolet's unusual entrance stands as a testament to the substantial precontact population of Green Bay. With the ratio of one warrior to four to five women and children, the four thousand to five thousand warriors at Green Bay suggest a surrounding population of sixteen to twenty thousand inhabi-

10. *JR,* XXIII, 278–279, esp. 279.

tants, a figure later substantiated by Fathers Marquette and Allouez. Green Bay's population was high before the arrival of Europeans. It was the Tadoussac of the midcontinent: a large trading village where corn was sent north in exchange for furs.[11]

Nicolet's 1634 journey did little to change the fur trade, but the western voyages of Médard Chouart Des Groseilliers and his brother-in-law, Pierre-Esprit Radisson, in 1660 dramatically changed it. When they returned to Montreal, surrounded by a convoy of sixty canoes carrying three hundred men—and loaded with two hundred thousand livres of peltry—news quickly spread about the wealth to be found in furs. The governor formally acknowledged the adventurers' contributions to the colony's prosperity but then fined them ten thousand livres and a fourth of their furs, amounting to fourteen thousand livres more, for leaving without permission. This voyage to the west threatened the profits of the Montreal merchants, whom the governor was eager to protect. The western fur trade was off to a rocky start, but Radisson and Groseilliers's voyages initiated the western trade, encouraging hundreds of young men to leave Montreal and trade in the western Great Lakes.[12]

Jesuit missionaries in the west also unintentionally spread good news about the Green Bay region. Father Allouez reported that, when he journeyed from Montreal to Michilimackinac and arrived at Green Bay, he was greeted by eight hundred warriors. He described the site as "a center for all the nations of these regions." He walked around the "beautiful Bay" and at the head discovered "the great Village of the Savages." This was a Potawatomi village with

---

11. Ibid. Jean Nicolet (Nicollet) de Belleborne was born ca. 1598 and died in a 1642 storm on the St. Lawrence River when his boat capsized. He was a friend of Champlain and Brulé and was drawn to New France by Champlain's program to train young men to live among and learn the languages of the Indians. He arrived in New France in 1618, and his marriage to a Native woman at Lake Nipissing produced a child named Madeleine Euphrosine Nicolet. He lived in the region for twenty-five years and became the "Interpreter and Agent for the Gentlemen of the Company of New France" (275).

12. Paul Chrisler Phillips, *The Fur Trade*, 2 vols. (Norman, Okla., 1961), I, 226; Gideon G. Scull, ed., *Voyages of Peter Esprit Radisson: Being an Account of His Travels and Experiences among the North American Indians, from 1652 to 1684* (Boston, 1885). For Intendant Jean Talon's belief that the western lakes afforded access to the Northwest Passage, see La Potherie, *Histoire*, in Blair, ed., *Indian Tribes of the Upper Mississippi Valley*, II, 294–295; [Jean Talon du Roy], "Envoi d'explorateurs a l'ouest du Canada pour prendre possession du pays: Nécessité de s'etablir sur le lac Ontario; extrait d'une lettre de Jean Talon au roy," Oct. 10, 1670, in Pierre Margry, *Découvertes et établissements des Français dans l'ouest et dans le sud de l'Amérique septentrionale, 1614-1698, mémoires et documents inedits*, 6 vols. (1879; rpt. New York, 1974), I, 82–83.

nearby villages belonging to the Petun, or Tobacco Huron, Fox, Chippewa, Illinois, Sauk, Miami, and Nipissing.[13]

By 1670, French officials at Versailles concluded that this world of Indian nations should be incorporated into an expanding French Empire. Versailles attempted to assert French authority by staging an elaborate "possession" ceremony at Bow-e-ting, later renamed Sault Ste. Marie by the French. Simon François Daumont, sieur de St. Lusson, Nicolas Perrot, and Father Claude Allouez lured fifteen different Indian villages to Bow-e-ting, including Ojibwe, Sac, Winnebago, Potawatomi, Menominee, and Chippewa. Most southern villages at Green Bay sent no one: conspicuously absent were the Illinois, Fox, Miami, Kickapoo, Wea, and Mascouten. Lusson spoke on behalf of the French king and "declared to [the upper nations] that henceforth, from the present, they were to be answerable to his Majesty, subjects to submit to his laws and follow his customs, they were promised all protection and assistance from his part against the incursion or invasion of their enemies." He failed to understand the social dynamics of this village world, where society was held together by bonds of kinship rather than through laws; it was Father Allouez who placed Lusson's speech within an Indigenous context. Allouez described notions of identity that rested on kinship and a French king who cared for his children like a father, one who used his power and strength on their behalf, a warrior who bloodied his hands in vanquishing their enemies. Father Allouez described the power of kinship ties and the vast wealth that their French father possessed in "warehouses containing enough hatchets to cut down all your forests, kettles to cook all your moose, and glass beads to fill all your cabins." This ceremony might have proclaimed the wealth of the French Empire, but Indians did not trust Lusson. Afterward, they removed and burned the document that they had signed and Lusson had nailed to the top of the French cross. The conspicuous lack of French military might on display could have led Indians to question Lusson's assurances of protection.[14]

13. "Relation of the Mission of Saint Esprit, among the Outaouacs, on Lake Tracy . . . ," in *JR*, L, 273, 297.

14. Nicolas Perrot arrived in New France in 1660 as a *donné* of the Jesuits, with whom he visited Indian tribes and became proficient in Native languages. By 1665, he was trading at Green Bay. He remained a trader in the western Great Lakes for almost thirty years (*Dictionary of Canadian Biography*, II, *1701-1740*, http://www.biographi.ca/en/bio/perrot_nicolas_2E.html). For a description of Lusson's speech, see "Procès-verbal de la prise de possession des pays situés vers les lacs Huron et Supérieur," June 4, 1671, in Margry, ed., *Découvertes et établissements*, I, 96-99; *JR*, LV, 109-111, 112-113; James A. Clifton, *The Prairie People: Continuity and Change in Potawatomi Culture, 1665-1965* (Iowa City, 1998), 46.

After Louis Joliet received permission to explore the Mississippi with Father Jacques Marquette in 1673, they set out from Green Bay on May 17 with two canoes and five men. Their journals confirmed the high population levels at Green Bay and the willingness of people, like the Miami, to lead them into uncharted lands. Famous for reaching the Mississippi, the explorers also identified the river's junction with the Ohio and Missouri. They began their return journey in mid-July by traveling northeast along the Illinois River to Lake Michigan.[15]

News of these voyages convinced many Frenchmen of the viability of long-distance travel in the western Great Lakes. In early 1679, shortly after news of Joliet and Marquette's discovery of the Mississippi reached New France, the sieur de La Salle's canoe brigade left Montreal with fourteen men and three women. René-Robert Cavelier, sieur de La Salle, had received the exclusive right from Versailles to explore the area between Florida and Mexico and "to endeavor to discover the western part of New France, and, for the execution of this enterprise, to construct forts wherever you shall deem it necessary." His brigade met *Le Griffon,* or the *Griffin,* at Fort Frontenac, which he had built to hold peltry, and the canoes followed the *Griffin* west across Lake Erie. They stopped first at Michilimackinac, and, by the time they reached Green Bay, the *Griffin* was fully loaded with furs. La Salle was heavily engaged in the fur trade, under the guise of exploration. He sent the *Griffin* back to Fort Frontenac while the rest of his party headed south from Green Bay. They landed on the southwestern shore of Lake Michigan, built a stockade at the mouth of the River of the Miami (now the St. Joseph), and then journeyed into Illinois lands.[16]

15. The history of the Marquette-Joliet journey is drawn from Joliet in Dablon's report of August 1, 1674, "Relation of the Discovery of Many Countries Situated to the South of New France, Made in 1673," in *JR,* LVIII, 93–109; and "Relation de la descouverte de plusieurs pays situez au midi de la Nouvelle-France, faite en 1673," in Margry, ed., *Découvertes et établissements,* I, 262–270. Joliet's account is reproduced in his map in the *Jesuit Relations,* LIX, 86; Marquette's is "Journal incomplet du P. Jacques Marquette, adressé au R. P. Dablon, supérieur des Missions," ibid., LXIX, 164–184; and see Frontenac's report, "Extrait d'une lettre de Frontenac à Colbert, en date du 11 novembre 1674," Nov. 11, 1674, ibid., I, 257.

16. John Anthony Caruso, *The Mississippi Valley Frontier: The Age of French Exploration and Settlement* (Indianapolis, 1966), 161. Overviews of La Salle's journey can be found in Isaac Joslin Cox, ed., *The Journeys of Réné Robert Cavelier, Sieur de La Salle,* 2 vols. (New York, 1905–1906), esp. II, 242. For general background on La Salle, see John Gilmary Shea, ed., *Discovery and Exploration of the Mississippi Valley; with the Original Narratives of Marquette, Allouez, Membré, Hennepin, and Anaste Douay* (1852; rpt. Memphis, Tenn., 2010), 1–17; Frederic Austin Ogg, *The Opening of the Mississippi: A Struggle for Supremacy in the*

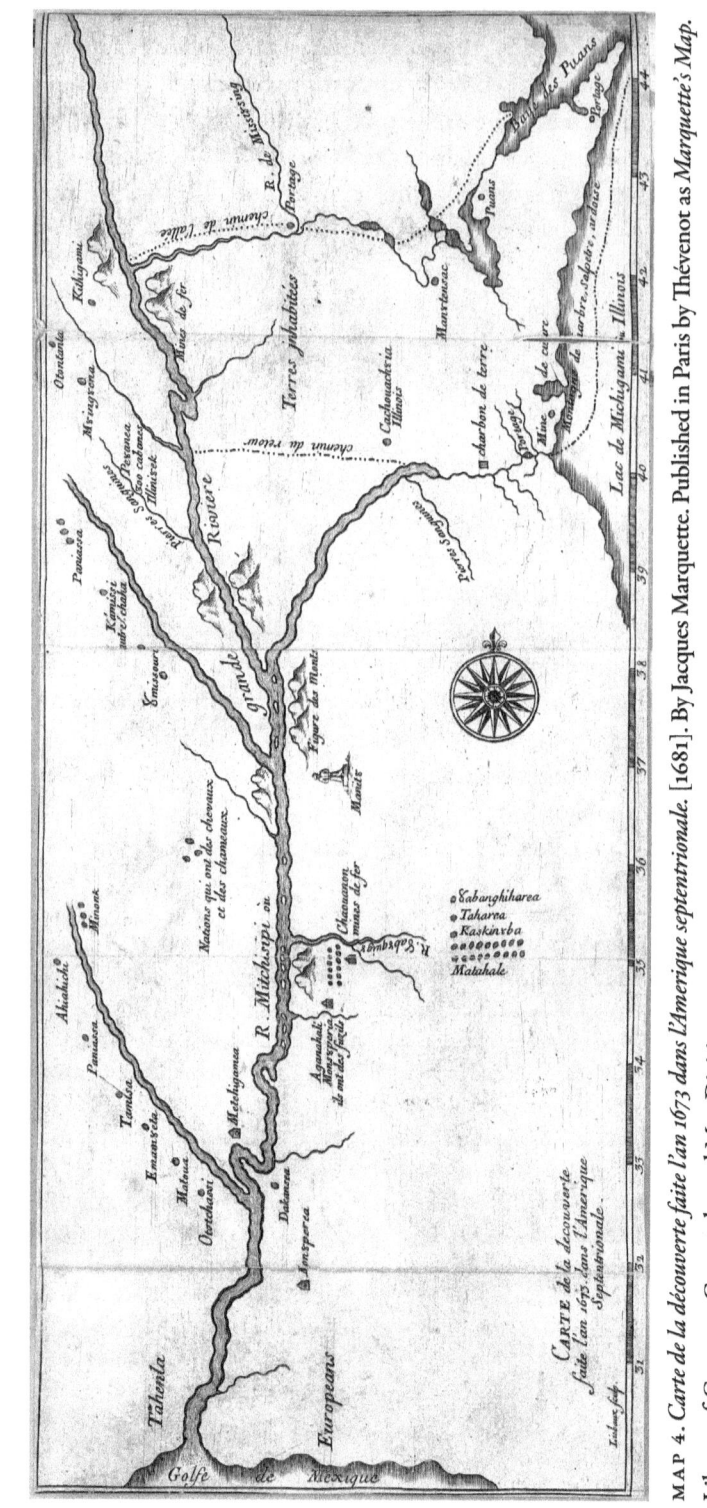

MAP 4. *Carte de la découverte faite l'an 1673 dans l'Amerique septentrionale.* [1681]. By Jacques Marquette. Published in Paris by Thévenot as *Marquette's Map.* Library of Congress, Geography and Map Division

FIGURE 5. "Building of the *Griffin*." Canada, ca. 1690. Engraving in *Voyage curieux du R. P. Louis Hennepin, missionaire recollect, et notaire apostolique* . . . (Leiden, 1704). Courtesy, Prints and Photographs Division, Library of Congress

These are some of the best known seventeenth-century voyages to the west, but there were many others, far too numerous to mention. This stream of explorers and travelers venturing west encouraged the growth of the fur trade in the region. Despite the profits to be gained from such trade, the Montreal governor, fearful of losing New France's young male population, attempted to limit western travel. Each year, only twenty-five fur traders received permits to head west. Each permit licensed three to four legal traders, who were accompanied by several canoes of trade goods. The ministry of marine believed that Montreal, not the western posts, should be the center of the trade. By limiting trade permits, New France unintentionally created a new group of illegal traders known as the *coureurs de bois,* or "runners of the woods." Legal and illegal traders left scant record of their travels. Names and probable des-

American Interior (New York, 1968); and Paul Chesnel, *History of Cavelier de La Salle, 1643– 1687: Explorations in the Valleys of the Ohio, Illinois, and Mississippi . . .* , trans. Andrée Chesnel Meany (1910; rpt. New York, 1932).

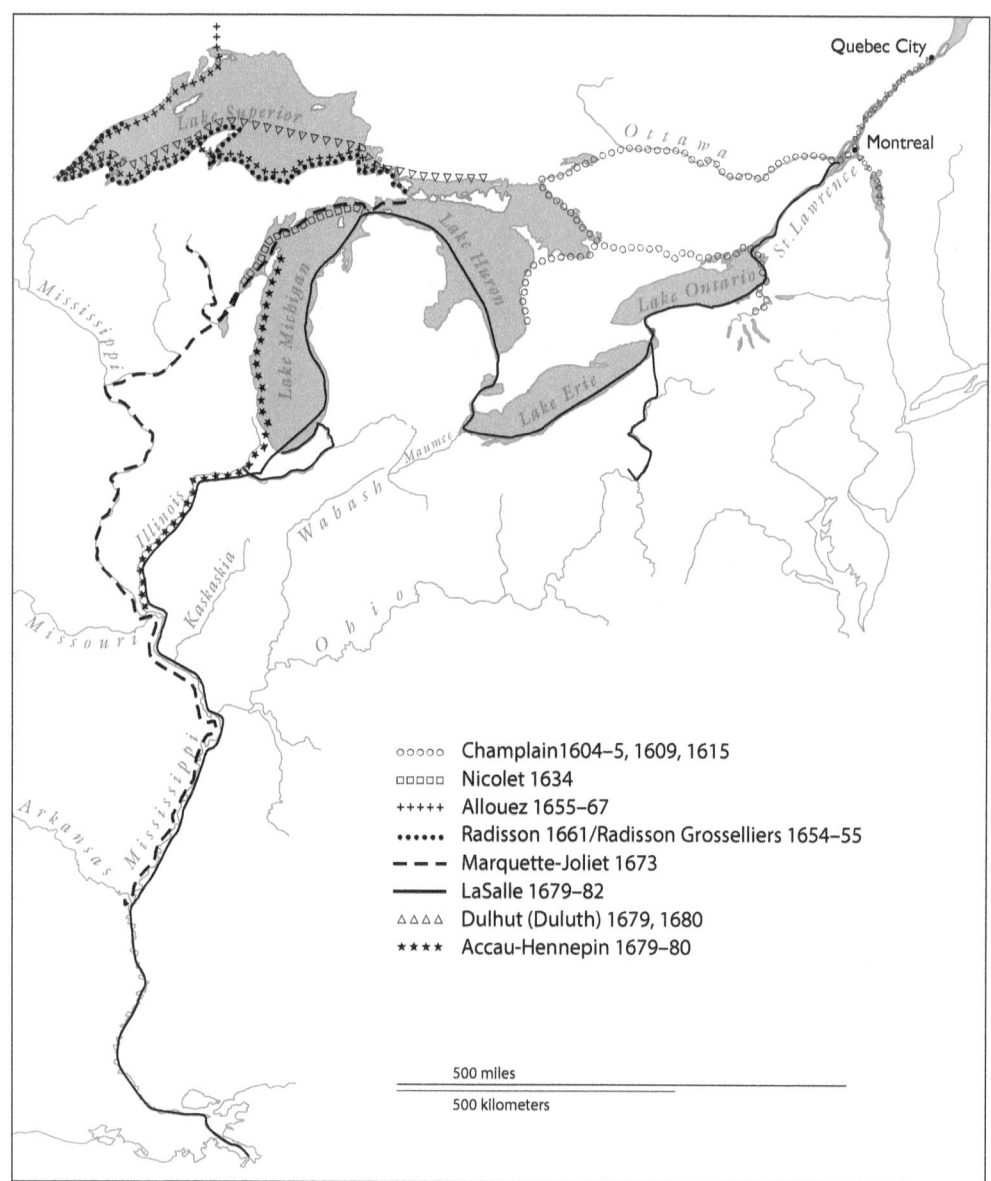

MAP 5. French explorers and the early exploration of New France. Drawn by Ellen White

tinations were carefully recorded on the permits of the legal traders, but we know little about their personal lives. Some of these returned and used their proceeds to purchase farmland, whereas many others remained traders and repeatedly journeyed west.[17]

SOCIAL DYNAMICS

Possession ceremonies by military men like St. Lusson fostered the European notion that Indians were being incorporated into the French Empire. Jesuits, like Father Allouez, and explorers, like Joliet and La Salle, better understood this Indian world and realized that it was notions of kinship that made this diverse village landscape into an intelligible world. European goods reinforced and extended existing kin-based alliances. Indians protected many of the Frenchmen who ventured west; they were often welcomed as friends and allies. Indigenous rituals preserved Europeans from danger. The calumet ceremony transformed dangerous pathways of encounter into avenues of welcome. When La Salle journeyed south from Green Bay, his canoe brigade was struck by a sudden, violent storm. This left his party in "great danger by stress of weather" and forced them "to throw ourselves into the water and carry our canoes on our shoulders to save them from being broken to pieces." They landed on an unfamiliar shore and found themselves surrounded by hostile Indians speaking an incomprehensible language. La Salle produced the calumet pipe, which transformed Frenchmen from enemies into friends. The Indians' reaction led Father Louis Hennepin to regard the calumet as "a symbol of peace."[18]

Indeed, the calumet served as a European passport into unfamiliar villages. The calumet ceremony involved specific rituals of greeting: villagers welcomed visitors with songs and dances, women welcomed them with bags of cornmeal, and then, amid this whirl of activity, Frenchmen joined Indians in the ritual smoking of the calumet. The pipe became "the God of peace and of war, the Arbiter of life and of death. It has but to be carried upon one's person, and displayed, to enable one to walk in safety through the midst of

17. Carolyn Podruchny, *Making the Voyageur World: Travelers and Traders in the North American Fur Trade* (Omaha, Neb., 2006); Grace Lee Nute, *The Voyageur* (New York, 1931); Grace Lee Nute, *The Voyageur's Highway, Minnesota's Border Lake Land* (St. Paul, Minn., 1944).

18. Cox, ed., *Journeys of La Salle*, 77; Father Louis Hennepin, "Account of the Discovery of the River Mississippi and the Ancient Country," in B. F. French, ed., *Historical Collections of Louisiana...*, I, *Historical Documents from 1678 to 1691* (New York, 1846), 200-201 (hereafter cited as *Hist. Colls. La.*).

Enemies—who, in the hottest of the Fight, lay down Their arms when it is shown." Both La Salle and Father Marquette were probably given calumets at Green Bay, most likely by the Potawatomi and Miami, and both men repeatedly used their calumets to avoid danger. Elaborate decoration on these pipes conveyed a message of peace: the pipe that La Salle carried was "adorned with feathers of all colors," but, more important, it was "interlaced with locks of women's hair." Feathers transported prayers to the Manitou, and the women's hair ensured that these strangers walked the pathway of peace. La Salle confidently believed that, throughout the Lake Michigan region, the "pipe is a safe-conduct amongst all the allies of the nation who has given it."[19]

The calumet restrained aggressive behavior, and the French were fully aware of its power. Father Hennepin and his two fellow Frenchmen were captured by Sioux warriors who were eager to torture and kill them. Following their first uncomfortable night in captivity, they were dismayed the next morning

---

19. *JR*, LXIII, 123; Hennepin, "Account," in French, ed., *Hist. Colls. La.*, I, 200–201, esp. 201. Juliana Barr shows how the European display of the figurative Mariá was visually translated by the Caddo as symbolizing a lack of hostility on the part of Europeans. With female hair attached to the calumet, the presentation of the pipe would have conveyed a similar image of peaceful intentions. See Barr, *Peace Came in the Form of a Woman: Indians and Spaniards in the Texas Borderlands* (Chapel Hill, N.C., 2007), 41; Hennepin, "Account," 201. The gendered nature of diplomacy was evident in American Indian communities. Cross-cultural negotiation was primarily a male responsibility, although inclusion of female representations signaled that diplomatic representatives came in peace. Barr demonstrates the use of female figures and inclusion of women and children in diplomatic parties as representative of peace, Kathleen DuVal maintains that hosting diplomatic receptions was a female responsibility because of their agricultural obligations, and Tracy Neal Leavelle shows how "Female spiritual power held meaning on a personal level and, given its focus on fertility and the life cycle, for the community as a whole." The presence of women's hair attached to the calumet would have signaled peaceful intentions by groups of unaccompanied men, especially groups of French explorers and traders, who did not speak the language. Anthropologists confirm this historical perception, and Ray DeMaille maintains, "Males and females were always expected to behave according to different patterns and to have different demeanors. Men were expected to be aggressive, women to be passive." Although there were examples of "warrior women" among Plains Indians that Beatrice Medicine describes, she also confirms the "idealized and normative patterns of female passivity and dependence in Plains Indian societies." See Barr, *Peace Came in the Form of a Woman: Indians and Spaniards in the Texas Borderlands* (Chapel Hill, N.C., 2007), 1, 13, 33; DuVal, *The Native Ground: Indians and Colonists in the Heart of the Continent* (Philadelphia, 2006), 20; Leavelle, *The Catholic Calumet: Colonial Conversions in French and Indian North America* (Philadelphia, 2012), 166–169; DeMallie, "Male and Female in Traditional Lakota Culture," in Patricia Albers and Beatrice Medicine, eds., *The Hidden Half: Studies of Plains Indian Women* (Lanham, Md., 1983), 238, and Medicine, "'Warrior Women': Sex Role Alternatives for Plains Indian Women," 276.

when a Sioux captain demanded that Hennepin relinquish his calumet. The Frenchmen felt that the loss of their pipe signaled their demise, but, instead, the Sioux captain used the calumet to transform the hostility of the Sioux warriors into protection that ensured the safety of the three Frenchmen. "It being delivered him, he filled it with tobacco, and made the rest who had been for putting us to death to smoke in it." Smoking the calumet by the enemy Sioux guaranteed that the Frenchmen were spared and regarded as friends.[20]

Throughout the seventeenth century, French explorers and fur traders survived because of these rituals and because Indian women supplied them with food. During the calumet ceremony, it was women who fed these strangers. More generally, obtaining adequate nourishment was inevitably a concern for explorers and traders, and women controlled access to village food supplies. Corn, in particular, was crucial for survival, and explorers who ran out of food were often saved by the corn in underground storage pits in Indian villages. To take one example, while building a fort on the Miami River, La Salle began to fear that his men would starve to death. After a series of unsuccessful hunting forays and many hungry days, La Salle was anxious to replenish their supply of corn. They headed south to the Illinois territory and stumbled on a vacant village. A brief search unearthed a large quantity of corn, which women had stored to seed their fields in the spring. La Salle stole forty bushels of the women's corn, but he dutifully left presents to compensate for the loss. He knew that he should "not meddle with the corn they had laid under ground for their subsistence, and to sow their lands with; it being the most sensible wrong one can do them."[21]

Europeans survived in the western Great Lakes because of the surplus corn that women grew and stored. Many traders were eager to do more than survive and enthusiastically established social relationships in villages where they traded. Indian men initially offered Frenchmen their sisters, daughters, and even their wives as consorts. During the initial years of the seventeenth-century trade, adoption became a widespread practice for incorporating strangers. When Hennepin was captured by the Sioux, chief Aquipaquetin adopted him "for his son, in the room of him he had lost in the war." Adoption was a problematic pathway following the large influx of French traders at midcentury and created social linkages that were so complex, disputes arose and were only resolved with great difficulty. The kinship obligations imposed by adoption and intermarriage fueled disputes and led to clashes among the various clans at Green Bay. Hennepin's account of this region described the

---

20. Hennepin, "Account," in French, ed., *Hist. Colls. La.*, I, 209.
21. Ibid., 203.

violence that could erupt when Frenchmen were incorporated into this kin-based world.

> A dispute arose between two Frenchmen and an old man, who was one of the leading men among the Pouteouatemis ... sharp words arose on both sides, and they came to blows. The Frenchmen were vigorously attacked ... and a third man came to the aid of his comrades. The confusion increased; that Frenchman tore the pendants from the ears of a savage, and gave him a blow in the belly which felled him.... At the same time the Frenchman received a blow ... which caused him to fall motionless.... There were three families interested in this contention — those of the Red Carp, of the Black Carp, and of the Bear. The head of the Bear family — an intimate of the Frenchman, and whose son-in-law was the chief of the Sakis — seized a hatchet, and declared that he would perish with the Frenchman, whom the people of the Red Carp had slain. The Saki chief, hearing the voice of his father-in-law, called his own men to arms; the Bear family did the same; and the wounded Frenchman began to recover consciousness. He calmed the Sakis, who were greatly enraged.

Intermarriage and adoption between villages and across clans created densely intertwined social linkages. This particular dispute was resolved when the Frenchman recovered and the man who had felled him was banned from the village. Adopting Frenchmen frequently recast normally peaceful interactions as volatile reactions. Adoption and intermarriage usually involved lengthy negotiations, but the desire for trade goods and the hasty adoption of traders had unpredictable consequences. A multitude of traders followed Radisson and Groseilliers's successful voyage into Green Bay — but so did conflict.[22]

UNDERMINING THE FRENCH FUR TRADE IN THE WESTERN GREAT LAKES

Reports of friendly Indians and vast quantities of furs not only led hundreds of coureurs de bois to head west but also encouraged English traders to head from Albany toward the Great Lakes. Even before the British arrived, the Dutch claimed that "numerous French Indians" traded at Fort Orange. Many coureurs de bois also found that English goods were of better quality and lower price than those at Montreal. New York's governor, Thomas Dongan, identified all western Indians as Odawa and encouraged intrusions on French lands, eagerly financing men who were willing to trade illegally at

---

22. Ibid., 211; La Potherie, *Histoire,* in Blair, ed., *Indian Tribes of the Upper Mississippi Valley,* II, 319–322.

Michilimackinac. As early as 1685, eleven English canoes arrived, guided by French deserters. The Odawa encouraged their return and, the next year, the Dutch trader Johannes Rooseboom and the French deserter Abel Merrior led ten canoes filled with British goods to the Straits of Mackinac. They were warmly welcomed by both the Odawa and Huron, who gladly traded prime coat beaver for reasonably priced British goods. Eager to obtain British cloth, they not only encouraged the traders to return but simultaneously sent word to the governor that they desired "that their enemies, the Seneca, open a path for them to come to Albany to trade." Governor Dongan publicly urged the Iroquois to establish an alliance with the "Ottawa, the Miami, and 'further Indians.'" Dongan planned to send two even larger trading expeditions the next year. The first ventured west in 1686 and included twenty canoes and fifty men; a second, much larger flotilla left in 1687. Indians and French fur traders from the Illinois Country attacked both expeditions, interrupting the first on Lake Huron and the second on Lake Erie. They seized the canoes filled with goods and captured and transported the English traders to Montreal and Quebec.[23]

Fearful that these English intrusions would undermine the economic foundations of the French Empire in the American interior, Governor General Denonville overreacted to the situation. He wasn't wrong to worry about the consequence of continuing British incursions, but his letters to Versailles overstated the danger: "Missilimakinac is theirs. They have taken its latitude; have been to trade there with our Outawas and Huron Indians, who received them cordially on account of the bargains they gave." He warned Versailles, "If the English continue their expeditions in this manner, and the king is unwilling that war be waged against them, nothing is to be expected for this Colony but its ruin." In addition to faulting Versailles for failing to declare war against

---

23. J. Franklin Jameson, ed., *Narratives of New Netherland, 1609–1664* (New York, 1909), 86; E. B. O'Callaghan et al., eds., *Documents Relative to the Colonial History of the State of New York*, 15 vols. (Albany, N.Y., 1853–1887), III, 510 (hereafter cited as *NYCD*); Helen Broshar, "The First Push Westward of the Albany Traders," *Mississippi Valley Historical Review*, VII (1920), 228–241, esp. 232. In 1682, James, duke of York, as lord proprietor of New York, appointed Dongan to govern the bankrupt colony. Dongan had served with the duke in France and was a fellow Catholic. He convened the first representative assembly of the province in 1683, which enacted the Charter of Liberties enunciating the form of government in New York. Following the Glorious Revolution, with the Protestant William of Orange in charge, Dongan returned to England in 1691 and, upon the death of his elder brother, inherited the earldom of Limerick under its first (1686) creation. He died in 1715, poor and childless. See Paul Chrisler Phillips, *The Fur Trade*, 2 vols. (Norman, Okla., 1961), I, 261–262; *NYCD*, III, 476.

Britain, Denonville blamed the Iroquois for luring away New France's Indian allies and the coureurs de bois for being "French libertines who carry their peltries to [Albany], deserting our Colony, and establishing themselves among the English." In Denonville's view, only war against the Iroquois would "avert from us a general Indian Rebellion which would bring down ruin on our trade and cause eventually even the extirpation of our Colony." For men like Denonville, long-distance English traders were a sign of Iroquois domination in the Great Lakes.[24]

Denonville failed to obtain the loyalty of Indians, and it was not long before he was relieved of his position. In 1689, Louis de Buade, comte de Frontenac et de Palluau, returned as governor general of New France, and he immediately tackled the Iroquois problem. He intended to thwart the Iroquois threat by securing the allegiance of Great Lakes Indians—loyalty he would gain by increasing the number of fur traders in the west. Frontenac was motivated not only by concerns about the English and Iroquois but also by the need to bolster his declining fortune. He dramatically expanded the trade by illegally sending large numbers of fur traders into the western Great Lakes, ignoring the royal order that prohibited him from engaging in the trade. The trade had been officially limited to twenty-five permits, or *congés,* and Frontenac disguised his actions by sending officers and *troupes de la marine* upcountry for military purposes. The flotillas of canoes sent west were purported to carry munitions and military supplies, but they were so laden with trade goods and brandy that there was little room for armaments. En route, many of these expeditions simply dumped their armaments overboard. Military canoes were completely unrelated to protection from the Iroquois; Frontenac even sent one detachment of 6 officers and 128 men west to bring back the furs traded in 1690. In these early decades of the trade, one canoe-load of trade goods produced well over a canoe-load of furs, and the military transported the surplus furs that traders were unable to carry back in their canoes to Montreal. The numbers of furs brought to Montreal increased dramatically within three years. In September 1693, when the Odawa arrived in Montreal with 187 canoes of peltry, Frontenac sent them back with a military contingent of 146 men, whose canoes were filled with trade goods. When Henri de Tonti, who had taken La Salle's place as Frontenac's trading partner, headed west to the Illinois in 1693, he was surrounded by a flotilla of 55 canoes, each loaded with trade goods. The same year, Frontenac sent another 140 military men into the western Great Lakes, claiming that their presence ensured the loyalty of the western Indians. He even recalled Olivier Morel de La Duran-

24. *NYCD,* IX, 309, 319.

taye, Michilimackinac's highly effective commandant, because Durantaye refused to engage in the trade. Frontenac replaced him with the sieur de Louvigny, who went west with 143 men and 4,000 livres of contraband goods. Only one month after Louvigny's arrival at Michilimackinac, he sent 4,500 livres of beaver to his wife in Montreal.[25]

Frontenac claimed that sending the military and goods upcountry would encourage the western Indians to attack the Iroquois, which would relieve the St. Lawrence settlements of repeated Iroquois assaults. In fact, the western Indians were interested in trade goods but not in serving as protectors of the French settlements. Montreal and Quebec were far from Green Bay and near Iroquois lands. Most villages clustered around Green Bay became more concerned with seeking allies among the Iroquois than making enemies of them. Worse, when novice fur traders began selling trade goods to the Sioux, they aroused the ire of the Indians at Green Bay. The Miami openly negotiated a separate peace as well as an alliance with the Five Nations against the Sioux, who were long-standing enemies. Far from encouraging France's Green Bay allies to press for war against the Iroquois, the activities of the French soldiers and fur traders actually fueled Green Bay Indians' fear of the Sioux and prompted overtures to the Iroquois.[26]

Frontenac's overzealous support of the western trade returned vast quantities of peltry to Montreal. The Company of the Farm, a royal monopoly, was obligated to buy all peltry from the traders, regardless of quality. Beaver was the mainstay of the fur trade, and the company accepted all beaver at a fixed price, regardless of the amount brought in or the state of the market in France. By 1696, the large numbers of furs received in Montreal left the Company of the Farm on the verge of bankruptcy. Indians had complied with the increased demand for furs by trapping all varieties of beaver, summer coat as well as prime winter coat, and the market was soon glutted with unsalable furs. Large canoe flotillas carried as many as 200,000 pelts. In 1695, two canoe fleets flooded the Montreal marketplace with furs—one flotilla carried 235,786 pelts and was worth 774,644 livres. Just two months later a second flotilla arrived at Montreal, carrying 615,273 livres of beaver. By 1695,

25. La Mothe Cadillac á [de Lagny, Michilimackinac, 1695], Catalogue des manuscrits de la collection Clairambault, DCCCLXXXII, 137, Bibliothèque nationale de France, Paris; Moreau de St. Méry, Relation de ce qui s'est passé en Canada depuis le mois de Septembre 1692 jusqu'au [Novembre] 1694 . . . 1695 [Frontenac], VII, 320, Archives Nationales, Colonies, Versailles, Paris (hereafter cited as ANCol.), C11A, 14, F3, 213, Mémoire sur le Canada, 1696.

26. Ibid.; W. J. Eccles, *Frontenac: The Courtier Governor* (1959; rpt. Lincoln, Neb., 2003), 283–284.

the Montreal warehouses had far more peltry than French manufacturers could absorb. A year later, in 1696, Louis XIV closed the posts of Michilimackinac, Green Bay, and St. Joseph and banned all fur traders from the west in an attempt to save the Company of the Farm. The king ordered the Indians to bring their furs directly to Montreal. Closing three posts dramatically reduced the supply of trade goods in the western Great Lakes, but western Indians were nonetheless reluctant to make the long journey to Montreal. Louis Phélypeaux, comte de Pontchartrain, the French minister of the marine, made Frontenac directly responsible for enforcing the ban on the western trade, writing to Frontenac and telling him that, lacking protection at court, he was no longer in a position to flout the king's wishes.[27]

The closure of the western posts dramatically changed the nature of the fur trade, encouraging Indians to establish links to British markets; prompting the opening of new trade routes and the involvement of new Indigenous trading partners; and enhancing the trading partnerships that the Iroquois had formed with several western villages. Although Frontenac warned Versailles that the Iroquois would quickly envelop the entire region, it was, in fact, the Miami who resettled in the Wabash and Miami River valley and took control of the fur trade. Other villages at Green Bay, including the Wea, Mascouten, and Kickapoo, also returned to the Wabash River valley, settling near Ouiatenon. The Miami soon established trading links with the Iroquois, and their control over the Maumee-Wabash portage positioned them as middlemen in the trade between the Wabash villages and the Iroquois to the east. Lacking support from the government in New France, the French traders who ignored the fur trade ban and remained in the west now found themselves heavily reliant on the Indians. They had to forge new relationships, and they increasingly relied on kinship ties to cement their alliances with specific communities.

Illegal traders were incorporated into Indian households through "marriage in the manner of the country." Marriage secured Indians' direct access to trade goods while enhancing women's power and prestige. The exchange process was defined by Indigenous standards of behavior; Indian women with

27. Frontenac to the minister, Nov. 12, 20, 1690, France, Canada, Correspondence generale, ANCol., C11, 11 F, 178; Phillips, *Fur Trade,* I, 195-196. Peltry that came from the Americas were purchased by the Company of the Farm and, as a result of the dramatic expansion of the trade under Frontenac, more than 140,000 livres a year of beaver were shipped to France. By 1695, there was a surplus of 3,500,000 livres in the French storehouses, and the trade was on the verge of bankruptcy. See W. J. Eccles, *The Canadian Frontier, 1534-1760* (1969; rpt. Albuquerque, N.M., 1979), 124-125; minister to Frontenac, Versailles, May 26, 1696, ANCol., XIX, 98-99.

extensive kin networks became highly desirable marriage partners. Women's kinship ties cemented alliances with other households as well as with nearby communities, and women with extensive kin networks often mediated for their fur trader husbands in the exchange process. During the nineteen years of the fur trade ban, a trader became increasingly dependent on his wife and her kin network. An illegal trader who found refuge in his wife's household accommodated to, and even assimilated into, a world structured by Native American custom and tradition. Native women did not marry out of their villages, and, instead, Frenchmen were incorporated as husbands, fathers, and brothers. The fur trade villages of the Ohio River valley evolved into a highly complex, kin-based world where individuality was subsumed under a larger, collective identity. This was a face-to-face world in which people were identified by their relatives; strangers were suspect. An encounter between strangers required lengthy introductions, necessitated by increasingly dense kin networks. The words used in most greetings indicated of whom one was a son or daughter or who one's mother's brothers were. When the names of family members were unknown, introductions were extended until a familiar name was identified, even as distant as the brother of one's mother's father's sister's son. It was the prominence of kin networks, rather than trade, that defined social acceptance and prominence.[28]

---

28. French traders were forced to comply with Indian protocol. In order to secure furs from kin, they were incorporated into that kin network through marriage; a woman who married out and was defined by her husband's world would have been of no use in securing furs for her husband. Exchange was defined by kinship relations and not by the marketplace. See Jennifer S. H. Brown, "Woman as Centre and Symbol in the Emergence of Métis Communities," *Canadian Journal of Native Studies,* III (1983), 39–46.

Both Richard White and Michael Witgen have written extensively about how diplomatic rituals were shaped by collective and individual identity and "envisioned community formation to be the result of the relationships between the members of an extended family." Witgen tells us, "Political alliance was expressed as kinship" and hence the necessity for defining one's relationship to kin during diplomatic negotiations. To successfully secure Indigenous allies, the French were forced to recognize the social politics of individual villages and were frustrated by what they considered "endless negotiation and ritual forms" in which the participant's positionality was embedded in the socially complex network of this village world. Even when the French were addressed as *Onontio,* the father, and sought to curtail and control the behaviors of their children (Indians), they proved unable to do so. Various officials repeatedly complained that diplomacy entailed being "a slave to these Indians, of hearing them night and day in council and in private," where ritual forms dominated verbal exchange and where the French would have preferred reducing their allies to subjects. See White, *Middle Ground,* 171–185; Michael Witgen, *An Infinity of Nations: How the Native New World Shaped Early North America* (Philadelphia, 2012), 75, 89, 135–138.

The closure of the western French fur trade coincided with British expansion of the Albany fur trade. French revocation of the Edict of Nantes (1685) and the renewed prosecution of Protestants led Huguenot French hatters to seek refuge in England. This greatly increased the demand for beaver in London. Moreover, western Indians preferred both the quality of cloth and the comparatively low prices that English traders offered for it. Once the Miami established trading alliances with the Iroquois, they increasingly withdrew from their alliances with the Illinois. As Miami villages along the western shores of Lake Michigan declined in size, the Miami population along the Wabash River valley and at the Maumee-Wabash portage increased. Well before the French signed the Great Peace of Montreal in 1701, the diminished supply of French trade goods in the western Great Lakes and access to British goods at Albany had dramatically changed the demographics and distribution of the Indian population in the western Great Lakes.

CLOSING THE WESTERN FUR TRADE

By the 1690s, most Miami, Wea, Mascouten, and Kickapoo returned to the Ohio River valley. French fur traders and officers loudly protested the post closures and, eventually, the minister of the marine modified the Versailles ban on the trade to allow two posts to remain open: Michilimackinac and St. Joseph des Miamis. The fur trade remained banned at these posts, however, and the remaining trade was left in the hands of the military commanders there. Despite orders to return to Montreal, most coureurs de bois, at least two hundred, remained in the west. Because French trade goods remained scarce and Montreal's price for beaver remained well below what the English paid at Albany, most illegal traders quickly discovered the advantages of trading with the British. Even before the 1696 fur trade ban, as mentioned above, many coureurs de bois had already discovered English goods to be a better deal than those at Montreal.[29]

Most Indian villages that returned to the Ohio River valley moved quickly to establish links to the British at Albany. The desire for British trade goods connected the Miami and Shawnee through trading alliances, and in 1691 and 1692, the Shawnee trading at Albany invited British fur traders to visit them in the Ohio River valley. In 1693, the Dutch trader Arnout Viele arrived in the valley. Viele was the official British interpreter from 1682 to 1692 and was known to have "lived a long time with the Indians and frequently converse[d] with them." When Viele found himself politically disgraced and removed as official interpreter, he left Albany and moved south to New Jersey. From there,

---

29. Eccles, *Canadian Frontier,* 128; *NYCD,* III, 510.

Viele journeyed across the mountains, canoed from the Allegheny River to the Ohio, and, guided by several Indians, carried trade goods to the west. In 1691, he arrived at the Wabash River and went north to Ouiatenon, where he traded among the Miami, Wea, Mascouten, and Kickapoo villages. He then descended the Wabash and continued west on the Ohio till he reached the Cumberland River. This river, which flows into the Ohio, crosses western Kentucky and stretches into Tennessee. Shawnee villages were clustered along the banks of this major southern waterway. Viele spent the winter among the Shawnee, and in spring 1692, he returned to Philadelphia accompanied by several hundred Shawnee and surrounded by a flotilla of canoes loaded with furs. His success, like that of Groseilliers and Radisson at Green Bay in 1660, offered proof that the newly emerging fur trade of the Ohio River valley could be highly profitable.[30]

In 1694, news of Viele's journey circulated through Albany and simultaneously passed along the official letter-writing grapevine that linked New France to Versailles. Henri de Tonti, who controlled the Indian trade in the Illinois Country, believed his profits threatened by the arrival of this British trader in the Ohio River valley. Sensitive to the balance of power in the region, Tonti claimed that Viele and the Shawnee were seeking an alliance with the Miami "to draw them to them, which will give them a strong foothold for the success of their enterprise, if he corrupts them." New France and Versailles paid scant attention to Tonti's warning. The French ministry of marine was unconcerned about these English incursions and uninterested in establishing a French presence in the Ohio River valley. Their focus was on acquiring prime coat beaver, best secured at the more northerly Lake of the Woods, and wanted Indians to transport that peltry directly to Montreal. At Versailles, Pontchartrain, French chancellor from September 1699 to July 1714, continued Jean-Baptiste Colbert's "compact colony" policy, which limited French settlement to the farmlands of the St. Lawrence River valley. Pontchartrain believed that New France should remain a farming colony rather than become a fur-trading venture. With French warehouses overflowing with furs, reopening the western trade made little sense. Besides, Pontchartrain's patience with French fur traders was long exhausted; he considered these Canadians bizarre and guided by "another spirit, other manners, other sentiments" than the people of France. These men, with no fixed abode and a willingness to illegally trade with the British, had little interest in farming.[31]

30. *NYCD*, IV, 51.
31. Margry, ed., *Découvertes et établissements*, IV, 4; Banks, *Chasing Empire*, 30; Dale Miquelon, *New France, 1701–1744: A Supplement to Europe* (Toronto, Ont., 1987), 11.

THE INDIAN FUR TRADE OF THE OHIO RIVER VALLEY

During the twenty-year span in which the western trade was closed, from 1696 to 1716, Indians in the Ohio River valley developed an independent fur trade, free of French restrictions. The officials of New France lacked interest in the events that unfolded in the Ohio region. They were missing out on a great opportunity. The extensive wetlands in the region north of the Ohio and especially the Great Black Swamp, which bordered the southern shore of Lake Erie, provided an almost endless supply of the types of peltry now in high demand in Europe. French market prices for beaver at Montreal remained depressed, whereas animals indigenous to the Black Swamp were in high demand: red and grey fox, otter, mink, American marten, raccoon, possum, and coyote. There were many villages clustered along the drylands that bordered the swamp. Although the origin of the swamp's name is obscure, nineteenth-century land speculators claimed that it referred to the rich, black soil. But the nickname probably emerged from early travelers, who were deterred by the forest's gloom and the vast expanse of stagnant swamp water. Stretching south of the Maumee River, the Black Swamp was 30 to 40 miles wide and 120 miles in length, submerging the land from the Sandusky River in the east to present-day Fort Wayne, Indiana, in the west. When rain fell or the spring thaw arrived, the area was water and muck. Water oozed underfoot in all but the hottest of summer months.[32]

The swamp was created twenty thousand years ago, when glaciers leveled the land and dug out the lowlands. Sand, earth, and rocks were left along the leading edges of the glacier and formed ridges known as moraines, preventing the increasingly stagnant water from draining west, north, and south. Glaciers pushed the soil out in front, depositing and compacting areas in Northwest Ohio, where the topsoil is often ninety feet deep. The glacial movement formed extensive lakes, far larger than present-day Lake Erie, and, as the lakes dried up, they created a shallow, northeastern slope of fewer than four feet per mile. Fine blue clay subsoil cupped the remaining water, and low beach ridges blocked drainage. When the Wisconsin Glacier melted ten thousand years ago, it left behind vast quantities of water that had no place to go; the area must have been a vast cattail marsh, crowded with waterfowl. Natural plant succession gradually transformed the marsh into a thick swamp forest. Ancient elm and ash trees grew with their roots in the standing waters, with

---

32. Sometime between 1671 and 1674, before Viele arrived in the Ohio River valley, there were four even earlier colonial traders — Thomas Batts, Robert Fallam, James Needham, and Gabriel Arthur — who had previously journeyed along the southern tributaries of the Ohio to trade with the Shawnee and Miami.

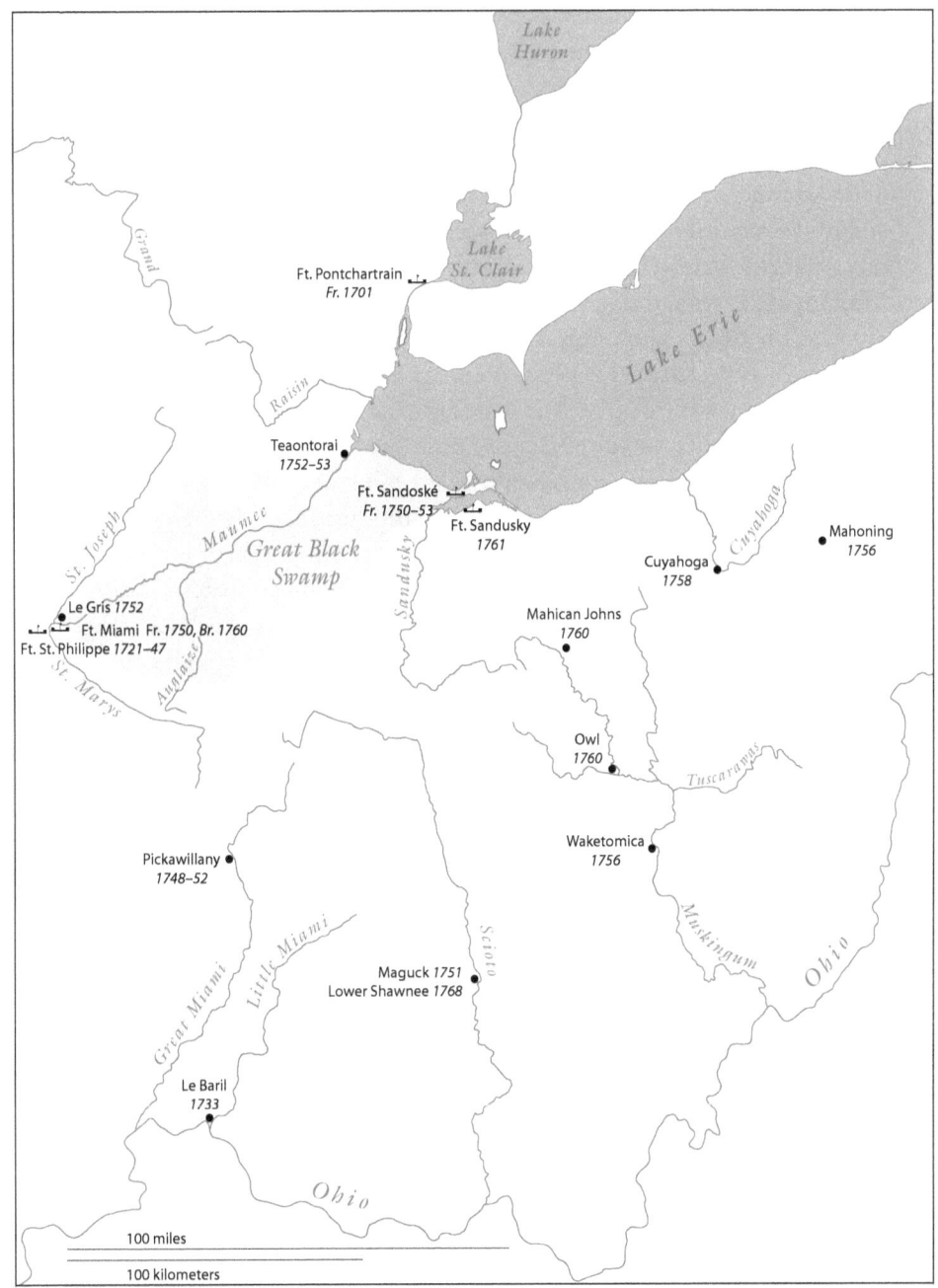

MAP 6. Great Black Swamp. Drawn by Ellen White

massive oaks and hickories on the sandy beach ridges. In contrast with the warmer Everglades, here the trees were broadleaf oak and ash, and they kept the floor of the forest in the dark. Windfalls often tumbled and uprooted the trees, a process that, coupled with the deep, heavy mud into which the tree fell, made this region almost impassable.

This swampland was a vast wildlife habitat, rich with fur-bearing mammals and freshwater fish. The monster muskellunge, a large, relatively uncommon species of fish that weighed as much as forty pounds, was indigenous to the Muskingum River and migrated into the watersheds that sustained the Black Swamp. The Muskingum watershed was linked to the Sandusky watershed, which was at the eastern border of the Black Swamp. The riverbanks flowing into the swamp were lined with an amazing assortment of freshwater mussels. Prodigious numbers of fur-bearing animals lived in the Black Swamp: bear, beaver, boar, bobcat, elk, cougar, deer, moose, buffalo, and timber wolf, but no animals were more highly prized by Europeans than the otters, American martens, muskrats, skunks, and raccoons that brought high prices in the marketplace and thrived in the swamp's waters and along its banks. Elk herds gathered along the rivers that fed the swamp; the Reverend David Zeisberger translated Muskingum to mean Elk's Eye, "because of the numbers of elk that formerly fed on its banks." Enormous flocks of passenger pigeons blackened the skies of the swampland, and, in 1806, pioneer ornithologist Alexander Wilson described a flock of more than two billion passenger pigeons that passed overhead for several hours and flew in a formation estimated to be 1 mile wide and 240 miles long.[33]

The swamp was the product of three poorly drained rivers: the Maumee, the Auglaize, and the Portage. The Maumee and Portage River watersheds in northwest Ohio and northeastern Indiana encompassed almost 1,500 square miles of swamplands. Indian villages bordered the swamp in a circular pattern. The Miami were settled at the Maumee-Wabash portage and along the Miami and Little Miami Rivers. The Huron (also called Wyandot) were located in villages along the Scioto, on lands east of the swamp, and they were settled as far south as the Ohio. The Black Swamp was the hunting ground for most of the villages in the Ohio River valley. In the west, the fur trade was

---

33. Claude Clayton Smith, *Ohio Outback: Leaning to Love the Great Black Swamp* (Kent, Oh., 2011); Emily Foster, ed., *The Ohio Frontier: An Anthology of Early Writings* (Lexington, Ky., 1996); Michael B. Lafferty, ed., *Ohio's Natural Heritage* (Columbus, Oh., 1979); Archer Butler Hulbert and William Nathaniel Schwarze, eds., *David Zeisberger's History of the North American Indians,* Ohio State Archaeological and Historical Society (Columbus, Oh., 1910).

dominated by the Miami, and to the east of the Black Swamp, the Wyandot were key players in the trade; farther downstream on the Ohio, at the mouth of the Scioto River, it was the Shawnee, who established Lower Shawneetown in the 1730s. The Shawnee had been scattered since the mid-seventeenth century and had lived among the Illinois at Fort St. Louis and the Creek in Alabama; others were in eastern Tennessee and trading with the Spanish at St. Augustine, and they had villages along the Potomac River in Maryland and eastern Tennessee. During the first decades of the eighteenth century, many Shawnee relocated to the Ohio River valley and established villages along the Scioto bordering the Black Swamp, allowing them to participate in the emerging fur trade.[34]

Unlimited access to the rich peltry of the Great Black Swamp encouraged the growth of an Indian-controlled fur trade. Indian women who processed the peltry increased their demands for new varieties of cloth, which encouraged the arrival of British traders from Albany and Pennsylvania's backcountry. Although few beaver pelts entered the Philadelphia market, Indian women processed vast quantities of other peltry, such as deer, fox, bear, otter, and bison, as well as the wildcats, muskrats, skunks, and wolves that were so plentiful in the Black Swamp. In 1701, British colonial traders returned with 953 bearskins, 799 wildcats, 3,811 fox skins, 5,525 raccoons, 783 minks, 791 deerskins, 261 otters, 100 wolves, and 547 beaver skins. Philadelphia and Albany captured a large portion of the furs harvested in the Ohio River, sup-

---

34. Berthold Fernow, *The Ohio Valley in Colonial Days* (Albany, N.Y., 1890), 54–55. Families among the Miami were distinguished by totems and usually resided in the same village. For their principal families, Miami totems included the Hare and the Crane; a third family totem was the Bear. The Serpent, Deer, and Small Acorn were the totems of the subtribes and included the Ouiatenon, Peanguichia, and Petikokia. In February 1721, Jacques-Charles Renaud Dubuisson arrived among the Miami, following the death of Jean-Baptiste Bissot de Vincennes. Dubuisson was to persuade the Miami to return to St. Joseph, but they refused; in August 1722, he returned to establish a garrisoned post at the Miami villages. He completed the post in May 1723, which he named Fort Saint Philippe des Miami, later shortened to Fort Miami. Governor Vaudreuil described it as one of the finest forts in the Upper Country. See Vaudreuil letter, Oct. 6, 1721, ANCol., C11A, 43, 328v–329v; Helen Hornbeck Tanner, *Atlas of Great Lakes Indian History* (Norman, Okla., 1987), 43–44, map 9. See also Charles Callender, "Miami," in Bruce G. Trigger, ed., *Handbook of North American Indians*, XV, *Northeast* (Washington, D.C., 1978), 684. Recent work on the Shawnee has been completed by Laura Keenan Spero, "'Stout, Bold, Cunning, and the Greatest Travellers in America': The Colonial Shawnee Diaspora" (Ph.D. diss., University of Pennsylvania, 2010); Stephen Warren, *The Worlds the Shawnees Made: Migration and Violence in Early America* (Chapel Hill, N.C., 2014); and Sami Lakomäki, *Gathering Together: The Shawnee People through Diaspora and Nationhood, 1600–1870* (New Haven, Conn., 2014).

plied in great part by the Black Swamp. Just west of Pennsylvania, newly resettled Delaware and Shawnee villages trapped numerous minks and raccoons, which went to Philadelphia. Throughout Europe, these types of furs remained in high demand, being used to trim the robes of civil and religious officials.[35]

Fur trade routes in the Ohio River valley were unfettered by French regulation and incorporated a diverse range of participants. English or Anglo-American traders arrived from Pennsylvania, New York, and the Carolina backcountry. The coureurs de bois ventured east to Albany and as far south as New Orleans and the Gulf Coast. In 1701, Biloxi's French commandant wrote of sixty northern coureurs de bois arriving in canoes filled with beaver pelts. Several hundred illegal French traders settled in Indian villages along the Wabash, Maumee, Miami, and Sandusky Rivers. The Indian population of the Ohio River valley increased dramatically as entire villages returned from Green Bay. Meanwhile, Indian groups east of the Appalachians were being pushed west by settler colonists in Maryland, Delaware, and Pennsylvania; these refugees established villages along the eastern Ohio and ventured as far west as the Little Miami and Sandusky Rivers.[36]

The region's ability to export peltry depended on the processing skills of women, who were increasingly the center of the households. Their social structure was changed by the incorporation of coureurs de bois. During the early years of the seventeenth-century fur trade, French traders at Green Bay relied on short-term relationships with Indian women to secure an entrée into Indian villages. Most of these relationships were transformed into long-term unions when villages returned to the Ohio River valley region. Along the Wabash, marriage after the "custom of the country" evolved to meet the needs of fur trade villages. Although the Jesuits denounced such marriages as immoral, these unions were far from casual or promiscuous. The coureur de bois who entered an Indian woman's household secured food, clothing, protection, and access to the peltry of his wife's kin.[37]

---

35. Bellomonte Memorial to the Board of Trade, 1704–1705, in *Journal of Commissioners for Trade and Plantations . . . ,* I (London, 1920), 686; Phillips, *Fur Trade,* I, 325; Richard Weyhing, "'Gascon Exaggerations': The Rise of Antoine Laumet dit de Lamothe, Sieur de Cadillac, the Foundation of Colonial Detroit, and the Origins of the Fox Wars," in Robert Englebert and Guillaume Teasdale, eds., *French and Indians in the Heart of North America, 1630–1815* (East Lansing, Mich., 2013), 77–112, esp. 109n.

36. Margry, ed., *Découvertes et établissements,* V, 353, 362; Phillips, *Fur Trade,* I, 301n; *NYCD,* IX, 712–713.

37. For descriptions of how marriage in the manner of the country, or *à la façon du pays,* became institutionalized as crucial to the fur trade, see Sylvia Van Kirk, *Many Tender Ties:*

Ouiatenon and Kethtippecanuck emerged as trading centers for villages clustered along the Wabash and engaged in a variety of supply activities that were important to fur traders and their northern Indian allies. They grew enough surplus corn to feed their households and visiting fur traders as well as enough to trade to northern villages when northern crop yields proved insufficient to last the winter months. Indian women also manufactured baskets, or mococks, from reeds in the wetlands, in which marketable goods such as corn and maple sugar were transported. Indian men were long-distance traders and were also engaged in a variety of other occupations. Many of them built the larger bark-clad canoes that were used in the deeper waters just south of Ouiatenon. As hunters, they supplied their own households with fresh meat and fish as well as with the peltry for processing. As the fur trade prospered, and the number of French, British, and colonial traders increased, many Indian men became provisioners for trading villages, like that of Kethtippecanuck. At this village, there were also fur trade presses, which safely stored furs until they could be shipped north to Detroit or south to Vincennes or New Orleans. The transport of large peltry harvests often depended on the manning of canoes and bateaux by Indians or, increasingly, their leading packhorses north and south along the Wabash foot trails that linked Vincennes, Ouiatenon, Kethtippecanuck, and Miamitown.

Fur trade activity was generally organized by household. A European trader who married an Indian woman had access to the broad range of labor available in her household, since women both owned the house and its contents and commanded the labor of those living in it. Women with extensive kin networks acquired greater quantities of fur. Indian women dried, compressed, and secured the peltry in packs. Each pack weighed about one hundred pounds. A pirogue, or boat, that was sufficiently large might carry forty

---

Women in Fur-Trade Society, 1670–1870 (1980; rpt., Norman, Okla., 1990), 28; see also Van Kirk, "The Custom of the Country," in Lewis H. Thomas, ed., *Essays on Western History* (Edmonton, Ont., 1976), 49–82. Jennifer S. H. Brown also discusses intermarriage between fur traders and Native women in *Strangers in Blood: Fur Trade Company Families in Indian Country* (1980; rpt. Norman, Okla., 1966). See also Jacqueline Peterson and Jennifer S. H. Brown, eds., *The New Peoples: Being and Becoming Métis in North America* (Winnipeg, Man., 1996), esp. Jacqueline Peterson, "Many Roads to Red River: Métis Genesis in the Great Lakes Region, 1680–1815," 37–73; Gary Clayton Anderson, "Joseph Renville and the Ethos of Biculturalism," in James A. Clifton, ed., *Being and Becoming Indian: Biographical Studies of North American Frontiers* (Prospect Heights, Ill., 1989), 59–81; John Mack Faragher, "Americans, Mexicans, Métis: A Community Approach to the Comparative Study of North American Frontiers," in William Cronon, George Miles, and Jay Gitlin, eds., *Under an Open Sky: Rethinking America's Western Past* (New York, 1992), 90–110.

packs, but this required four men to manage the voyage. Along the Wabash River, such a vessel, under the management of skillful boatmen, was propelled fifteen or twenty miles a day against the current. In the eighteenth century, furs were transported north to Miamitown on horseback along the pathways to the Maumee-Wabash portage. Packs carried over the portage to the head of the Maumee were often placed in pirogues or in keelboats and transported to Detroit.

Along the Wabash River, the corn harvest was the crucial summer activity, whereas processing peltry for the fur trade was a winter task. Because animals had the thickest and most luxuriant coats during the winter months, this meant trapping them in ice-clad or frozen ponds. Women's production of waterproof clothing, especially leggings and moccasins, was essential: hunters who lived in wintering camps were outdoors for extended time periods, and protection from the elements allowed their survival. Almost all Indian men relied increasingly on traps to capture fur-bearing animals, but the traps were far from reliable. They were set in both shallow and deep water, either beneath or partially above the surface. Traplines, the route along which a trapper set his traps, were in proximity and checked frequently, often two to three times a week, to prevent escape.

A hunter's work ended only after the animal was removed from the trap and skinned. This required a small, sharp axe and chopping block. The hunter quickly removed the feet and cleaned the outer two inches of the pelt, leaving as much of the fat tissue as possible on the carcass. At this point, the men returned to the wintering camps and turned the process over to the women who had accompanied them. Women cleaned and stretched the skins, which required tremendous patience and time. Well-processed pelts could be exchanged for larger quantities of better quality trade goods.

Women processed most pelts by fleshing them over a rounded and pointed board that was several feet long and held at a 45-degree angle between the floor and their chest. This was grueling work; these women leaned over the beam and drew a sharp knife back and forth across the skins to remove the connective tissue and muscle. Traders acquired knives designed for this purpose, usually ten to twelve inches long and sharply honed. Because the thickness of the pelt varied, women drew the knife slowly along the pelt, careful not to pierce the skin. The thinnest section of the pelt was often turned over to processing by older women, who used their teeth to process the fragile sections. Indian women then stretched the pelt; if it was beaver, they would stretch it in an oval shape. If moisture was trapped between the skin and the drying board, it damaged the pelt. Moisture also caused the pelt to dry too slowly, which could ruin the pelt. For this reason, the initial cleaning process often took place within a warm shelter so that the fur dried quickly and thoroughly and was ready to be stretched.

Women stretched beaver skin around a circular hoop made from the small limbs of pliable tree branches. Pelts of different shape, such as otter, required rectangular stretching frames. The skin was tied with string made from animal gut, at one-inch intervals, completely around the edge of the pelt to secure it to the hoop. Women then further cleaned the pelt of fat and moisture with a fleshing tool, a scraper with rounded corners, or they used an old, curved knife blade. Many elderly women possessed the skills that came with long years of experience but did not travel to the wintering camps; furs were often returned for final processing to the home villages. In the late spring, after several months of drying, the furs were ready for the market. In exchange for furs women secured the metal awls essential to processing furs as well as the cooking utensils that replaced stone, bone, and pottery implements and the manufactured cloth that they transformed into clothing for their households.

Marriage to traders provided tangible advantages: more material items, higher status, and enhanced power as intermediaries. Indian village headmen encouraged the formation of marital alliances between Indian women and traders in the interest of group welfare. Households with large numbers of women were the most efficient in processing furs, and this probably meant that serial polygamy remained a crucial part of many fur-processing households. Through marriage, the trader was drawn into the Indian woman's kinship circle and, in turn, into a moral universe as a predictable human being. Kinship responsibilities regulated his behavior. John Lawson, an eighteenth-century naturalist, noted that this archetypal trader was "seldom without an *Indian* Female for his Bed-fellow." Among the Cherokee on the removal roll of 1835, intermarried whites and their children were slightly less than 23 percent of the population. Intermarriage took place even earlier in the Great Lakes region, where the Jesuits complained of the practice and endorsed the ban on fur traders in the west to prevent marriage to Indian women. In a world where they were strangers and at risk, Frenchmen depended on their Indian relatives for labor and protection in transporting the winter peltry to market. Women were more than the processors of peltry. Late-eighteenth-century records openly praised women's contributions on trading journeys with their husbands, and one trader attributed another trader's failure to an absence of Indian women's involvement. Women were also skilled interpreters who demanded and received extra additional gifts to insure their involvement. Additional costs were overlooked, and fur trade correspondence reveals that these women demanded and received preferential treatment. One post commander, George Simpson, who rose to prominence in the Hudson's Bay Company, accorded his Chipewyan female interpreter special privileges and "felt obliged to give in to her demands for extra rations and preferential treatment in order to prevent her defection, and he was amazed by this woman's resourcefulness." Traders were completely dependent on the households of their wives; they acquired both fluency in Indian languages and familiarity with Indigenous behavioral standards, usually dressing in Indian fashion. When French military men or envoys entered these Wabash Indian villages during the 1720s, these French traders often served as cultural mediators. Men once dismissed as outlaws often later reappear in the written record as translators or mediators for Indians, newly legitimate employees of New France.[38]

Before European arrival, most Indian villages were patrilineal, and generally women moved into the households of their husbands' mothers. Since Indian women did not marry within the same clan, most moved into their husband's village. But with the 1690s arrival of illegal French traders, or coureurs des bois, Indian women remained within their home villages. The return of villages from Green Bay and refugees from the east led to rising population levels. The concurrent expansion of agricultural fields and the success of the

---

38. Van Kirk, *Many Tender Ties,* 84. Indian women are most frequently thought of as cultural mediators, but French men also played a similar role in Indian villages. For one of the first discussions about cultural mediators, see Clara Sue Kidwell, "Indian Women as Cultural Mediators," *Ethnohistory,* XXXIX (1992), 97–107. See also Brown's *Strangers in Blood* (esp. 65, 127) and Van Kirk's *Many Tender Ties* as part of the expanding literature on cultural mediators in the fur trade. For a parallel male figure, see James H. Merrell's description of Andrew Montour, son of Madame Montour and an interpreter and go-between, in "'The Cast of His Countenance': Reading Andrew Montour," in Ronald Hoffman, Mechal Sobel, and Fredrika J. Teute, eds., *Through a Glass Darkly: Reflections on Personal Identity in Early America* (Chapel Hill, N.C., 1997), 13–39; Nancy L. Hagedorn, "'Faithful, Knowing, and Prudent': Andrew Montour as Interpreter and Cultural Broker, 1740-1772," in Margaret Connell Szasz, ed., *Between Indian and White Worlds: The Cultural Broker* (Norman, Okla., 1994), 44–60; Jon Parmenter, "Isabel Montour: Cultural Broker on the Frontiers of New York and Pennsylvania," in Ian K. Steele and Nancy L. Rhoden, eds., *The Human Tradition in Colonial America* (Wilmington, Del., 1999), 141–159. "Bed-fellow": John Lawson, *A New Voyage to Carolina,* ed. Hugh Talmage Lefler (Chapel Hill, N.C., 1967), 35–36. Frenchmen involved in the trade relied on Indian dress both because of its practicality and because it signified acceptance within an Indian village. Dressing in Indian fashion was common practice in the fur trade and entailed donning waterproof moccasins, leggings, and outer garments. Much has been written about cultural cross-dresssing, which is yet another aspect of how dress changed with the mixing of different cultures, and this will be more fully discussed in Chapter 5, "Picturing Prosperity."

Wabash River fur trade led to highly productive households that were increasingly composed of a majority of women.[39]

Pierre Roy is a good example. In 1703, when the fur trade ban was most effective, Roy married a Miami woman at Ouiatenon, Marguerite Ouabankikoué. She was the daughter of the Miami leader Pacanakoma, and this relationship gave Roy an entrée into the fur trade. His wife provided him the protection of her household and, simultaneously, access to the peltry of her kin. His access to trade goods and familiarity with Native people and customs led him to become a well-known and respected fur trader. Because his wife was the daughter of a prominent leader, Roy became an interpreter for visiting Frenchmen. We first learn of him in 1721, when Captain Jacques-Charles Renaud Dubuisson went to the Maumee-Wabash portage with orders for all fur traders to leave the village. Although Roy left with his wife, children, and property and wintered at Detroit, the Detroit post was close to her Miamitown relatives, and they probably returned to the region the next spring. Around 1731, Roy was living with his wife and children at Montreal. Relying on his wife's illness as an excuse, he petitioned New France officials for permission to return to the Wabash River valley so that his wife could recover her health. At this time, Roy also formed a company with the commandant at Miamitown for the trade of that post. The original agreement establishing their partnership identified Roy's wife as Miami. Roy "represented to us that his wife, who is of the Ouiatenon nation, and who has been continually ill for the two years that she came to live in this colony, wished to return to her country to recover her health and to take with him her three children and to take with him three Frenchmen, Joseph Larrivé, Louis Goulet, and François Seran to man the canoes." Roy "declared he is taking the things necessary for his housekeeping, his clothes and those of his family, with a hundred pounds of flour, three hundred pounds of biscuit, two pots of brandy, fifteen pots of wine, and two pots of strawberry brandy, and that his entire merchandise consists of only one hundred pounds of powder, one hundred pounds of lead, nine ells of woolen cloth, a gross of knives, and two pounds of vermillion." Although Roy was forbidden to trade with the Indians, his canoe was laden with trade goods rather than household products. His woolen cloth, knives, and vermilion had more value in trade than in housekeeping. By 1740, Roy and Marguerite Ouabankikoué had returned to Ouiatenon and her mother's household, and their involvement in the acquisition and exchange of furs

---

39. See Smith, "The Matrifocal Family," in Goody, ed., *Character of Kinship*, 124–125. See also Olwig, "Women, 'Matrifocality,' and Systems of Exchange," *Ethnohistory*, XXVIII (1981), 59–78.

had led their two young sons to become traders and interpreters among the Miami.[40]

Other Indian households at Ouiatenon also absorbed illegal traders through marriage. In the 1710s, the coureur de bois Jean Richard became an official interpreter, translating for both sieurs de Vincennes, father and son. Richard had lived in the west since 1702, when the western trade was outlawed. He was incorporated into his wife's Ouiatenon household, which ensured his involvement in the fur trade, and the linguistic skills he learned from his wife and kin led to his persistence in the region.[41]

Throughout the southern Great Lakes, Indian women's marriages to French fur traders became commonplace. Even Antoine de la Mothe Cadillac, despite his belief that Indian culture was inferior, proposed that a garrison be kept at Detroit where the soldiers should be permitted to marry Indian women, cementing Indian relations to the French regime. His proposal reflects the reality of fur trade society, where marriage — whether performed after the custom of the country or legitimated by a priest — was integral to the exchange process. Even after the fur trade reopened in 1716, many legal French traders continued to marry into Indian households and to remain there to raise their children. Many Frenchmen had legitimate families in Montreal as well, and some were military men, like Jean-Baptiste Bissot de Vincennes. He had married a French woman in Montreal in 1696 and had four daughters and three sons with her. After serving in the west, however, he chose to move from Montreal and live permanently among the Miami from 1712 until his death in 1719. His primary responsibility was to prevent the Indians from falling under English control, but this would have been difficult without becoming an integral part of that community. Leadership came from village elders, not outsider Frenchmen.[42]

40. "No. 7. Extract of the Memoir of M. the Marquis de Vaudreuil, governor and lieutenant for the King in France, to serve as instructions for the Sieur Dumont, half-pay ensign in the troops maintained in Canada, detached until further orders to go to command in the country of the Ouiatanon and at the Rivière des Miamis, August 26, 1720," in Frances Krauskopf, ed. and trans., *Ouiatanon Documents,* Indiana Historical Society, *Publications,* XVIII, no. 2 (Indianapolis, 1955), 165–168. For a detailed examination of the family and descendants of Pierre Roy and Marguerite Ouabankikoué, see Karen L. Marrero, "Founding Families: Power and Authority of Mixed French and Native Lineages in Eighteenth-Century Detroit" (Ph.D. diss., Yale, 2011).

41. "No. 12. Permission to Jean Richard, Sepetember 3, 1722" (in margin: "Richard, permit for Ouiatanon, Took out sixteen pots of brandy for the four men, left September 9"), in Krauskopf, ed. and trans., *Ouiatanon Documents,* 172–174.

42. In 1680, when the French population of New France remained at ten thousand,

The English had been tangentially involved as early as 1689 in trading at Wabash villages like Miamitown and Ouiatenon. French goods at Montreal were more than double the Albany prices. As early as 1689, Indians trading at Albany exchanged two beaver pelts for a gun, whereas a gun was worth five beaver at Montreal. The situation continued to worsen, and the most popular fur trade items, such as red trade cloth and manufactured shirts, were generally double the Albany prices. The English had a distinct economic advantage in the fur trade because they manufactured strouds, the coarse woolen blankets that were a staple of the trade. That advantage proved so great that Frenchmen were often forced to resort to the purchase of English strouds to maintain the viability of the exchange process. With the western trade closed, New France became too weak to interrupt this shift to English trade goods. Even the presence of active military posts, like those at Detroit and among the Illinois, did not disrupt the illegal trade.[43]

Coureurs de bois who refused to return to Montreal became crucial participants in the development of this Ohio River valley fur trade. In the Montreal market, their Indian kin became the go-betweens for illegal traders, who feared that they would be arrested by French authorities. Indeed, French policy alienated many coureurs de bois, usually considered rebellious men to begin with, and coupled with their spatial alienation of living in an Indian world, they became increasingly amenable to Indian rather than French ways. The French closure of the western trade had saved the Company of the Farm but simultaneously transformed western Frenchmen into Indian allies and English trading partners. They established trading connections to Albany and more distant trading posts, such as the English posts in the Caro-

---

French Minister Jean-Baptiste Colbert urged the Christianization of the Indians and their intermarriage with Frenchmen. These efforts often failed because young Frenchmen came to prefer Indian lifestyles to the westernized lifestyles of the French at Montreal, see W. J. Eccles, *France in America* (1972; rpt. East Lansing, Mich., 1990); Jean Delanglez, *Frontenac and the Jesuits* (Chicago, 1939). Both the Chevaliers and Chouteaus are well-known examples of legal French traders who brought their families into the west and whose children and later descendants married Indian women, raised families, and remained in the western country. For more information about the Chevalier and Chouteau families, see Tanis C. Thorne, *The Many Hands of My Relations: French and Indians on the Lower Missouri* (Columbia, Mo., 1996); and Susan Sleeper-Smith, *Indian Women and French Men: Rethinking Cultural Encounter in the Western Great Lakes* (Amherst, Mass., 2001), 47–48.

43. Arthur H. Buffington, "The Policy of Albany and English Westward Expansion," *Mississippi Valley Historical Review*, VIII (1922), 356–357; Helen Broshar, "The First Push Westward of the Albany Traders," ibid., VII (1920), 228–241; Phillips, *Fur Trade*, I, 301, 314; *NYCD*, IX, 712–713.

lina backcountry and the new French center in New Orleans. In the seventeenth century, the French had introduced kettles, knives, and metal products to Indians; now, in the eighteenth century, increasing Indian demand for cloth coincided with the growth of the English cloth industry. In addition, as illegal traders took up residence in Indian households, few trade goods came directly from Montreal. In villages where there were no coureurs de bois, Odawa, Miami, and Illinois began functioning as fur traders. It was the Odawa, also middlemen of the trade, who brought prime coat beaver from more remote northern regions to exchange for trade goods at Albany. Unintentionally, the movement of French traders to Albany, Philadelphia, New Orleans, and the backcountry Carolina posts encouraged Indians to exercise greater independence. Their desire for European goods led them to journey to far-off posts themselves if coureurs de bois were not making the journeys for them. Indians in the Ohio River valley emerged as independent traders engineering a vast exchange of furs for cloth. Even when the French attempted to reestablish their control over the trade by opening Detroit, they often failed to provide the type of cloth that Indian women demanded in exchange for peltry. The English supplied the lighter-weight cloth required by the Indian trade in the southern Great Lakes, as opposed to the heavy woolens the French produced for the northern trade in beaver. Banning fur traders from the west introduced Indians to English competition and encouraged them to search for favorable exchange rates for their peltry. Market-savvy Indians skillfully discerned the trade advantages at different trading posts. In the end, the fur trade ban encouraged Indian resettlement in the Ohio River valley, with its vast supply of peltry, encouraged illegal French traders to marry into Indigenous kin networks and refocused the western trade to a region little explored by the French and thoroughly controlled by Indians.[44]

44. "Extrait d'une lettre de Champigny au ministre," Nov. 4, 1693, in Margry, ed., *Découvertes et établissements,* VI, 55; see also "1697: Le Sueur's Mines on the Mississippi," in Reuben Gold Thwaites, ed., *The French Regime in Wisconsin,* part 1, *1634–1727,* State Historical Society of Wisconsin, *Collections,* XVI (Madison, Wis., 1902), 173; "Correspondance entre M. de Vaudreuil et la Cour," in *Rapport de l'archiviste de la province de Québec pour 1947–1948* (Quebec, 1948), 298–299.

3

REOPENING THE WESTERN TRADE

Versailles had little interest in the Ohio River valley until the beginning of the eighteenth century, when increased amounts of peltry found their way into English hands. Coureurs de bois and Odawa were already trading at British posts, transporting furs from the western Great Lakes across Lakes Huron and Ontario to exchange at Fort Albany. Following France's closure of the western trade, fur-laden Miami and Shawnee canoes began floating down the Maumee and Sandusky Rivers to Lake Erie and north across the lakes to the English posts. This was part of a long, unprotected frontier that extended from Fort Frontenac to Fort St. Louis in the Illinois Country. Governors Frontenac and Denonville had both seen the advantages of constructing a fort at the straits; Denonville had sent Olivier Morel de La Durantaye to build a post on the east bank of the river, but it was soon abandoned. It was Antoine de la Mothe Cadillac who traveled to Versailles and obtained permission to build the new post.

This chapter focuses on the founding of Detroit and its impact on the Indian fur trade in the Ohio River valley. The fort, conveniently located on the Detroit River, drew illegal traders and Indians from the Ohio River valley. Indians obtained better prices for their peltry by pitting the English against the French. Although the new post procured a greater share of the trade for New France, it also intensified the conflict between the English and French. The new post also dramatically changed the lives of the coureurs de bois who had remained illegally in the west. The men who had sought refuge in Indian villages became the translators and mediators that Cadillac relied on to negotiate with the Indians. No longer outlaws, they became respectable Frenchmen as France moved farther south in the lands north of the Ohio and established trading outposts at Miamitown, Ouiatenon, and Vincennes.

FOUNDING DETROIT, 1701

The ban on the western trade might have saved the Company of the Farm by reducing the glut of furs in Montreal, but French officials remained preoccupied with the problems of the Iroquois, the Albany traders, and the large number of coureurs de bois operating in the west. The hundreds of illegal traders who refused to return to Montreal troubled the minister of the marine, who doubted the loyalty of these renegades. More generally, officials in Versailles had begun to question the economic profitability and strategic importance of New France. In the midst of these discussions, Cadillac arrived at Versailles to petition for the establishment of a new post at Detroit. He promised that this fort would eliminate the region's contraband trade, interrupt Iroquois excursions to the west, and resituate and concentrate the interior trade of the Great Lakes at Detroit. Cadillac claimed that the new post would reshape the scattered Indian population and reposition them at the French establishment. Instead of heading into the west, fur traders would be drawn to the new site. The post was intended to allay Versailles's traditional anxiety over the westward expansion of New France by reshaping the pays d'en haut into a more compact colony. Once the market for peltry recovered, of course, Cadillac intended to profit from the trade in furs.[1]

In convincing Versailles policymakers that the creation of the Detroit post would be the remedy for many of New France's problems, Cadillac employed a Francocentric strategy that was to reconfigure the pays d'en haut and refocus the colony around one central place. Cadillac argued that relocating Indians from the Great Lakes region to Detroit would also provide a new source of Indian allies for the French Army, as effective as the Iroquois were for the English. To Versailles, impending warfare on the European front made this notion of accessible Indian allies an attractive prospect. However, the relocation of diverse tribes at Detroit drew France into the struggles and alliances

---

1. Richard Weyhing, "'Gascon Exaggerations': The Rise of Antoine Laumet dit de Lamothe, Sieur de Cadillac, the Foundation of Colonial Detroit, and the Origins of the Fox Wars," in Guillaume Englebert and Robert Teasdale, eds., *French and Indians in the Heart of North America* (East Lansing, Mich., 2013), 79. For recent explorations of Detroit's early history, see Catherine Cangany, *Frontier Seaport: Detroit's Transformation into an Atlantic Entrepôt* (Chicago, 2014); and Karen L. Marrero's dissertation, "Founding Families: Power and Authority of Mixed French and Native Lineages in Eighteenth-Century Detroit" (Ph.D. diss., Yale University, 2011); Brian Lee Dunnigan, *Frontier Metropolis: Picturing Early Detroit, 1701–1838* (Detroit, 2001). See also Timothy J. Kent, *Ft. Pontchartrain at Detroit: A Guide to the Daily Lives of Fur Trade and Military Personnel, Settlers, and Missionaries at French Posts*, 2 vols. (Ossineke, Mich., 2001), I.

of the Great Lakes, a fight that it could ill afford. Indians had little intention of serving French interests, although they expected that the French would mediate the disputes French meddling had set in motion at Detroit. Cadillac had recruited Indians without regard to the conflicts that had long divided them. Relocating the Miami, Huron-Petun, and Odawa alongside each other was disastrous—Cadillac made no attempt to ensure that their quarrels over earlier killings were resolved nor to offer restitution to cover the bodies of those killed. Violence broke out almost immediately between the Odawa, Miami, and Wyandot and rapidly escalated, which resulted in dead Indians and Frenchmen. By 1706, "a Recollect missionary and a French soldier of the garrison were killed in an intertribal quarrel" outside the gates of Fort Pontchartrain. Detroit became a disastrous and dangerous area for the Miami, who relocated to villages that distanced them from the fray. Rather than remain enmeshed in Detroit's disputes, the Miami moved to the Maumee-Wabash portage. They had been enticed from the St. Joseph post by Cadillac, but now preferred to join their kin at Miamitown.[2]

The varied agendas of distinct Indian communities challenged Cadillac's skills as a mediator, and he failed to bring together peoples who were not traditional allies. Instead, Cadillac's policies brought chaos to the newly founded post and led to the outbreak of the Fox Wars, which spread to the larger region, affecting the Illinois, New France's most loyal allies. Western Indians who came to Detroit to trade did not cooperate with Cadillac's vision of an

2. The idea of founding a post at the Straits of Detroit did not originate with Cadillac. At the end of the seventeenth century, both governor of New France Jacques-René de Brisay Denonville and his successor, Louis de Buade, comte de Frontenac, thought a new outpost at Detroit would be advantageous to the French fur trade. It was to be across the lake from Fort Frontenac and along the Detroit River, where the straits joined Lake Huron to Lake Erie. This route would link the Huron and the Odawa and thwart Iroquois passage into the western Great Lakes. Olivier Morel de La Durantaye, who replaced the weak and ineffectual Governor La Barre, sent Sieur de Duluth to build this new post on the Detroit River. Duluth was hesitant to follow Denonville's orders, and although he eventually began building a post on the east bank of the river, it was soon abandoned. See Reuben Gold Thwaites, ed., *The Jesuit Relations and Allied Documents: Travels and Explorations of the Jesuit Missionaries in New France, 1610–1791*, 73 vols. (Cleveland, 1896–1901), LXII, 274; Weyhing, "'Gascon Exaggerations,'" in Englebert and Teasdale, eds., *French and Indians in the Heart of North America*, 95; [M. de Lamothe Cadillac], "Description of Detroit: Advantages Found There," Michigan Pioneer and Historical Society, *Collections*, 29 vols. (Lansing, Mich. 1886–1912), XXXIII, 133; Richard White, *The Middle Ground: Indians, Empires, and Republics in the Great Lakes Region, 1650–1815* (New York, 1991), 82–90; James A. Clifton, *The Prairie People: Continuity and Change in Potawatomi Indian Culture, 1665–1965* (Iowa City, 1998), 87.

alliance of hundreds, if not thousands, of Indians who could be mobilized at Detroit. They were not an effective counterweight to the Iroquois, and Cadillac's promise to Versailles in 1698 proved hollow.³

The western trade of the Iroquois did decline in the late seventeenth and early eighteenth centuries, although this was more likely a result of Iroquois involvement in interimperial warfare. The Iroquois supplied warriors to the English during both King William's War (1689–1697) and Queen Anne's War (1702–1713). Despite their proclaimed neutrality, the Iroquois remained allies of the British, and this drew Iroquois attention and men away from the western trade. Prolonged Iroquois absence enabled the Potawatomi, Odawa, and Miami to become middlemen in the fur trade, which increased their involvement with English traders from New York and Pennsylvania.⁴

In 1710, Cadillac was relieved of his command at Detroit and assigned the governorship of Louisiana. He was replaced by Jacques-Charles Renaud Dubuisson. Once the violence surrounding its establishment was resolved, Detroit had distinct advantages for the Indian trade in the Ohio River valley. The post placed French goods at the disposal of Indians and provided a more direct link to the French in Montreal. Simultaneously, the presence of a French fort near the entrance to Lake Erie shielded Miamitown and villages along the Wabash from Iroquois intrusion. Despite the advantages that Albany possessed, especially the lower price of British trade goods, Detroit's location at the nexus of rivers flowing into Lake Erie allowed the French to retain control over a considerable part of the fur trade. Governor Philippe de Rigaud, marquis de Vaudreuil, described Detroit as enabling the French to control *"un commerce considerable."*⁵

THE WESTERN FUR TRADE REOPENED

In 1716, when they discovered that the oversupply of peltry had been ruined in storage, French officials reopened the western trade. Before this,

---

3. Brett Rushforth, *Bonds of Alliance: Indigenous and Atlantic Slaveries in New France* (Chapel Hill, N.C., 2012), 200–201; White, *Middle Ground*, 148–159; R. David Edmunds and Joseph L. Peyser, *The Fox Wars: The Mesquakie Challenge to New France* (Norman, Okla., 1993), 62–85; Andrew Keith Sturtevant, "Jealous Neighbors: Rivalry and Alliance among the Native Communities of Detroit, 1701–1766" (Ph.D. diss., College of William and Mary, 2011).

4. Paul Chrisler Phillips, *The Fur Trade*, 2 vols. (Norman, Okla., 1961), I, 318, 319. For a discussion of the Odawa's long-term involvement in the trade, see Michael A. McDonnell, *Masters of Empire: Great Lakes Indians and the Making of America* (New York, 2015).

5. Archives Nationales, Colonies, Versailles, Paris (hereafter cited as ANCol.), C11, 21, F21 (emphasis added); Cangany, *Frontier Seaport*, 22.

only three posts remained open in the southern Great Lakes but forbidden to trade: Fort Chartres in the Illinois Country, Fort St. Joseph, and Detroit (Fort Pontchartrain). The license system revoked in 1696 was restored.

The reopening of the western trade called attention to the need to establish a fort in the Ohio River valley. Pierre Dugué, sieur de Boisbriand, the commandant of the Illinois District, was the first to alert the French government to the importance of asserting control over the region. That need was becoming apparent because of rising competition from the British, who were now venturing as far west as the Wabash and increasing their overtures to the Miami. The death of the elder Vincennes in 1719 had allowed English traders to establish a foothold at Miamitown. Boisbriand's first petition of 1718 stressed the importance of the Maumee-Wabash portage because it was the shortest water route from Montreal to the Illinois Country, as well as from Montreal to New Orleans. If New France lost control of it, French fur traders going from the former city to the latter would be forced to make a circuitous journey through Lake Huron to the Straits of Michilimackinac, south along the Lake Michigan shoreline, and then down either the Illinois or St. Joseph River to reach the Illinois Country and the Mississippi. This would almost double the length of the journey through the portage.

With the reopening of the western trade, the governor of New France was given the authority to garrison as many posts as he felt were necessary in the Upper Country. During the 1720s, the French began reestablishing and opening small garrisons at Ouiatenon, Miamitown, and Pimitoui (Pimiteoui) on the Illinois River at Peoria and rebuilding the larger Fort de Chartres on the Mississippi. Versailles was interested in curtailing British competition, but minimal French support left these small perimeter outposts incapable of offering much opposition to British overtures. French officials were also unable to decide whether permits were an effective means of controlling the western trade. They vacillated. In 1715 and 1716, they reestablished a very limited permit system for fur trading. They then revoked this system in 1719, only to reestablish it yet again in 1728.[6]

Despite these newly established posts, French traders continued to live in an Indian world and generally acquired the habits and lifestyles of their adoptive households. They followed Indian customs and behaved like their Indian neighbors, a process apparent at the smaller village outposts and forts throughout the Ohio River valley region. The coureurs de bois who found

---

6. Helen Hornbeck Tanner, *Atlas of Great Lakes Indian History* (Norman, Okla., 1987), 39; Frances Krauskopf, ed. and trans., *Ouiatanon Documents,* Indiana Historical Society, *Publications,* XVIII, no. 2 (Indianapolis, 1955), 140–141.

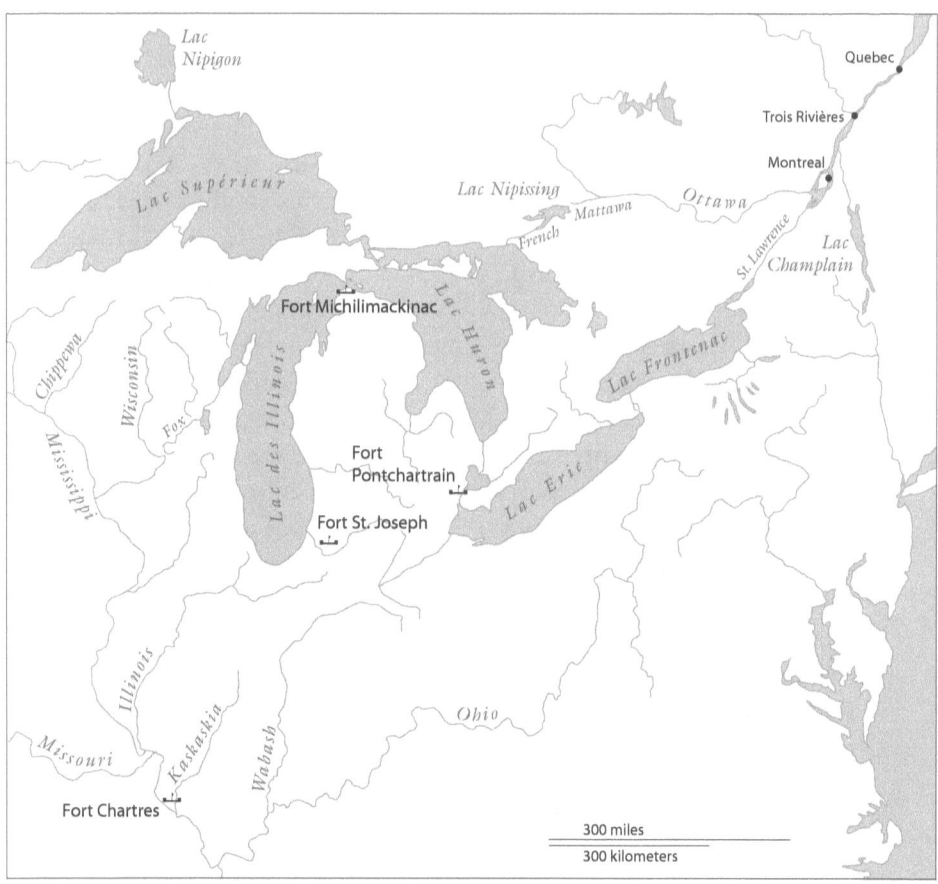

MAP 7. Early French forts, 1720. Drawn by Ellen White.

refuge in his wife's household accommodated to and even assimilated into her household and kin network. Because Native women did not marry out, marriage, either sacramentally sanctioned or "in the manner of the country," transformed Frenchmen into Indian husbands, fathers, and brothers.

Moreover, French officials ultimately failed to establish control of the Ohio River valley fur trade. During the fur trade ban, Indians established new commercial routes that extended beyond French territorial boundaries. The Albany trade routes were the most viable, but Indian alliances with different nations and colonies opened up additional sources of trade goods. The Shawnee established new villages close to Philadelphia, where they could exchange peltry acquired from the Shawnees' Ohio River valley allies, like the Miami and Delaware. Coureurs de bois, Miami, and Illinois, as well as their allies, transported furs from the western Ohio Valley to backcountry posts in

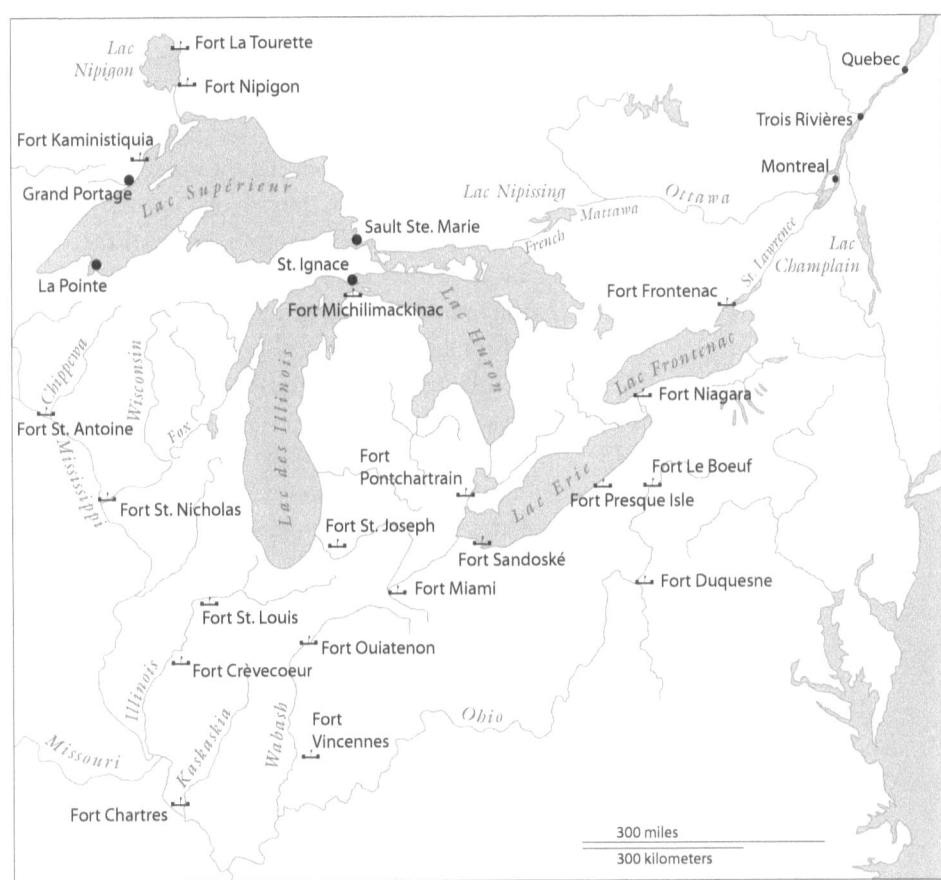

MAP 8. French forts, 1634–1763. Drawn by Ellen White

the Carolinas. The Tennessee River served as the primary route to Carolina, whereas the Piankeshaw and Wea traveled along the Cumberland to reach the same posts. Although the French appointed knowledgeable men in crucial Indian villages, the distant policymakers at Versailles failed to heed the advice of their agents, often dismissing them as greedy fur traders.[7]

In the absence of clear and informed guidance from France, the extension of

---

7. Furs from the Ohio Country are further explored in Verner W. Crane, "The Tennessee River as the Road to Carolina: The Beginnings of Exploration and Trade," *Mississippi Valley Historical Review*, III (1916–1917), 3–18; Crane, "The Southern Frontier in Queen Anne's War," *American Historical Review*, XXIV (1918–1919), 379–395; and more recently in Eric Hinderaker, *Elusive Empires: Constructing Colonialism in the Ohio Valley, 1673–1800* (Cambridge, 1997), 35.

a French presence into the Ohio River valley was haphazard. A good example is the founding of a French outpost at Ouiatenon by the young François-Marie Bissot de Vincennes. Jean-Baptiste Bissot de Vincennes's eldest son was sent by the governor of New France to visit the Wea village at Ouiatenon and convince them to return to their former lands. He was then eighteen or nineteen, having lived among the Miami since he was thirteen. French officials wanted the Wea to settle closer to Lake Michigan, and Vincennes journeyed there from Miamitown with a contingent of ten soldiers. When the Wea refused to move, Vincennes solved the problem by taking up residence at Ouiatenon with his men and a small number of traders. They settled in the midst of five thousand Indians, and Vincennes constructed a small house near the Indians' fort at Ouiatenon. The ten men who accompanied him probably took up residence in Indian households. The French were numerically insignificant and continued to face competition from the English, who traded intermittently along the Wabash. Vincennes shaped what was to become a familiar pattern of interaction with fur trade Indians: small numbers of French soldiers and traders established outposts in or near Indian villages; these men had access to trade goods and were welcomed as long as they respected and honored Indigenous cultural norms.

Lack of French trade goods undermined Vincennes's authority at Ouiatenon. His continual pleas for additional goods reflected his need to further the diplomatic goals of his position, but they also masked his own agenda of personally profiting from the fur trade. Although Governor Vaudreuil sent Vincennes one canoe annually with five men and twenty pots of brandy, as well as an additional thirty pots for his personal use, the large village population at Ouiatenon did not find this sufficient to retain their allegiance. Nor did they view these limited goods as satisfactory for sustaining the symbolic gift giving that reaffirmed their alliance with the French. Gift giving occurred within a public ceremonial context and was thus subject to open scrutiny. Vincennes lamented, "On account of the nearness of the English, it has been impossible for me to bring together all these nations because there has always been a lack of merchandise in this place." The visible stinginess of their French father in Montreal made it difficult to secure Indian loyalty.[8]

---

8. Sieur de Vincennes to the Department of the Marine, Mar. 7, 1733, in Pierre-Georges Roy, *Sieur de Vincennes Identified,* Indiana Historical Society, *Publications,* VII, no. 1 (Indianapolis, 1932), 82, 91–93, esp. 92; John D. Barnhart and Dorothy L. Riker, *Indiana to 1816: The Colonial Period* (Indianapolis, 1971), 80; Pierre-Georges Roy, *Le Sieur de Vincennes, Fondateur de l'Indiana et sa famille* (Lévis, Que., 1919), 92; Marcel Mauss, *The Gift: The Form and Reason for Exchange in Archaic Societies* (New York, 1990), xiv–xv.

The Indians' world, not dictates from New France, defined everyday life for Vincennes. When Indian warriors returned from battle, they expected Vincennes to cover the bodies of the dead warriors with presents. The giving of gifts eased the loss of men in warfare and allowed Vincennes to secure captured enemy warriors. He purchased prisoners of war to seal agreements in future diplomatic exchanges. As slaves, these prisoners labored for Vincennes; if returned to their villages, they averted future hostilities. Vincennes's awareness that his standing in the Indian world depended on trade goods drove his repeated requests to French officials to send him more. During wartime, his pleas were especially plaintive: "When these nations return and when all the prisoners, which they have taken are given to us, it will be necessary to pay for this sort of thing as well as to look for the dead if we lose any one." Vincennes asserted, "Nothing is possible in this place with so few troops. I need thirty men with an officer," but French administrators at Montreal turned a deaf ear to his pleas.[9]

Driven to look elsewhere for help, Vincennes secured additional financial support through his friendship with Boisbriand, the Illinois District commandant, who lived at Kaskaskia. Vincennes was a frequent visitor to the community, which led him to marry the daughter of a French merchant and trader living there. With Boisbriand's support, Vincennes received funds from the Louisiana governor, Jean-Baptiste Le Moyne de Bienville, aid made possible by the division of New France into the provinces of Upper and Lower Canada during the 1730s. Upper Louisiana (la Haute-Louisiane) began north of the Arkansas River, and Lower Louisiana (la Basse-Louisiane) south of it. The Wabash River valley became a crucial link between Canada and the Mississippi Valley. Fur traders reached New Orleans from the Great Lakes by traversing the Maumee-Wabash portage and following the Wabash River to the Ohio and west to the Mississippi. When Louisiana and Montreal vied for Vincennes's support, he played these officials against each other. In 1730, he secured financial support from New Orleans; he was promoted to a half-pay lieutenant and received an annual stipend. In return, Vincennes agreed to ship Wabash River valley furs to New Orleans. Vincennes was also sent Jesuit fathers and several Frenchmen, as well as two canoes of trade goods. By 1732, Vincennes had erected a stockade fort at Ouiatenon, and when the Indians living there refused to grant him land, Vincennes countered by establishing a

---

9. Natalie Maree Belting, *Kaskaskia under the French Regime* (Urbana, Ill., 1948), 10–18; Edward G. Mason, *Illinois in the Eighteenth Century: Kaskaskia and Its Parish Records; Old Fort Chartres; and Col. John Todd's Record Book*, Fergus Historical Ser., no. 12 (Chicago, 1881), 15.

new post, Vincennes, which he named in honor of his father. The Vincennes post was farther south on the Wabash, closer to the Ohio River. Boisbriand had recommended the establishment of this new post as a means of strengthening French fortifications along the Ohio and deterring English fur traders from expanding westward. With his new salary, Vincennes purchased additional trade goods and secured from the Indians their promise to trade with him, send their furs to New Orleans, and side with the French in times of crisis. Several Mascouten villages relocated downriver to the new fort, with a sizable population remaining at Ouiatenon. It was probably Wea, Piankeshaw, Kickapoo, Miami, and a remaining Mascouten village, which Vincennes described as the "five nations who compose four villages of . . . sixty men carrying arms, and all of them could furnish from six to seven hundred men."[10]

Shortly after Vincennes arrived at Ouiatenon, another small French post was established at the Miami village near the Maumee-Wabash portage. In 1721, Jacques-Charles Renaud Dubuisson arrived in the west with a supply of trade goods, eight soldiers, and sixty-four pots of brandy, half of which were for his men and half for his personal use. Dubuisson was a stranger, unfamiliar with the Miami language. Montreal ordered Vincennes to send Sieur Nicolas Ladouceur, his interpreter from Ouiatenon, to accompany the French contingent out to the new post. Like other Frenchmen who had married into Indian households, Ladouceur was a familiar presence among the Miami. It was Ladouceur who led the newcomers into Miamitown and ensured that the new arrivals were greeted as friends.[11]

Although Dubuisson completed a stockade fort by the following spring, Indians maintained control over the entrance to the portage from Lake Erie. Portage access was through a wide-mouthed river bordered by extensive marshes that obscured both the entrance and banks of the river. The marshes bordering the Maumee River were more than ten leagues long and required several days to negotiate; they were controlled by the Miami, who guided strangers to the river's entranceway when allowing them access to the portage.

The Maumee-Wabash portage, which led to the Wabash on the west and the Miami and Little Miami Rivers on the east, served as a crucial crossroads for the western half of the Ohio River valley. The Miami River geographi-

---

10. Andrew R. L. Cayton, *Frontier Indiana* (Bloomington, Ind., 1996), 17–18; Shirley S. McCord, *Travel Accounts of Indiana, 1679–1961: A Collection of Observations by Wayfaring Foreigners, Itinerants, and Peripatetic Hoosiers,* Indiana Historical Collections, XLVII (Indianapolis, 1970), 6; Belting, *Kaskaskia under the French Regime,* 10–18; Mason, *Kaskaskia and Its Parish Records,* 15.

11. Congé à Nicolas Ladouceur, le 8 août 1721, Registre des congés, ordonnances, et arrêts conservé aux Archives judiciaires se Montréal, 9072.

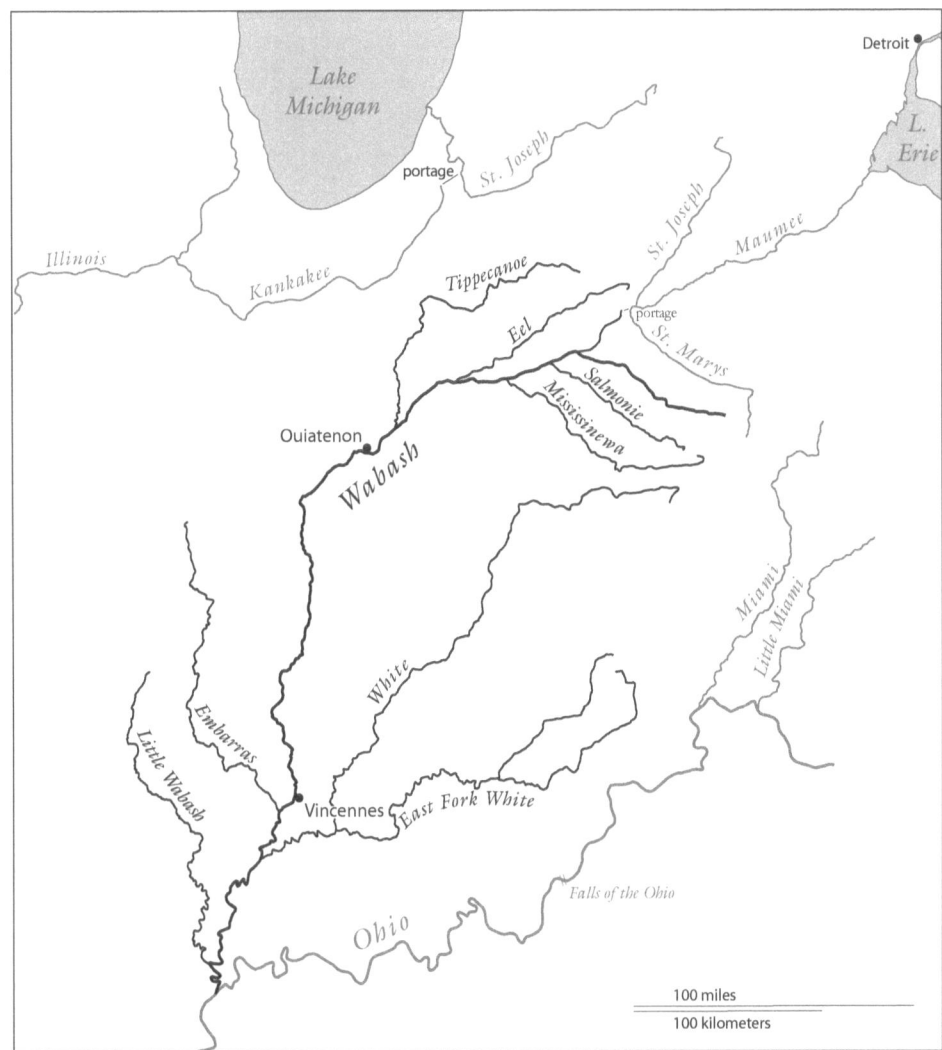

MAP 9. The portage of the Maumee and Wabash Rivers. Drawn by Ellen White

cally separated English and French traders, with English working the eastern half of the Ohio River and Frenchmen securing furs from villages west of the Miami River. The Black Swamp reinforced the geographical division of the Ohio River valley into two sections. Although the French appeared confident that the new fort at the Maumee-Wabash portage would prevent further British incursions into the region, their inability to meet Miami demands for trade goods led the Miami as well as the French traders to continue exchanging their furs at Albany rather than heading north to Detroit or Montreal,

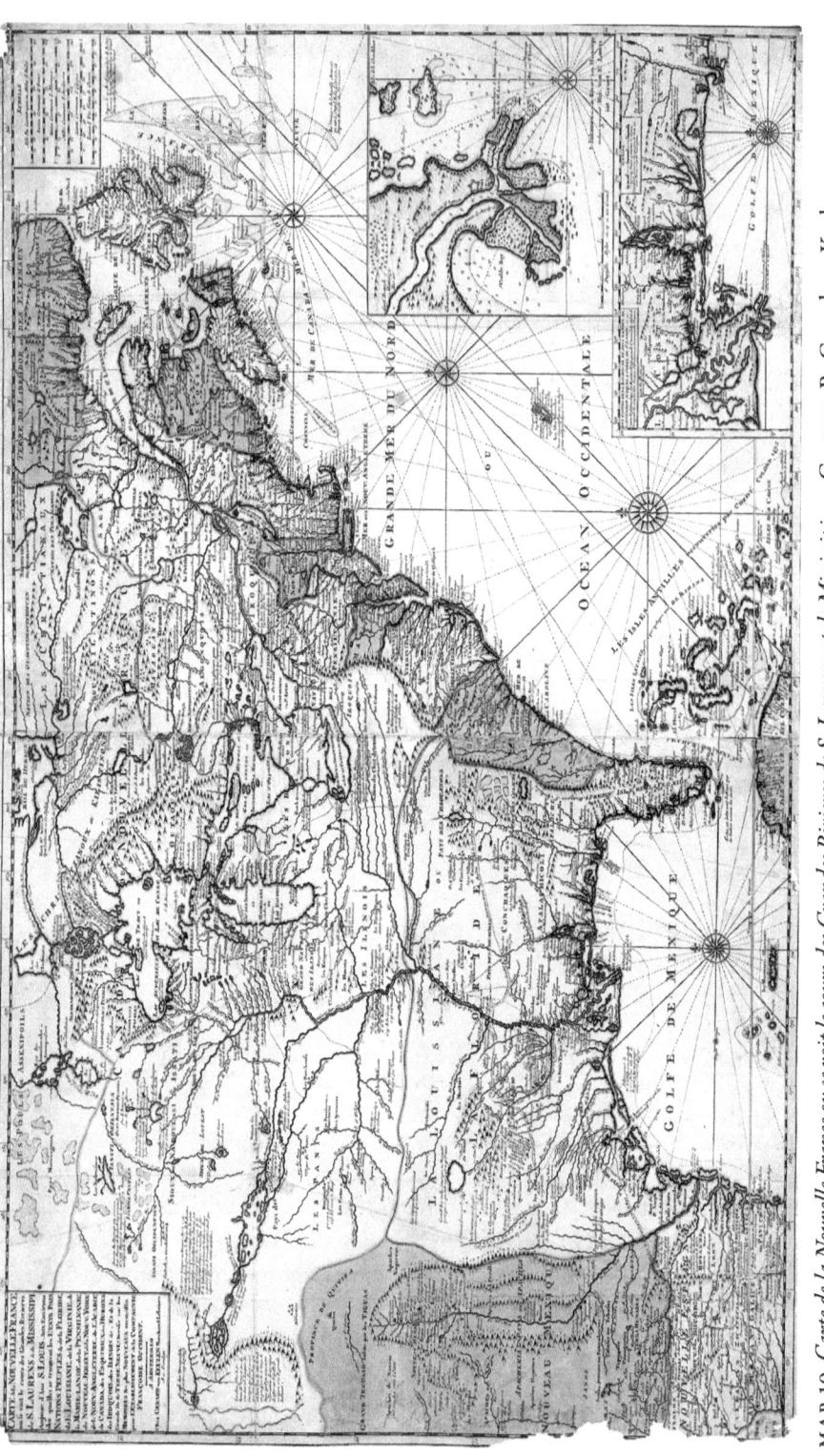

MAP 10. *Carte de la Nouvelle France ou se voit le cours des Grandes Rivieres de S. Laurens et de Mississipi. . . .* Ca. 1720. By Gerard van Keulen. Courtesy of the Collections of the Louisiana State Museum, Gift of Dr. and Mrs. E. Ralph Lupin, Jr.

where trade goods were more expensive. English traders rarely ventured west of the Little Miami River, but when they did, the Miami traded with them farther south along the Little Miami, closer to the Ohio.

THE OHIO RIVER VALLEY AND THE
PROVINCES OF UPPER AND LOWER CANADA

The division of the Ohio River valley into English and French spheres of influence transformed the Wabash River valley into a borderland in which Indians controlled the fur trade. In 1732, when the new fort at Vincennes was established downriver from Ouiatenon, it drew French fur trade families as well some Piankeshaw villages, which moved to the Vermilion River, adjacent to the new site. Throughout the 1730s, Indians were drawn to the Wabash River valley by the availability of French trade goods shipped to Vincennes from New Orleans. Increased trade goods shifted Indian loyalty from Montreal to Louisiana and drew Indians from the Wabash villages into Franco-Indian conflicts originating in the lower Mississippi Valley, such as those between the French and the Creek and Chickasaw. When "the Chickasaws ... killed six Frenchmen in the Wabash country," Vincennes raised a force of Indian allies to join Bienville in a joint retaliatory strike. Vincennes gathered Frenchmen and Indians from along the Wabash and from Kaskaskia in the Illinois Country to fight alongside forces from Louisiana. Bienville's offensive met with disaster. Vincennes was captured, along with Pierre d'Artaguiette, who commanded the Illinois District of the province of Louisiana, the Jesuit Father Antoine Senat, and Indian warriors from the Wabash villages. The Frenchmen were burned at the stake near present-day Tupelo, Mississippi, in 1736. Reverberations reached deep into the Wabash River valley villages, where the deaths of warriors who had fought alongside Vincennes multiplied the number of matrifocal households.[12]

As Indians descended the western waters of the Ohio and its tributaries, they would have come upon the posts established by Vincennes linking the region's trade to New Orleans. Initially, Vincennes, Ouiatenon, Kaskaskia, and Cahokia supplied both peltry and agricultural goods. Later, Kaskaskia and Cahokia became agricultural suppliers, whereas Vincennes and Ouiatenon

---

12. Sieur de Vincennes to the Department of the Marine, Mar. 7, 1733, in Roy, *Sieur de Vincennes Identified,* 91–93; Barnhart and Riker, *Indiana to 1816,* 80; Daniel H. Usner, *Indians, Settlers, and Slaves in a Frontier Exchange Economy* (Chapel Hill, N.C., 1992); McCord, *Travel Accounts of Indiana,* 4–5. Vincennes had left a wife and two young daughters. His daughters were appointed guardians among the French at Kaskaskia. See Belting, *Kaskaskia under the French Regime,* 91–92, 96.

continued as suppliers of peltry. That division of labor and provision of commodities remained viable well into the nineteenth century. Despite the departure of the Piankeshaw in 1732, the population at Ouiatenon remained large, with the combined villages able to supply six to seven hundred warriors. In contrast, the modest fort at Ouiatenon was designed to facilitate the fur trade, and no large-scale, long-range French settlement was established at this fort. These small, penurious outposts with a handful of soldiers typified the French structures that stood along the trading routes of the Ohio River valley, most of them characterized by extreme poverty. Outside the posts, Indian villages expanded and prospered, dwarfing the French both in population and in the extent of their settlements.[13]

At Ouiatenon, Indian villages retained their distinctive ethnicities. Each village was distinguished by different dialects of the Miami language, a particular ritual calendar, and a unique history. The Wea, Kickapoo, Mascouten, Miami, Shawnee, and Piankeshaw villages were within a half-mile to twenty miles of the fort. Many French and English traders collectively referred to the residents of these Indian villages as "Ouiatenons" or "Wabash Indians," but that terminology is misleading: archaeological excavations have demonstrated the distinctiveness of these separate villages. The largest of the early-eighteenth-century villages was that of the Wea, located opposite Fort Ouiatenon on the Wabash River, beneath Wea Creek. The Miami, Kickapoo, Mascouten, Shawnee, and Piankeshaw lived in individual settlements while the culturally related Mascouten and Kickapoo shared two villages on the north shore of the Wabash, about a mile or two from Fort Ouiatenon. Both claimed that their lands stretched westward to the forks of the Illinois River. The Kickapoo consisted of three principal groups: the largest of the groups included the Vermilion band, whose villages and land stretched from Ouiatenon to the Vermilion River, whereas the Prairie bands ranged throughout the central Illinois country. The name of the third band of Kickapoo is unknown, but we do know that they were the first to migrate west, settling about twelve leagues from St. Louis.[14]

13. Sieur de Vincennes to the Department of the Marine, Mar. 7, 1733, in Roy, *Sieur de Vincennes Identified*, 91–93, esp. 92; Michael Strezewski et al., *Report of the 2006 Archaeological Investigations at Kethtippecanunk (12-T-59), Tippecanoe County, Indiana* (Fort Wayne, Ind., 2007), 1.

14. James R. Jones III, "An Archaeological Survey of an 18th Century Wea Village Near Fort Ouiatenon, in Tippecanoe County, Indiana," *Proceedings of the Symposium on Ohio Valley Urban and Historic Archaeology*, III (Louisville, Ky., 1985), 105–116; Vergil Noble, "Excavations at Fort Ouiatenon," Preliminary Report, 1977–1980, 1982 Field Seasons, Tippecanoe County Historical Association, Lafayette, Ind.; Noble, "Functional Classification and

Although several Miami villages were initially located near the first Indian fort at Ouiatenon, they moved upriver early in the eighteenth century, perhaps at the time of a measles outbreak in late fall 1732. The size or extent of these Miami villages during their time near the fort is not known, although there are references to the Miami village of Atihipe-Catouy along the Wabash.[15] About this same time, the French established a trading community at the old Indian village at Kethtippecanuck. This trading village became a mixture of Euro-American and Native inhabitants, whereas villages adjacent to Fort Ouiatenon were exclusively Native. It appears that the villages at Ouiatenon refused to provide lands to Europeans. There was little need for outside assistance since, by the 1720s, Indian women in these Ouiatenon villages yielded, probably, the largest quantity of peltry.

When Sabrevois arrived in the Ohio River valley in 1718, he focused on the luxuriant agrarian landscape and overlooked the complex river routes that crossed the region and connected it with lands beyond the river basin. The multiplicity of navigable tributary rivers made it impossible for the French to establish defensible boundary lines. Their continuing ignorance about the tributary rivers of the Ohio encouraged Indians to circulate freely along these riverways, plying peltry at many trading villages and pitting French and British fur traders against each other. Versailles's knowledge of the eastern Ohio remained scanty because the minister of the marine considered French control over the short stretch of the Ohio from the Wabash to the Mississippi sufficient to dominate the Ohio as a whole. The Ohio was almost a thousand miles long, but French maps depicted it as an insignificant tributary of the

---

Intra-Site Analysis in Historical Archaeology: A Case Study from Fort Ouiatenon" (Ph.D. diss., Michigan State University, 1983); Judy D. Tardoff, "1978 Report of Archaeological Investigations at Fort Ouiatenon 1794 and 1795," Tippecanoe County Hist. Assoc.; Tardoff, "1980 Excavations at Fort Ouiatenon, 1974–1976 Field Season, Preliminary Report," ibid.; Paul L. Stevens, "'One of the Most Beautiful Regions of the World': Paul Des Ruisseaux's *Mémoire* of the Wabash-Illinois Country in 1777," *Indiana Magazine of History,* LXXXIII (1987), 374-375.

15. Pierre Margry, *Decouvertes et éstablissements des Français dans l'ouest et dans le sud de l'Amerique septentrionale, 1614–1754, memoires et documents originaux,* 6 vols. (Paris, 1876–1886), IV, 597, 661–662, anon. trans., Great Lakes–Ohio Valley Ethnohistory Collection, Glenn A. Black Laboratory of Archaeology, Indiana University, Bloomington; Donald J. Berthrong, *Indians of Northern Indiana and Southwestern Michigan* (New York, 1974); Erminie Wheeler-Voegelin, Emily J. Blasingham, and Dorothy R. Libby, "An Anthropological Report on the History of the Miami, Wea, and Eel River Indians . . . ," MS on file, Great Lakes–Ohio Valley Ethno. Arch., 130 (later edited and published as Wheeler-Voegelin, Blasingham, and Libby, *Miami, Wea, and Eel River Indians of Southern Indiana . . .* [Garland, N.Y., 1974]).

Wabash. Early French explorers ignored the Ohio River valley. There were no Marquettes or Joliets who left the Mississippi, journeyed through Indian villages, and spoke Native languages. Versailles had relied on La Salle's inaccurate observations, formed because he had gone no farther east along the Ohio than the Kankakee Marsh. The age of exploration had ebbed before the French had fully mapped and described much of the Great Lakes region, especially the southern tier of river systems that formed the Ohio River basin. Much of the strength of the French colonial system in North America rested on the exploratory journeys and descriptive reports French officials had received from their military officers and missionary priests. They had few such reports for the Ohio Valley, and it was only in 1749 that Father Joseph Pierre de Bonnecamps accompanied the Pierre-Joseph Céloron de Blainville expedition and completed the first map of the Ohio Valley.

The complex interconnections of the Ohio to its tributary river systems protected Indians' hunting grounds and communications networks. The riverine landscape was their habitat, and the many-channeled navigability that made it useful to them baffled French officials in the ministry of marine. The multiplicity of tributary rivers that were part of the Ohio's river network made it possible for many Indians and French traders to reach Albany relatively undetected. By the last decade of the seventeenth century, as much as one-half or even two-thirds of the Canadian beaver trade had left the purview of New France and was secured by English traders. By 1725, two Albany traders believed that 80 percent of the beaver peltry shipped from New York to London was the work of illegal French traders.[16]

The Ohio was the most important river route east of the Mississippi, and the French had left it and most of its adjacent lands and tributary rivers unexplored, unsecured, and resistant to French influence. Perhaps the French explained their understanding of the Ohio River within their familiar framework of less complicated river systems, which were shorter and had fewer tributaries. The longest river valley in France was the Loire, which flowed 619 miles through France. Not only was this French river more than 300 miles shorter than the Ohio, but there were far fewer tributary rivers linked to the Loire; the Ohio had at least eighteen major tributary rivers. It spanned almost a third of a continent and was home to many culturally varied Indian villages. There was no nation-state demarcating the region's larger boundaries for out-

---

16. Jean Lunn, "The Illegal Fur Trade out of New France, 1713–60," *Report of the Annual Meeting of the Canadian Historical Association,* XLVIII (Ottawa, Ont., 1939), 61–76. Lunn's doctoral work on the New France economy remains an important reference for this period. See also White, *Middle Ground,* 125.

siders. The Ohio River valley, with its diverse Indian population, had a multiplicity of intertwined and overlapping borders that belied the French conception of Indians as nations with distinct territorial borders. In *The Common Pot,* Lisa Brooks argues that, whereas European systems of land tenure were about fixing and bounding space, this could not be done in the Ohio River valley, where the Indians sought to bolster a much older vision: "The land itself was held in common, consisting of a network of shifting riverside villages within a larger shared hunting territory of grasslands and forests, all fed and connected by the Ohio River and its tributaries, enabling an efficient and diplomatic use of resources." The presence of highly fertile landscape niches in the Ohio River valley enabled a multiplicity of Indians to settle together closely, and their access to the Black Swamp encouraged their involvement in the fur trade. This conceptualization of the land encouraged movement and migration and led the Shawnee and Delaware to settle among the Miami at Miamitown. This pattern of coexistence replicated itself throughout the region.[17]

Navigating the Great Lakes entailed extensive use of the adjacent waterways. To access the land south of the lakes, much less control it, required familiarity with this riparian landscape. The paths and trails that paralleled the multiple rivers and interconnected this region privileged Indigenous knowledge, which was embedded in the various place-names, stories, and songs that demarcated the land. Stone shapes, trees with distinctively shaped limbs or marks on trunks, and rock drawings recalled past events and identified the distinct pathways. Local knowledge rendered these places meaningful to Native people in stories that associated memories with specific physical attributes in the landscape. Endowing the land with social importance enabled them to unravel the tangle of rivers, streams, and creeks that characterized the Ohio River valley.

The Miami tell us that they emerged from the rivers adjacent to the St. Joseph, near the present-day Wabash. This origin myth speaks directly to the importance that rivers played in Miami life.

Mihtami myaamiaki nipinkonci saakaciweeciki ("at first, the Miamis came out of the water"):

It is with these words that the very first Myaamia story begins. This story describes our emergence as distinct and different people onto Myaamionki, our traditional homelands. In this story, our people emerge from the waters

17. Lisa Brooks, *The Common Pot: The Recovery of Native Space in the Northeast* (Minneapolis, 2008), 124.

of Saakiiweesiipiwi [St. Joseph River, near South Bend, Indiana] at a spot we call Saakiiweeyonki [the Confluence]. Our history as people began here, but this emergence was not easy. The people had to struggle out of the water as they grasped and pulled their way onto the bank. This struggle at the river's edge marked the end of an undescribed, but likely challenging, journey.[18]

Rivers were the highways of all seventeenth-century Indian people. They led to new places, bringing Indians west to secure trade goods and, eventually, fostering their ascendancy in the Ohio Valley region. Most likely, the Miami traveled west from the St. Joseph to the Wabash and then headed south to the Ohio and to Illinois Country.

Forbidding to fur traders and missionaries, this riverine landscape was even more problematic for French policymakers who had never been to the Americas. Looking at French-constructed maps, which depicted New France and the northern region as the center of the North American continent, officials in Versailles could easily have thought that control over the St. Lawrence River and the Great Lakes was tantamount to domination of the continental interior. But the St. Lawrence, which the French considered the heart of their territory, was frozen for half of the year and was not a viable means of controlling trade along the multiplicity of routes in and out of the Great Lakes. The Great Lakes were equally problematic because gales buffeted their waters from November to March, and summer storms frequently made the lakes impassable.[19]

FUR TRADE PROBLEMS

As discussed in the previous chapter, growing involvement in the fur trade brought changes to villages along the tributary rivers of the Ohio and increased the number of matrifocal households. Along the Wabash, the demographic balance of Indian households changed when fur traders and Indian warriors were drawn into deadly conflicts as French allies during the Chickasaw Wars. These wars had a deadly impact on the Wabash River valley when Sieur de Vincennes recruited several hundred Wea, Piankeshaw, and Miami warriors. The female-to-male ratio of the Wabash villages increased dramatically following the Chickasaw victory over French forces in 1736, when hundreds of French traders and Indians from Vincennes and the Wabash basin

---

18. George Ironstrack, "A Myaamia Beginning," Aug. 13, 2010, Myaamia Project, Miami University, esp. https://myaamiahistory.wordpress.com/2010/08/13/a-myaamia-beginning.

19. Keith Basso, *Wisdom Sits in Places: Language and Landscape among the Western Apache* (Albuquerque, N.M., 1996), 31.

lost their lives. Such changes within the household aside, the Wabash River valley remained a series of agrarian villages where women expanded their cornfields along the river bottoms to feed a growing population. Despite the loss of men, population levels swelled as Indians moved into the region. Feeding them required more female labor, as did the processing of furs. The wetlands surrounding the Wabash were rich in small peltry and, as the fur trade expanded, the number of women required to process those pelts multiplied.[20]

Along with warrior mortality, village insobriety became an increasingly apparent problem in the 1730s as a result of trade with the English. Liquor was an important part of the exchange process and generally marked the opening of a prospective transaction. New France officials attempted to limit the trade in liquor to what voyageurs themselves consumed on their journey to outlying posts. Of course, should voyageurs abstain from their pots of brandy and redirect them to the exchange process — rare though we might imagine this to be — there was little that officials could do. Most of the time, drinking was confined to evening revelries, but when voyageurs began drinking while pad-

---

20. White, in *The Middle Ground*, contends that access to trade goods empowered warlike young men and displaced elders, transforming villages into unruly republics and enhancing hostilities in the Ohio River valley (see chap. 5, "Republicans and Rebels," 186–222). Accounts of this battle organized by Governor Bienville are contradictory. Bienville's account is in "Bienville's Letters to Maurepas," in Dunbar Rowland and A. G. Sanders, eds., *Mississippi Provincial Archives, 1729–1740*, 3 vols., I, *Wars with the Natchez and Chickasaw Indians* (Jackson, Miss., 1932), 222–227, 297–310, 311–316. An eyewitness account of the battle by Drouet de Richardville, an expedition member who was taken prisoner, is "Report of Richardville on D'Artaguiette's Expedition against the Chickasaws," in Caroline Dunn and Eleanor Dunn, eds. and trans., *Indiana's First War*, Indiana Historical Society, *Publications*, VIII, no. 2 (Indianapolis, 1924). Roy's *Sieur de Vincennes Identified* has another account on 98–108. These three appear to be the most accurate of the multiple accounts available about this battle. Even the historical marker depicting the event in Tupelo, Miss., has the dates inaccurately recorded.

Bienville ordered Pierre d'Artaguiette, the military commander of Upper Louisiana, to march his troops south from Fort de Chartres to attack the Chickasaw villages in present-day Mississippi, where he would meet Bienville and his force from Lower Louisiana. Bienville was late, and to feed his large number of Indian allies, d'Artaguiette assaulted the village of Ogoula Tchetoka on May 25, 1736. The Chickasaw were aware of the French approach and were heavily armed. D'Artaguiette was accompanied by thirty French regulars, one hundred militia, and almost three hundred Illinois, Wea, Miami, and Piankeshaw who were led by Chief Chicagou and Sieur de Vincennes. Twenty-one of the French were captured, of whom nineteen, including d'Artaguiette and Vincennes, were executed by burning. Few Indians escaped the Chickasaw wrath. See Spencer Tucker, ed., *The Encyclopedia of North American Indian Wars, 1607–1890: A Political, Social, and Military History* (Santa Barbara, Calif., 2011), 580.

dling, canoe journeys were interrupted because the men were unfit to travel. New France officials attempted to make sure that canoes loaded solely with brandy did not depart from Montreal. In contrast, initially, English officials turned a blind eye to the amount of liquor that became part of the exchange process and paid little heed to canoes leaving their posts loaded with rum and brandy.[21]

The founding of Fort Miami magnified the alcohol problem. The village had access to Albany and was the stopping place for Detroit fur traders journeying into the Ohio River valley or returning at the end of the season. A 1732 incident there indicates the extent to which liquor and sporadic outbreaks of disease could threaten this region, as well as the steps that Indians took to interrupt and counteract the spread of alcohol and epidemic disease. The trouble began with the arrival of fifteen or sixteen Miami canoes from Albany with four hundred casks of brandy. The Miami intended to reach out to the Wea at Ouiatenon by combining the calumet ceremony with a fall feast. The Miami had invited the Wea to join the celebration, as a means of removing the thorns in the pathway of their relationship. Feasts took place before Indians departed for their wintering camps, when households left their villages and broke into smaller units to hunt and trap. Most camps consisted of no more than two or three households, and they remained isolated until the spring. During this significant celebration in their ritual calendar, the Miami spent five or six days feasting and drinking. With the arrival of both the Wea and, later, the Piankeshaw, the Miami needed large amounts of liquor. During the third day, the ceremonies and evening revelry were briefly interrupted by the outbreak of disease. Two men who had been unwell during the previous day's festivities died during the night. Both were buried the next day and, following these initial deaths, another four men died every day for three more weeks. On the fifth day, the Miami found the skin of a human hand in one of the casks. They were appalled — but even this did not halt the course of their festivities.[22]

---

21. Carolyn Podruchny, *Making the Voyageur World: Travelers and Traders in the North American Fur Trade* (Lincoln, Neb., 2006), 183; Peter C. Mancall, *Deadly Medicine: Indians and Alcohol in Early America* (Ithaca, N.Y., 1995), 154–164.

22. Knowledge about this comes from the newly appointed commandant, Nicolas-Marie Renaud (d'Arnaud) Davenne de Desmeloises (1696–1743) (also referred to as sieur Darnaud), who assumed command of the Miami post in late October 1732. It was the evening's revelries that horrified the French commander. Sieur Darnaud was aghast that the Indians continued to drink after so many deaths; he felt they had ignored his warnings because "brandy was a greater chief than I" ("Extract of a Letter Written to M. the Marquis de Beauharnois by the Sieur Darnaud, Commandant at the Miami," Oct. 25, 1732, in Krauskopf, ed. and trans., *Ouiatanon Documents,* 181–182). See also Nancy Shoemaker ed., *Clearing a Path: Theorizing*

When the Piankeshaw arrived to participate in the calumet ceremony, the commandant of the Miami post, the sieur Darnaud, warned them not to drink the brandy because, he claimed, the British had poisoned it. The Indians scoffed at Darnaud's warning and eagerly participated in the feasting. They then remained only a couple of days before departing. Although the Piankeshaw had, at first, dismissed Darnaud's warning, they soon realized that disease was ravaging the Miami festivities, and they tried to get away before it was too late. They failed. Darnaud reported to Montreal that among the Piankeshaw "some are dying of it every day." The Miami had intended for these extended festivities to secure peace with the Wea. Instead, 150 of the Wea who came to dance the calumet with the Miami died; this was a significant population loss. Only when the Wea left for their winter camps did the outbreak end.[23]

This was one of the worst outbreaks of epidemic disease that occurred along the Wabash. One French missionary described it as "'a sort of measles' with stomach pains . . . reaching the Seneca country." Given that the Miami had traded their furs with the Seneca for the four hundred kegs of rum, the Seneca most likely spread the disease to the Miami, who subsequently spread it to villages in the Wabash River valley. When the surviving Wea and Piankeshaw returned to Ouiatenon, they endangered the nearby villages. Most villages had gone to their winter camps, but those that remained quickly left the area. The Shawnee village, which had recently taken up residence at Ouiatenon, moved to the lower mouth of the Miami River.[24]

Wabash villages were generally ten to fifteen miles apart, and when disease broke out, unaffected villages often isolated themselves to ward off its further spread. Many villages at Ouiatenon were spared crippling epidemics because they depended on French fur traders to transport their furs to market. Incorporating these French traders also had a distinct advantage, for many French traders carried an immunity to the viral diseases that could cripple Indian villages. Fortunately, many French fathers passed their immunity to their children.

---

the Past in Native American Studies (New York, 2002), xi; Stewart Rafert, *The Miami Indians: A Persistent People, 1654–1994* (Indianapolis, 1996); Bert Anson, *The Miami Indians* (1970; rpt. Norman, Okla., 1990); Elmore Barce, *Land of the Miamis* (Fowler, Ind., 1929).

23. "Extract of a Letter Written to M. the Marquis de Beauharnois by the Sieur Darnaud, Commandant at the Miami," Oct. 25, 1732, in Krauskopf, ed. and trans., *Ouiatanon Documents*, 182; ANCol., C11A, 57, 348–350; Joseph L. Peyser, "It Was Not Smallpox," *Indiana Magazine of History*, LXXXI (1985), 159–169.

24. "Extract of a Letter Written to M. the Marquis de Beauharnois by the sieur Darnaud," Oct. 25, 1732, in Krauskopf, ed. and trans., *Ouiatanon Documents*, 182.

In fact, the Indians who moved to the Ohio River valley found themselves in a unique position. Disease proved far less disruptive than along the Atlantic seacoast. Geography protected them because there were only three entranceways into the Ohio River valley: the Cumberland Gap, dominated by the Shawnee, the Allegheny / Monongahela River entrance through Iroquois lands, and the western Ohio / Mississippi confluence, controlled by the Illinois Confederacy. There were large Indian villages along the river valley perimeter, and they did become the demographic targets of epidemic disease. In contrast, interior Indian villages along the Ohio tributaries were protected by their isolation, even when disease outbreaks afflicted gatekeeper villages. The Iroquois, Illinois, and Shawnee had substantial village populations that bore the brunt of the disease. Epidemic diseases spread to the Ohio's interior villages in cluster patterns; outbreaks never spread unchecked along the entire length of the Ohio River valley. In the central region of the river valley, disease outbreaks were limited. A localized smallpox outbreak occurred among the Miami from 1731 to 1733; it was not until 1787 that another smallpox epidemic occurred, when disease spread among the Wyandot at Detroit and Upper Sandusky. Instead, it was the Iroquois and the Illinois outside the central Ohio River valley region who suffered repeated and multiple epidemics, along with the Shawnee villages clustered north of the Cumberland Gap.[25]

---

25. David S. Jones, "Virgin Soils Revisited," *William and Mary Quarterly*, 3d Ser., LX (2003), 703–742. The ongoing discussion over Indian populations in North America has long revolved around the issue of how epidemic disease affected Indian populations. In many of the initial studies, historians claimed that twenty million Indians died in epidemic outbreaks, a number that has caused great debate. Two important works framed this debate: Alfred W. Crosby, *The Columbian Exchange: Biological and Cultural Consequences of 1492* (Westport, Conn., 1972); and William H. McNeill, *Plagues and Peoples* (New York, 1976). See also Crosby, "Virgin Soil Epidemics as a Factor in the Aboriginal Depopulation in America," *WMQ*, 3d Ser., XXXIII (1976), 289–299; Crosby, *Ecological Imperialism: The Biological Expansion of Europe, 900–1900* (New York, 1986). Subsequent narratives followed, which provided for the bio-imperial ascent of Europe, the most well-known being Jared Diamond's *Guns, Germs, and Steel: The Fate of Human Societies* (New York, 1997); more particular to Indian history is Noble David Cook's *Born to Die: Disease and New World Conquest, 1492–1650* (New York, 1999). These findings elicited a discussion about the number of Indian inhabitants at and following contact, an issue hotly debated in books such as Russell Thornton, *American Indian Holocaust and Survival: A Population History since 1492* (Norman, Okla., 1987).

One of the worst outbreaks came during the Seven Years' War, when smallpox-infected blankets were distributed to the Indians from Fort Pitt. But even this outbreak was primarily confined to the eastern area of the Ohio, largely afflicting villages located along the Muskingum and Scioto Rivers; see Helen Hornbeck Tanner, *Atlas of Great Lakes Indian*

Environmental factors were also crucial in determining the impact and transmission of epidemic disease. Epidemics had far lower mortality rates where people were well fed. Malnutrition is most frequently associated with high death rates. Diseases caused by deficiencies, like rickets, were common; rarer was the onslaught of viral diseases, like smallpox and measles, that led to high mortality rates. In the Ohio River valley, where malnutrition was unusual, epidemic disease outbreaks did not level villages. When disease did strike these communities, they experienced higher survival rates. Moreover, regular trade with coastal villages precluded the presence of virgin soil disease among the Ohio River valley Indians; intermittent but sufficient contact with eastern coastal villages meant enough exposure to viral diseases to develop immunity, but not so much that epidemics could devastate the valley. Disease resistance also developed through contact with European traders in the Green Bay region, and intermarriage with traders introduced new immunities into the Indian gene pool. Simplistic generalizations about American Indian susceptibility to European diseases do not apply to eighteenth-century Ohio Valley Indians. By the mid-eighteenth century, population levels had increased dramatically, and many Indian villages had achieved high levels of prosperity, as we shall see in the next chapter.[26]

THWARTING FRENCH IMPERIALISM

Indian communities frustrated French attempts to control and refocus the fur trade at Detroit. Versailles, hampered by an inability to understand the geography of the region, did not realize that the far-reaching river

---

History (Norman, Okla., 1986), 169–174. Tanner also mapped "Epidemics among Indians: 1630–1880," ibid., 169–174. For more information about understanding the nature of disease during contact, see Arthur C. Aufderheide, "Summary on Disease before and after Contact," in John W. Verano and Douglas H. Ubelaker, eds., *Disease and Demography in the Americas* (Washington, D.C., 1992); Clark Spencer Larsen, "In the Wake of Columbus: Native Population Biology in the Postcontact Americas," *Yearbook of Physical Anthropology*, XXXVII (1994), 109, 114.

26. Tanner, *Atlas of Great Lakes Indian History*, 169–174. Historians like Alfred Crosby, William H. McNeill, Henry Dobyns, and Noble David Cook popularized the inaccurate claim that "no immunity led to the devastation of the American Indian" population and that "nothing more unique than the familiar forces of poverty, malnutrition, environmental stress, dislocation and social disparity" led to high mortality rates. These same circumstances are present in our twenty-first-century world, and, when epidemic diseases strike impoverished villages in developing nations, populations experience equally appalling high death rates. Unfortunately, this belief in the power of virgin soil epidemics to almost completely level entire villages has blindly shaped how we envision encounter between Indians and Europeans. See Jones, "Virgin Soils Revisited," *WMQ*, 3d Ser., LX (2003), 735, 740–741.

systems of the Ohio River valley allowed Indians to surreptitiously transport their peltry to posts at Oswego and Albany as well as to the English backcountry posts of the Carolinas. Ironically, Detroit's position at the straits worked to Indigenous advantage, serving as a convenient outpost where Indians comparison-shopped French trade goods to those available at British posts. Cadillac convinced Versailles officials that founding Detroit would halt contraband trade, but instead, fur traders and Indians avoided the new post by traveling along the islands in the strait or by silently gliding past the fort during the nighttime hours. Cadillac's promised Algonquian-speaking military alliance did not materialize. Up close and personal, the French appeared far less powerful than their British competitors. The French lacked the military presence and power of their imperial rivals and eventually, most Ohio Valley Indians failed to support the French during the Seven Years' War. Instead of fostering unity among western Indians, Cadillac's misguided policy of locating Indian villages in proximity to Detroit created long-standing animosities that alienated New France's Indian allies. Both the Miami and Potawatomi returned to their former villages and refused to return to Detroit.

When Detroit traders and merchants supplied the goods that Indians most desired, Detroit was a viable exchange port. The goods offered by Detroit merchants and traders were influenced by the demographic shift to greater numbers of matrifocal households along the Wabash. Women's increased involvement in this trade fostered the expansion of the cloth trade. As we shall see, more than 70 percent of the trade goods shipped to Detroit consisted of cloth; Indian women increasingly sought new types of cloth, incorporating silks and calicos into their wardrobes, and demanded silver ornaments to highlight and decorate their clothing. Detroit's demography changed as larger numbers of silversmiths were drawn there. Simultaneously, this Indian-controlled fur trade produced a golden age of Indigenous prosperity and drew Indians from the east to the Ohio River valley region. The Ohio's fertile landscape meant accommodating refugee villages from the east and, as population levels increased, entrepôt trading villages emerged at Ouiatenon, Kethtippecanuck, Miamitown, and Sandusky. Indians transported their peltry to these villages, and traders fostered a continuation of a face-to-face exchange process. Detroit had the potential to create a depersonalized trade, but that failed to emerge because of the evolution of Indian-controlled sites of exchange in the Ohio River valley. What becomes evident in the following chapters is the extent to which webs of community drew Indians and traders into an increasingly close-knit world, where the loyalties of traders aligned with those of the Indians rather than the interests of the French Empire.

4

WEBS OF COMMUNITY

"The Gris and Turtle Came to Us and Breakfasted with Us as Usual"

In June 1763, Fort Michilimackinac soldiers and officers were watching Indians play lacrosse in front of the fort gates. The match was in honor of King George's birthday. At a critical moment, the ball landed near the open gates, and the players rushed toward the fort. As they threw down their sticks, Indian women passed the players hatchets from beneath their blankets. The warriors seized Captain Etherington and Lieutenant Leslie, who had been watching the game. In another instant, Lieutenant John Jamet, fifteen British soldiers, and a trader named Tracey were dead. Two other soldiers were wounded; the rest of the garrison was taken prisoner. Two weeks earlier, in mid-May, Fort Sandusky had been captured and burned by the Wyandot, who killed nearly all of its soldiers, ransoming only Ensign Paully, the commander. Later in May, Fort St. Joseph also fell. The Potawatomi killed eleven soldiers and the post commander, Ensign Schlösser. Only three men remained to be taken prisoner and ransomed. Two days after Fort St. Joseph fell, an Ensign Holmes leaving Fort Miami was shot to death. Threatened with torture, his men opened the fort gates to the Indians. In mid-June, when Ensign Price and thirteen men attempted to escape Fort Le Boeuf by the rear entrance, Indians set the fort on fire. Five men died. Eight grueling days afterward, Price and seven of his men reached safety at Fort Pitt, which was also attacked but not taken. Led by Ensign Christie, the twenty-four-man garrison at Fort Presque Isle briefly resisted the assault by two hundred warriors, thought better of it, and quickly surrendered. They were carried off to Detroit for ransom. When Fort Venango fell on June 20, its Indian assailants killed Lieutenant Gordon and all of his men. The garrison of L'Arbre Croche hastily abandoned it on June 21, in advance of a feared Indian attack. Only Fort Ouiatenon was spared this type of violent confrontation: the Wea simply walked in, and Lieutenant

Edward Jenkins and his fifteen British soldiers surrendered to them. The Wea never fired a shot nor raised a tomahawk. By the end of June, six weeks after the first onslaught began, the only unsubdued British soldiers in the western Great Lakes were those under siege at Detroit.[1]

The uprisings in spring 1763, known as Pontiac's Rebellion, proved a bitter lesson for the British about how to govern the Indian people of the Great Lakes. Twelve British forts were besieged, eight fell, many British soldiers died, and several English and Scots-Irish traders were killed. Most, but not all, of the officers were ransomed. Although Detroit was the only fort west of Niagara to remain under British control, it suffered a debilitating four-month siege. Pontiac's Rebellion brought together numerous warriors from diverse villages for the common design of driving the British from Indian lands, a vivid reminder that the western Great Lakes region remained Indian Country. Britain had defeated France in the Seven Years' War, but the Anglo-French negotiations that transferred Indian lands excluded representatives of the Indian communities inhabiting them. Lands were the bargaining chips of European empires, but the distance that made them easy to cede also made them hard to control. In the Great Lakes, European empires existed with the consent of Indians who manipulated imperial rivalries to meet their own goals. In this world where imperial power was tentative and fragile, Indians could influence imperial designs and colonial realities—at the walls of a frontier fort, if not at the table of a foreign ministry. Britain's victory in the Seven Years' War gave it hegemony in the western Great Lakes, but not authority.[2]

---

1. Gregory Evans Dowd, *War under Heaven: Pontiac, the Indian Nation, and the British Empire* (Baltimore, 2002), 93. Other descriptions of the rebellion can be found in Keith R. Widder, *Beyond Pontiac's Shadow: Michilimackinac and the Anglo-Indian War of 1763* (East Lansing, Mich., 2013); Francis Jennings, *Empire of Fortune: Crowns, Colonies, and Tribes in the Seven Years' War in America* (New York, 1988); the classic Howard H. Peckman's *Pontiac and the Indian Uprising* (1947; rpt. Detroit, 1994); and, more recently, William R. Nester, *"Haughty Conquerors": Amherst and the Great Indian Uprising of 1763* (Westport, Conn., 2000). Fort Niagara, on the Niagara River at the mouth of Lake Ontario, was heavily fortified and not attacked.

2. With the end of hostilities following the Seven Years' War, Britain gained possession of the fortifications and outposts of Canada. Lieutenant John Butler left Detroit on December 10 and arrived at Ouiatenon on January 18, 1761. Butler and his rangers remained until October 25, 1761, when Ensign Holmes of the 80th Foot (Gage's Light Infantry) and fifteen men of the 60th Foot (Royal Americans) relieved the rangers. Near the end of 1761, Jenkins commanded twenty men of the 60th at the Ouiatenon garrison. See François Furstenberg, "The Significance of the Trans-Appalachian Frontier in Atlantic History," *American Historical Review*, CXIII (2008), 650; Juliana Barr, *Peace Came in the Form of a Woman: Indians and Spaniards in the Texas Borderlands* (Chapel Hill, N.C., 2007); Kathleen DuVal, *The Na-*

Britain attempted to take control over the Great Lakes region by redeploying its military to the conquered French forts. British troops closest to the frontier, including two regiments of Highland Scots, were sent to end the siege at Fort Pitt. But although these Scots came from a fiercely militaristic culture, they were ill equipped to deal with this populous and diverse Indian world, and relieving Fort Pitt did not establish British control over the remaining western posts. Instead, when British forces attempted to push west from the Forks of the Ohio, they encountered renewed resistance. Colonel Henry Bouquet ventured no farther west than the eastern borderlands of the Little Miami River valley. His negotiated peace was with villages already in the sphere of British fur traders. In the Wabash River valley and Illinois Country, Indians remained in rebellion. French forces at Fort de Chartres, located in the northern district of Louisiana, the seat of French control in Illinois Country, continued to resist British intrusion. At the end of the Seven Years' War, the fort remained under the command of a French officer, Louis Groston de Saint-Ange et de Bellerive.[3]

---

tive Ground: Indians and Colonists in the Heart of the Continent (Philadelphia, 2006); Pekka Hämäläinen, *The Comanche Empire* (New Haven, Conn., 2008); Brian Delay, "Independent Indians and the U.S.–Mexican War," *AHR,* CXII (2007), 39.

3. Henry Bouquet was born in 1719 in Switzerland. In 1755, the British minister at The Hague succeeded in getting him to take the lieutenant colonelcy of the first battalion in the newly formed Royal American regiment, and he left for America in 1756. He defended the British colonies during the French and Indian War, participated in the capture of Fort Duquesne, and became famous for the role he played during Pontiac's Rebellion. In the autumn of 1764, Bouquet, as commander of the fort (renamed Fort Pitt), subdued the Indian uprising and forced the Shawnee, the Seneca, and the Delaware to sue for peace and return more than two hundred captives. See Allen Johnson et al., eds., *Dictionary of American Biography,* 20 vols. (New York, 1928–1937), II, 480–481. Thirty manuscript volumes of his writings can be found in the British Museum, transcribed and calendared in Douglas Brymner's *Report on Canadian Archives* (Ottawa, Ont., 1889) as the Bouquet Collection. Much of this material is reprinted as Michael Shoemaker et al., eds., "Bouquet Papers," in Michigan Pioneer and Historical Society, *Collections,* 29 vols. (Lansing, Mich., 1886–1912), XIX, 27–295.

Louis Groston de Saint-Ange et de Bellerive was born in Montreal in 1700. In 1720, he followed his father to Fort St. Joseph. In 1723, he accompanied the explorer Étienne de Véniard along the banks of the Missouri and Platte Rivers. He assisted in the construction of Fort Orleans. Louis served as a military officer until 1736, when his father asked the governor of Louisiana, Jean-Baptiste Le Moyne de Bienville, to promote him to lieutenant and commander of Fort Vincennes, replacing François-Marie Bissot de Vincennes, who had been killed by the Chickasaw. Louis remained commander of the fort until 1764 and surrendered Fort Vincennes to the British under the terms of the Treaty of Paris of 1763. He then assumed command of Fort de Chartres. On October 10, 1765, he surrendered Fort de Chartres

The British mounted several expeditions to secure control of Fort de Chartres. In 1764, they attempted to ascend the Mississippi from New Orleans. Repeated Indian attacks convinced them to return to New Orleans. Finally, in 1765, Indian agent George Croghan was dispatched from Fort Pitt, accompanied by Alexander Fraser and soldiers from the Seventy-Eighth Highlanders; they headed west along the Ohio River and into Illinois Country. Fraser ultimately reached Chartres, but not before many of his men were captured by different Illinois villages along the way. Most of the Highland regiment eventually escaped and fled to New Orleans. Meanwhile, Croghan and his men had stopped at the mouth of the Wabash, near Vincennes. Here, they were attacked and the survivors taken prisoner and marched overland to Ouiatenon. Pontiac had Croghan released, and at Ouiatenon, the two men reached an agreement for peace. Croghan played a pivotal role in negotiating an end to Pontiac's Rebellion, but it was clear that the fort at Ouiatenon would remain in Native hands. It was never regarrisoned. Eventually, several British traders took up residence at Kethtippecanuck, near Ouiatenon, where they worked alongside the French and Spanish.[4]

---

to Captain Thomas Sterling (Stirling) and the British. He took his regiment to Saint Louis, Missouri, and in 1770 he turned his authority over to Pedro Josef Piernas but continued as an adviser to work with the Indians. In 1770, he swore allegiance to the Spanish governor and became a captain in the Spanish infantry, where he served until his death in 1774. See Donald Chaput, "Groston (Grotton) De Saint-Ange et de Bellerive, Louis," *Dictionary of Canadian Biography,* IV (Toronto, Ont., 1966–), 315–316.

4. Vergil E. Noble, "Ouiatenon on the Ouabache: Archaeological Investigations at a Fur Trading Post on the Wabash River," in John A. Walthall, ed., *French Colonial Archaeology: The Illinois Country and the Western Great Lakes* (Urbana, Ill., 1991), 67–68. George Croghan was an Irish-born fur trader living in the Ohio Country, a representative to the Iroquois Council, a land speculator in Pennsylvania and New York, and a British Indian agent in colonial America. He was born of English parents in Ireland in about 1717 and emigrated to the province of Pennsylvania in 1741. His successful trading posts in Native American villages emulated the French. Croghan was fluent in Delaware (an Algonquian language) and probably Mohawk (an Iroquoian language), which were spoken by the two major groups of people in the eastern region of the Ohio River valley. In 1764, Croghan was in England supporting the establishment of a strong Indian department. When he returned to the colonies, he was placed in charge of opening the Illinois Country following Pontiac's Rebellion. Croghan moved from Carlisle, Pennsylvania, to the Pittsburgh frontier in 1758, where he acquired extensive tracts of Indian land. He patented more than 250,000 acres of former Indian lands in central New York. His greatest rival as a land speculator was George Washington. See Allen Johnson and Dumas Malone, eds., *Dictionary of American Biography,* IV (New York, 1930), 556–557. Most of Croghan's journals and many of his letters are found in Illinois State Historical Library, *Collections,* X, XI (Springfield, Ill., 1915–1916); E. B. O'Cal-

Following the Ouiatenon peace agreement, the British again turned their attention to the capture of Fort de Chartres. From Fort Pitt, Captain Thomas Stirling led a detachment of 100 Forty-Second Highlanders west to secure control of the fort. They traveled down the Ohio, ascended the Wabash, and stopped at Ouiatenon on October 10, 1765. The prosperity of these agrarian villages caught the attention of the soldiers, and like previous outside observers, they praised the tremendous fertility of the women's river-bottom cornfields. They described a highly populated village with "vast and extensive plains or Meadows on its banks, abounding with incredible quantities of all kinds of game." They met "numerous Tribes of Indians [who] live on its banks: the Piankashaws, part of the Kiquapous and Musqatons, Ouiatanons etc." After several days' rest, the military continued on to Fort de Chartres, which they finally secured from Bellerive. The French commander led his men to St. Louis, where they eventually enlisted in the Spanish Army. Many French families departed for Kaskaskia or Vincennes, but despite the British presence, many others remained.[5]

Although the fall of Quebec in 1759 had marked the end of the official French presence in the Great Lakes, Britain soon discovered the difficulty of establishing sovereignty over the area. Numerous groups, including colonial squatters, traders, land speculators in the east, and Spanish authorities in the west, posed threats. Spain reigned over St. Louis and western Louisiana, as well as the Mississippi River and New Orleans, while Spanish fur traders worked in the western Ohio River valley. To reap the profits of the fur trade, the British had to maintain the integrity of Indian lands. In the Royal Proclamation of 1763, the British government committed itself to the defense of the Ohio Valley and the restriction of encroachment on Indian lands by both speculators and settlers. Ohio River valley lands were placed under the control of Quebec's imperial authorities, and, in the hopes of addressing Indian grievances, the proclamation dismissed the claims of Virginia, Pennsylvania, and Connecticut

---

laghan et al., eds., *Documents Relative to the Colonial History of the State of New York...*, 15 vols. (Albany, N.Y., 1853–1887), VI–IX; and Reuben Gold Thwaites, ed., *Early Western Travels: A Series of Annotated Reprints of Some of the Best and Rarest Contemporary Volumes of Travel...*, 32 vols. (Cleveland, 1904–1907). I. A. T. Volwiler's "George Croghan and the Western Movement, 1741–1782," *Pennsylvania Magazine of History and Biography*, XLVII (1923), 28–57, is a full biography of his life.

5. Robert Girard Carroon, ed., *Broadswords and Bayonets: The Journals of the Expedition under the Command of Captain Thomas Stirling of the 42nd Regiment of Foot, Royal Highland Regiment (the Black Watch) to Occupy Fort Chartres in the Illinois Country, August 1765 to January 1766* ([Springfield?], Ill., 1984).

to lands west of the Appalachians. The British hoped this would strengthen commercial ties between the Indians of the Ohio River valley and Quebec.

But the proclamation failed to regulate the Indian trade, with oversight of the trade and issuance of licenses falling to the colonial governors. They were too busy to pay attention, and most traders along the Wabash and Maumee Rivers remained unlicensed. The coureurs de bois and their descendants continued to dominate the region, garnering contempt from the English traders. Croghan, deputy superintendent of Indian affairs in the region, disparaged them as "a lazy indolent people, fond of breeding mischief, and spiriting up the Indians against the English."[6]

AGRARIAN AND FUR TRADE VILLAGES ALONG THE WABASH

Following Pontiac's Rebellion, four villages came to dominate the trade in the western Ohio River valley: Vincennes, Ouiatenon, Kethtippecanuck, and Miamitown. They were all located on or near the Wabash, within two to three days of each other by canoe. The Wabash was one of the most navigable rivers in the western country, and John Filson, who traveled down it in 1785, viewed the Wabash as "promis[ing] Considerable advantage by trade." At the rebellion's end, Ouiatenon was the most prosperous; the post at Miamitown was in ruins. William Johnson, then the British superintendent for the Northern Department, described Ouiatenon as one of the most desirable trading posts in the west.[7]

By the 1760s, Indian villages were primarily agrarian or, like Vincennes, Kethtippecanuck, and Miamitown, largely engaged in the fur trade. Villages throughout the Ohio River valley were crucial to the collection of furs, and, following the conquest of Canada, most British traders took up residence at Detroit or Miamitown while a scattering of others lived and traded at Vincennes, Kethtippecanuck, and the Glaize. Conditions had changed since the

---

6. George Croghan, "A Selection of George Croghan's Letters and Journals Relating to Tours into the Western Country—November 16, 1750-November 1765," in Thwaites, ed., *Early Western Travels*, I, 150.

7. John Filson, "The Discovery, Settlement, and Present State of Kentucky," in Gilbert Imlay, *The Discovery, Settlement, and Present State of Kentucke . . . to Which Is Added an Appendix, Containing . . . The Adventures of Col. Daniel Boon . . . the Whole Illustrated by a . . . Map of Kentucky, Etc.* (Wilmington, Del., 1784), 11. George Croghan, who visited the portage in 1765, has left an excellent description of it in his journal. See Croghan, "A Selection of George Croghan's Letters and Journals," in Thwaites, ed., *Early Western Travels*, I, 148-150; Oscar J. Craig, *Ouiatanon: A Study in Indiana History*, Indiana Historical Society, *Publications*, II (Indianapolis, 1893).

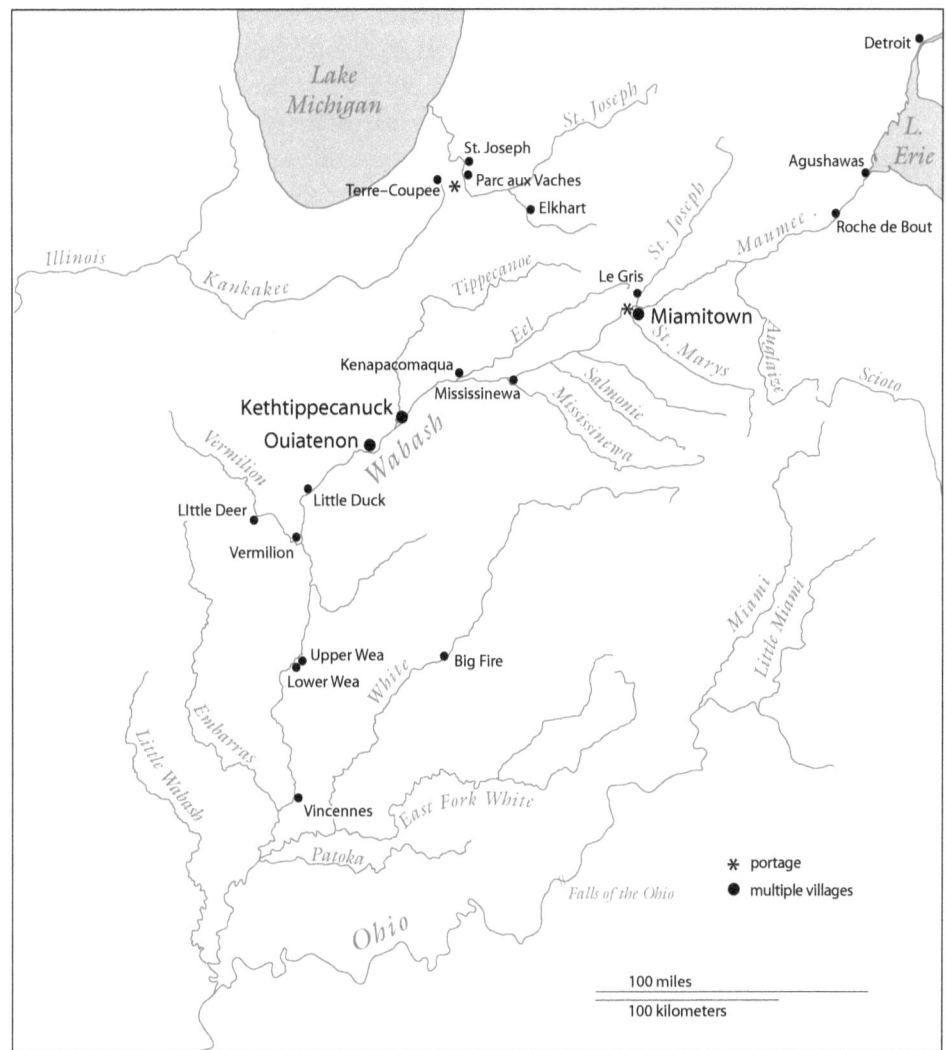

MAP 11. Villages along the Wabash River valley. Drawn by Ellen White

late seventeenth century, when the illegal French traders were incorporated into Indian households and villages. Now the remaining Frenchmen were joined by traders from St. Louis and Albany, but most of these were not integrated into Indian families. Two trading sites, Kethtippecanuck and Miamitown, were old precontact villages. Vincennes, surrounded by one Miami village and several Piankeshaw villages, was often referred to as Post St. Vincent, with French, Spanish, British, and Anglo-American traders working and living there.

The Miami had long occupied Miamitown. The first Frenchman, Jean-Baptiste Bissot de Vincennes, arrived around 1712, and Commandant Jacques-Charles Renaud Dubuisson built the first French fort here in 1721. Miamitown was later referred to as Kekionga—an inaccurate name but a common designation on American maps. Kekionga is a possible corruption of "Kiskakon," the name for an Ottawa village that might have been located here before the Miami established control over the Maumee-Wabash portage. The first fort was probably located on the high bluff that overlooked the river, to secure it from spring flooding. Indian women cultivated fields along the river; spring floods ensured long-range soil fertility. To the east was the Black Swamp, which provided plentiful, edible plants and was at the heart of the region's fur trade. The Miami River, with its numerous tributaries, especially the nearby St. Marys River, provided an inexhaustible supply of fish. The St. Marys was known as the *mameewa siipiiwi*, or Sturgeon River, because these huge fish spawned there in the spring.[8]

Fort Miami existed until 1747, when it was destroyed by English-allied Huron warriors under Chief Nicholas. The attack occurred when the commandant, Ensign Douville (Dagneau), and most of the soldiers were away at Fort Detroit. The Huron sacked the fort and burned it to the ground. In summer 1749, Captain Pierre-Joseph Céloron de Blainville rebuilt it, with the help of several French traders and the Miami. The second assault on the fort took place in 1752, when two soldiers from the French garrison were captured outside the fort and killed. At the close of the Seven Years' War, the French garrison formally surrendered Fort Miami to Ensign Holmes and his men. The British shortly lost control of the fort in 1763, during Pontiac's Rebellion, and it was destroyed by the Indians. The importance of the site led to the rebuilding of the town, which reemerged under the British as a highly successful fur-trading village. After it was rebuilt, the Shawnee and the Delaware established villages there.[9]

---

8. Calvin M. Young, *Little Turtle (Me-She-Kin-No-Quah): The Great Chief of the Miami Indian Nation* ... (Greenville, Oh., 1917), 31–32. Jacques-Charles Renaud Dubuisson named the post Fort Saint Philippe des Miami, in honor of his patron saint. The governor general Philippe de Rigaud, marquis de Vaudreuil, shortened the name to Fort des Miami, then Les Miami. Many people have assumed that Kekionga was an early Miami name for their town near the headwaters of the Maumee, but this name does not appear in any records until the arrival of the Moravian missionary David Zeisberger, who wrote it down in 1784 as "Gigeyunk." Josiah Harmar, following his defeat here in 1790, transformed the name into English, referring to the town as "Kegaiogue." See Michael McCafferty, *Native American Place-Names of Indiana* (Urbana, Ill., 2007), 74–81.

9. It would be attacked later in 1780 by Augustin Mottin de La Balme, a French cavalry

Miamitown quickly emerged as the largest and most important trading village in the Ohio River valley. Its location at the portage that linked the Maumee and Wabash Rivers housed the most diverse group of villages in the valley. The Maumee-Wabash portage was the shortest route from Canada to the Mississippi, linking the distant ports of Montreal and New Orleans. The nine-mile-long portage became navigable with the snow melts of the early spring and the seasonal rains of the early fall, and traders easily canoed from the Maumee to the Wabash. Other routes from the Great Lakes to the Mississippi were longer and navigation through Michigan's lower peninsula or the southern end of Lake Michigan more difficult; spring ice floes made the Chicago entry treacherous.

Croghan described the 240-mile journey from Miamitown to Ouiatenon as three days by canoe, when the river was at its height. Trade goods and furs were generally transported along the river trails that bordered the Wabash. Kethtippecanuck was several miles north of Ouiatenon, and it was here that most traders stopped to exchange trade goods for furs. This trading village assumed greater importance following Pontiac's Rebellion, when the Indians captured Fort Ouiatenon and the post was abandoned by the British. Indians in the Ouiatenon villages allowed the fort to disintegrate, and most fur traders moved upriver to Kethtippecanuck.[10]

While Miamitown drew its importance from the riverways, the grassy plains that surrounded Ouiatenon supported extensive bison herds that provided buffalo robes for the fur trade and meat to sustain the large village populations. The many streams and rivers that intersected the Wabash created a multiplicity of wetlands, with large numbers of fur-bearing animals. The British estimated a population of at least three thousand warriors. This would have corresponded to nine thousand to twelve thousand total inhabitants. Fur traders generally estimated the population as five thousand to seven thousand Indians. Later, President Washington and Secretary of War Henry Knox believed that ten to twelve thousand Indians resided in the villages along the banks from Miamitown to Ouiatenon. Ouiatenon also marked the geographical start of deepwater navigation. Here, the lighter barques and canoes that carried trade goods between Montreal and the Miami River were

---

officer who came to the new United States of America to assist with the Revolutionary War. The force raided the stores but was soon destroyed by Little Turtle, and the goods were returned. The coalition at Miamitown remained true to their British allies even after the area was ceded to the United States at the close of the war.

10. "A Selection of George Croghan's Letters and Journals," in Thwaites, ed., *Early Western Travels,* I, 150.

exchanged for larger ones that were needed for the deeper waters of the lower Wabash.[11]

Two to three days south of Ouiatenon lay Vincennes. Fur traders approached the village through a wide savanna that extended eight miles to the town. A few trees dotted this landscape, but the savanna generally consisted of three- to four-foot umbelliferous plants, which were wild herbs, and plants like parsley, leeks, and parsnips. The fort at Vincennes, initially erected to safeguard the trade from British intrusion, now traded with the larger posts of St. Louis and New Orleans. In 1765, Croghan described it as "one of the finest situations that can be found. The country is level and clear, and the soil very rich, producing wheat and tobacco. I think the latter preferable to that of Maryland and Virginia." Most houses were clustered in the village, and residents farmed in small gardens near their dwellings. A great, common field of almost five thousand acres stretched across the prairie lands below the village.[12]

Vincennes was adjacent to the overland Buffalo Trace (Alanantowamiowee), and following the fort's completion, the inhabitants of several Piankeshaw villages from Ouiatenon established new settlements here. The fort was probably founded not far from the former outpost of the sieur Juchereau. In 1702, Juchereau, along with thirty-four Canadians, traded for buffalo hides with American Indians where the Buffalo Trace crossed the Wabash. The exact location of Juchereau's trading post is uncertain. In the first two years, his traders collected an astounding thirteen thousand buffalo hides, but the post was abandoned when he died. The French-Canadian settlers left for Mobile (in present-day Alabama), then the capital of Louisiana. By the mid-eighteenth century, bison hunting had shifted east to the Buffalo Trace, which led to Kentucky's grass prairies.

The increased trading activity transformed Indian village life. Women's involvement in the fur trade changed the styles of houses that were being built and dramatically altered clothing styles as well, as discussed in the next chapter. Women owned the dwellings, which, by the mid-eighteenth century, con-

---

11. Noble, "Ouiatenon on the Ouabache," in Walthall, ed., *French Colonial Archaeology*, 68; Craig, *Ouiatanon*, Indiana Historical Society, *Publications* II, 327–328.

12. Croghan journeyed from Vincennes to Ouiatenon and traveled by horseback. The road was smooth, and he commented on the fertility of the landscape, but the trip was probably three days, as opposed to the two-day canoe ride downriver. See "A Selection of George Croghan's Letters and Journals," in Thwaites, ed., *Early Western Travels,* I, 140–141; Lee Burns, *Life in Old Vincennes,* Indiana Historical Society, *Publications,* VIII (Indianapolis, 1929), 437–438.

stituted bark-clad houses, log structures, and post-frame buildings. Traditional oval lodges covered with rush mats had disappeared. Bark-clad houses were generally built by Indian women, but log structures and post-frame buildings required the help of men. Most of these structures, whether in trading or agrarian villages, were surrounded by orchards and small vegetable gardens; cultivated apple, peach, and plum trees were commonplace. Mulberry trees and wild plum trees grew naturally along the banks of the Wabash. Women's cornfields stretched along low-lying river bottoms, with horses and cattle kept on the opposite bank. Horses roamed loose on the adjacent grassy plains and forests; men tied tinkling bells to their manes to locate them. Most Indian horses were quite small, selected because they were light enough to travel on the soggy soil of the bordering wetlands. Domesticated livestock were rare, although women owned some cattle at both Vincennes and Kethtippecanuck.

To English eyes, such villages appeared disordered, derelict, and impermanent; in reality, Indian women's agricultural techniques gave them a stronger footing than that of many English towns. Few villages corresponded to the pastoral ideals of the English countryside, where cultivated fields were surrounded by fences, and grain crops were planted in plowed, linear rows. Indian corn was planted in hills, each mound surrounded by nitrogen-replenishing bean plants. Once the corn was tall and ripe, the difference from cultivated fields became difficult to discern. Cornfields were well tended and free of weeds. Indian women's farming methods ensured long fertility for those fields and a solid agricultural foundation for the villages. All of these villages had a collection of outlying buildings where furs and surplus grains were stored. Much to the chagrin of many English observers, the villages lacked barns, and there were few domesticated animals. Vincennes, Ouiatenon, and Kethtippecanuck were also connected by horse trails, which transported furs north to Miamitown or south to Vincennes.[13]

Most outsiders described Indian lands as underutilized and noticed little or nothing about Indian women's work. Instead, they focused their attention on the French inhabitants. In Ouiatenon, Miamitown, and Vincennes, Croghan

13. This trade was especially apparent in the Great Lakes, where the Wabash and Kankakee River valleys remained viable fur trade regions until late in the nineteenth century. See Charles Callender, "Miami," in Bruce G. Trigger, ed., *Handbook of North American Indians,* XV, *Northeast* (Washington, D.C., 1978), 681–689; Jane Mt. Pleasant, "The Paradox of Plows and Productivity: An Agronomic Comparison of Cereal Grain Production under Iroquois Hoe Culture and European Plow Culture in the Seventeenth and Eighteenth Centuries," *Agricultural History,* LXXXV (2011), 462; Milo Milton Quaife, ed., *The Indian Captivity of O. M. Spencer* (Chicago, 1917), 44–45.

considered the French planters to be failures, wastrels of a remarkably fertile landscape. His comments on Vincennes with its eighty or ninety families typified all the villages that housed these lazy Frenchmen. They might live in "one of the finest situations that can be found," but they "are an idle lazy people, a parcel of Renegadoes from Canada, and are much worse than the Indians."[14]

ENTREPÔTS OF TRADE

Trading communities were located at river confluences; both Kethtippecanuck and Miamitown were on major riverways, just three days apart by canoe. Firsthand narratives and correspondence provide a robust portrait of Miamitown, confirmed and enriched by Kethtippecanuck's extensive archaeological excavations. Kethtippecanuck, at the convergence of the Wabash and Tippecanoe Rivers, covered at least 13.5 acres, but only a small section of this site has been unearthed. Today, Kethtippecanuck is open-space parkland, which allows for ongoing digs at the site; such investigation is impossible at Miamitown, which has been displaced by Fort Wayne. Combining the evidence for the two towns allows insight into these diverse village worlds where Indian women and men shared daily life with Europeans.

Kethtippecanuck was connected to the densely populated villages surrounding Ouiatenon, and people traveled easily from one village to the other. Most Indian residents were either traders, laborers, or hunters. They bartered food and fresh meat for trade goods; when the spring arrived, hunters brought their peltry in from the wintering camps. The French traders generally lived at Kethtippecanuck year round, whereas the English and Spanish traders usually arrived in the fall and departed in the spring. Written descriptions recount an ongoing, indeed, almost constant, stream of Indians arriving and departing throughout the year. Most French fur traders moved twenty-five kilometers upstream to Kethtippecanuck following Pontiac's Rebellion, when the Wea captured the fort at Ouiatenon. Three prominent traders, Toop Maisonville, Lamoureus fils, and Piere Clairmont, moved from Ouiatenon to Kethtippecanuck after the rebellion, according to the 1767 British census.[15]

Archaeologists have described Kethtippecanuck as a "thriving, substantial, multiethnic settlement with agricultural fields, livestock at pasture, and

14. "A Selection of George Croghan's Letters and Journals," in Thwaites, ed., *Early Western Travels*, I, 141.

15. James R. Jones, "Kethtippecanuck: A Mixed 18th Century Village Near the Mouth of the Tippacanneoe River; Recent Research," paper presented at the 1987 Indiana Historical Society Meeting, Indianapolis; Jones, "Acculturation at Historical Aboriginal Sites in Tippecanneoe County, Indiana: The Artifactual Evidence," *Michigan Archaeologist*, XXXVIII (1992), 105–120.

a number and variety of permanent structures inhabited by French and English traders and Native Americans from several Great Lakes groups." Kethtippecanuck was a long-established village site with shell-tempered pottery fragments, confirming the village's precontact occupation. Indians lived here during the Archaic, Middle Woodland, Late Woodland, and Late Precontact periods.[16]

More than 28,000 artifacts, 15,481 historic and 12,909 prehistoric, have been recovered, despite the village's destruction by Kentucky militia forces in 1791, its occupation by thousands of followers of Tecumseh and the Prophet, and its repurposing by white farmers who plowed the fields and fenced it as pastureland. "That so much remains, even in a damaged, scattered and fragmentary state, is evidence for how substantial and comfortable Kethtippecanuck must have once been, meriting the observation by William Clark that 'these Indians appear to be wealthy,' when he recorded the destruction of the town in 1791 in his journal."[17]

The village had "about 120 houses, 80 of which were shingle roofed ... the best houses belonged to French traders, whose gardens and improvements round the town were truly delightful . . . there was a tavern, with cellars, bar, public, and private rooms; and the whole marked a considerable share of order, and no small degree of civilization." The tavern was the focus of this trading village, and here visitors, traders, and Indians roomed and shared meals together. It was probably surrounded by a large number of dwellings with a variety of building styles: French poteaux-en-terre, log houses, and bark cabins. Large quantities of corn were stored at the village, and scattered throughout the community were "bear's oil, kettles, [and] plows." Salt was stored and either sold by the merchants or used to preserve meat. Most of the salt was processed by the Wea and Kickapoo from Kentucky's salt flats when they crossed the Ohio and hunted along the Buffalo Trace. Cattle and hogs were kept by many village residents. When the Americans leveled Kethtippecanuck in 1791, they destroyed almost 1,000 bushels of corn, which led the raiders to conclude that this was a prosperous Indian trading village.[18]

---

16. Michael Strezewski et al., *Report of the 2006 Archaeological Investigations at Kethtippecanuk (12–T–59), Tippecanoe County, Indiana* (Fort Wayne, Ind., 2007), 133.

17. Ibid.

18. George Imlay, "A Topographical Description of the Western Territory of North America, 1793," in Harlow Lindley, ed., *Indiana as Seen by Early Travelers: A Collection of Reprints from Books of Travel, Letters, and Diaries Prior to 1830* (Indianapolis, 1916), 12; Lyman Draper Manuscript Collection, 63 J 141, microfilm, 1949, State Historical Society of Wisconsin, Madison; Strezewski et al., *Report of the 2006 Archaeological Investigations at Kethtippecanunk*, 178.

The extensive architectural artifacts unearthed included the structural elements from numerous buildings, such as bricks, stones, nails, door hardware, and furnishings. Ubiquitous across the site and present in every unit and level of the excavation was mud daub, which was hardened and preserved by the fire that destroyed Kethtippecanuck in 1791. Extensive chinking and large quantities of hand-wrought nails found during the excavation suggest large, impressive structures. In the eighteenth century, when hand-wrought nails were at a premium, the quantities located here suggest that the people intended to remain for a prolonged period of time. In the center of this village, Indians and fur traders lived in proximity. The intermingling of European and Indian artifacts adjacent to the remains of housing structures suggests they were neighbors, not simply trading partners. Native roasting pits for tubers or roots, broken or recycled kettles reworked by Native craftsmen for adornment and tinkling cones are found in the midst of such European artifacts as iron nails, brass tacks, trigger guards, white clay pipe fragments, a candle snuffer, tin-glazed earthenware, bottle glass, and a trade ring.[19]

A large variety of imported kitchen goods were also found at the Kethtippecanuck site, such as those used to prepare and serve food. Indians and Euro-Americans shared meals served on "French faience, English creamware, and English salt-glazed stoneware," evidence that Indians who lived in trading villages enjoyed a more European way of life, influenced by the presence of luxury trade goods. At the nearby Wea village, where there were no fur traders, archaeological digs yielded higher frequencies of beads, stone pipes, and modified European artifacts, such as tinkling bells or cones, which Indians fashioned from iron or brass kettles to decorate women's shirts or to tie to horses' manes.[20]

In Kethtippecanuck as well as Miamitown and the surrounding villages, Indians served as the village provisioners: men provided geese, ducks, venison, and fish, while women supplied mussels, wild and domesticated vegetables, herbs, maple sugar, salt to season food, and strawberries, blueberries, and pawpaws to incorporate into stewpots, breads, and desserts. By the mid- to late eighteenth century, Indian hunters had transformed dining tables into multi-

---

19. Strezewski et al., *Report of the 2006 Archaeological Investigations at Kethtippecanunk*, 141–143, 179.

20. Neal L. Trubowitz, "Native Americans and French on the Central Wabash," in John A. Walthall and Thomas E. Emerson, eds., *Calumet and Fleur-de-Lys: Archaeology of Indian and French Contact in the Midcontinent* (Washington, D.C., 1992), 257; Ian W. Brown, "Certain Aspects of French-Indian Interaction in Lower Louisiane," ibid., 23.

course feasts, creating groaning boards of gastronomy. Dinners were an endless round of meat and fowl, which at one sitting included "pheasants, grouse, elk, venison, and even buffalo." With the adjacent grass plains at Ouiatenon, the Wea would have supplied bison meat to both Miamitown and Kethtippecanuck. The Quakers who visited Miamitown in 1804 and 1805 also described lengthy dinners in which they were served well-roasted turkey as well as boiled turkey. Food remained so plentiful that the Quakers commented on the "very fat and healthy looking children" of Miami women. It was very clear from the Americans who later burned down Kethtippecanuck that they viewed these Indians as "very wealthy."[21]

In March 1788, when Revolutionary War veteran William Biggs was captured by the Kickapoo and Wea while traveling through Illinois Country, he was held at a number of villages and sugar camps along the Wabash. While living at Kethtippecanuck, he arranged his ransom and subsequent release. During that time, he lived with a French baker and "had plenty to eat ... good light bread, bacon and sandy hill crains, boiled in leyed corn, which made a very good soup." Corn and wheat came from Indian women, whereas men provided the meat, waterfowl, and fish that transformed meals into memorable daily feasts. Since Biggs paid his own ransom, he was given extensive freedom toward the end of his captivity, which allowed him to visit with several village residents. He met several fur traders, including a Frenchman named Ebert, a Spanish trader named Bazedone, and an English trader named John McCauslin. Material artifacts excavated at this site confirm the presence of this diverse fur-trading population. A fob seal used to stamp documents, for instance, probably belonged to McCauslin. It was decorated with a Masonic coat of the Premier Grand Lodge of England and was in use from 1717 until 1813. Biggs eventually traveled with a French trader and his wife to their home in Vincennes. The Frenchman explained to him that "they had moved up to that Kickapoo town in the fall of the year in order to trade with Indians that winter."[22]

---

21. Milo M. Quaife, ed., *A Narrative of Life on the Old Frontier: Henry Hay's Journal from Detroit to the Mississippi River,* State Historical Society of Wisconsin, *Proceedings* (Madison, Wis., 1915), 208–261 (hereafter cited as *Henry Hay's Journal*); Daniel K. Richter, "'Believing That Many of the Red People Suffer Much for the Want of Food': Hunting, Agriculture, and Quaker Construction of Indianness in the Early Republic," *Journal of the Early Republic,* XIX (1999), 601–628; Draper MSS, 63 J 141.

22. Strezewski et al., *Report of the 2006 Archaeological Investigations at Kethtippecanuck,* 2–4; Judith Dunn Tordoff, "An Archaeological Perspective on the Organization of the Fur Trade in Eighteenth-Century New France" (Ph.D. diss., Michigan State University, 1983);

Kethtippecanuck was not an open trading village. Traders who failed to secure the permission of village chiefs at Miamitown were imprisoned. Antoine Lasell, a French trader from Detroit, arrived unannounced and was immediately captured by the Wea. They accused him of supporting the Americans against the British. He was rescued when he sent a petition to Le Gris, signed by Little Egg (a Wea chief) and The Sirropp (a Peoria chief), as well as ten French traders: Diaum Payette, Jean Cannehous, Lamoureux, Etienne Pantonne, Henri Rainbeare, Jacque Dumay, Toop Maisonville, Lamoureus fils, Piere Clairmont, and Jean Coustan. Le Gris had warned fur traders not to travel to Kethtippecanuck without first obtaining his permission. He knew Lasell but was unaware of the Frenchman's journey there; had Le Gris known, he would have sent "one of my Chiefs with him, or given him a belt, as a Guard and which would have prevented anything of this happening." Instead, Le Gris arranged for Lasell's release by sending three warriors, including Little Turtle.[23]

Peltry from Kethtippecanuck, along with that of Miamitown and Vincennes, went to the larger trading towns of St. Louis, Detroit, and Albany. In trading villages along the Wabash, Indians and Euro-American fur traders lived side by side. (In contrast, earlier French coureurs de bois and their descendants had inhabited and remained based in multiple smaller agrarian villages from which they brought furs acquired from their kin network to market.) Most of the new traders who arrived in the last half of the eighteenth century were seasonal residents who rented rooms over taverns or in boardinghouses, where Indians also lodged. The more successful traders built log or wood structures, where they lived during the winter season. In the spring, most returned to larger trading centers like Detroit and St. Louis, depositing their furs with merchants who shipped them to Montreal, New Orleans, and ultimately London. A Mr. Pyatt and his wife lived at Kethtippecanuck during the winter season but returned to their home in Vincennes in the spring. Pyatt arrived in Vincennes with his furs carried by a drove of horses he had purchased from the Indians. His wife hired a large, flat-bottom boat and four Frenchmen to transport their household furnishings. Spanish

---

Trubowitz, "Native Americans and French on the Central Wabash," in Walthall and Emerson, eds., *Calumet and Fleur-de-Lys,* 256; Frederick Haldimand, "State of the Settlement at St. Vincents on the Ouabache," in Frederick Haldimand Papers, Indiana Historical Society Library, Indianapolis; *Narrative of William Biggs, While He Was a Prisoner with the Kickepoo Indians...*, Garland Library of Narratives of North American Indian Captivities, XXXVII (1826; rpt. Garland, N.Y., 1977), 21.

23. Henry Hay, *Fort Wayne in 1790,* ed. Milo Milton Quaife, Indiana Historical Society, *Publications,* VII (Greenfield, Ind., 1921), 323.

FIGURE 6. "Nan-Matches-Sin-A-Wa, 1839, Chief Godfroy's Home." By George Winter. Courtesy of Tippecanoe County Historical Association, Lafayette, Ind. Gift of Mrs. Cable G. Ball

traders also lived at Kethtippecanuck for the winter season and returned to St. Louis in the spring with their furs.[24]

One of the more prominent traders at Kethtippecanuck was the Frenchman Gabriel Godfroy, who married a Miami woman and whose son Francis later became a Miami chief. The elder Godfroy's trading house was burned down by the Kentucky militia in 1791, and he rebuilt his home on the Wabash. Later, his son Francis would build a house on the nearby Mississinewa, in the same timber frame construction as his father's home. George Winter, who sketched Francis Godfroy's Mississinewa house in 1839, described it as "a fine two story frame building for trading purposes on the *bank* between the canal and Wabash river, at the town of Peru . . . he built a substantial trading house at 'Nan-matches-sin-wa,' which was well stocked with merchandise peculiarly adapted to the Indian purchaser." The sketch was later completed as a water-

---

24. *Narrative of the Captivity of William Biggs among the Kickapoo Indians in Illinois in 1788, Written by Himself* (New York, 1922), 33, 35; George Winter, "Journal of a Visit to Deaf Man's Village, 1839," rpt. in Howard H. Peckham, *The Journals and Indian Paintings of George Winter, 1837–1839* (Indianapolis, 1948), 151–196.

color and provides a snapshot of some of the house styles that might have characterized Kethtippecanuck.[25]

Under British rule, population levels surged at the trading villages; but during the French era, these villages had had large numbers of Indians and far fewer fur traders. Even the founding of Detroit failed to draw large numbers of Frenchmen to the southern Great Lakes. In 1701, 100 French settled among 1,200 Indians at Detroit. Despite ongoing disputes, the Indian population level continued to increase, but after thirty years, there were still fewer than 200 Frenchmen. By 1750, there were only 450 non-Indian people at Detroit, and even by 1765 there were only 801 French inhabitants. Total population levels greatly increased during the British period: to 1,367 in 1773; 1,500 in 1776; 2,144 in 1778; and 2,653 in 1779. Farther south, Miamitown eclipsed Kethtippecanuck in importance and emerged as a key trading village in the Ohio River valley. In the 1767 English census of Wabash villages, Miamitown was the smallest, but, a decade later, it had a far larger number of traders as well as sizable Shawnee and Delaware communities. Indians from Ouiatenon as well as Miami, Odawa, Ojibwe, Potawatomi, Cherokee, and Seneca who had wintering camps in the Black Swamp generally traded at nearby Miamitown. Although many Ouiatenon villagers remained loyal to the traders at Kethtippecanuck, Miamitown emerged as the largest trading village north of the Ohio, where diverse Indian groups spoke different languages and behaved and thought differently but were motivated by similar economic goals. Each sought to obtain the most desirable trade goods for their peltry.[26]

Miamitown was, in other words, Kethtippecanuck writ large. Manners, formality, and social etiquette were a captivating blend of Indigenous and European customs; this was a lively, informal world where Indians and traders were social intimates and trading partners. Miamitown turned into an important communications center for the entire Ohio River valley, a place where Indians gathered to exchange news and gossip. At the treaty of Greenville,

25. George Winter, "Journal of a Visit to Deaf Man's Village, 1939," in Sarah E. Cooke and Rachel B. Ramadhyani, eds., *Indians and a Changing Frontier* (Indianapolis, 1993), 120; *Henry Hay's Journal,* 236n; Michigan Pioneer and Historical Society, *Collections,* VIII, 283–285, XXIV, 106, 107, 166, 273.

26. Brian Leigh Dunnigan, "'The Prettiest Settlement in America': A Select Bibliography of Early Detroit through the War of 1812," *Michigan Historical Review,* XXVII (2001), 1–20; Dunnigan, *Frontier Metropolis: Picturing Early Detroit, 1701–1838* (Detroit, 2001), 19, 20, 22, 31; Wilbur Edel, *Kekionga! The Worst Defeat in the History of the U.S. Army* (New York, 1997); *Military Journal of Major Ebenezer Denny: An Officer in the Revolutionary and Indian Wars* (Philadelphia, 1860); Basil Meek, "General Harmar's Expedition," *Ohio Archaeological and Historical Publications,* XX (1911), 86–87; *Henry Hay's Journal,* 208–261.

Little Turtle spoke of this village as "That glorious gate through which all the good words of our chiefs had to pass from the north to the south and from the east to the west." There was no military presence to restrain communications; here, the benefits of aligning with the British, Americans, or even the Spanish were openly discussed. Indians stopped at Miamitown before they went off to hunt or arrived when they had sufficient peltry to exchange. In addition, many Indians walked from the nearby Delaware and Shawnee villages or strode along the pathways that linked the villages of Little Turtle and Le Gris to Miamitown. They came to barter produce and visit with friends. As in Kethtippecanuck, Indian hunters supplied the food for Miamitown's cooking pots. Men were the provisioners of fresh meat and fish, and women supplied corn, rice, dried seeds and berries, and vegetables. Market activity extended beyond the fur trade: Indian women bartered food for trade goods. Indians also transported food to share with others or carried the raw ingredients, which others prepared for them. There was little formality associated with these social interactions. Indians dined with French residents, traders, or other Indians. They enjoyed breakfast and dinner together and, like the French residents and fur traders who lived here, ate and drank, often to excess.[27]

Miamitown's whirl of social activity was vividly described by the young British trader Henry Hay when he arrived there shortly before the 1789 Christmas season. The Miami guided him through the marshlands that masked the Maumee River entrance; his journey lasted almost two weeks. He was warmly received at Miamitown and quickly incorporated into the round of social events that characterized daily life. Hay was greeted by the French families "sans ceremonie," and he considered the French traders "decent and polite." He relished this social interaction and became known for playing the flute, accompanied by his friend John Kinzie, another Detroit trader, who was an accomplished fiddle player. These two men were especially popular at Indian gatherings, where they also undoubtedly provided the musical entertainment.[28]

Hay's father, Jehu, was well liked by the Indians of Miamitown, having been in the Indian service, and he had raised Henry among the Indians. Welcoming Henry as the son of an old friend, the Delaware provided him with

---

27. *Henry Hay's Journal*, 208–257; Helen Hornbeck Tanner, "The Glaize in 1792: A Composite Indian Community," *Ethnohistory*, XXV (1978), 15–39, rpt. in Peter C. Mancall and James H. Merrell, eds., *American Encounters: Natives and Newcomers from European Contact to Indian Removal, 1500–1850* (New York, 2000), 404–425; *Narrative of Biggs*, 21; Jones, "Acculturation," *Michigan Archaeologist*, XXXVIII (1992), 105–120; Young, *Little Turtle (Me-She-Kin-No-Quah)*, 31–32.

28. *Henry Hay's Journal*, 218–219.

a personal servant: a white captive Irishman born in Tipperary. The captive secured Henry's food, prepared it, served him, and also attended to young Hay's personal hygiene. The Irishman made sure that Hay's clothes were clean and brushed and his linens carefully laundered. The servant had been captured by the Delaware to provide information about the number and location of newly arriving settlers and troop movements at Fort Washington (present-day Cincinnati). The Delaware intended to return him in the spring; in the meantime, the Irishman spent the winter with Henry.[29]

Winter was a lively season with holiday celebrations that stretched from the week before Christmas to the New Year, and the influx of Indian visitors reached unprecedented heights. Most of the celebrating was far from pious, and Miamitown became a riotous festival. Hay thoroughly enjoyed village social life, reveling in its late-night festivities. He celebrated in the spirit of the community, and on December 26 he "got infernally drunk . . . with Mr. Abbott and Mr. Kinzie — Mr. A. — gave me his daughter Betsy over the bottle. Damnation sick this morning in consequence of last night's debashe — eat no breakfast — Kinzie and myself went to mass and played as usual. — Mrs. Ranjard gave us a cup of coffee before mass to settle our heads." Hay's account typified the behavior of many male fur traders. Drunkenness was commonplace, and Hay and Kinzie attended Mass intoxicated, sobered by the Frenchwomen who plied them with coffee. Neither man was chagrined about his behavior and, when Mass was over, Hay went visiting at a French household. He flirted freely with two young women while the adults excused themselves and left the young people to amuse themselves. Hay frequently noted in his journal that "the old people were out of the way."[30]

Miamitown celebrated New Year's Day in the French fashion. Houses overflowed with Indian guests: it was then "a common custom among them to flock in about that time from their wintering places, to Salute." By the first of the year, there were more Indians than Hay "could ever have thought." He added to the merriment of the holiday by tossing three rounds of powder and shot into the fireplace. The loudness of the subsequent explosion tremendously pleased his French and Indian guests: his stunt was one small contribution to a rowdy week of ongoing celebrations. When Hay failed to join in the New Year's Eve celebrations, the revelers came to him: at 3:00 a.m., men and women arrived in his room unannounced. Hay was shocked to discover

---

29. Jehu Hay had been a member of the Indian Department. Henry had probably come to Miamitown either under the purview of the British government or as a trader, perhaps working for William Robertson, a Detroit merchant. See *Henry Hay's Journal*, 212.

30. Ibid., 217–226.

that "one lady came to shake hands with me when in bed." By the next morning, having recovered from this stunning lack of etiquette, Hay engaged in another round of social visits, walking through the village, calling on "the Principal families," and displaying proper French frontier etiquette by "kiss[ing] all the Ladies young and Old." The next two days he spent with his Indian visitors, who also ate, danced, and drank with other Indians as well as with the French residents and visiting traders. Then, pretty well exhausted, the Indians headed back to their wintering camps, after "thanking us for the reception they received."[31]

Hay's raucous lifestyle centered on card playing and dancing. He played cards with "the principal People of the Village" and with his Indian friends, often at late-night parties; on January 16, it was 4:00 a.m. by the time he returned home from one of these, "rather Drunkish." The next day brought a more formal party, where he danced with "all the Decent Ladies of this place" at the home of the La Salles, an important fur-trading family who lived in the midst of the Indians. On the day after that, French and Indian villagers partied at a much more public dance, where they gathered to celebrate the queen's birthday. Hay and Kinzie entertained the guests by singing "God Save the King."[32]

Henry Hay's observations went beyond the social life of Miamitown, and he also described several preemptive strikes against settler communities along the Ohio. War parties frequently returned to Miamitown to exchange news about the encroaching American settlements or to display their captives. Hay described one of Little Turtle's raids on the Columbia City settlement, three-fourths of a mile below the Little Miami, where the Indians secured two captives, an elderly white man and a young African American. The Indians tortured and killed the white man, but Little Turtle incorporated the African American into his nearby village. The public torture and death of an elderly white man was a message, as Indians attempted to intimidate encroaching American settlers and secure British support against those settlements. Several other war parties also returned during Hay's visit. When Le Gris arrived from a raid along the Ohio, the residents at Miamitown responded by housing Le Gris's warriors in several French homes, assigning a few to each house. At Hay's boarding house, Le Gris found room for six Indians, whom he placed there in "a very polite manner." Shortly after Le Gris departed, the Shawnee chief Captain Johnny arrived, accompanied by warriors from his own village

---

31. Tanner, "The Glaize in 1792," *Ethnohistory*, XXV (1978), 15–19; *Henry Hay's Journal*, 318, 320–321.
32. *Henry Hay's Journal*, 239.

as well as a party of Miami warriors. These groups went directly from Miamitown to their wintering camps.³³

Miamitown was thus the core of the Indian communication network in the Ohio River valley. Most Indians were welcomed as friends, and they shared meals and daily conversation with residents and visitors. Hay welcomed leaders like Le Gris and Little Turtle, who "came to visit us and breakfasted with us as usual" or, in the afternoon, "drank tea, also madeira." Much of Hay's perspective was influenced by Little Turtle. These men sat and enjoyed themselves and probably watched the continuing stream of Indian men and women who transported large quantities of turkey, deer, bear, and raccoon along the pathways to provision Miamitown. Most arrived in the morning or the afternoon and left later that day, returning to their villages with news about the raids and the resistance to American encroachment.³⁴

What echoes through the pages of Hay's journal is the sense of a face-to-face world. Sociability and the exchange of trade goods were dynamically intertwined. Indians were friends and, frequently, relatives. They were simultaneously customers and consumers. Miamitown was an intimate world where economic transactions were mediated by social interaction. Outsiders were welcome, especially visiting traders who were part of the ongoing exchange process. When Indians transported their peltry to Miamitown, traders like Henry Hay competed directly with other fur traders. According to Hay, these traders were ruthless competitors, and he complained that "everyone tries to get what he can either by fowle play or otherwise—that is by traducing one another's characters and merchandise." No complaints came from the Indians—or at least none have come down to us—who profited from the competition and secured a bountiful supply of trade goods.³⁵

Long-established French traders who were part of Indian households frequently stopped at Miamitown on their way to Detroit or Albany with their furs. Their system of wintering with Indians had originated during the early years of trade and continued throughout the eighteenth century. They provided Indians with goods in advance of the wintering season, then gathered their furs in the spring. Although villages like Miamitown grew as they incorporated new fur traders, Frenchmen who had married into matrifocal households and gathered furs from their Indian kin were the ones retaining access to larger quantities of better quality peltry.³⁶

---

33. Ibid., 217.
34. Ibid., 228–229.
35. Ibid., 224.
36. Tanner, "The Glaize in 1792," *Ethnohistory*, XXV (1978), rpt. in Mancall and Mer-

New traders moving into the Great Lakes often hired Indian women to aid them in competition with established French traders. John Askin successfully relocated to the Great Lakes in the early 1760s and purchased a female slave familiar with the trade. When he moved to Michilimackinac in the mid-1760s, he hired Sally Ainse, an Oneida woman trading at Detroit, to help him capture a greater share of the northern market. Ainse, the former wife of Pennsylvania's Andrew Montour, had moved to the Great Lakes to trade among the Odawa; Askin noted at one point in his journal that she "went in a Boat for the Grand Traverse or to meet the Ottaways." Several years later, Detroit trader John Porteous encountered Sally in a canoe laden with goods, on her way to winter among her people at Long Point, Ontario. Sally had been born in an Oneida village, where she returned following her divorce from Montour. She had first traded along the Mohawk River in 1759, then moved to Detroit, entered the northern Great Lakes trade with Askin, and moved back to Detroit. Her Detroit commerce likely centered on the Moravian Indian settlement, with people she probably knew from her days in Pennsylvania. Askin supplied her with trade goods worth three thousand pounds in 1783. Montague Tremblay, another Detroit trader, supplied her with cheese, sugar, rum, coffee, green tea, shirts, petticoats, and earbobs. She amassed sufficient capital to purchase two houses and land inside Fort Pontchartrain. The 1779 Detroit census reveals that her property included "one male and three female slaves, four horses, three cows, and one hundred pounds of flour." Sally Ainse had evolved from fur trader to merchant.[37]

Like John Askin, James Sterling also moved from Albany to Detroit, where he married a woman who "has been raised to trade from her infancy and is

---

rell, eds., *American Encounters*, 312–313, 315, 317, 351–353. Gail D. MacLeitch describes how trading towns worked among the Iroquois in *Imperial Entanglements: Iroquois Change and Persistence on the Frontiers of Empire* (Philadelphia, 2011).

37. At. S. De Peyster, "Merchandize and Liquors for Detroit," Michigan Pioneer and Historical Society, *Collections*, XIX, 588–589; M. M. Quaife, ed., *The John Askin Papers*, 2 vols. (Detroit, 1928–1931), I, 50, 52, 194; Justin M. Carroll, "John Askin's Many Beneficial Binds: Family, Trade, and Empire in the Great Lakes" (Ph.D. diss., Michigan State University, 2011); Frederick C. Hamil, "Sally Ainse, Fur Trader," *Detroit Algonquin Club Historical Bulletin*, III (1939), 2–6, 14; Donna Valley Russell, *Michigan Censuses, 1710–1830 under the French, British, and Americans* (Detroit, 1982), 42, 55. Sally Ainse received land from the Moravian village along the Thames River. The Moravians had abandoned their lands along the Ohio and secured permission to move across the Detroit River at the entrance to Lake Erie, where Amherstburg now stands. Sally was given lands on the north side of the river, between the mouth of the river and the forks. See Hamil, "Fairfield on the River Thames," *Ohio History*, XLVIII (1939), 2–3.

generally allowed to be the best interpreter of the different languages at this place." Marie-Angelique Cuillerier's knowledge and relationship with Indian communities gave Sterling an entrée into the fur trade. Sterling wrote to his Albany partner, "The Indians flock here daily since our marriage and lament our not having Indian goods, as they would trade nowhere else but here, if we could supply them." Angelique continued to work as an independent trader while Sterling worked as a merchant, supplying the British garrison at Detroit. Sterling often sent Angelique's peltry to John Duncan, his British agent at Fort Niagara, while she purchased silver ornaments from her husband's eastern suppliers. Angelique's trade differed from most of her competitors' because she focused on acquiring the eye-catching clothing that Indian women manufactured. Often, Sterling secured items from Angelique that he gave to influential British officials, such as a beaver blanket that he sent to Colonel John Vaughan at Niagara.[38]

For recently arrived traders like Askin and Sterling, Indian and mixed-ancestry women were crucial links to Indian communities. Askin purchased a female Indian slave who had ties to a prominent Michilimackinac fur trade family, the Bourassas. Manette (Monette) became the mother of two of his children, and he later incorporated them into his familial kin network. Askin freed Manette in 1766, about the same time that Sally Ainse began trading for him. These women opened the trade for the newcomers.[39]

TACUMWAH: MIAMI WOMAN AND FUR TRADER

Following twenty years of marriage, Tacumwah, a Miami woman, publicly and successfully challenged her French husband's authority over the fur trade as well as his control over the Maumee-Wabash portage. The British commander-in-chief, General Thomas Gage, granted the Maumee-Wabash portage, long controlled by the Miami, to Joseph Drouet de Richardville and his partner, Maisonville, after they rescued several British traders during Pontiac's Rebellion. Tacumwah had married Richardville during the Seven Years' War and incorporated him into the Indigenous kin networks of the Ohio

---

38. James Sterling to John Duncan, Feb. 26, May 31, 1765, Sterling to John Vaughan, July 17, 1765, in James Sterling Letter Book, 1761–1765, 1931.M–125, William L. Clements Library, University of Michigan, Ann Arbor; Susan Sleeper-Smith, *Indian Women and French Men: Rethinking Cultural Encounter in the Western Great Lakes* (Springfield, Mass., 2001), 64. See also Walter S. Dunn, Jr., *Frontier Profit and Loss: The British Army and the Fur Traders, 1760–1764* (Westport, Conn., 1998).

39. Justin M. Carroll, *The Merchant John Askin: Furs and Empire at British Michilimackinac* (East Lansing, Mich., 2017), 3, 23, 77–78, 83n, 106, 115, 119–120, 121n, 253, 258.

River alley. They had two sons and two daughters, who were raised in Miami communities but also integrated into the larger Catholic kin network that linked French and Indian traders at Detroit. Tacumwah's eldest son later became one of the Miami's most notable and powerful chiefs, considered the richest man in early-nineteenth-century Indiana.[40]

This dispute was symbolic of the larger issues about whether Native communities or European traders would control this regional fur trade. Tacumwah's extensive and powerful Indigenous kin network made it possible for her to challenge her husband's authority in this face-to-face world. She was a member of the Crane clan and the half-sister of Little Turtle and Pacanne, both well-known war chiefs among the Miami. Pacanne and Tacumwah shared the same father, Pacanne dit Roy, who was half French and half Miami, but they had different Indian mothers. Tacumwah and Little Turtle shared the same Mahican mother but had different fathers.[41]

In 1774, Tacumwah challenged Richardville when he refused to give her the furs from the winter season. Their dispute erupted when Tacumwah left Richardville and moved in with Charles Beaubien, a fur trade competitor. In eighteenth-century British society, property was controlled by the husband, whereas in Indigenous households property belonged to the woman. Tacumwah had followed the traditional Indian pathway to divorce and simply moved out of Richardville's house and into the home of his rival. Richardville did not contest their divorce, but he claimed control over the furs from the season's hunt. Tacumwah insisted that the furs belonged to her. Pacanne appealed to British authorities on her behalf, turning to Detroit's recently appointed English commander, Captain Robert Lernoult. He requested that Lernoult act

---

40. Sleeper-Smith, *Indian Women and French Men,* esp. 38–53. Jean Baptiste de Richardville was born about 1761 to Tacumwah and Joseph Drouet de Richardville in Miamitown. He was also known as Pinšiwa in Miami (meaning Wildcat, also spelled "Peshewa") and was known to the Americans as Joseph Richardville. He served as a powerful chief in a position chosen by women. For an extensive discussion of Richardville, see Karen L. Marrero, "Founding Families: Power and Authority of Mixed French and Native Lineages in Eighteenth-Century Detroit" (Ph.D. diss., Yale University, 2011), 278–310.

41. Kinship is often difficult to decipher, but the work of historians Karen L. Marrero and Bradley J. Birzer shows how these meaningful links emerged and how they would influence British decision making in the Ohio River valley. See Marrero, "'She Is Capable of Doing a Good Deal of Mischief': A Miami Woman's Threat to Empire in the Eighteenth-Century Ohio Valley," *Journal of Colonialism and Colonial History,* VI (2005), special issue, online journal, Project Muse, 1532–5768, https://muse.jhu.edu/article/192180; Birzer, "Entangling Empires, Fracturing Frontiers: Jean Baptiste Richardville and the Quest for Miami Autonomy, 1760–1841" (Ph.D. diss., Indiana University, 1999).

as judge and mediator to decide "the fairness of [the] property settlement." In explaining the circumstance of their dispute, Pacanne relied on British prejudices about French fur traders to disgrace Richardville and establish Tacumwah's control over the portage. Ironically, the Francophobic rise of English officers following Pontiac's Rebellion encouraged Indian leaders like Tacumwah, Pacanne, and Little Turtle to overturn General Gage's imperial-level decision making and restore Native control over crucial waterways.[42]

Of the five primary actors in this story, four were men. All of the men — Lernoult, Pacanne, Richardville, and Beaubien — were present for the drama that unfolded, whereas Tacumwah, despite being the main character, did not appear at the hearing. Her absence allowed Pacanne to portray her as the domestic ideal of Indian motherhood, which proved remarkably similar to the maternal behaviors attributed to Englishwomen. Pacanne cleverly sidestepped the reality of his sister's authority at Miamitown: she acted as head of her clan until her son came to adulthood, and she was an active fur trader. Instead, Pacanne depicted Tacumwah as a caring, maternal figure whose only concern was the health and safety of her children.[43]

---

42. "Copy of a Council Held at Detroit 18th September 1774 by Pacan Chief of the Miamis Indians with Five Others of the Chiefs and Principal Men of His Nation in the Presence of Richard Berringer Lernoult Esquire . . . ," Thomas Gage Papers, 1754–1807, American Series, CXXIII, Clements Library. See also Marrero, "'She Is Capable of Doing a Good Deal of Mischief,'" *Journal of Colonialism and Colonial History*, VI (2005); Marrero, "Founding Families." Sir William Johnson, superintendent of Northern Indian Affairs, had recommended to Gage that Alexis Maisonville be given control over the portage in 1764. Johnson considered this a means of overseeing Miami activity in the region. See Johnson to Maisonville, Fort Stanwix, Oct. 8, 1771, in James Sullivan et al., eds., *The Papers of Sir William Johnson*, 14 vols. (Albany, N.Y., 1921–1965), XII, 930–931; Richard White, *The Middle Ground: Indians, Empires, and Republics in the Great Lakes Region, 1650–1815* (New York, 1991), 212–213. The Miami were patrilineal, but leaders were chosen from the chief's sister's line, and thus the headman's nephew could expect to succeed to that position. If there were several nephews, it was the headman's sister who chose among her sons. See Harvey Lewis Carter, *The Life and Times of Little Turtle: First Sagamore of the Wabash* (Urbana, Ill., 1987), 19.

43. Tanis C. Thorne, "For the Good of Her People: Continuity and Change for Native Women of the Midwest, 1650–1850," in Lucy Eldersveld Murphy and Wendy Hamand Vener, eds., *Midwestern Women: Work, Community, and Leadership at the Crossroads* (Bloomington, Ind., 1997), 95–120; Susan Sleeper-Smith, "Women, Kin, and Catholicism: New Perspectives on the Fur Trade," *Ethnohistory*, XLVII (2000), 430. For English views on women's place in the domestic sphere, see Michael McKeon, *The Secret History of Domesticity: Public, Private, and the Division of Knowledge* (Baltimore, 2005); Marilyn Francus, *Monstrous Motherhood: Eighteenth-Century Culture and the Ideology of Domesticity* (Baltimore, 2012).

Tacumwah was far from the subservient wife that Pacanne so vividly described in his story to Lernoult; her presence at the hearing probably would have worked against her. As we know from Henry Hay's journal, she was a shrewd and seasoned trader who traveled through the Miami wintering camps garnering the choicest furs. Pacanne neglected to mention Tacumwah's trading skills and centered his argument on the vivid image of Richardville as a dissolute, Indianized French trader. Pacanne reinforced British stereotypes about Frenchmen and played on Lernoult's prejudices by describing Richardville as lazy, lacking incentive and discipline, and living as a dissipated Indian. Pacanne contextualized this contest within the familiar English frameworks of patriarchy and family responsibility, further magnifying Richardville's sins by noting his failure to provide for either his wife or children. Tacumwah became the hapless victim whose husband refused to support his own family. Pacanne claimed that Tacumwah was entirely supported by her Miami relatives; they supplied her with furs that she then sold to support her children, a dire situation when Tacumwah was denied access to those furs. We can hear Pacanne's theatrically anguished voice in Lernoult's journal as he describes this reprobate Frenchman who stole the food from the mouths of his own children. Pacanne drew on the language of negative epithets that British military officers associated with French traders, calling Richardville "slothful, vicious, and indolent," so "lazy [that he] does nothing but sit and smoke his pipe."[44]

Pacanne tried to increase sympathy for Tacumwah by describing Richardville's relationship with his sister as physically abusive. The Richardville household became a place where Tacumwah feared for her life and the safety of her children. Pacanne claimed that because Tacumwah had no choice, she was forced to seek refuge at the home of a more honorable Frenchman, Captain Beaubien. Beaubien then reinforced Pacanne's description of Richardville when he appeared as a witness on Tacumwah's behalf. "Richardville sought to kill me long before the squah left him. I believe it proceeded from his jealousy. But he abused the squah so much that she could no longer live with him, and she left him for that reason. I believe a large part of the bad treatment she has met with is on my account and I thought myself under an obligation to provide for her. For this reason, I took her to live with me sometime after she left Richardville. I did this with the consent of her Brother Pacanne and their family."[45]

44. Marrero, "'She Is Capable of Doing a Good Deal of Mischief,'" *Journal of Colonialism and Colonial History*, VI (2005); Hay, *Fort Wayne in 1790*, ed. Quaife, 298. Lernoult had characterized the French as "Rebels to a man" during his second assignment to Detroit (Lernoult, Mar. 26, 1779, Michigan Pioneer and Historical Society, *Collections*, X, 328).

45. "Copy of a Council Held at Detroit," Aug. 14–31, 1764, Gage Papers, Amer. Ser.,

The finale to this drama was not surprising: Captain Lernoult granted Tacumwah the furs that she claimed and went beyond the scope of this property dispute to award Tacumwah control over the Maumee-Wabash River portage. Pacanne's vivid portrayal resonated so successfully with English prejudices that Richardville was driven from the portage site. Tacumwah's decision to tell this tale through the authorial voice of her brother was a wise one. He situated Tacumwah's problems within an English grasp of social relationships and family responsibilities, especially those associated with marriage and the dependence of a wife and children. Lernoult's prejudices about Frenchmen and his own patriarchal tendencies led him to protect a woman who had been neglected and abused by her indolent, pipe-smoking French Indian husband. Pacanne had successfully cast Richardville as even more lazy than the "average" Indian.

Despite his long experience, Richardville had violated Indigenous norms of behavior. The issue was larger than a struggle over peltry. He had profited from the Maumee-Wabash portage and reduced Miami profits by denying Pacanne and Tacumwah the right to carry goods across it. Indeed, if Richardville had violated the hereditary rights of the Miami and engrossed the financial benefits that should have accrued to them, then opposition and exclusion were expected outcomes. Rather than allow the situation to flare into warfare, the Miami sought to reestablish their hereditary right to the portage through peaceful means. The Miami, relying on Tacumwah, took advantage of a political "moment" in which they used British military officers to establish Miami rights over their lands and to reassert Indian hegemony over French fur traders.

This 1774 event also suggests how British military officers were manipulated to serve Indian interests. Richardville and Maisonville had received control over the Maumee portage from General Gage more than ten years before Tacumwah's 1774 petition. By the time Lernoult heard Tacumwah's case against Richardville, Gage was no longer the governor general of Canada. That same year, the powerful William Johnson died. Faced with no political opposition from higher levels, the Francophobic Captain Lernoult gladly served as judge and jury in a case that pitted Indians against French fur traders.[46]

Imperial governance rested on everyday decision making by men like Lernoult, men known for their dislike of French fur traders. Their biases had been

---

CXXIII; Marrero, "'She Is Capable of Doing a Good Deal of Mischief,'" *Journal of Colonialism and Colonial History*, VI (2005).

46. Johnson to Maisonville, Fort Stanwix, Oct. 8, 1771, in Sullivan et al., eds., *Papers of Sir William Johnson*, XII, 931.

intensified by Pontiac's Rebellion, when the kin network of the French fur trade became apparent. Although France had been defeated, French people remained, and the treachery of numerous Frenchmen became apparent when most refused to aid beleaguered English fur traders.[47]

Tacumwah's appeal to Lernoult for justice demonstrates how anti-French sentiments influenced British Indian policy. Traders like Croghan had repeatedly warned their British superiors that the French traders living in the midst of Indians were more dangerous than the Indians. Croghan not only described the French as far more lazy than Indians, but even French houses acquired the "slovenly" traits of Indian life. This English disdain for the French appears in marked contrast to descriptions recorded for these same villages a decade later by the American geographer Thomas Hutchins. Whereas Croghan described Vincennes as a derelict and unproductive place, Hutchins saw a thriving village with sixty French families who "raise[d] Indian Corn,—Wheat; and Tobacco of an extraordinary good quality;—superior, it is said, to that produced in Virginia. They have a fine breed of horses ... and large stocks of Swine, and Black Cattle. The settlers deal with the natives for Furs and Deer skins to the amount of about 500l. annually. Hemp of a good texture grows spontaneously in the low lands of the Wabash, as do Grapes in the greatest abundance ... Hops large and good ... All European fruits;—Apples, Peaches, Pears, Cherrys, Currants, Goosberrys, Melons, etc. thrive well." Many British officers longed for their orderly English countryside, while Americans viewed the lush fertility of this river valley as ripe for western expansion. Resources mattered greatly to Americans; often the people who lived here were invisible because they lacked the incentive to transform the land.[48]

Many British officers continued to believe that Pontiac's Rebellion had been French inspired. Henry Gladwin, who commanded at Detroit during the revolt, felt that Pontiac's Rebellion was entirely the work of disaffected French traders. Even General Gage fell behind this reasoning. He wrote to the Board of Trade that French, Canadians, and Spanish had stirred up the Indians by circulating rumors that the British were intent on depriving Indians of their lands. That Indians could assert their independence from the French was, in the eyes of many British traders, unimaginable. There is no doubt

---

47. Noble, "Ouiatenon on the Ouabache," in Walthall, ed., *French Colonial Archaeology*, 68.

48. Albert T. Volwiler, *George Croghan and the Westward Movement, 1741–1782* (Cleveland, 1926), 186; Thomas Hutchins, *A Topographical Description of Virginia, Pennsylvania, Maryland, and North Carolina, Comprehending the Rivers Ohio, Kenhawa, Sioto, Cherokee, Wabash, Illinois, Misissippi, Etc. . . .* (London, 1778), 28–29; Burns, *Life in Old Vincennes*, 437–438.

that French traders who married into Indian villages and established linkages through kinship ties were more sympathetic trading partners than nonaligned British traders who lacked Indian kin. British traders quickly discovered that, at villages like Ouiatenon, Indian women were reluctant marriage partners. Instead, the British found it more agreeable to take up residence at trading villages like Kethtippecanuck or Miamitown or to supply the French traders entrenched in Indian households.[49]

Indians shaped daily life in the face-to-face world of these trading villages. Change was ongoing: newcomers were incorporated, populations multiplied, and village life was defined by evolving kin relations. But these changes occurred within the framework of an Indian world, one that was increasingly shaped by Miami hegemony over the Wabash region. Intermarriage had blurred social borders and created new pathways to authority and power, but for generations of children born to Indian mothers and French fathers, the Indians and French were so completely enmeshed that outsiders "had difficulty in ascertaining the racial and cultural borders, if any truly existed, between the two."[50]

49. Gladwin was a British army officer who was commander at Detroit when it was besieged during Pontiac's Rebellion. He had previously served in the disastrous campaign of Edward Braddock and in other actions in the French and Indian War. In 1764, he asked to be returned to England and was subsequently made a major general in 1780. He died in 1791. See Peter E. Russell, "Henry Gladwin," *Dictionary of Canadian Biography Online*, IV, *1771–1800,* http://www.biographi.ca/en/bio/gladwin_henry_4E. Thomas Gage (1719?-Apr. 2, 1787), was a British general, best known for his role as military commander in the early days of the Revolutionary War. Born to an aristocratic family in England, he entered the military service, was assigned to North America, and first saw action during the French and Indian, or Seven Years', War. See S. F. Wise, "Thomas Gage," ibid., http://www.biographi.ca/009004-119.01-e.php?&id_nbr=1895. See also John Clarence Webster, ed., *The Journal of Jeffery Amherst: Recording the Military Career of General Amherst in America from 1758 to 1763* (Chicago, 1931), 315; Gage to Lord Egremont, Aug. 28, 1763, Colonial Office, 42/24, 192, PAC, National Archives, Kew, U.K. British trade goods were shipped directly from London to Montreal and then carried by canoe to the lakes. Even here, the nature of the trade changed as larger freight canoes were constructed to bring increased quantities of trade goods into the Great Lakes. Multiple locations emerged along the Saint Lawrence that produced the *canots de maître,* which were large canoes usually thirty feet in length that carried twelve to twenty men, plus baggage and merchandise. Most frequently, a dozen voyageurs paddled these canoes, which carried up to four tons of trade goods. These freight or transport canoes paddled well in winds that left smaller boats on the shore (White, *Middle Ground,* 137).

50. R. David Edmunds, "George Winter: Mirror of Acculturation," in Sarah Cooke and Rachel B. Ramadhyani, eds., *Indians and the Changing Frontier: The Art of George Winter* (Indianapolis, 1993), 23–41.

Whitehall replaced Versailles, but official correspondence continued across the ocean slowly, making effective governance as challenging as it had been for the French. Imperial decision making rested on the reports of a military hierarchy, which were transmitted first to the governor general and then over the Atlantic to Whitehall. Most problematic in this chain of command were British field officers and their preconceptions about the French. General Gage considered the French system of trade not "worthy of our imitation" and implemented a regulated system of trade by having military officers at five interior posts: Kaministiquia, Michilimackinac, Green Bay on Lake Michigan, Detroit, and Ouiatenon. By limiting the exchange of furs to military posts, Gage thought that he was eliminating French traders, but it was actually the Indians he distanced and alienated. Gage's system was a complete failure and led to continued confrontation with Indians. Pontiac's Rebellion forced the British to honor Indigenous patterns of exchange, although they misread and misunderstood this as a social and economic landscape created by the French. To remain profitable, exchange had to remain a village-level process under the British, and they did not curtail or remove French traders.[51]

British military officers also stripped bare many of the processes of social formation that had facilitated exchange under the French. When the Quebec Act was passed in 1774, it permitted the practice of Catholicism. At Green Bay, Michilimackinac, Fort St. Joseph, Cahokia, and Kaskaskia, Indian women had refashioned and incorporated the kin-based networks of Indian villages into a Catholic, fictive kin network that exchanged furs for trade goods. But the British officers who abhorred Catholicism did little to encourage its practice or to foster the religious and social middle ground of fictive kin. Such prejudices ensured that there were never more than four priests in the western Great Lakes; with so few of them, this social link between French traders and Indian communities slowly disintegrated. Indian women's ability to act as godmothers had brought newly baptized Indians into the trade, but the disappearance of Catholic missionary priests hindered the expansion of those networks.[52]

The British had long believed that, following the French defeat, they would monopolize the profits of the fur trade. They continued to strive toward this state of financial bliss, and it was not until 1812, when fur trade profits in the Canadian Northwest outstripped those of the Ohio River valley, that

---

51. Gage's report is reprinted in Michigan Pioneer and Historical Soceity, *Collections,* XIX, 16–19.

52. Sleeper-Smith, *Indian Women and French Men,* 23–53; George Paré, *The Catholic Church in Detroit, 1701–1888* (Detroit, 1951), 224.

the British left the valley fur trade. Following the American Revolution, the British openly defied the Treaty of Paris and refused to relinquish the western posts of the Great Lakes to the Americans, a refusal arising in part from pursuit of a profitable fur trade. Desire to retain the profits of the fur trade and their prejudices against Frenchmen would lead the British Empire down a disastrous pathway. With the exception of the Iroquois, there were few Indians who fought for the British during the Revolutionary War. The British presence offered Indians a variety of trade goods, and in the mid-eighteenth century, fur traders exchanged British luxury goods for Indian peltry, which lasted until the War of 1812.

Tacumwah's new trading partner, Charles Beaubien, had access to trade silver, which became the most desirable trade good commodity in the Great Lakes. The fur trade initially exchanged furs for European goods like iron kettles, but by the early eighteenth century, with basic necessities met, manufactured cloth reflected the change in Indian demand, and by the mid-eighteenth century, the fur trade incorporated the silver trade.

For important headmen like Pacanne, silver objects were part of everyday dress. Henry Hamilton's sketch of Pacanne depicts his roach haircut and the silver bands around his arms. Trade silver earrings hang down from his earlobes, and silver brooches decorate the sleeves of his shirt. Vast amounts of silver were integral to the trade; we know the cities where these silver objects were made, who manufactured them, what they were worth, and how they were worn by Indians. In the next chapter, we glimpse this highly prosperous Indian world, where trade goods had transformed Indian dress, their houses, and the villages in which they lived.

FIGURE 7. "Pecan, a Native American Chief of the Miami Tribe." Ca. 1776–1778. From Henry Hamilton, "Drawings of North American Scenes and Native Americans," MS Eng 509.2. Houghton Library, Harvard University

5

PICTURING PROSPERITY

The decline of Indian communities has often been blamed on the destructive impact of the fur trade, an explanation that has masked the far more deleterious impact of American and Canadian greed for Indian land in the nineteenth century. Forced removal from their homelands to barren reservation lands proved far more disruptive than exchanging peltry for European goods. Because fur trade stereotypes are difficult to displace, this chapter identifies and reassesses the more destructive biases of the fur trade literature in order to reestablish the positive role of the fur trade in Indian life in the Ohio River valley.

Most fur trade stereotypes assume Indian demise and blame fur traders and merchants for enriching themselves while impoverishing Indians. Supposedly lured to trade goods by the primitive and nomadic nature of their society, Indians' dependence on European goods purportedly reduced them to poverty and destroyed the fabric of daily life. But, as we have seen in the previous chapter, Indians in the Ohio River valley fur trade were well dressed, lived in substantial houses, and experienced unprecedented prosperity.

The fur trade has also been blamed for rampant alcoholism in Indian communities, as unscrupulous traders plied Indians with liquor and cheated them of their furs. The destructive relationship between alcohol and the eighteenth-century fur trade has been exaggerated. This is not to deny that Indians drank to excess, but alcohol in the fur trade served compensating economic, diplomatic, and religious purposes. In the exchange economies of Indian villages, alcohol sealed the terms of agreement, a crucial factor when traders provided goods in advance of the wintering season. Most traders, especially French ones, extended goods on credit to Indians. The next spring, Indians reimbursed traders from the bounty of their winter hunt. Alcohol reinforced these agreements and, more important, sealed alliances. As we have seen in Chapter 3, the Miami combined fall festivals with the calumet ceremony and used alcohol to seal the pathway to peace with the Wea and Mascouten. Although disease undermined the outcome of the ceremonies, the Miami did achieve a lasting peace with the two communities. Alcohol also served other purposes: from a religious perspective, drinking to excess replicated the visions associated with fasting and called forth one's guardian spirit. When alcohol abuse became problematic, Indians developed strategies to deal with these problems, and many moved their villages to escape its ravages. Alcohol was damaging to Indian communities, but not devastating.[1]

Supplying Indians with firearms has been considered one of the most destructive aspects of the exchange process, but exhaustive studies of the French fur trade have demonstrated that guns were a minor part of the trade and that what Indians really wanted, demanded, and received was European cloth. Guns were crucial to warfare, not hunting. Steel traps secured small peltry, and deer were best hunted with bows, since powder burns ruined the pelts. Traditional methods of securing game remained critical in the fur trade. The almost endless supply of peltry in the wetlands and swamplands was exchanged for equally large quantities of manufactured cloth. This led to a flowering of Indian clothing styles and situated Indian women at the heart of the fur trade. Women not only processed all the furs but also created new styles of clothing; they perfected existing designs and redesigned and embellished the manufactured European clothing that came into their households. The revolution in Native dress placed women at the center of the fur trade, enhancing their authority.[2]

1. Peter C. Mancall, *Deadly Medicine: Indians and Alcohol in Early America* (Ithaca, N.Y., 1995), 42–61; Gail D. MacLeitch, *Imperial Entanglements: Iroquois Change and Persistence on the Frontiers of Empire* (Philadelphia, 2011), 35; Maia Conrad, "Disorderly Drinking: Reconsidering Seventeenth-Century Iroquois Alcohol Use," *American Indian Quarterly*, XXIII, nos. 3–4 (1999), 1–11.

2. Dean L. Anderson, "Variability in Trade at Eighteenth-Century Outposts," in John A. Walthall, ed., *French Colonial Archaeology: The Illinois Bounty and the Western Great Lakes* (Urbana, Ill., 1991), 218–236; Anderson, "The Flow of European Trade Goods into the Western Great Lakes Region, 1715–1760," in Jennifer S. Brown, W. J. Eccles, and Donald P. Heldman, eds., *The Fur Trade Revisited: Selected Papers of the Sixth North American Fur Trade Conference, Mackinac Island, Michigan, 1991* (East Lansing, Mich., 1994), 93–115; Rob B. Mann, "'True Portraitures of the Indians, and of Their Own Peculiar Conceits of Dress': Discourses of Dress and Identity in the Great Lakes, 1830–1850," *Historical Archaeology*, XLI (2007), 37–52; Robert S. Du Plessis, "Cloth and the Emergence of the Atlantic Economy," in Peter A. Coclanis, ed., *The Atlantic Economy during the Seventeenth and Eighteenth Centuries: Organization, Operation, Practice, and Personnel* (Columbia, S.C., 2005), 72–94; Sophie White, *Wild Frenchmen and Frenchified Indians: Material Culture and Race in Colonial Louisiana* (Philadelphia, 2012), 4.

Many historians believe that the fur trade led Indians into the abyss of environmental destruction, as they overhunted wildlife, driving the beaver and the white-tailed deer to near annihilation. But beavers are far from extinct, and today's ubiquitous whitetail deer are considered a nuisance in many suburban neighborhoods and a danger on the nation's highways. One well-known historian has viewed Indians as violating the sacred bonds that they had with animals by killing them for their pelts, which led the animals to reciprocate by spreading epidemic diseases. Indians have even been condemned as more environmentally destructive than Euro-Americans for this supposed overhunting. For a long time, fur trade historians assumed that the shift to a trans-Mississippi trade occurred because Indians eliminated fur-bearing animals from lands east of the river. In fact, this shift into the Rocky Mountain West and Canadian Northwest took place because settlers appropriated Indian lands and interrupted Indigenous trapping and hunting. Furs simply became cheaper to harvest in the West rather than the East.[3]

These long-held biases then crept into the New Indian history that emerged in the 1960s and 1970s, when historians came to believe that the extinction of animals left indebted Indians with nothing to trade but their land. In the Great Lakes and Ohio River valley, however, Indian debt was not a result of the fur trade as such, but was usually associated, instead, with manipulative and dishonest merchants. In the Early Republic, the federal government relied on treaty making to extinguish title to Indian lands. Those agreements were sealed by gift giving; corrupt merchants charged exorbitant rates for the goods they supplied to the government and subsequently lobbied the government to pay these debts from the proceeds of land sales. No merchants were more dishonest than the House of Ewing in Indiana, which made a fortune supplying the government with goods at treaty conferences and speculating in Indian lands. While his fellow merchants went bankrupt supplying settler colonists, George Ewing wrote to his brother, "I swear I will have nothing to do with white people, I go for Indian skins—Indian specie, Land, and Treaty allowances in future—Thus my object is singled out, Settled and fixed so I know what to do."[4]

---

3. Calvin Martin, *Keepers of the Game: Indian-Animal Relationships and the Fur Trade* (Oakland, Calif., 1982); Shepard Krech III, *The Ecological Indian: Myth and History* (New York, 2000).

4. Francis Jennings, *The Invasion of America: Indians, Colonialism, and the Cant of Conquest* (1975; rpt., Chapel Hill, N.C., 2010), 102; James Axtell, "The First Consumer Revolution," *Beyond 1492: Encounters in Colonial North America* (New York, 1992), 147–149; Axtell, "The English Colonial Impact on Indian Culture," *The Indian and the European: Essays in the Ethnohistory of Colonial North America* (New York, 1981), 272–315; W. G.

Only in the last decade of the twentieth century did historians begin to seriously question these negative assumptions about the fur trade and Indians. Today, the fur trade is viewed as just one part of a much broader arena of interaction between Europeans and Indians. New France, for one, often sacrificed the profits of the fur trade. Incorporating Indians into French alliances and extending French influence across the colonial landscape proved more important. The fur trade led to interdependence and linked French power to securing the support of Indian allies. Indians remained able to feed, clothe, and shelter themselves without the assistance of the French or, later, the British. Interaction with Europeans was not a downhill slope toward dependence but created a middle ground between Indians and Europeans. Increasingly, the persistence, in fact, the renaissance of Indian societies in the present-day Great Lakes has led to revisions in the fur trade's history.[5]

EVOLUTION OF THE CLOTH TRADE

Although Indian villages along the Wabash were similar to others along the Ohio's tributary network, the Wabash is unique because it affords ample written and archaeological evidence for a reevaluation of the fur trade's impact on the larger region. Rather than demise, the fur trade brought affluence and prosperity to these villages. Indians were drawn here in the late seventeenth century by trade goods available at Albany and by access to the rich peltry of the region's extensive wetlands. Population dramatically increased. In the 1750s, there were twelve villages along the Wabash; by the 1790s, more than twenty.[6]

The expansion of the fur trade along the Wabash provided one avenue through which Indian villages successfully adapted to a changing social landscape and a new economic world. Well before European settlement, Indians had eagerly traded with Old World sailors and fishermen. The goods they received dramatically influenced dress. In those early years of the trade, Europeans looked on in astonishment as Indians cut up metal kettles and transformed them into tinkling bells, hung crucifixes from their necks, transformed

---

Ewing to G. W. Ewing, Nov. 14, 1839, Ewing Family Papers, Indiana State Library, Indianapolis; Robert A. Trennert, Jr., *Indians on the Middle Border: The House of Ewing, 1827–54* (Lincoln, Neb., 1981), 77–78.

5. Richard White, *The Middle Ground: Indians, Empires, and Republics in the Great Lakes Region, 1650–1815* (New York, 1991), 115–119.

6. Helen Hornbeck Tanner, *Atlas of Great Lakes Indian History* (Norman, Okla., 1987), 84–91; Neal L. Trubowitz, "Native American and French on the Central Wabash," in John A. Walthall and Thomas E. Emerson, eds., *Calumet and Fleur-de-Lys: Archaeology of Indian and French Contact in the Midcontinent* (Washington, D.C., 1992), 243.

house keys into earrings, and wove elongated copper tubes into their hair as ornaments. European trade goods that were highly prized quickly spread to distant villages in the Great Lakes, long before the arrival of Europeans. Copper kettles, knives, and glass beads were traded among Native peoples early in the seventeenth century. Exactly when trade goods arrived remains a matter of speculation. Some researchers suggest that foreign objects and materials were present in protohistoric interior sites as early as 1600 — certainly no later than the end of the first quarter of that century in the western Great Lakes. These early trade goods had a social function that was lacking in European society. They were given as gifts, sealed alliances, affirmed marital relationships, and dried the eyes of grieving families, which we know from the Jesuits and from military commanders like Vincennes. Trade goods retained this social dimension, and both the French and English established and maintained Indigenous alliances through the giving of trade goods. Some were crafted to acknowledge the social position of the Indian leaders who sealed those agreements. At the signing of the Treaty of Greenville in 1795, Deaf Man, a Miami leader from the Wabash River valley, was presented with a pipe tomahawk wrought in iron, steel, and curly maple and embellished with decorated silver. The blade of the tomahawk was topped with a pipe, perhaps symbolizing the end of warfare and the start of peace. The tomahawk was then passed down through several generations and eventually purchased from a descendant of Deaf Man and given to the Detroit Institute of Arts. Elaborate pipe tomahawks were symbolic and had little useful function.[7]

An analysis of the types of trade goods transported into the western Great

7. Gift exchange was a "total social fact" that extended beyond its voluntary and individualistic facade and, according to Marcel Mauss, constituted a complex social affair. See Mauss, *The Gift: The Form and Reason for Exchange in Archaic Societies* (1954; rpt. New York, 2000); David W. Penney, *Art of the American Indian Frontier: The Chandler-Pohrt Collection* (Seattle, 1992), 223-226, esp. plate 148, "Miami presentation tomahawk," 224; Kathleen L. Ehrhardt, *European Metals in Native Hands: Rethinking Technological Change, 1640–1683* (Tuscaloosa, Ala., 2005); Chris Gosden, *Archaeology and Colonialism: Cultural Contact from 5000 B.C. to the Present* (Cambridge, 2004), 85; P. Nick Kardulias, "Negotiation and Incorporation on the Margins of World-Systems: Examples from Cyprus and North America," *Journal of World-Systems Research*, XIII (2007), 55–82; Ronald J. Mason, "Rock Island: Historical Indian Archaeology in the Northern Lake Michigan Basin," *Midcontinental Journal of Archaeology (MCJA)*, special paper no. 6 (Kent, Oh., 1986), 211-212; Penelope B. Drooker, "Madisonville Metal and Glass Artifacts: Implications for Western Fort Ancient Chronology and Interaction Patterns," ibid., XXI (1996), 145-190; Robert Mazrim and Duane Esarey, "Rethinking the Dawn of History: The Schedule, Signature, and Agency of European Goods in Protohistoric Illinois," ibid., XXXII (2007), 145-200; White, *Middle Ground*, 122.

Lakes offers a glimpse of how the fur trade changed with the increased availability of European goods. When base metal objects, such as kettles, reached a saturation point, they were supplemented by trade cloth. Initially, trade goods enhanced adornment and status, and only when metal goods were sufficiently numerous were they used for their intended, utilitarian purposes. There is abundant evidence that the volume of trade goods coming into the Great Lakes increased dramatically after 1720, when British and French competition intensified and large transport canoes, *canots de maître,* began to carry much greater quantities of goods into the Great Lakes. The volume of goods entering the Ohio River valley dramatically expanded because Indian villages had access to British traders at Albany; colonial traders from Pennsylvania, Virginia, and the Carolinas; Spanish and French traders from St. Louis; and French fur traders who carried or shipped goods from Montreal to Miamitown, Kethtippecanuck, Vincennes, and Detroit.[8]

Cloth quickly became the most desirable item of exchange as Indian women, who processed the furs, increased the demand for it. Both French and English manufacturers wove specific types of cloth to meet the explicit demands of Indian women. Colonial merchants transmitted instructions back across the Atlantic to England and France in which they carefully detailed the color, style, and even the weave of the cloth meant for Indian consumption. As competition between the French and the British intensified, overseas merchants were continually cautioned by fur traders about the quality of the goods they manufactured and shipped west for the Indian trade. Traders frequently returned goods rejected by Indians, who were highly selective consumers. Indians demanded their cloth in specific colors: "un drap bleu, une raye blanche large comme le petit doight proche de la lizière, et a l'écarlatine rouge." Initially, England surreptitiously imported goods from the French to meet the demands of their Indian customers. As early as 1682, the Hudson's Bay Company's board of directors obtained French blankets and had manufacturers use these as models for the Indian trade. This familiar French cloth was produced cheaper in British mills, and the quality improved when Protestant craftsmen migrated from France to England following the revocation of the Edict of Nantes in 1685. Supportive policies from the English crown allowed the woolen industry to produce superior cloth. A 1701 report from New France claimed that Indians preferred English cloth because those manufacturers more successfully replicated the particular hues favored by Indians. By November 1713, Governor Vaudreuil and the intendant of New France, Michel Bégon, sent a joint letter to Versailles complaining about the

8. White, *Middle Ground,* 137.

excessive price of French cloth and warning that Indians were trading with the British because their goods were cheaper and of better quality. "The fur trade is also considerably diminished by the excessive prices of the merchandise, the English profit from this disagreeable circumstance, draw among them the Indians as much by the cheap prices as by the character of the merchandise which they supply them especially 'des draps de Limbourg et Ecarlatines.'"[9]

By 1714, the situation became so desperate for New France officials that they recommended French suppliers obtain their cloth directly from England. The Quebec merchants pleaded with Versailles for English cloth: "You informed us last year that His Majesty had given orders to have goods manufactured in the kingdom to imitate them which is very much desired ... Srs. De Vaudreuil and Bégon believe that if they could not be obtained in France of this quality it is important for sustaining the Colony that His Majesty should permit them to be sent from England to France to be unloaded on the armed vessels for this colony." In 1714, English cloth was sent to the Quebec merchants, and the next year, when French manufacturers imitated the British cloth, Indians detected the substitute cloth and refused to trade. During the Seven Years' War (1756–1763), with a diminished supply of French trade goods, most Ohio River fur traders simply obtained their cloth directly from English posts such as Albany. The few Quebec merchants who were able to

---

9. Philippe de Rigaud de Vaudreuil served as the governor general of Canada from 1703 to 1725, and Michel Bégon de la Picardière as intendant of New France from 1712 to 1726. See Arthur J. Ray, "Indians as Consumers in the Eighteenth Century," in Carol M. Judd and Ray, eds., *Old Trails and New Directions: Papers of the Third North American Fur Trade Conference* (Toronto, Ont., 1980), 255–271; Gail D. MacLeitch, *Imperial Entanglements: Iroquois Change and Persistence on the Frontiers of Empire* (Philadelphia, 2011), 34–37; Axtell, "First Consumer Revolution," in Axtell, *Beyond 1492*, 125–151; Harold A. Innis, *The Fur Trade in Canada: An Introduction to Canadian Economic History* (1930; rpt. Toronto, Ont., 1956), 78–79; Herbert Heaton, *The Yorkshire Woollen and Worsted Industries: From the Earliest Times up to the Industrial Revolution* (Oxford, 1920), chap. 8, "From the Restoration to the Industrial Revolution: The Period of Progress," 248–281, especially the section entitled "Progress of the Woollen Industry during the Eighteenth Century," 276–281; see also primary accounts, such as Cadwallader Colden, "A Memorial concerning the Fur Trade of the Province of New-York: Presented to His Excellency William Burnet, Esq. ...," in David Hosack, ed., *Memoir of DeWitt Clinton, with an Appendix, Containing Numerous Documents Illustrative of the Principal Events of His Life. . . .* (New York, 1829), 232–245. Colden discussed the English superiority in commodities such as woolens and the disadvantage of the French. He claimed, "The *Strouds* (which the *Indians* value more than any other Cloathing) are only made in *England,* and must be transported into *France* before they can be carried to *Canada*" (Colden, *The History of the Five Indian Nations of Canada Which are Dependent on the Province of New York* [New York, 1747], 32).

supply acceptable cloth did so through circuitous routes. "Escarlatines from England are an indispensable necessity for the beaver trade in Canada. To get these escarlatines, which they have up to the present tried in vain to imitate in France, the Company is obliged to bring them from England to Holland and from Holland to France on neutral boats."[10]

European goods for Indian customers complemented and enhanced traditional crafts rather than displacing existing practices. Cloth was an ideal trade item, and Indian women who lived at Miamitown and Kethtippecanuck had access to both British and French trade goods. Even colonial merchants sought an increasing share of the fur trade profits and often advertised in terms that would make their wares attractive to Indian women. One Philadelphia merchant, who supplied Pennsylvania and Virginia traders, claimed that he had "an assortment of Goods, suitable for the Indian trade, consisting of Indian blanketing ... best French match coats, best blue, red, and black London strouds, white and purple napt halfthicks, [and] ... ribbons, calicoes, linens, [and] vermillion." Anglo-American merchants successfully competed with London by supplying the types of cloth in colors Indian women preferred. Women used ribbons to embellish leggings and, like men, painted their bodies with vermilion. John Heckewelder, the Moravian missionary, described Indian dress and the ways in which Indian women were circumspect in ornamenting their bodies: "The women make use of vermilion in painting themselves for dances, but they are very careful and circumspect in applying the paint, so that it does not offend or create suspicion in their husbands; there is a mode of painting which is left entirely to loose women and prostitutes."[11]

By the mid-eighteenth century, luxury goods had become a crucial part of the Indian trade: silk cloth and ribbons, brocades, tea, fine china, silverware, and tea services. At the end of the Seven Years' War, the fur trade entered an expansionary period. British merchants annually supplied about £135,000 sterling in manufactured goods to fur traders, and, in return, they grossed more than 100 percent profit from furs. In June 1762, Governor Murray of

---

10. Innis, *Fur Trade in Canada*, 79, 86.

11. MacLeitch, *Imperial Entanglements*, 34–36; *Pennsylvania Gazette* (Philadelphia), Dec. 26, 1771. The scarlet and blue cloth woven in the Stroud, or Stroudwater valley of Gloucestershire, retained market popularity with Indians throughout the eighteenth century. Merchants supplying the Indian trade remained in contact with Bristol, which was closer to Gloucestershire and where the cloth was exported more cheaply than in London. For a detailed description of this cloth, see Ruth F. Butler, "Social and Economic History," in William Page, ed., *The Victorian History of the County of Gloucester*, 2 vols. (London, 1907), II, 160, 163–164; John Heckewelder, *History, Manners, and Customs of the Indian Nations Who Once Inhabited Pennsylvania and the Neighboring States* (Philadelphia, 1876), 203.

Canada estimated the fur trade returns from the three major posts: Detroit amounted to 350,000 livres, Michilimackinac was 250,000, and St. Joseph, 60,000. Detroit emerged as North America's most important fur-trading center, drawing its furs directly from the Ohio River valley and extending its market reach south along the Wabash to Vincennes and into the Illinois Country.[12]

As we have seen, Detroit's expansion as a fur trade center and the growth of Miamitown and Kethtippecanuck depended on the Black Swamp and the Wabash River valley and their supply of peltry. Matrifocal households along the Wabash processed large numbers of furs, enabling Indian women to exert a greater influence over the types of trade cloth received in the exchange process. Indian women's skills in scrapping, stretching, and processing peltry determined the amount and types of European trade goods available to their households. Poorly processed furs yielded far fewer trade goods and less desirable trade cloth. When these households of women made clothing, they also influenced the types and range of trade cloth available to them. They created lavish clothing styles and made apparent the successful involvement of their villages in the fur trade, as well as the prosperity of their own households.

We might as well call the fur trade the cloth trade. An analysis of the Montreal Merchants' Records, which contain all the goods shipped into the western Great Lakes during the French regime, shows that more than 60 percent of fur trader expenditures went toward cloth. These invoices detail the amount and types of goods transported from 1715 to 1760, with the specific amounts for each of the western posts. We know the traders, their destinations, and the types of goods carried; and for each piece of cloth, we know the type, size, color, material, and even the place of manufacture. Organizing the trade goods into functional categories shows how Indians used these goods. The largest functional category in this Montreal analysis was cloth and the items needed to transform it into clothing: scissors, thread, and needles. At posts such as Michilimackinac, cloth expenditures accounted for 72.04 percent of a trader's outfit, while at Detroit these percentages were even higher, at 75.58 percent. Most surprising is the low percentage of weapons shipped west. Firearms constituted less than 5 percent of the items brought into by the Great Lakes by French fur traders. Alcohol also played a minimal part in the exchange process. At a post like Ouiatenon, it represented less than 0.2 percent of trader expenditures. Weapon expenditures rank eleventh out of

---

12. Paul Chrisler Phillips, *The Fur Trade*, 2 vols. (Norman, Okla., 1961), I, 546; Michigan Pioneer and Historical Society, *Collections*, 29 vols. (Lansing, Mich., 1886–1912), XIV, 141.

the thirteen functional categories. Traders going to Detroit spent so little on weapons that firearms were not even ranked as a category (Table 1).[13]

Indian woman who could cut, sew, and embellish trade cloth quickly emerged as significant people in their households and community. Clothing became the everyday display of women's handiwork. It was also a measure of the status of a household and even reflected the well-being of an entire village. Women produced clothing for the entire family, and although men knew the rudiments of sewing and could repair or even replace their moccasins, it was women who created the clothing styles that characterized Indian dress in the eighteenth-century Ohio River valley.

Archaeological evidence found in villages along the central Wabash supports the presence of increasingly elaborate forms of Native dress. Cloth disintegrated, but the beads that decorated it remained behind. In the Wea village at Ouiatenon, archaeologists uncovered more than one hundred glass beads in thirteen tubular and seed-embroidery varieties during the first season of excavation. White and ruby red were the most frequent varieties, but there were a multiplicity of other colors of beads, including red-orange, lemon yellow, yellowish green, moderate green, bright green, turquoise, royal blue, and a tubular bead that was white with a red stripe. Even if the evidence of trade cloth has perished, the numerous and colorful beads that adorned the clothing show us the heavily ornamented nature of dress.[14]

Indian women were far more than ordinary seamstresses. Their ability in cutting and joining cloth and their embroidery and beadwork transformed Indian dress into distinctive apparel. Crucial to fur trader inventories were needles and scissors, which converted fine cottons, "worsted strouds" (woolen cloth), and printed cotton or calico into elegant items of clothing. The older women of a household taught young girls how to work with beads and porcupine quills, which required great skill and patience; the embroidery, cutwork designs, ribbonwork, and a multitude of enhancements were practiced and perfected by the older women. Ornamentation was not superficial but possessed symbolic implications, openly expressing the potential for spiritual

---

13. Anderson, "Flow of European Trade Goods," in Brown, Eccles, and Heldman, eds., *Fur Trade Revisited*, 93–117.

14. Walthall and Emerson, *Calumet and Fleur-de-Lys*, 250; Kenneth E. Kidd and Martha Ann Kidd, "A Classification System for Glass Beads for the Use of Field Archaeologists," *Canadian Historic Sites: Occasional Papers in Archaeology and History* (Ottawa, Ont., 1970), I, 45–89; Francis Flavin, "The Adventurer-Artists of the Nineteenth Century and the Image of the American Indian," *Indiana Magazine of History*, XCVIII (2002), 1–29; Gary L. Fogelman, *Glass Trade Beads of the Northeast*, Pennsylvania Artifact Series, booklet no. 70 (Turbotville, Pa., 1991).

TABLE 1. *European trade goods in the western Great Lakes, 1715–1760; rank ordered by trader expenditure*

DETROIT

Ranking	% all Invoices
1. Clothing	75.58
2. Hunting	11.91
3. Alcohol use	4.83
4. Cooking & eating	4.28
5. Adornment	1.73
6. Grooming	.54
7. Tobacco use	.50
8. Woodworking	.46
9. Digging / cultivation	.09
10. Maintenance	.07
11. Amusements	.02
12. Weapons	—
13. Fishing	—

OUIATENON

1. Clothing	55.04
2. Hunting	20.08
3. Cooking & eating	7.22
4. Alcohol	6.95
5. Adornment	5.62
6. Woodworking	2.25
7. Grooming	1.24
8. Tobacco use	1.20
9. Digging / cultivation	.10
10. Amusements	.08
11. Weapons	.02
12. Fishing	.01
13. Maintenance	—

GREEN BAY

1. Clothing	65.08
2. Hunting	18.09
3. Cooking & eating	4.59
4. Alcohol	4.37
5. Adornment	2.95

TABLE 1. *Continued*

6. Woodworking	2.39
7. Tobacco use	1.61
8. Grooming	.87
9. Weapons	.19
10. Digging / cultivation	.07
11. Maintenance	.06
12. Fishing	.03
13. Amusements	.01

Source: Susan Sleeper-Smith, *Indian Women and French Men: Rethinking Cultural Encounter in the Western Great Lakes* (Amherst, Mass., 2001), 126, after Dean L. Anderson, "The Flow of European Trade Goods into the Western Great Lakes Region, 1715–1760," in Jennifer S. H. Brown, W. J. Eccles, and Donald P. Heldman, eds., *The Fur Trade Revisited: Selected Papers of the Sixth North American Fur Trade Conference, Mackinac Island, Michigan, 1991* (East Lansing, Mich., 1994), 107.

---

power as well as the cultural values of Indigenous communities. Cloth resonated with the social, religious, and economic orientation of everyday life. The color and luster of trade cloth gave dress its symbolic value. White and sky blue symbolized purity, peace, the powers of the intellect, and prophetic clarity. Red represented the animate and emotional aspects of life, the destructive nature of armed conflict, and, simultaneously, it promised its wearer spiritual benefit and protection. Even "trinkets and baubles" that Europeans dismissed as trivial possessed symbolic meaning and visually expressed underlying cultural values. Crystal, glass, and silver corresponded with spiritual purity and prophetic clarity. Art historians and Native people have studied trade goods and especially cloth, linking the colors to symbolic meaning and demonstrating the continuity in clothing styles to ongoing ceremonies, such as the Dream Drum and Ghost Dance religions. Over time, dress symbolized ethnic solidarity and differentiated Indian people from the dominant culture. Revitalization movements, such as the Midewiwin, or Grand Medicine Society, stressed the wearing of formal dress and remained crucial to the Ojibwe, where it originated, and spread south among the Potawatomi and other nations in the southern Great Lakes. Mide priests were elegantly clad in elaborate garments and decorative accessories that symbolized their office and power and reflected their connections to traditions and lifeways of the fur trade era. Even present-day public events, like powwow, are highly visible statements that reflect the elaborate traditions of eighteenth-century dress and express the continued vitality of Native American cultures and the negotiated space that exists between white and Native worlds.[15]

The distinctive clothing styles fashioned from trade cloth earned women respect and admiration within their villages. Clothing was highly prized and passed down from one generation to the next. Although we cannot identify these women by name, their tribal identity or clan membership is often evident from the specific embellishments of the moccasins they created. Women created distinctive clothing styles, and everyday items, such as leggings, breechcloths, shawls, and dresses, were transformed through their intricate designs. They acquired the knowledge associated with clothing manufacture: some became proficient in embroidery and cutwork, whereas others relied on beadwork and quillwork to enhance the beauty of their clothes. Any one or a combination of these features transformed cloth into striking designs. Dress was distinctively fashioned to reflect both status and authority for the wearer as well as the creator. These ornate forms of dress were apparent during ceremonial occasions, when different types of cloth were reserved for specialized varieties of dress. In the Midewiwin, which spread throughout the Great Lakes in the eighteenth century, women fashioned elaborate dress for mide priests, accessorizing it with beadwork sashes, bandoliers, and shoulder bags to symbolize their office and power. Elaborate dress was also worn by the candidates and described by Joseph Nicollet when he attended an Ojibwe Midewiwin ceremony in 1837.

> The candidate, man or woman, will make his appearance dressed in the richest, the most beautiful and classical costume of his sex in line with the customs of his nation. A stranger cannot but admire the taste and artfulness revealed by the Chippewa in their way of reconciling elegance with the customs and requisites of modesty and decency.... To them [the Chippewa], these celebrations are a matter of national pride for which men and women prepare themselves long in advance.[16]

When outside observers attended dances, they recorded and often sketched the elaborate clothing worn by the participants. Although this clothing was

---

15. Jocelyn Riley, *Her Mother before Her: Winnebago Women's Stories of Their Mothers and Grandmothers; A Resource Guide* (Madison, Wis., 1995); Penney, *Art of the American Indian Frontier*, 26, esp. 35–65.

16. Martha Coleman Bray, ed., *The Journals of Joseph N. Nicollet: A Scientist on the Mississippi Headwaters with Notes on Indian Life, 1836–37*, trans. André Fertey (St. Paul, Minn., 1970), 209.

frequently buried with its wearer, some valued items were given to household members and close friends. Later, this clothing was often acquired by museums. Today, extensive archives of clothing from the eighteenth-century fur trade are held in Midwestern museums — the Detroit Institute of Arts, the Cranbrook Institute of Science, the Milwaukee Public Museum, the Minnesota Historical Society, and the Field Museum of Natural History in Chicago. Large numbers of these items came from the Ohio River valley.

The seventeenth- and eighteenth-century fur trade world built upon the material richness of the precontact world of the Ohio River valley. Men were the artisans, held in regard because they could skillfully fashion precious stones, minerals, and copper goods into grave goods; their carving and metalwork reflected the status and authority of the deceased. Women had long created garments from animal skins, but the appearance of European manufactured cloth transformed their work, providing them the authority and status formerly accorded male artisans. The great variety of cloth in the fur trade offered them a visible outlet for their creativity, and when cloth was intended for women, they secured more than half the trade goods. At Detroit, almost three-fourths of the trade goods consisted of cloth, most of it transported to the Ohio River valley. Women received a wide assortment of cloth that ranged from coarse cottons to fine linens and silk. Europe produced new fabrics, buttons, beads, and shirts to participate in an expanding global economy, and the Atlantic economy's reach extended into the Ohio River valley, where it created a flowering of Indian dress. Manufactured cloth encouraged women to create intricate garments that signified identity through one's clothes. The color, fabric, and style of clothing in combination with bodily adornments, posture, and manners conveyed the sense of being Indian. Clothing adorned their bodies in specific ways to create a sense of self, of belonging and being part of an Indian world. The act of dressing spoke to their identity as Miami, Shawnee, Wea, Kickapoo, and to the multiplicity of other Native people who lived in this region. For instance, the Shawnee became known for the way in which calico cloth was worn by both men and women (Figure 8). Women manipulated imported goods to create this language of appearance. Dress was not merely a surface phenomenon; people were not just mannequins for their clothes. Shawnee women adapted what was initially a male clothing style from the Cherokee by lengthening blouses and shirts to extend the garment just below the knee.[17] John Heckewelder traveled along the Ohio and de-

17. George R. Hamell, "The Iroquois and the World's Rim: Speculations on Color, Culture, and Contact," *American Indian Quarterly*, XVI (1992), 451–469; Hamell, "Strawberries, Floating Islands, and Rabbit Captains: Mythical Realities and European Con-

scribed how cloth, ornament, and wealth were interrelated in the region. "The wealthy adorn themselves besides with ribands or gartering of various colours, beads and silver broaches. These ornaments are arranged by the women, who, as well as the men, know how to dress themselves in style." Eventually, dress reflected increasing notions of Pan-Indian identity, linking diverse people across the broad span of the Ohio River valley.[18]

Shawnee women began to wear match coats made from cloth but tied in the middle by a string or waistband, and they decorated the edges, sleeves, and bosoms of their calico blouses with an abundance of silver brooches. Men also wore calico shirts with a sash or tied a separate cloth worn around their waists with strings to hold up their leggings. Over their shoulders, they displayed a blanket or robe of various colors and frequently adorned with beads, which they confined by a belt around their body. Both men and women wore leggings and stockings, which they often festooned with streamers of silk ribbons.[19]

David Zeisberger, who lived among the Delaware, described the social distinctions visible in dress.

> Their dress is light; they do not hang much clothing upon themselves. If an Indian has a Match-coat, that is a [wool] blanket of the smaller sort, a shirt and a birch clout [breech cloth], and a pair of leggins, he thinks himself well dressed. In place of a blanket, those who are in comfortable circumstances and wish to be well dressed, wear a stroud, i. e., two yards of blue, red or black cloth which they throw lightly over themselves and arrange much as they would a Match-coat. Trousers they do not wear; but their

---

tact in the Northeast during the Sixteenth and Seventeenth Centuries," *Journal of Canadian Studies*, XXI (1986 / 1987), 451–469; Archer Butler Hulbert and William Nathaniel Schwarze, eds., *David Zeisberger's History of the North American Indians*, Ohio State Archaeological and Historical Society (Columbus, Oh., 1910), 118; see also Heckewelder, *History, Manners, and Customs*; Penney, *Art of the American Indian Frontier*, 49–54.

18. This perspective relies on the work of social archaeologists who explore the intersection of Native people and material culture; see esp. Michael S. Nassaney and Eric S. Johnson, "The Contributions of Material Objects to Ethnohistory in Native North America," in Nassaney and Johnson, eds., *Interpretations of Native North American Life: Material Contributions to Ethnohistory* (Gainesville, Fl., 2000), 1–30; Diana DiPaolo Loren, *In Contact: Bodies and Spaces in the Sixteenth and Seventeenth-Century Eastern Woodlands* (Walnut Creek, Calif., 2008); Robert W. Pruechel and Lynn Meskell, "Knowledges," in Pruechel and Meskell, eds., *A Companion to Social Archaeology* (Oxford, 2004), 3–22.

19. Gail DeBose Potter, "The Matchcoat," *Museum of the Fur Trade Quarterly*, XXXIII, no. 4 (Winter 1997), 2–3; Edwin Earle Sparks, ed., *Incidents Attending the Capture, Detention, and Ransom of Charles Johnson, of Virginia* (Cleveland, 1905), 114.

FIGURE 8. Linen shirt with pierced brooches. Worn by Miami, Shawnee, and Potawatomi women and men. Top brooch is ten centimeters in diameter. Hebenstreit Collection, Ethnologisches Museum, Staatliche Museen, Berlin / Art Reource, NY

hose [leggings], reaching considerably to above the knee and held together by a piece of strowd and extending only to the feet, to some extent supply the place of trousers. If they desire to go in state, they wear such hose with a silken stripe extending from top to bottom and bordered with white coral [beads].[20]

At treaty conferences, the speakers and the men and women who attended were splendidly dressed, and their images were often captured in sketchbooks and later on canvas. These depictions are proof of the widespread Indian use of European trade cloth, to which Indian women added meaningful forms of ornamentation, such as colored ribbons, beads, and trade silver. The fur trade

20. Hulbert and Schwarze, eds., *Zeisberger's History*, 15; see also Diana DiPaolo Loren, *The Archaeology of Clothing and Bodily Adornment in Colonial America* (Gainesville, Fl., 2010), 3–4.

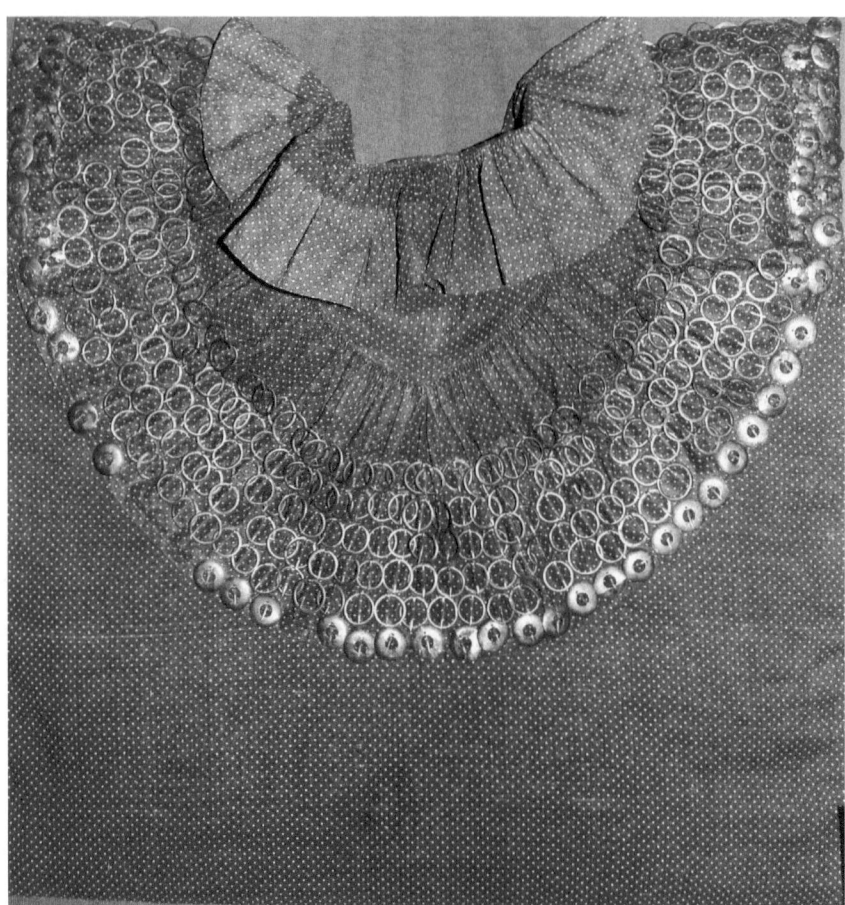

FIGURE 9. Woman's blouse with silver brooches, Miami. Cranbrook Institute of Science. Photography by Tom Stapleton

transformed Indians into remarkably colorful figures. Both men and women displayed the type of dress that most Europeans would have reserved for formal events in sophisticated urban settings. The contrast in clothing styles became noticeable in the late-eighteenth-century Ohio River valley. Most settler colonists wore drab outfits of homespun cloth, owning no more than one or two items of undecorated and rather plain clothing. Indians, on the other hand, wore prized cottons and imported silks, often as part of everyday dress. Places like Detroit, Miamitown, Ouiatenon, and Vincennes emerged as the sources for fashionable cloth and luxury adornments, such as beads and trade silver. Clothing that was initially intended to keep the body warm and dry now emerged as the visual embodiment of one's identity as Indian. This

FIGURE 10. Woman's blouse, Potawatomi. Ca. 1890. Cotton, German silver, and ribbons. American School (19th century) / Detroit Institute of Arts, USA / Founders Society Purchase with funds from Founders Junior Council / Bridgeman Images

fashion, which combined European trade cloth in a distinctive way, was recognized as the "Indian fashion."[21]

Heckewelder, who lived and traveled among Indians, described the dress of the more prosperous Indians:

> Those of the men principally consist in the painting of themselves, their head and face principally, shaving or good clean garments, silver arm spangles and breast plates, and a belt or two of wampum hanging to their necks. The women . . . line their petticoat [with] blue or scarlet cloth blankets or covering with choice ribands of various colours, or with gartering, on which they fix a number of silver broaches, or small round buckles. They adorn their leggings in the same manner; their mocksens . . . are embroidered in the neatest manner, with coloured porcupine quills, and are besides, almost entirely covered with various trinkets; they have, moreover, a

---

21. Mann, "'True Portraitures of the Indians,'" *Historical Archaeology*, XLI (2007), 46; Richard Smith, *A Tour of Four Great Rivers: The Hudson, Mohawk, Susquehanna, and Delaware in 1769*, ed. Frances W. Halsey (1906; rpt. New York, 1989), 149–150.

FIGURE 11. Shawnee coat. Courtesy, Minnesota Historical Society, no. 66.27.1

number of little bells and brass thimbles fixed round their ancles, which, when they walk, make a tinkling noise, which is heard at some distance; this is intended to draw the attention of those who pass by, that they may look at and admire them.[22]

The specific types of clothing that Indian women created and wore in the Ohio River valley influenced clothing styles throughout the Great Lakes. One of the most important aspects of eighteenth-century clothing was ribbonwork: long, woven bands of cloth that were cut and then sewn to emphasize the shape, color, and texture of the garment. Ribbonwork panels were usually lined with a lightweight cotton backing and then attached to trade cloth. This needlework style disseminated via garments that women gave to secure alliances or on clothing that recently married women carried into households outside their home village. Designs invented by one group were often borrowed by other villages. Observances like the Green Corn Ceremony, celebrated throughout the agrarian villages of the Ohio River valley, displayed clothing and facilitated the exchange of new styles of dress and decoration. Miami women were among the first to develop and apply ribbon appliqué work, or cutwork, to their clothing. Their technique involved tight, geometric patterns of cut cloth that were sewn onto the main piece of cloth in a shingled pattern. These same methods were integrated into Potawatomi clothing and then copied by Ojibwe women, who used ribbonwork in the manufacture of their clothes.[23] In Figures 12, 13, and 15, we see three examples: first, the original Miami technique; then the eastern Chippewa (Ojibwe) adoption of that technique; finally, the technique's inclusion into the western Ojibwe hood. These changes in style spread throughout the Great Lakes, traveling along the same water routes used by Indians and fur traders. When the eastern Chippewa (Ojibwe) at Walpole Island applied ribbonwork to their clothing, it spread westward across the Great Lakes and was soon adopted by the Lake Superior Ojibwe. Cutwork techniques were similar: women cut cloth into simple shapes and then sewed it onto an underlying cloth. Usually the applied cutwork was outlined with simple glass beads. In prosperous villages, the techniques of fashioning clothing with cutwork became more and more elaborate. Between 1754 and 1779, fur traders in Pennsylvania, Illinois, and Indiana stocked silk ribbons for the fur trade. The wool cloth referred to as

22. Heckewelder, *History, Manners, and Customs*, 203.
23. Susan M. Neill, "Emblems of Ethnicity: Ribbonwork Garments from the Great Lakes," in Nassaney and Johnson, eds., *Interpretations of Native North American Life*, 147; Donna Kathleen Abbass, "Contemporary Oklahoma Ribbonwork: Styles and Economics" (Ph.D. diss., Southern Illinois University, 1979).

FIGURE 12. Miami skirt. Ring brooches and cutwork applied to black wool trade blanket, tied at the waist and opened in front. A trade blouse or shirt was worn on top of the skirt. Cranbrook Institute of Science. Photography by Tom Stapleton

FIGURE 13. Wearing blanket, Potawatomi culture, 1860–80 (wool and silk). Native American / Detroit Institute of Arts, USA / Bridgeman Images

FIGURE 14. Chippewa leggings. Ca. 1840. Wool cloth, glass beads, silk ribbon, bast fiber straps, and thread. American School (19th century) / Detroit Institute of Arts, USA / Founders Society Purchase with funds from Founders Junior Council / Bridgeman Images

strouds and calicos were a longtime staple of the fur trade. In the 1740s, the silk ribbons that further embellished dress were added to trader inventories in the Ohio River valley. At this same time, silver brooches were also becoming increasingly popular.[24]

Eighteenth-century Miami women incorporated cutwork into their moccasins, as indicated by Figures 16 and 17. Many of the earliest moccasins can be identified by the tight, organized designs and fastidious workmanship of specific women. Later, when nineteenth-century clothing became bold and extravagant, few women achieved the technical skill and ability of these early

---

24. Rachel K. Pannabecker, "Ribbonwork of the Great Lakes Indians: The Material of Acculturation" (Ph.D. diss., Ohio State University, 1986).

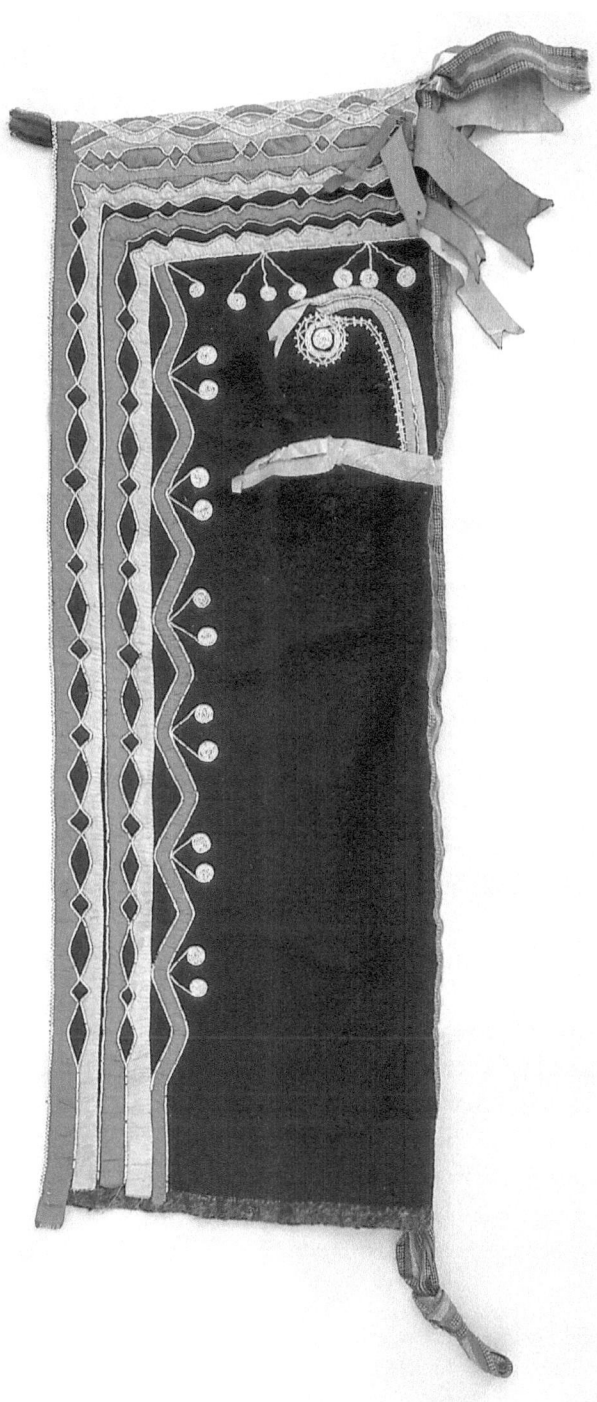

FIGURE 15. Chippewa hood. Ca. 1840. Wool, glass beads, and silk ribbon. American School (19th century) / Detroit Institute of Arts, USA / Founders Society Purchase with funds from Founders Junior Council / Bridgeman Images

FIGURE 16. Miami moccasins. Purchased by Milford G. Chandler from a descendant of Meshinga Mezhas of Wabash, Indiana. Cranbrook Institute of Science. Photography by Tom Stapleton.

designs. John Long, another eighteenth-century Great Lakes fur trader, remarked on moccasins, "Mohawks at the Grand River near Niagara are preferred for their superior workmanship and taste, and are sometimes sold so high as four dollars a pair [!], but in general they may be purchased without ornaments for one dollar."[25]

Indian women increasingly relied on manufactured cloth to create an Indian style of dress that came to characterize most of the fur trade villages of the western Great Lakes and many beyond the region. During the seventeenth century, when trade goods first became accessible in the Ohio River valley, Indian women applied traditional decorative techniques to cloth. As imported cloth became more available, much of what was formerly considered "fancy" clothing became incorporated into everyday dress. These new, expres-

25. James Sterling to John Duncan, May 31, 1795, Sterling to John Vaughan, July 17, 1765, both in James Sterling Letterbook, William L. Clements Library, Ann Arbor, Mich.; Milo Milton Quaife, ed., *John Long's Voyages and Travels in the Years 1768–1788* (Chicago, 1922), 47.

FIGURE 17. Cutwork moccasins. Cranbrook Institute of Science. Photography by Tom Stapleton

sive forms of dress spread west through intertribal trade, traveling from the Ohio River valley to the Mississippi and then from St. Louis to the far reaches of Indian villages in the Plains in the eighteenth century. Intertribal trade also took place between contrasting resource areas, such as between the Miami and Potawatomi and the Ojibwe, where prime coat beaver came south in exchange for corn and clothing, with exchanges frequently sealed through gift giving. Women who excelled in the manufacture of garments did not confine their work to families and relatives but produced items intended as gifts or for exchange and sale. The value of women's work was crucial to the intertribal trade in prepared hides and finished garments, with travelers commenting on the active trade in decorated shirts, leggings, and robes. The potential for trade was a strong incentive for productivity; women who produced specialized garments or who skillfully processed large numbers of hides were accorded higher status. Intertribal trade privileged these women while the fur trade increased the types of materials that women had access to. Fur traders on the Plains supplied the same types of cloth that were first exchanged in the Ohio River valley. One traveler noted that a quilled robe made by a member of a quilling society was worth a pony among the Arapaho or Mandan (Hidatsa). Just as peach pits made their way from Florida to the Ohio River valley and spread west across the Mississippi, well-crafted garments followed the same trade routes.[26]

26. John C. Ewers, *Indian Life on the Upper Missouri* (Norman, Okla., 1968), 21; Mary Jane Schneider, "Women's Work: An Examination of Women's Roles in Palins Indian Arts and Crafts," in Patricia Albers and Beatrice Medicine, eds., *The Hidden Half: Studies of Plains Indian Women* (Lanham, Md., 1983), 114; William C. Sturtevant, "The Meanings of Native American Art," in Edwin L. Wade, ed., *The Arts of the North American Indian: Native Traditions in Evolution* (New York, 1986), 28–33.

After the War of 1812, when Americans arrived in present-day Indiana, they were so diligently engaged in remaking this landscape into settler homesteads that they discounted the Indians who lived in nearby agrarian villages. Most Indian villages were surrounded by extensive wetlands, landscapes that held no interest for most incoming Americans. But the more curious newcomers, like George Winter, who lived in Lafayette, Indiana, near the former village of Kethtippecanuck, sketched nearby Indians, who remained well into the nineteenth century. Winter's work provides visual confirmation of their astonishing dress and even the prosperity of their villages. In his sketchbook he quickly rendered many of the Miami and Potawatomi he encountered and then recorded in his journal the intricate details of their dress. Later, he would transform many of his black and white sketches to canvas, carefully detailing the striking colors of their dress. Winter came to know many of these people and was often included in their festivities. One evening in the early 1830s, Winter sketched the Potawatomi headman, Wewissa, or We-saw, as he danced around the fire. Winter's journal provides the narrative description of those events and a vivid picture of those women who had created We-saw's elegant dress:

> We-saw, a chief, was called upon to open the dance. . . . he commenced dancing around the stakes and fire and to the tapping of the drum. . . . As he danced around he muttered something in Indian, by way of encouragement to others to follow. . . . The squaws, who had been merely passive spectators to the dance, joined in, a dozen very superbly dressed, heightened the effect and beauty of the scene. . . . They wore red and black blankets, as their rich mantles are called. Which are made of superfine broadcloth decorated with colored ribbons and silver ornaments, are very costly, and are worn over the head, covering the body very gracefully, reaching nearly to the ground. . . . Some of the squaws were encumbered with many rows of beads, that I verily believe would weigh ten pounds. . . . Their nether garments were also made of cloth, handsomely bordered with many colored ribbons shaped into singular forms.

There are very few rich renderings of this social landscape by outside observers. Winter offers us rare, dramatic evidence about the nature of their attire and about the physical landscape of Indian villages.[27]

Indian fashion favored certain colors and fabrics, and European traders adjusted their stock to include them. Traders provided woolens in shades of

---

27. Howard H. Peckham, *The Journals and Indian Paintings of George Winter, 1837–1839* (Indianapolis, 1948), 109–110.

FIGURE 18. "Wewissa," or Wesaw. By George Winter. Courtesy of Tippecanoe County Historical Association, Lafayette, Ind. Gift of Mrs. Cable G. Ball

blue, red, and black and often included serge and striped calicoes in "lively Colours to satisfy their many Indian customers." Manufactured clothing demonstrated Indian men's fondness for long, linen hunting shirts that were made in England, which they wore as outer garments and which extended down to their knees. Indian women frequently dyed much of this ready-made clothing, applying plant dyes to produce a range of colors.[28]

Clothing also functioned quite effectively in allowing Indians to judge the attitudes of strangers. The buckskin or linen shirt was widely associated with Indians, and to cross from the south shore of the Ohio to the north shore and into Indian country required "a Calico shirt made in the Indian fashion, trimmed with Silver Brooches and Armplates." Properly attired strangers were assured hospitality. By donning Indian apparel to enter a village, strangers proclaimed their status as friends rather than enemies. White captives experienced this same type of visible transformation following their adoption. When Benjamin Allen was captured by the Shawnee, they took him to their wintering camp at the Licking River and demanded that he remove his clothes. "They brought two calico hunting shirts, sort of red with half the arm worn off, and put them on me ... then tied on a blanket around me, with a buffalo tug; and then tied a piece of blanket round my head. They then patted me on my head, and said, 'Indian.'" Allen's new clothing was the initial step in his adoption.[29]

Clothing also provided Indians the capacity to address a transnational audience, one that included Americans and Englishmen. Different forms of clothing suggested different types of performances. When Indian leaders visited Philadelphia or London, they dressed for the occasion, clad in their finest American clothing (Figures 19, 20), but when they arrived back in their home villages, they donned Indian dress. Joseph Brandt, the loyalist Mohawk who moved his village and his Iroquois followers to southern Ontario, wore American-style clothing when he conducted business with Euro-Americans, but in his community, he wore Indian clothing and painted his face. Historian Timothy Shannon has argued, "The goods that passed between Europeans and Indians, like the rituals involved in their exchange, created a language of speech, deportment, and appearance that crossed cultural barriers." The visual language of Indian dress became more and more apparent in the last decade of the eighteenth century and the first decades of the nineteenth,

---

28. Ibid., 21.

29. *The Journal of Nicholas Cresswell, 1774–1777* (London, 1925), 103; Elizabeth A. Perkins, *Border Life: Experience and Memory in the Revolutionary Ohio Valley* (Chapel Hill, N.C., 1998), 91.

FIGURE 19. "Ca-Ta-He-Cas-Sa — Black Hoof, Principal Chief of the Shawanoes."
Courtesy, Prints and Photographs Division, Library of Congress

FIGURE 20. "Thayeadanega, Joseph Brant, the Mohawk Chief." 1776. By George Romney. Brandt wears ring brooches as earrings and silver wrist bands at his elbows. National Gallery of Canada (no. 8005)

as Indian delegations went to the nation's capital to meet with members of Congress, the president, and religious supporters like the Quakers. Portraits of many of these Indian visitors were commissioned by Thomas Loraine McKenney, who served as the superintendent of Indian trade under Presidents Madison, Monroe, John Quincy Adams, and Jackson. Many of these Indian men and women were depicted in American, rather than Indian, dress. Clothing helped bridge the differences in culture and language that complicated communication. Indian involvement in European-Indian trade and diplomacy manipulated clothing to their advantage. On the New York frontier, Sir William Johnson and Mohawk leader Hendrick used clothing to convey their power and authority. "Johnson's and Hendrick's attention to self-presentation thus contributed to their power. Realizing that an impressive outfit, a well-orchestrated entrance, or a ceremonial presentation of a gift could speak volumes, Johnson and Hendrick used the nonverbal language of appearance to negotiate cultural borders." Henry Schoolcraft, an Indian agent who negotiated with the Ojibwe, confirmed the role that dress played for chiefs engaged in treaty negotiations.

> At dinner to which I invited him, at my tent, and also during the public council following it, he appeared in native costume. But after the close of the council and before we embarked, he came down to the lake shore, to bid us farewell dressed in a blue military frock coat, with red collar and cuffs, with white underclothes, a linen ruffled shirt, shoes, and stockings, and a neat citizen's hat. To have uttered his speeches in this foreign costume, might have been associated in the minds of his people, with the idea of servility; but he was willing afterwards to let us observe, by assuming it, that he knew we would consider it a mark of respect.[30]

In the Ohio River valley, Winter frequently sketched Indians in conversation, in their villages, and along the pathways leading to adjacent villages. His sketches reveal the distinctive nature of dress that was now part of daily life. Also visible are many of the stylistic innovations related to dress: long shawls were added to the clothing of both men and women, while men wound fancy trade cloth into turbans to cover their heads.

SILVER

During the earliest years of the French trade, silver became prominent as a commodity and quickly replaced shell ornamentation (Figure 23). It proved so popular in the western Great Lakes that Montreal and Quebec silversmiths were soon melting down silver coins to produce ornaments. Fearing that the fur trade would quickly absorb the colony's hard currency, the

---

30. Timothy J. Shannon, "Dressing for Success on the Mohawk Frontier: Hendrick, William Johnson, and the Indian Fashion," *William and Mary Quarterly*, 3d Ser., LIII (1996), 26; Phillip P. Mason, ed., *Schoolcraft's Expedition to Lake Itasca* (East Lansing, Mich., 1958), 56. McKenney's images of Indian visitors were on display at the Smithsonian Institution, where they were destroyed by fire in 1865.

FIGURE 21. Untitled (Indian women on hilltop). By George Winter. Courtesy of Tippecanoe County Historical Association, Lafayette, Ind. Gift of Mrs. Cable G. Ball

New France governor, Claude de Ramezay, in 1704 warned, "There will be much embarrassment in future for the commerce of the country when there is no more money." In Quebec, it became illegal for any "goldsmiths, jewelers and other artificers in gold or silver, to deface any money coins for the purpose of employing them in their products, on pain of the galleys for life."[31]

Silver became such a ubiquitous feature of the exchange process that its presence is the single best criterion for dating archaeological sites during the Late Historic period, from 1760 to 1820. By the end of the eighteenth century, trade silver brooches were a common medium of exchange in the Ohio

---

31. William Henry Carter, *North American Indian Trade Silver* (London, Ont., 1971), 36–37; George Irving Quimby, *Indian Culture and European Trade Goods: The Archaeology of the Historic Period in the Western Great Lakes Region* (Madison, Wis., 1966), 91–102.

FIGURE 22. "Indian Burial, Kee-Waw-Nay Village, 1837." By George Winter. Courtesy of Tippecanoe County Historical Association, Lafayette, Ind. Gift of Mrs. Cable G. Ball

River valley. Trade silver transformed female clothing and embellished male bodies. Silver manufactured for the trade included gorgets, brooches, crosses, armbands, wristbands, and earbobs. Less common were earwheels, hair pipes, hair plates, animal effigies, lockets, hatbands and crowns, and cradle board decorations. Silver worn by women quickly absorbed the largest portion traded in the Ohio River valley.[32]

32. In O. M. Spencer's captivity narrative, he noted that the woman with whom he lived "received presents of venison and skins and brooches, the common circulating medium

FIGURE 23. "Saga Yeath Qua Pieth Tow, King of the Maguas." 1710. By Jan Verelst. This is an ancestor of Joseph Brant who was presented to Queen Anne in 1710. His shell earbobs presage the shape of future trade silver ornaments. Library and Archives Canada / John Petre collection / c092418k

TABLE 2. *Trade silver shipped to George Morgan*

6 hair plates	@ 30 / 180.0	7 doz. & 4 large do.	5. ea 440.0
4 ditto	@ 25 / 100.0	13 doz. smaller do.	2 for 5 / 32.10
4 ditto	@ 20 / 80.0	201 brooches	2 for 5 / 255.0
23 ditto	@ 15 / 345.0	24 heart brooches	4 for 5 / 30.00
2 ditto	@ 10 / 20.0	19 medals	5 / ea 95.00
51 hair pipes	@ 5 / 255.0	53 silver Morris bells	2 for 5 / 132.10
11 pair ear bobs	@ 5 / 55.0	4 wrist bands	5 / ea 20.00
25¾ doz. silver rings	6 for 5 / 257.10	27 small heart drops	8 for 5/10.10
18 doz. smallest brooches	8 for 5 / 135.0	5 moon shells	15 / 75.00
15 doz. smallest crosses	8 for 5 / 112.10	50 rings with stones	2 for 5 / 125.0
6 doz. & 2 larger do.	4 for 5 / 92.10	[glass]	
35 ditto larger do.	2 for 5 / 87.10		
£2941.10			

Source: George Morgan at Ft. Pitt to His Partners in Baynton, Wharton and Morgan in Philadelphia, Oct. 18, 1767, Baynton, Wharton and Morgan Papers, Historical Society of Pennsylvania.

Silver brooches, large, medium, and small, transformed Indian women's daily dress. They were the most frequent item in mid-eighteenth-century fur trade ledgers, and they are among the most abundant silver items in contemporary museum collections. Silver brooches were such a common item of the trade that they remain readily available in antique gift shops or at auctions. Most of the brooches that museums acquired came from archaeological excavations, primarily in the Ohio River valley and Great Lakes region. Once the French left the Ohio River valley fur trade and backcountry, colonial traders went west to meet the increasing demand for trade goods. The item most frequently ordered was trade silver. George Morgan's extensive order for silver ornaments is typical of the orders received by Philadelphia merchants.

During the last decade of the eighteenth century, when Indians' access to their homelands was being contested by the government, Indian women used silver, especially brooches, as one means of securing wealth. Such brooches were easily detached from clothing and used as currency. The most popular brooch forms were circular, ornate discs or round, pierced brooches with a

---

among them." See Milo Milton Quaife, ed., *The Indian Captivity of O. M. Spencer* (Chicago, 1917), 86; Quimby, *Indian Culture and European Trade Goods*, 93.

hinged pin that fastened the brooch to the garment. Plain, circular brooches were also popular but lacked the cut perforations and were often embellished with simple, geometric designs. These round brooches were often worn in groups to produce a massed effect, a look reminiscent of chain mail or flexible armor.[33]

The vast quantity of silver ornaments that entered the Great Lakes was produced by an identifiable group of men. The silversmiths who skillfully crafted ornaments of good quality signed their work with a personalized mark or symbol. Most silver ornaments were imported directly from Montreal silversmiths, but there was also a fair quantity of silver manufactured in London, using a well-established system of hallmarks and date letters that identifies the year of manufacture. Silver ornaments were also fashioned by the Spanish and by silversmiths in Philadelphia, Boston, and New York, where most were produced without any systematic form of identification. Indicative of the importance of the silver trade was the sizable number of silversmiths who relocated to the Great Lakes. John Kinzie settled among the French and Indians at the Glaize on the Maumee River and was both a silversmith and fur trader in the Ohio River valley. He joined a substantial circle of silversmiths, most of whom lived and worked in Detroit. The best known were Garret Greverat, who died in 1790; Dominique Riopelle, who frequently appeared in fur trade account ledgers; Amable Maillou, who was the earliest known silversmith working at Detroit; and Lafertie, who became a Detroit resident and purchased a house and lot from the Forsythe fur-trading company. Antoine O'Neal, François Ranvoyzé, Jacques Page, and Michel Lavasseur also worked as silversmiths in the Great Lakes. The popularity of silver encouraged the British to rely on it as a reward for their most faithful allies. In 1781, the British Indian Department at Detroit had more than 18,600 silver ornaments in inventory. That year, when the British met with the Miami at Detroit, they specifically requested silver gifts: "We hope you be good enough to give us in profusion of that Shining Metal, an ornament which draws the attention of the Warriours."[34]

The amount of silver that Indians wore amazed the first settler colonists, especially the Kentuckians. Squatters relied on the valuable silver ornaments plundered during Indian raids to secure household necessities: in return for

---

33. James W. Van Stone, "Indian Trade Ornaments in the Collections of the Field Museum of Natural History," *Fieldiana,* N.S., XIII (Chicago, 1989), 1–40, esp. 5.

34. [Frederick Haldimand], "At a Conference Held by Maj'r A. S. De Peyster Commandant of Detroit and Dependencies etc. etc. etc. with a Party of Miamis Just Arrived from the Miamis Town," Oct. 29, 1781, Haldimand Papers, Michigan Pioneer and Historical Society, *Collections,* X (Lansing, Mich., 1887), 532–533.

FIGURE 24. Trade silver eagle brooch. Private collection. Photography by Jacki Hawthorne

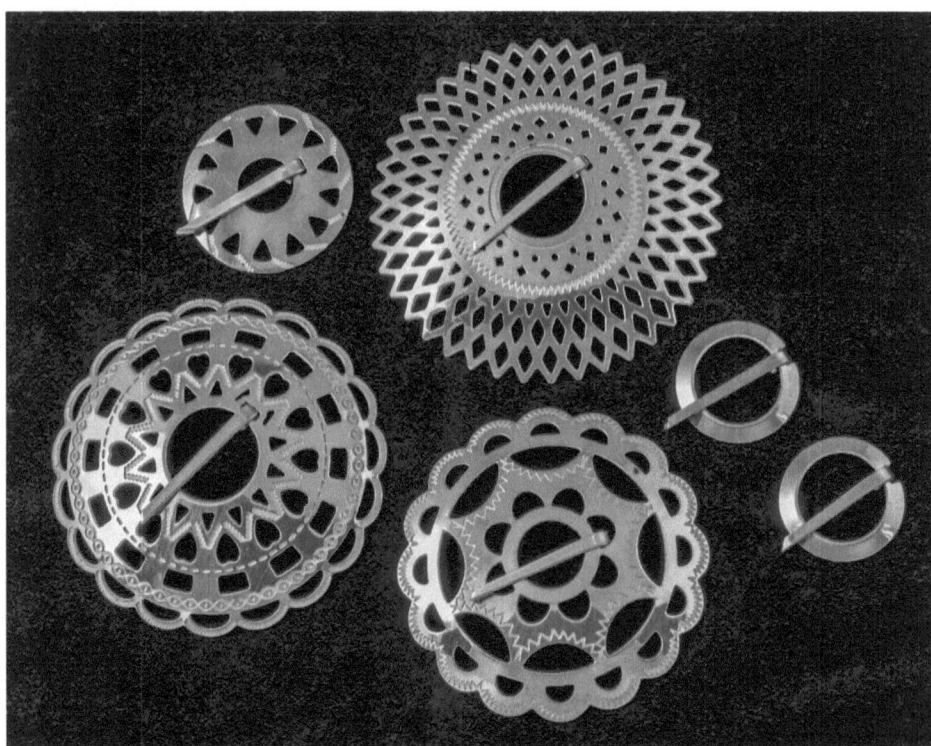

FIGURE 25. Pierced brooches. Private collection. Photography by Jacki Hawthorne

"3 silver broaches," Samuel Shepard "bought a rifle gun and a small copper kettle." On Joseph Bowman's campaign in 1779, two soldiers described a man's shirt that held 110 silver brooches and a woman's outfit that had "five hundred silver brooches stuck in her shift, stroud, and leggings." On this foray across the Ohio, militia leader Josiah Collins recalled that it took three days to divide the booty from an Indian village, where they also secured "163 head of horses . . . [and] one squaw's gown in which were 1,100 silver brooches." Winter sketched Indian women who had silver brooches so closely aligned that they bore the appearance of silver shawls. Henry Hamilton's sketch of Pacanne (Figure 7) showed off the silver ornaments in his ears and around his neck. Indian men wore silver ornaments plaited in their hair, and many Indians wore the silver bracelets on their arms, silver half-moon gorgets around their necks, and silver bands around their upper arms.[35]

The most prolific silversmiths were located in Montreal. Narcisse Roy,

35. "Extracts from the Journal of Samuel Shepard," Apr. 10, 1787–Dec. 3, 1796, M–683, microfilm, Special Collections, University of Kentucky, Lexington; Perkins, *Border Life*, 131.

FIGURE 26. Native American earrings. Ca. 1800. Silver. American School (19th century). © Chicago History Museum, USA / Bridgeman Images

Robert Cruikshank, and Joseph Schindler produced vast quantities of silver ornaments for the trade. Between August 1797 and April 1801, the McGill Company of Montreal, one of the most important trading firms in the Great Lakes, spent more than 4,184 pounds sterling for silver ornaments. In 1801, Narcisse Roy received 342 pounds sterling in payment for about 9,000 silver ornaments. That same year, Robert Cruikshank, who had several apprentices, produced and supplied more than 49,000 silver pieces for the trade. If we are to assume that the volume of production stayed constant for a ten-year period, Cruikshank produced more than one million pieces of trade silver in his lifetime. It is highly unlikely, given preindustrial forms of production, that one smith could have produced this many objects. Cruikshank did, however, employ a large number of apprentices. All his pieces were handmade, and after

Picturing Prosperity 201

being formed and cast, they still had to be hand-finished and engraved. These silver pieces were crafted to reflect the demands of specific chiefs; animal symbols indicated clan membership.[36]

Indians attached value to trade goods that were far beyond the utilitarian meaning that Europeans attributed to a new gun, a shirt, or a metal tool. In fact, many trade items, such as guns and tomahawks, were transformed into works of art by silversmiths. Many of these items are now housed in museum collections. Indians paid high prices for these valued objects (Table 3). By the end of the eighteenth century, silver items transcended the ethnic distinctiveness of different Ohio River villages. Indeed, for outsiders, the use of silver made it difficult to distinguish Miami from Potawatomi, Shawnee from Delaware, or Wea from Kickapoo. The growing similarity in eye-catching silver decoration and in clothing styles paralleled the evolving Pan-Indian movement, which emerged at the end of the Revolutionary War. Increasingly, clothing styles led to a homogeneous Indian appearance. For Indians in the Ohio River valley, identity was apparent from the decoration applied to moccasins, such as the cutwork style of the Miami or the beadwork patterns of the Delaware. Tenkswatawa (Figure 27) railed against European trade goods, but his dress reflected the trends apparent in Indian villages in the Ohio River valley, Great Lakes, and along the Atlantic coastal region.

CRAFTING A PAN-INDIAN WORLD

At the end of the eighteenth century, Indian dress flourished as cloth, glass beads, silk ribbons, and silver were reshaped for Indian consumption. European trade goods were incorporated into clothing and signified the economic and spiritual well-being of the households and villages in the Ohio River valley. The patterns that arose during this era remain a crucial part of Native dress; the regalia of ceremonies and powwows enables American Indians to literally clothe themselves in their unique heritage.

The daily interaction among American Indians and French, English, and Spanish fur traders brought together very different people. When the fur trade was at its eighteenth-century height, Indigenous dress exhibited hybrid cultural forms, and these new styles spread rapidly westward to other villages. The syncretism of dress was indicative of the dramatic changes in American Indian lives in the Great Lakes region. Rather than leading down the path to ruin, the fur trade exposed Indians to European trade goods, which they acquired and appropriated for their own use and to which they gave new meanings. Native agency remained at the fore, and the power relations between

---

36. Quimby, *Indian Culture and European Trade Goods,* 93, 99.

TABLE 3. *Trade silver values at Albany*

Indian Goods	To be Sold for—
Large Silver arm Bands	4 Beaver or 5 Bucks
Small Ditto Ditto	3 Beaver or 4 Bucks
Wrist Bands	2 Bucks
Womens Hair Plates	3 Beaver or 4 Bucks
Silver Brooches	1 Rac[c]oon
Large Cros[s]es [up to 5½"]	1 Small Beaver or Med. Buck
Ear Bobs	1 Doe

Source: "Regulations for the Trade at Fort Pitt," in James Sullivan et al., eds., *The Papers of Sir William Johnson* (Albany, N.Y., 1891), III, 532.

the Indians and their foreign visitors were not yet unequal. In the early eighteenth century, the few Europeans who lived in this highly populated Indian world found intermarriage the most frequent path to acceptance into village life. With the rise of trading villages like Kethtippecanuck and Miamitown, traders with an array of goods became welcome commercial partners, and the intrusion of the marketplace created impersonal exchanges when marital alliances were no longer crucial to acceptance. During this same period, the hybridization of cultures became increasingly apparent. The images displayed in this chapter, the written historical records, and the archaeological evidence reflect a past in which change was part of daily life for Indians. Indian identity has often been elided or silenced in the documentary record because of our static portraits of traditional Indians and our belief that authentic Indians were unchanging. We tend to categorize the eighteenth-century Ohio River valley as inhabited by Indians and by Europeans cast as different and oppositional cultures when, in fact, their dress, lifestyles, and even occupations were in flux. We strip Indians of their Indianness simply because they were as prone to change as any group of human beings or because we see their adoption of selected French practices as a sign of their aspiring to be Frenchmen. Instead of addressing the remaking of social practices from an Indigenous perspective, we transform Indians into French, métis, or a static peoples separated into unbridgeable ethnic categories. Rarely do we imagine the evolution of a new social world as Indians integrated diverse peoples into their cultures. The pictures displayed in this chapter are not those of a vanishing race but of a colorful, multiethnic society fashioned by a vibrant fur trade world.

In the nineteenth century, the villages of the Great Lakes world were drawn

FIGURE 27. "Tens-Kwau-Ta-Waw, the Prophet." By Henry Inman, after a painting by Charles Bird King. In Thomas L. McKenney and James Hall, *History of the Indian Tribes of North America: With Biographical Sketches and Anecdotes of the Principal Chiefs,* 3 vols. (Philadelphia, 1848–1850), II, plate opposite 47. Photo Courtesy of the Newberry Library (Ayer E.77M.131)

FIGURE 28. "The Son, a Miami Chief." 1827. By James Otto Lewis. Completed at the Treaty of Mississinewa, Indiana, in 1827. Wisconsin Historical Society, Madison, WHS-26901

FIGURE 29. "Nicholas Vincent Tsawanhonhi, Principal Christian Chief, and Captain of the Huron Indians...." By E. Chatfield. Vincent wears a gold medal presented to him by George III; beneath is a silver medal given to him by George II. He wears silver arm and wrist bands and a silver nose ornament. McCord Museum M20855

FIGURE 30. Cherokee portrait. Ca. 1791. By William Hodges. Courtesy of Hunterian Museum at the Royal College of Surgeons of England

together into a larger Pan-Indian world—the work, not so much of Tecumseh and Tenskwatawa, but of earlier women's involvement in the fur trade: women facilitated intermarriage, processed huge quantities of peltry, demanded and secured large amounts of cloth, and transformed trade cloth into beautiful dress that first displayed and ultimately eased the ethnic divisions of the various villages that settled in the Ohio River valley. Which traders were incorporated into this village world was determined by the people who lived there; women were central to decision making, selecting which outsiders to include in their households.

FIGURE 31. "Mas-saw in Fulton County." 1837. By George Winter. Courtesy of Tippecanoe County Historical Association, Lafayette, Ind. Gift of Mrs. Cable G. Ball

When growing divisions in material wealth threatened to splinter villages and fragment this diverse world, Indians, rather than outsiders, took measures that leveled those disparities. Villages intervened to level and reallocate individual accumulations of wealth. In his captivity narrative, William Biggs described how the Kickapoo attempted to redistribute the lopsided accumulation of material goods: "I was taken to that town, there was a number of Indians went from that town to the old Kickapoo trading town. They took me with them to dance what is called the 'Beggar's Dance'. It is a practice for the Indians every spring, when they come in from their hunting ground, to go to the trading towns and dance for presents; they will all go through the streets and dance before all the traders' doors. The traders then will give them presents, such as tobacco, bread, knives, spirits, tomahawks, etc." In this Indian world, authority and respect emerged from generosity, not the individual accumulation of wealth.[37]

As we shall see, Indians from the northern Great Lakes and the eastern seaboard came from great distances to defend this village world from the United States' armed intrusion. The fur trade established new pathways of trade that linked villages in the northern Great Lakes with those in the Ohio River valley. When corn harvests failed in the north, Indian villages along the Wabash provided surplus corn. In exchange, the Ojibwe provided winter furs or highly prized eagle feathers. Clothing was exchanged along these same pathways, and marital alliances sealed and expanded those trade routes.[38]

Between the Seven Years' War and the Revolutionary War, most of the remaining Shawnee and Delaware moved west and settled adjacent to the Miami. Some were also incorporated into the Wyandot villages at Fort Sandusky; others were absorbed into established Shawnee and Delaware villages. Populations increased dramatically because of the large number of refugees but also because of natural increases among existing Indian populations. Except for the Illinois to the west, most villages recovered from the initial onslaught of diseases associated with encounter.

This population increase was endangered by Anglo-American newcomers moving into the region before Indian lands were ceded. Well-dressed Indians living in prosperous villages were an enticing target for Americans who squatted on Indian lands and who considered Indian people fit objects for plunder. They regarded Indians as "savages" — despite the material evidence to the contrary.

---

37. *Narrative of the Captivity of William Biggs among the Kickapoo Indians in Illinois in 1788, Written by Himself* (New York, 1922), 31. See also Matthew Brayton, *The Indian Captive: A Narrative of the Adventures and Sufferings of Matthew Brayton in His Thirty-Four Years of Captivity among the Indians of North-Western America* (Fostoria, Oh., 1896).

38. John L. Comaroff and Jean Comaroff, *Ethnography and the Historical Imagination* (Boulder, Colo., 1992); Mann, "'True Portraitures of the Indians,'" *Historical Archaeology*, XLI (2007), 49.

6

PLUNDER AND MASSACRE

PLUNDER

An incredible variety of trade goods were coming into the Ohio River valley by the middle of the eighteenth century. The appearance of Indians and the transformations in their daily lives reveal the unprecedented level of luxury goods introduced into the exchange process by fur traders. Indian leaders welcomed English traders, American visitors, and Indian captives into their homes to sit down and share afternoon tea with their families. Well-known leaders, such as Black Hoof, Little Turtle, and Blue Jacket, enjoyed many of the same luxuries as wealthy colonists along the Atlantic seaboard. Under the English, Indians became consumers of tea and displayed the material accoutrements associated with tea drinking. China teapots rested on silver trays, surrounded by silver spoons and elegant cups. Many chiefs' homes were tastefully decorated: visitors remarked on the elegance of the interior furnishings, and one visitor was surprised to discover that his Indian host slept in a curtained bed. This new world of the luxury trade was apparent in British military diplomacy. During the Revolutionary War, Indians demanded an increasingly steep price in trade goods to seal their alliances with the British. By 1780, Governor Haldimand was angered by the amount of money expended on presents to the Indians and considered the cost of gift giving to have far exceeded the benefit. Instead of recognizing Indians' choices in these exchanges, Haldimand blamed fur traders for creating a desire for luxury goods among Indian consumers and inflating the cost of diplomacy. He believed that "indulgence has created wants with the Indians, which otherwise they would never have experienced, such as fine Saddles and many Luxuries, carefully exhibited to their view by the grasping Trader[s]." During the Revolutionary War, when Indians were drawn to their former French allies, Indian loyalty along the Wabash and in the Illinois Country could only be bought by the British with masses of trade goods. The British had lost control over Kaskaskia, Cahokia, Prairie du Rocher, and St. Philip in 1778 and Vincennes in 1779. In 1780, Arent DePeyster, the commander at Detroit, relied on a sufficient quantity of goods to secure the allegiance of the Indians in the Illinois Country and along the Wabash River. The Wabash Indians came across as "high and insolent" and far from cooperative, but DePeyster's strategic gift giving paid off. The American alliance with France and Spain posed the threat of invasion by enemy partisans at St. Louis, but the upper Wabash villages, led by Little Turtle, successfully thwarted Augustin Mottin de La Balme's 1780 French expeditionary force. The defeat propelled Little Turtle to prominence as a victorious war chief, although his loyalty to the British came at a steep price. The Wabash villages collected 638 yards of scarlet cloth, 180 pieces of crimson and scarlet strouds, more than 3,000 yards of tinsel lace, 1,080 yards of calico, 1,575 yards of linen, 24 bales (950 pairs) of blankets, 2,142 yards of strouds, 638 yards of scarlet strouds, as well as vast quantities of tobacco, looking glasses, vermilion, and copper and brass kettles. Warriors were almost fully armed with four hundred to five hundred Indians acquiring 380 guns. This exorbitant cost of Indian loyalty shocked Haldimand, leading him to question DePeyster's expenditures.[1]

Wabash villages were reluctant British allies, angered by the Treaty of Fort Stanwix in 1768, when Sir William Johnson and his deputy George Croghan met with the Six Nations, and Iroquois negotiators relinquished all claims to the lands south of the Ohio. The treaty line ran near Fort Pitt and followed the Ohio as far east as the Tennessee River in what is now western Pennsylvania, Kentucky, West Virginia, and New York. The Shawnee vigorously protested this cession, which encompassed rich hunting lands shared with the Cherokee, Wyandot, Huron, Ojibwe, Odawa, and Miami. They now viewed the British government with resentment and suspicion.

When George Rogers Clark seized Fort Vincennes from the British in 1779, Ohio Indians, still bitter about the Treaty of Stanwix, failed to come

---

1. Milo Milton Quaife, ed., *The Indian Captivity of O. M. Spencer* (1917; rpt. New York, 1961), 46–48; Anne Crabb, "'What Shall I Do Now?' The Story of the Indian Captivities of Margaret Paulee, James Hoy, and Jack Callaway, 1779–ca. 1789," *Filson Club History Quarterly*, LXX (1996), 376; Arent DePeyster to Frederick Haldimand, May 27, 1781, "Account of Sundry Goods for Indian Presents Sent to Detroit Addressed to Major DePeyster Commanding There," in Michigan Pioneer and Historical Society, *Collections*, X (Lansing, Mich., 1887), 481–485. The Miami lost five warriors in the confrontation with La Balme, but thirty Frenchmen died—including La Balme himself. See Andrew R. L. Cayton, *Frontier Indiana* (Bloomington, Ind., 1998), 147–148; Bradley J. Birzer, "French Imperial Remnants on the Middle Ground: The Strange Case of August de la Balme and Charles Beaubien," *Journal of the Illinois State Historical Society*, XCIII (1998), 132–133.

MAP 12. Fort Stanwix treaty line, 1768. Drawn by Ellen White

to British lieutenant governor Henry Hamilton's aid. Pacanne, who had traveled with Hamilton to Vincennes, watched silently as Clark's men recaptured the fort. Young Tobacco, the leader of the nearby Piankeshaw village, even offered Clark the support of 100 warriors. It was not surprising that, following Clark's victory, DePeyster would be willing to pay the high price needed to gain Indian support and counter American advances west of the Appalachians.

Sadly for the Indian villages along the Wabash that had aided or refused to fight against Clark, his seizure of Kaskaskia and Vincennes was to have dire consequences for western Indians. Many Virginians who fought alongside Clark remained in the west, built fortified settlements south of the Ohio, and brought new levels of brutality to the region. Violence escalated as newly recruited militia marched west to join Clark's forces, plundering Indian camps and villages. Many backcountry men had heard stories from colonial frontier traders about affluent Miami and Shawnee villages; others had raided

212 *Plunder and Massacre*

Indian encampments and villages during their overland travels to Vincennes. Clark's recruiters promised these volunteers the loot to be gained from attacking Indian communities. Fifteen-year-old Daniel Trabue accompanied his brother's militia unit and described the wealth to be had from such ventures. When the militia accidentally stumbled on a small Indian group, the Indians fled, and the Americans ransacked their camp. The Americans immediately detoured to Booneville to sell their ill-gotten gains: "We found 7 packits, 5 boughs and arrows, 3 shot bags and powdir horns, several blankets, several new shirts, new fine leggans full of silver Broaches, brich cloaths full of silver broaches, one brass kittle, and many other things. . . . We sold the Indean plunder in the Fort on Munday at vandue and it Fetched Fifty shillings for each man. Lucust got no part of the plunder. The negro boy got his shear. I bought some of this plunder, some nise wamp um and a shot bag and powder horn, etc." Looting proved a valuable source of income, with militia units often ignoring their orders to march west in haste.[2]

George Rogers Clark modeled how he expected his militia followers to deal with Indians. Rather than negotiate with them, Clark scorned, intimidated, and killed. In one instance, he tomahawked four British allied Indians, scalped them, and — if British rumors were true — shook hands with Lieutenant Governor Hamilton with blood still on his hands. The capture of Vincennes led to constant demands for plunder from his militia, who desired "some enterprise [that] might be undertaken, to enable them to perform some exploit. Detroit was their object." Clark shared his men's desire to conquer Detroit, but he lacked the resources needed to launch a successful campaign. He was hampered by supply shortages and distractions. He had encouraged his men to raid prosperous villages along the lower Wabash, and they quickly discovered the appeal of plundering nearby Indian towns rather than trudging toward distant Detroit.[3]

Well-dressed and well-supplied Indians on the north bank of the Ohio contrasted in appearance with the impecunious militia accompanying Clark and the squatters occupying the Kentucky grasslands. Crossing the river into Indian Country was a profitable venture for many penniless Kentuckians. Though it was often obscured by racial antipathy, greed inspired American raids along this Indian frontier. Many of Kentucky's earliest settlers possessed

---

2. Chester Raymond Young, ed., *Westward into Kentucky: The Narrative of Daniel Trabue* (Lexington, Ky., 1981), 46–47.

3. Craig Thompson Friend, *Kentucke's Frontiers* (Bloomington, Ind., 2010), 105–106; John D. Barnhart and Dorothy L. Riker, *Indiana to 1816: The Colonial Period* (Indianapolis, 1971), 208; Cayton, *Frontier Indiana*, 84.

little beyond the clothes that they wore as they headed west. There was substantial profit to be made when raiders secured Indian clothing, household goods, and, especially, trade silver ornaments. Auctions took place regularly along the Kentucky frontier as returning raiders sold the booty and then divided the profits among themselves. Kentuckian Josiah Collins noted that his involvement in a successful raid across the Ohio gained him a share of "163 head of horses . . . [and] one squaw's gown in which were 1,100 silver brooches." When Colonel John Bowman launched an expedition against the Shawnee town of Chillicothe in May 1779, shortly after the capture of Vincennes, the participants first "agreed to have a sale of the horses and other booty and then make an equal division of the amount realized." In addition to securing 163 horses, the participants also acquired "strouds, clothes, leggings, shirts, . . . and a great variety of English goods."[4]

Loot from Indian villages transformed the lives of poor, white settlers like Samuel Shepard. He came home from Bowman's expedition with a kettle and three silver brooches, which he bartered for "a rifle gun and a small copper kettle." When plunder from the raid was auctioned, it netted each of the raiders "about one dollar," which most men used to purchase food. Shepard purchased "19 ½ weight of bacon which was the largest quantity of provisions I ever owned at one time." Indian plunder provided three things that allowed poor whites to survive on the frontier: a gun, a cooking pot, and food. The raid also ensured Samuel Shepard's continued involvement in future raids: with the gun he acquired, he would have a more active role in the attacks and secure a larger share of the spoils; without a gun, Shepard could only have watched as his fellow raiders returned home "loaded with Indian plunder such as camp kettles, blankets, and so on."[5]

---

4. Friend, *Kentucke's Frontiers*, 105–106; Barnhart and Riker, *Indiana to 1816*, 208; Cayton, *Frontier Indiana*, 84; John Dabney Shane, interview with Josiah Collins, [1841], Lyman Draper Manuscript Collection, 12 CC 66, microfilm, reel 76, State Historical Society of Wisconsin, Madison. Bowman, along with Benjamin Logan and Levi Todd of the Kentucky County militia, attacked the town from two sides but were eventually repulsed. The Shawnee remained secure and undefeated inside a blockhouse, but the town was completely looted, and the raiders auctioned the plunder. See John Dabney Shane's interview with Collins, Draper MSS, 11 CC 103, reel 76; Bayliss Hardin, ed., "Whitley Papers, Draper MSS, Kentucky Papers, Volume 9," *Register of the Kentucky Historical Society*, XXXVI (1938); Henry Hill, "Bowman's Campaign, 1779," Ohio Archaeological and Historical Society, *Publications*, XXII (1913), 502–509, 517–519.

5. "Extracts from the Journal of Samuel Shepard," Apr. 10, 1787–Dec. 3, 1796, M-683, microfilm, Special Collections, University of Kentucky, Lexington; Young, ed., *Narrative of Daniel Trabue*, 46–47.

Many of the Indians who camped along the Ohio were less fortunate, losing their lives as well as their belongings. Increasingly, to justify their depredations, Anglo-American frontiersmen portrayed Indians as volatile and desperate savages. Kentuckians became well known for their brutality. Hugh McGary killed an Indian who wore a shirt like that of his dead stepson and then chopped the Indian up and fed him to the dogs. "Savage Morgan" earned his name following a fatal scuffle with an Indian, whose corpse he then flayed, tanned, and transformed into a razor strop. In 1778, on an Indian raid across the Ohio, Daniel Trabue described the sentiments of a bloodthirsty companion who "wishd he could come up with the indians. He wanted so bad to have the chance of killing them. He said he knew he could kill 5 him self. He Could shoot. He could Tomerhack and make use of his butcher knife and slay them."[6]

Much of this brutality came west with the militia, inspired by both Clark and colonial officials. The governor of Pennsylvania, Joseph Reed, encouraged the scalping of Indians. Pennsylvania put a hundred-dollar bounty on Indian scalps and Kentucky men complied, even digging up Indian graves and scalping the corpses. Reed's broadside encouraged the intimidation of Indians: "The savages are not to be trusted gained or preserved on any other Principle than Fear." If the principle of fear depended on the killing of Indians, intimidation could verge on extermination.[7]

The warfare that enveloped the Kentucky frontier became an ecological crisis in the 1780s, when vast numbers of animals were slaughtered along the Buffalo Trace. Great herds of elk, deer, and bison followed this shale fault line south to the center of Kentucky, in search of salt licks and canebrakes. Bison packed down the soils, creating mile-wide stretches of land that became known as the barrens. Once Clark and the militia were ensconced at Vincennes, these well-worn pathways acquired a new meaning, becoming ready-made footpaths for people eager to reach the rich bluegrass country of central Kentucky. Indians had carefully nurtured this landscape to enhance animal life; they burned forestlands intentionally to get rid of woody undergrowth and to create the luxuriant grasslands and pasturelands that attracted and fed wild animals. These lands supported the wildlife that was at the core of Indians' existence. Whereas Indians revered the animals and transformed the entire animal into edible or usable products, settler colonists brought a disregard for the life of wild animals. One early settler reported, "Many a buffalo

---

6. Elizabeth A. Perkins, *Border Life: Experience and Memory in the Revolutionary Ohio Valley* (Chapel Hill, N.C., 1998), 136; Friend, *Kentucke's Frontiers*, 103.

7. Friend, *Kentucke's Frontiers*, 106; Young, ed., *Narrative of Daniel Trabue*, 45.

was killed by the whites, and only a little rump taken out, or a thigh bone for the marrow." Kentuckians had depleted the great herds in less than a decade of hunting. European demand for buffalo robes and deerskins pushed the price of peltry to new levels and fostered this senseless animal slaughter. Animals were skinned for their furs, and hundreds of carcasses were left to rot along the buffalo trace and at the salt licks. The quest for greater profits led many Kentucky hunters to carry their furs to Natchez and New Orleans. Frequently, it was not even profit that drove men to kill but, rather, "many a man killed a buffalo, just for the sake of saying so." Although deerskins were more profitable, it was the tales of buffalo hunting that testified to one's manhood. Attempts to protect animals from annihilation and destruction gave way to increasingly violent reactions by Indians staunchly preserving their way of life and appeasing the spirits of the massacred animals. The dismemberment of animals and the failure to consume the meat jeopardized the spiritual relation between wildlife and Indians. Fearing that animals would simply not return and submit to sacrifice probably led Indians to retaliate on their behalf. Contrary to Indigenous belief systems, settler colonists did not hold that animals had any higher spiritual essence, nor did they share the idea that animals would refuse to return when their killing lacked purpose.[8]

In one example of Indians' desperate response to Anglo-American overhunting, after defeating a Kentucky militia force at the Blue Licks in 1782, the Indians scattered forty dismembered bodies along the Alanantowamiowee to inspire terror in those who traveled along that pathway. Violence became a symbolic act meant to dissuade Americans from appropriating Indian lands and destroying their food supply. Brutality was a conscious act, employed as a military tactic against encroaching settler colonists. Anglo-Americans understood mutilation as a tactic meant to instill fear, failing to see the emblematic significance of acts like scalping, which Indians saw as appropriating the spiritual identity of the victim. "Terror," as a word, did not come into common use until the end of the eighteenth century, when the French Jacobins employed "terror" to describe their own revolutionary activities. But Indians and settler colonists had long understood what it meant "to terrorize" their adversaries.[9]

From 1782 to 1786, the situation further degenerated as the United States government attempted to force Indian land cessions. In 1784, at the nego-

---

8. "Deposition of Col. Robert Patterson," 1810, 6 BB 32, Shane's interview with Joshua McQueen, ca. 1840, 13 CC 121; Stephen Aron, *How the West Was Lost: The Transformation of Kentucky from Daniel Boone to Henry Clay* (Baltimore, 1996), 54–55; Friend, *Kentucke's Frontiers*, 102–103.

9. Aron, *How the West Was Lost*, 31–32; Friend, *Kentucke's Frontiers*, 102.

tiations of the second Treaty of Fort Stanwix, the United States pressured the Iroquois to cede the lands south of the Ohio, which confirmed the previous cession in 1768 to Great Britain. The U.S. treaty extended the western boundary line to the Mississippi. This same attitude prevailed the next year, when Congress sent George Rogers Clark, Arthur Lee, and Richard Butler to the Ohio Country to obtain lands north of the Ohio. Most Indians living north of the Ohio refused to attend the treaty conference, and the United States chose to negotiate with other Indians who had no claim to these lands: the Delaware (Lenape), the Ottawa, and the Ojibwe also signed the treaty, though they could claim only small parcels of land at the mouth of the Sandusky River. It was the Shawnee and Miami who had the greatest claim to these lands. The Miami refused to attend the negotiations, and U.S. demands for the cession of the southern and eastern parts of present-day Ohio met with resistance. Shawnee chief Captain Johnny told the negotiators that the Shawnee were "strong, unanimous, and united in determination" not to cede any lands north of the Ohio and warned that all settlers should remain on U.S. lands south of the Ohio. The U.S. emissaries refused to negotiate and threw black and white strings of wampum on the table, demanding that the Indians choose one color or the other. White wampum represented the pathway to peace; black was the pathway to death and destruction. Following Captain Johnny's departure, Moluntha, an old Shawnee chief, asked his people to reconsider, and he along with several others signed the Treaty of Fort McIntosh. In November, Colonel Benjamin Logan and nine hundred Kentucky militia invaded the newly ceded treaty lands. They ascended the Miami River and burned seven Shawnee villages. Most of the Shawnee had moved north to Miamitown, and the men who had remained were murdered and scalped. The militia took thirty women and children as prisoners. Moluntha, clutching the treaty in his hand, surrendered but was quickly dispatched with a tomahawk through his skull.[10]

10. Colin G. Calloway, *The Victory with No Name: The Native American Defeat of the First American Army* (New York, 2016), 43–44. The United States initially considered the Indians conquered nations and therefore demanded the cession of land based on the doctrine of conquest. Indians were not reimbursed for those lands under the Treaty of Fort Stanwix or the McIntosh treaty. In 1789, Secretary of War Henry Knox attempted to find a way back from the violence engulfing the Ohio River valley and formulated a new policy in which the Indian nations were independent, but the United States was to have the sole right of treaty negotiation with them. Indians were to be paid by the federal government for the purchase of their lands. Treaties made with the Indians after the Revolutionary War are discussed in Dorothy V. Jones, *License for Empire: Colonialism by Treaty in Early America* (Chicago, 1982), 120–186, esp. 168; Joyce G. Williams and Jill E. Farrelly, *Diplomacy on the*

By July 1786, Indians were attempting to control the violence by confronting the perpetrators. An Indian force of several hundred warriors surrounded Vincennes and demanded that the French join them in eliminating the Virginians from their settlement. The French refused, then attempted to pacify the Indians by smoking the calumet and offering them gifts of condolence. The warriors knew the perpetrators but left Vincennes without securing the Virginians in question. They did, however, burn Daniel Sullivan's fields, shoot at his house, and warn him that they would punish him when they returned. Sullivan had infuriated the Indians by leading the mob that had killed and scalped a sick Indian and dragged his body around town "Like a pig on the tail of a horse." The French also considered Sullivan dangerous and "pernicious to the public peace."[11]

The death of Moluntha, the murder of Shawnee men, the capture of women and children, and the continuing presence of American marauders at Vincennes led to a large gathering of furious Indians at Brownstown, a Wyandot town near Detroit, in December 1786. The Shawnee, Miami, Delaware, Huron, Ojibwe, Potawatomi, Odawa, Piankeshaw, Wea, Cherokee, and Mingo Iroquois there sent a message to Congress declaring the McIntosh treaty to be "void and of no effect." They blamed the new nation for kindling "your council fires where you thought proper without consulting us" and cautioned the "thirteen United States" that they would "defend those rights and privileges which have been transmitted to us by our ancestors." The signatories were now presenting themselves as a "Confederated Council Fire" to rally resistance to colonizing intruders.[12]

Indiana-Ohio Frontier, 1783–1791 (Bloomington, Ind., 1976); Reginald Horsman, *Expansion and American Indian Policy, 1783–1812* (East Lansing, Mich., 1967); Walter M. Mohr, *Federal Indian Relations, 1774–1788* (Philadelphia, 1967). In Johnson v. McIntosh (1823), the U.S. Supreme Court declared that Britain had based its claim to North American lands on the doctrine of discovery and that the United States, as its legitimate successor, now held legal title to Indian lands. See David E. Wilkins, *American Indian Politics and the American Political System* (Lanham, Md., 2002), 103–118; Josiah Harmar to Henry Knox, Nov. 15, 1786, in William Henry Smith, ed., *The St. Clair Papers: The Life and Public Services of Arthur St. Clair; Soldier of the Revolutionary War, President of the Continental Congress; and Governor of the North-Western Territory; with His Correspondence and Other Papers,* II (Cincinnati, Oh., 1881), 18–19.

11. Leonard C. Helderman, ed., "Danger on the Wabash: Vincennes Letters of 1786," *Indiana Magazine of History,* XXXIV (1938), 456–457; Beverley W. Bond, Jr., ed., "Two Westward Journeys of John Filson, 1785," *Mississippi Valley Historical Review,* IX (1922–1923), 326–327; Helderman, "The Northwest Expedition of George Rogers Clarke, 1786," ibid., XXV (1938–1939), 317–334.

12. "Speech of the United Indian Nations, at Their Confederate Council, Held Near the

The lands west of the Appalachians were chaotic and ungovernable because of the ongoing Kentucky raids on Indian villages and increasingly severe Indian retaliation. Many of Clark's former militia had remained at Vincennes and terrorized the Indians as well as the fur traders and Frenchmen living there. In 1787, reports from Henry Knox, the secretary of war, and John Jay, the secretary of foreign affairs, recommended the United States establish a governmental presence in the west, at Vincennes. Congress authorized the raising of militia forces to send to the Ohio River valley. In 1787, Knox authorized General Josiah Harmar to establish order by dispossessing "the men who had illegally taken control of Vincennes." Harmar, a thirty-one-year-old veteran of the Revolution, organized the First American Regiment. He was to establish federal authority, and, as he traveled to Vincennes, Harmar was also to build additional small fortifications along the river, despite his limited resources.[13]

Harmar feared that this sizable army traveling along the Ohio would be perceived with hostility by the Indians. Before beginning his journey west, he wrote to the French at Vincennes and asked them to warn the Indians of his advance: "I would wish you, Gentlemen, to inform the Indians that the United States wish to live in peace with them, and that they may not be alarmed at this movement; likewise to apprize them of troops being on their way to the Post, not a set of villains but regulars, and sent by the authority of the Grand Council of the Empire, in order to preserve good faith with them." In sharing information about his arrival with the French residents at Vincennes, Harmar was also sharing news about the government's desire to bring peace to the troubled region, an approach that appealed to the French and especially to the Indians. Harmar arrived at Vincennes on July 17, 1787, with a portion of his troops; the remaining men arrived by water on August 5.[14]

The army was to foster the peaceful resolution of conflicts and to avoid using force in calming this troubled region. Harmar received Knox's permission to distribute gifts in his conversations with the Indians. Both Washington and Knox were eager to avoid an Indian war. Many Wabash villages and

---

Mouth of the Detroit River," Nov. 28, Dec. 18, 1786, in United States Congress, *American State Papers: Documents, Legislative and Executive, of the Congress of the United States . . . ,* 38 vols. (Washington, D.C., 1832), Class II, *Indian Affairs,* 2 vols., ed. Walter Lowrie et al., I, 8–9 (hereafter cited as *ASPIA*).

13. Gayle Thornbrough, ed., *Outpost on the Wabash, 1787–1791: Letter of Brigadier General Josiah Harmar and Major John Francis Hamtramck and Other Letters and Documents Selected from the Harmar Papers in the William L. Clements Library,* Indiana Historical Society, *Publications,* XIX (Indianapolis, Ind., 1957), 7–13.

14. Harmar to J. M. P. Le Gras and François Bosseron, June 19, 1787, ibid., 23–24.

the leaders at Miamitown were also interested in peace. Raids along the lower Wabash disrupted the fur trade, destabilized villages, and devastated their inhabitants. The raid on Chillicothe had reduced a prosperous Shawnee village to ashes and scattered its residents. Most Shawnee moved north, establishing villages near Miamitown, which also began to function as an arena of collective decision making where Indian leaders determined how to respond to the spreading violence. Little Turtle, Captain Johnny, and Le Gris focused on displacing squatters who intruded on lands north of the Ohio: they burned cabins and killed or kidnapped the intruders. But even as these retaliatory raids took place, leaders discussed the possibility of peaceful coexistence with the Americans. With news of Harmar's impending arrival in hand, the Miami leaders from Miamitown and the Ouiatenon villages decided to respond peaceably rather than ignite further violence. Pacanne was sent to meet with Harmar. As he journeyed south along the Wabash, he shared news of his approaching meeting with the Americans. He met Harmar at the Falls of the Ohio, probably at Fort Steuben. Harmar and Pacanne then journeyed north along the Wabash to Vincennes, with Pacanne's warriors assuring the American army safe passage. Pleasantly surprised by the appearance of Vincennes, Harmar arrived on August 7, 1787, at a "very considerable village situated on the Wabash about one hundred and twenty miles from the mouth." There were "four hundred houses (log and bark), outhouses, barns etc. The number of the inhabitants about nine hundred (souls) French, and about four hundred (souls) Americans." In reality, there were 520 French people, a scattering of Spanish traders, and 103 male American inhabitants, who were "generally lawless refuges and vagabonds who squatted on public land in and around the surrounding village." For the past nine years, Vincennes had been characterized by "all the excesses that can be the result of self-created authority, wanton aggression, and boundless tyranny." The French believed that it was "high time to wash off the stain that the conduct of a lawless mob may, in the eyes of foreigners, have impress'd on the American character." Harmar blamed the lawlessness on Clark and the American traders who encouraged Clark's followers to plunder Indian villages. French residents confirmed Harmar's impressions, telling him, "We are too well convinced that the merchants and especially the traders, men of low and interested principles, stop at nothing and would rather spill rivers of blood than loose the only trade by which they can live."[15]

Harmar constructed Fort Knox at Vincennes and attempted to restore

---

15. Barthélemi Tardiveau to Harmar, Aug. 6, 1787, Harmar to Knox, Aug. 7, 1787, ibid., 13, 33, 36.

order by beginning the review of French land claims and restraining American assaults on the French traders and merchants. While at Vincennes, Harmar journeyed west to Illinois Country on a diplomatic visit to Indian and French villages, guided by Pacanne and the Miami chief La Demoiselle. Following an exhausting seven-day march, they arrived at Kaskaskia, where Harmar was warmly received by the French and by Jean Baptiste de Coigne, chief of the Kaskaskians. Eager to assure Knox and his Washington superiors of his success, Harmar described Coigne's speech as "expressive of the greatest friendship for the United States." Coigne presented Harmar with a calumet, which led to his welcome by the Peoria. Next, Harmar stopped at Cahokia, Ste. Genevieve, and Prairie du Rocher, speaking with the French, who were also pleased to see him. Harmar met with the Spanish governor at St. Louis, and upon his return to Vincennes, the Kaskaskians as well as the Miami leaders, their warriors, and several Frenchmen accompanied him. Shortly after Harmar's return, 120 Piankeshaw and Wea Indians arrived from the lower Wabash. Harmar's gifts sealed their bonds of friendship with the United States. He told them that "it was the wish of Congress to live in peace and friendship with them." Several days later, they replied to his speech and "in strong figurative language expressed their determination to preserve perfect peace and friendship with the United States. . . . They presented me with a number of calumets and wampum." He sent these gifts to Secretary Knox, which included "a rich otter skin."[16]

On October 1, Harmar departed again for Fort Washington and left two companies under the command of Major John Francis Hamtramck, with orders to construct a new post. They completed Fort Knox the next year. Hamtramck appeared the ideal commander for this region, since he was French Canadian, born in Quebec, and had entered the army to fight in the Revolutionary War. When Americans at Vincennes ignored his orders, he relied on French cooperation to maintain discipline. Harmar's warm reception had also encouraged Pacanne to establish a new village near La Demoiselle. Since 1785, Pacanne's people had lived intermittently near Vincennes, where he had served as Clark's intermediary with the Wabash villages. The U.S. Army's presence provided a sense of security and an opportunity to open a new path

16. La Demoiselle was the son of the Piankeshaw chief killed at Pickawillany in 1752. He had established his village twenty to thirty miles northwest of Vincennes and had been a guide for John Filson, the Kentucky cartographer, in 1785. See Harvey Lewis Carter, *The Life and Times of Little Turtle: First Sagamore of the Wabash* (Urbana, Ill., 1987), 75; George R. Wilson and Gayle Thornbrough, *The Buffalo Trace,* Indiana Historical Society, *Publications,* XV, no. 2 (Indianapolis, 1946), 192; Harmar to Knox, Nov. 24, 1787, in Thornbrough, ed., *Outpost on the Wabash,* 47–52.

to peace with Americans. While Pacanne's warriors began clearing land for planting fields, Pacanne returned to Kaskaskia for a meeting with the British commissioner of Indian affairs. The ninety-five men under Hamtramck's command appeared sufficient to halt future Kentucky intrusions. Unfortunately, Hamtramck failed in his charge. Pacanne's men became the first victims of the government's peace policy. Patrick Brown, a self-proclaimed Indian fighter who had survived "many frontier scrapes," organized sixty men from Nelson County to plunder the Wabash Indians. They began their journey by traveling overland to Vincennes. On their way, they stopped to rob, then murder, several men at Indian villages. When Brown arrived at Fort Knox, he bragged to Hamtramck that "he was after Indians and had killed nine that morning." He proudly displayed their scalps as well as twenty captured horses from Pacanne's village. The attack outraged Hamtramck, and he ordered the Kentucky raiders out of Vincennes; he later claimed that he was powerless to stop the intruders because only nine of his men were fit for service. Hamtramck told Harmar, "I could have prevented him with the canon of the fort, but did not think the affair of sufficient consequence to spill blood." Instead, Hamtramck dispatched Captain Ferguson to inform Brown that the Indians "were employed in the service of the United States and under the protection of the US government." Brown dismissed Ferguson and refused to return Pacanne's horses. When Hamtramck reported the incident to Harmar, he described Pacanne's men as having been brutally murdered and scalped while "in a pacific state and under the protection of the United States." Sadly, Hamtramck was more infuriated by the disregard for his authority and by "the humiliating necessity of letting him keep the horses." He complained to Harmar: "Never was my feeling so much wounded before."[17]

Brown's attack on Pacanne's fledgling village ended all hopes of establishing peaceful relations with the Indians. The murder and scalping of nine Miami men on a peace mission reverberated throughout the river valley. The army presence at the newly constructed fort was to bring peace, but the army had little interest in protecting Indians. Previous raids, frequently blamed on the lawlessness of squatter colonists, now proved that the cost of peace would be paid with Indian lives. Pacanne's reputation as a diplomatic mediator had been earned by his work with the British at Detroit, but he failed in his attempt to

---

17. For Pacanne's relationship with George Rogers Clark, see Richard White, *The Middle Ground: Indians, Empires, and Republics in the Great Lakes Region, 1650–1815* (New York, 1991), 427–429; Carter, *Life and Times of Little Turtle*, 75–76; John Francis Hamtramck to Harmar, Aug. 31, 1788, in Thornbrough, ed., *Outpost on the Wabash*, 114–116; Cayton, *Frontier Indiana*, 125.

reach out to the Americans. Hamtramck neglected to arrest the murderers, even when Brown's men paraded through town with the bloody scalps of the nine slain Miami men. Hamtramck also failed to prevent Brown's men from heading north to slaughter more Indians. Just north of Vincennes, the raiders killed and mutilated a young Indian woman and her child.

When Hamtramck called together the remaining Indians at Vincennes, he "explained to them who those people were, and took every possible measure to persuade them that it was not done by any lawful authority, and that I disapproved of their conduct." His excuses were feeble and unhelpful. Hamtramck tried to justify his actions to Harmar by telling him that the use of the fort's cannons against Brown's men would have resulted in "spilling American blood." For Hamtramck, the murder of Indians was not an affair of "sufficient consequence" to justify injuring Kentucky's outlaws. The message was clear: American men were not to be punished for killing Indians.[18]

With his village destroyed, horses stolen, and nine men murdered, Pacanne left Vincennes to join the survivors at the Ouiatenon villages along the Wabash. Hamtramck's unwillingness to halt the Kentucky raiders or secure the stolen horses seemed to convince Pacanne that peace with the Americans was no longer possible; he would make no future overtures. He traveled slowly through the villages along the river, perhaps to share news of the massacre.

Hamtramck's refusal to imprison and punish the perpetrators or to secure the stolen horses offered proof that reconciliation with Americans was problematic. Hamtramck's letter was not sent forward by Harmar; neither Washington nor Knox had any knowledge of the event. Harmar's effusive descriptions of his warm reception left the administration with little comprehension of how this Vincennes massacre had changed Indian attitudes toward Americans. The executive and legislative branches of the new government viewed Indian lands as the solution to the ongoing financial crisis, expecting the sale of Indian lands to pay off the crippling debts of the Revolutionary War and secure the new nation's prosperity. Washington erroneously believed that the Indians would beat a hasty retreat when faced with a deluge of settler colonists, thinking that "they [the Indian nations] will be as ready to sell, as we are to buy." He underestimated the resolve and resilience of the Indian peoples north of the Ohio.[19]

In fact, as the Indian population grew, the Ohio River was considered

---

18. Hamtramck to Harmar, Aug. 31, 1788, in Thornbrough, ed., *Outpost on the Wabash*, 116.

19. John C. Fitzpatrick, ed., *Writings of George Washington from the Original Manuscript Sources, 1745–1799*, 39 vols. (Washington, D.C., 1931–1944), XXVII, 136, 140.

an increasingly important boundary line between Indian Country and the United States. Many Shawnee moved to Miamitown, on the fringe of the Great Black Swamp and at the portage of the Wabash and Maumee Rivers. As we have seen, this important village was a thriving trading metropolis, a commercial stronghold that emerged as the armed bulwark of Indian resistance. Hundreds of refugees had resettled in this rich landscape that amply sustained a growing population. Miamitown had dramatically expanded; along the interconnected riverways, thousands of Indians, pushed from their homelands by settler intrusion, were welcomed onto Miami lands. These included Shawnee, Delaware, Nanticoke, and Conoy from the Potomac Bay region, Chickamauga Cherokee from Tennessee, as well as Mohawk, Cayuga, and Seneca, who were often classified as Mingo.[20]

On December 18, 1786, the representatives of this confederacy of Indian nations, which linked the refugees and permanent residents, forwarded their demands to Congress, demanding revocation of the McIntosh treaty and elimination of settlement north of the Ohio. Despite the warning, Congress moved forward that spring with its first grand speculative land scheme. It granted the Ohio Company five million acres of land at the intersection of the Ohio and Scioto Rivers for a bargain price of sixty-six cents per acre. Once paid for in military warrants and depreciated government securities, Congress had effectively sold Indian lands for twelve cents an acre.[21]

With the passage of the Northwest Ordinance in 1787, the government transformed communally held, unceded Indian lands into private property. Colonizing schemes proposed by Congress, the states, and the president divided the lands north of the Ohio and east of the Great Miami River into the Virginia Military District, the U.S. Military District, the Connecticut Western Reserve, the Seven Ranges, and the Fire Lands, and sold large parcels to the Symmes and Ohio Companies. Congress was attempting to make money through the sale of vast tracts to private land companies. Many Ohio Company officers were Revolutionary War veterans, and they agreed to assume the cost of surveying the land. Washington's desire to people the west with respectable leaders coincided with Congress's desire to save the cost of public land surveys and to begin repaying the national debt. Meanwhile, the presi-

---

20. Calloway, *Victory with No Name,* 27; Helen Hornbeck Tanner, "The Glaize in 1792: A Composite Indian Community," *Ethnohistory,* XXV (1978), I, 15–19.

21. Andro Linklater, *Measuring America: How the United States Was Shaped by the Greatest Land Sale in History* (New York, 2003), 80–81. R. Douglas Hurt estimates the cost per acre as even lower, at 8.5 cents an acre. See Hurt, *The Ohio Frontier: Crucible of the Old Northwest, 1720–1830* (Bloomington, Ind., 1996), 157.

MAP 13. Tribal locations north of the Ohio River valley, 1779–1794.
Drawn by Ellen White

dent and states continued rewarding Revolutionary War soldiers with land warrants; most failed to move west and sold their warrants to land speculators, who purchased them on credit, resold land in small lots, and accumulated capital for future, ever larger purchases. In the end, congressional land speculators, the president, and the land speculators of Boston, New York, and Philadelphia reaped the largest profits from the sale of Indian lands. Incoming

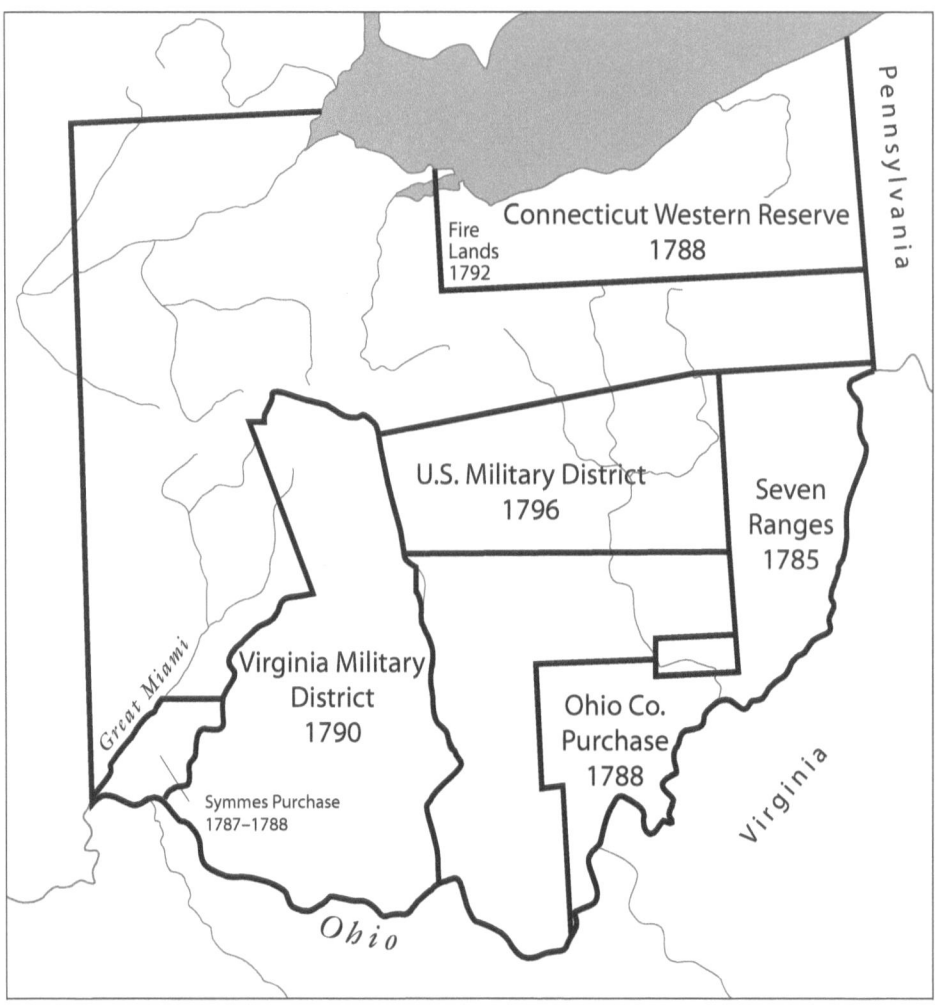

MAP 14. Land divisions in Ohio, by approximate date of first settlement.
Drawn by Ellen White

settler colonists secured fertile tracts of land but faced hostile Indian neighbors.[22]

In 1787, the Ohio Company claimed lands along the Muskingum; military warrant lands were established between the Scioto and the Little Miami. Cleves Symmes, head of the Ohio Company, then made a second large purchase of Indian lands with his partner, Elias Boudinot; they secured an addi-

22. Daniel M. Friedenberg, *Life, Liberty, and the Pursuit of Land: The Plunder of Early America* (Buffalo, N.Y., 1992), 277.

tional one million acres along the Miami and Scioto Rivers. They set aside forty thousand acres for their personal use, while Symmes advertised and sold his new lands, which he referred to as the "Miami Purchase." Selling eight hundred acres opposite the mouth of the Licking River, he began to lay out the small town of Losantiville, later Cincinnati. There, in spring 1789, Shawnee from Miamitown and other smaller confederated villages met with Symmes. The Indians pointedly asked Symmes if he had been sent there by the thirteen United States. Symmes, anxious to claim authority over the lands, showed them the flag and the seal of his commission. After listening to Symmes explain the symbolism of the seal, a Shawnee leader rejected the white man's assertion that an eagle holding a tree in one claw and a bundle of arrows in the other symbolized, respectively, peace and the power to punish enemies. The Shawnee countered with another interpretation:

> He could not perceive any intimations of peace from the attitude the Eagle was in; having her wings spread as in flight; when folding of the wings denoted rest and peace. That he could not understand how the branch of a tree could be considered as a pacific emblem, for rods designated for correction were always taken from the boughs of trees. That to him the Eagle appeared from her bearing a large whip in one claw, and such a number of arrows in the other, and in full career of flight, to be wholly bent on war and mischief.[23]

Indians scoffed at the idea that the Americans wished to live in peace with them. Pacific overtures to the United States had been rebuffed, first by the brutal invasion of Shawnee lands and the murder of Moluntha in 1786, then by the Vincennes massacre of Pacanne's men in 1787. The eagle was the very embodiment the United States' warlike intentions. Indians along the Wabash saw no point in attending the general peace conference at Fort Harmar that Arthur St. Clair, now governor of the Northwest Territory, attempted to assemble in 1788. They told Hamtramck, "Altho' Gov. St. Clair should promise them peace, that the Kentuck people would brake it immediately." Not surprisingly, Indians living along the Wabash and at Miamitown refused to send representatives to the conference. Only the Iroquois, Wyandot, Delaware, Odawa, Chippewa, Potawatomi, and Sauk Indians attended, but these men did not speak for the Miami, the Shawnee, or the multiplicity of diverse villages north of the Ohio River. From the standpoint of the Americans, this

---

23. Beverly W. Bond, Jr., *The Correspondence of John Cleves Symmes: Founder of the Miami Purchase* (New York, 1926), 75; Paul A. W. Wallace, ed., *Thirty Thousand Miles with John Heckewelder* (Pittsburgh, 1958), 275.

was a crucial treaty conference. The United States was to announce a major change in Indian policy: instead of demanding land cessions, the U.S. would pay the Indians for the lands they ceded. At the Fort Harmar meeting, St. Clair would compensate the Indians for the lands that they had previously ceded at the Fort Stanwix and Fort McIntosh conferences. Although the payments were small, the right of conquest disappeared from future negotiations with the Indians.[24]

Despite this provision, the peace conference did nothing to repair Indians' relations with the Americans. The Fort Harmar negotiations again went forward without the Indians who actually occupied the lands north of the Ohio. The Indians who attended the conference declared that these were Miami lands, and the Ohio River was the legitimate boundary between United States territory to the south and Indian Country to the north. St. Clair remained adamant that the boundaries negotiated at the McIntosh treaty be reaffirmed. He dropped all efforts at reconciliation and threatened an attack if the Indians in attendance failed to agree to the McIntosh treaty boundary line. The haughty disregard for people who felt they had legitimate claims to these lands encouraged Indians to fight rather than negotiate. St. Clair's speech only increased their militancy:

> The United States would have been justified to all the World to have Marched their Armies into Your Country and punished you in an exemplary manner, but they gave an example of Clemency. They considered that the War had Spread Misery over many Country's and were desirous to prevent its Spreading wider. They offered You peace upon the Condition of Surrendering a Part of Your Country. . . . If there were ever engagements that Should be binding upon Mankind, they were these, for the U.States, not only buried the rememberances of past injuries but made a generous division of the Ceded Country.[25]

When the conference ended in January 1789, the Indians present signed two separate treaties. The Wyandot and western Indians signed one, and the Iroquois, the other. The Wyandot received $6,000 worth of trade goods for the cession of Miami and Shawnee lands; the Iroquois received $3,000. On

---

24. Fort Harmar later became Marietta, Ohio. The fort was in southeastern Ohio at the mouth of the Muskingum River, where it joined the Ohio River. See Hamtramck to Harmar, Aug. 31, 1788, in Thornbrough, ed., *Outpost on the Wabash*, 117–119; Francis Paul Prucha, *The Great Father: The United States Government and the American Indians*, 2 vols. (Lincoln, Neb., 1984), 19.

25. Draper MSS, 23 U 75–142, microfilm, 134–135.

May 2, St. Clair sent the treaties to President Washington, who forwarded them to Congress, insisting that these treaties be ratified by the Senate. Washington hoped this would assure the Indians that they possessed political parity with the United States government. But the formalities of eastern governance lacked meaning in a western landscape where government inaction allowed Kentucky raids on Indian villages. Although the treaty included restrictions on white settlement, they were of no consequence.[26]

Believing the peace conference was a turning point in Indian policy, Harmar and St. Clair began 1790 hoping for peace with the western Indians. St. Clair requested that Hamtramck forward his speech to the Indians then living along the Wabash and, in particular, to the Miami.

> I have inclosed a speech to the Indians of the Wabash and those of the Miami village, which I must take the liberty to request you will get forwarded to them. . . . It is much the wish of the general government that peace may be established with those people, and the trial to effect it must be made. Should it fail, there is no doubt but an attempt must be made to chastise them.[27]

The absence of Indians from the Wabash villages and Miamitown at the treaty conference raised doubt in Washington's mind about whether they were "most inclined for war or peace." Undertaking Hamtramck's charge to deliver St. Clair's speech, Pierre Gamelin found that the message enraged the nearby Piankeshaw, and he ventured no farther north than the Vermilion River. He returned to Vincennes, where his ambassadorial duties were assumed by his brother, Antoine. Rephrasing St. Clair's speech to sound more appeasing, Antoine journeyed to several of the villages along the Wabash and asked the Ouiatenon villages for their opinion about the reversal in American policy, but they simply deferred their reply until he conferred with the Indians at Miamitown. Other villages offered the same answer, making it clear that Antoine would receive only one response, and it would come from the Indians gathered at Miamitown. Despite the reshaping of St. Clair's speech in more diplomatic language, the governor's arrogant tone and threat of chastisement were impossible to disguise. Because of the outrage that Moluntha's murder and the Vincennes massacre had created and the continuing assaults on villages along the lower Wabash, Indians in the Ohio River valley were

---

26. Francis Paul Prucha, *American Indian Treaties: The History of a Political Anomaly* (Berkeley, Calif., 1994), 55–58.

27. Arthur St. Clair to Hamtramck, Fort Steuben, Jan. 23, 1790, in Smith, ed., *St. Clair Papers,* II, 130–131.

prejudiced against Gamelin's peace overtures. These grievances were unassuaged by condolence ceremonies. The Miami, Delaware, and Shawnee gave Gamelin an unequivocal response, backed by their Indian allies and by French and British traders. Distrust was palpable, and Blue Jacket denounced the Americans who wanted "to take away, by degrees, their lands." In the end, the Miami provided Antoine Gamelin with nothing more than the promise that they would send their answer to Vincennes within the month.[28]

Gamelin's mission was a failure. The Indians' refusal to attend St. Clair's peace and the deferral of peacemaking decisions to Pacanne and the Miami left Washington and Knox baffled. In this increasingly hostile Indian landscape, shifts in federal treaty and land policy meant nothing. The Indians found proffers of peace absurd. Even Hamtramck began to sympathize with the Indians' vulnerable position. He wrote repeatedly to Harmar and expressed concern for the Wea, who faced recurring attacks from the Kentuckians. The Wea were not the aggressors, he assured Harmar; he had met with them and was certain "of their good intentions." When Hamtramck cautioned the Wea not to attack Kentucky settlements, he remained confident that they were not violating the peace.[29]

Hamtramck found himself and, in a larger sense, the United States increasingly powerless in the face of Kentucky aggression. Kentuckians disregarded his authority as he continued to rely on persuasion rather than force, and they failed to execute his orders to halt the attacks. One year after the Vincennes massacre, the Kentuckians returned to enlist the support of the Americans living at Vincennes, and the two groups jointly renewed attacks on the Wabash villages. Again in 1789, Hamtramck wrote to Harmar expressing his outrage at the insolence of the Kentuckians in ignoring his orders:

> In my last I had the honor to inform you of an expedition made by the people of Kentuck against the Wabash Indians. A Party of them now in this place on their return to Kentuck. This expedition consisted of 220 men who have gone near the Weeya, killed 12 Indians. All this great campaign has done in 16 days. It may be call'd a provocation for I am well persuaded that they will pay for it and perhaps this village. Some Americans of this village were with them. Mr. Daniel Sullivan and one Mr. Duff and others. Mr. Duff was walking this day in the streets with two scalps fastened on

---

28. George Washington to St. Clair, Oct. 6, 1780, ibid.; Cayton, *Frontier Indiana*, 142–143.

29. Hamtramck to Harmar, July 29, 1789, in Thornbrough, ed., *Outpost on the Wabash*, 178–179.

a stick. . . . It is very mortifying to me to see the authority of the United States so much sneered at and not having sufficient power to chastise the aggressors.[30]

Hamtramck complained repeatedly to Harmar and described the ongoing attacks on July 29, August 14, and August 17, 1790. Harmar ignored Hamtramck's letters. He failed to even forward them to Knox until October 1790. Although Hamtramck's reports were brushed aside, Congress, Washington, and the War Office paid close attention to the stream of petitions from outraged settlers in Kentucky and Ohio. They described vicious attacks by the Wabash and Miami Indians who had killed and pillaged their houses without reason; they portrayed the Indians as barbarians and demanded their annihilation. Rufus Putnam, who lived not far from Cincinnati, organized a letter-writing campaign to his friend and former military commander, President George Washington. Putnam encouraged multiple, lengthy petitions from former army officers. He was heavily invested in the Ohio Company, as were many of his colleagues. The attacks and kidnappings, they claimed, were making settlement impossible.[31]

The confederated villages at Miamitown considered American settlements north of the Ohio as intrusions on their land; they had never ceded these lands to the United States. The Indians organized a relentless series of attacks on the squatters. The Miami and Shawnee harassed, killed, and kidnapped settler colonists struggling to establish homesteads around Fort Washington. Putnam's emotional depictions of kidnappings included endless reporting of people being murdered by the Indians. The numbers were exaggerated in all the accounts, and the ongoing Kentucky attacks on Indians went unmentioned. Perhaps most politically significant, violence in the west was stemming the tide of migration, jeopardizing land sales. Washington and Knox decided to act. From their perspective, the hornet's nest was at Miamitown. But their plans to strike the Indians in their heartland were hampered by limited funding. Washington chose General Harmar to lead the attack, but Harmar would have to rely primarily on recruits rather than the regular army.

30. Ibid., 183.
31. "Copy of a Letter to the President, July 24, 1790," "Letter to Mr. Ames [Secretary at War], 1790," "Unaddressed Letter, Jan. 6, 1791," "Gen. Knox Letter, Jan. 27, 1791," "Copy of a Letter to Gen. Knox, March 8, 1791," "Copy of a Letter to Gen. Knox, Marietta, March 14, 1791," all in Rowena Buell, comp., *The Memoirs of Rufus Putnam and Certain Official Papers and Correspondence* (Boston, 1903), 232–252.

HARMAR'S DEFEAT

Harmar was a mediocre military officer who had never led men into battle but had been promoted to brigadier general. He and his wife enjoyed a frontier social life centered around Fort Washington, where rumors circulated about his alcoholism. Plagued by misinformation, Harmar considered Miamitown a series of small, weak, disorganized villages and chose to begin offensive operations with a direct attack. Confident that this would be an "easy" victory, he also believed that a successful campaign would ensure his political future in the army. Harmar understood little about Indian society in the Ohio River valley, and he appreciated neither the economic nor the political importance of Miamitown. It was well protected by war villages of the Miami, by Little Turtle and Le Gris's villages, and by peace villages farther west along the Wabash. Equally problematic for the Americans was the large number of potentially available Miami warriors: the Miami had allies spanning the one-thousand-mile length of the river and stretching into the western Great Lakes, extending to the northern and western shores of Lake Michigan, and including the Odawa and Ojibwe.

Harmar's planned offensive was naive in its approach to Miamitown, and his forces lacked the discipline needed to defeat the Miami warriors. Since funds to secure regular troops were lacking, volunteers were recruited from the Kentucky and Pennsylvania backcountry. Even then, Harmar fell short of the quota when he mustered his troops at Fort Washington on September 30, 1790. His army was plagued by disciplinary problems, and most of the recruits were untrained. Volunteers lacked the professionalism of the regular army, and even the regular army's discipline was questionable. Additional army members had been recruited from the cities, but most were unfamiliar with frontier life or Indian warfare. It was difficult to recruit young men into the military, which was compounded by vociferous opposition to a standing army. Farmers were reluctant to part with the labor of their young men, forcing army recruiters to seek soldiers from unemployed laborers in urban centers, who knew little about the west. "Jackson Johonnet," though possibly an apocryphal account of a soldier from Boston, provides an insight into recruitment.

> A young officer came into my room, and soon entered into conversation on the pleasures of a military life, the great chance there was for an active young man to obtain promotion, and the grand prospect opening for making great fortunes in the western country. His discourse had the desired effect; for after treating me with a bowl or two of punch, I enlisted,

with a firm promise on his side to assist me in obtaining a sergeant's warrant before the party left.[32]

The methodical, disciplined officers from the regular army scorned the young, impulsive, and disorderly volunteers and gave them little training. The more experienced recruits from the Kentucky militia were even more difficult: they were routinely insubordinate and openly resisted the hierarchical notions associated with effective military command. The Kentucky volunteers challenged even the most basic assumptions of military discipline — they were prone to mutiny and routinely headed home despite orders to the contrary. Also taxing were rivalries among the Kentucky militia officers. Harmar had to work with a factionalized militia divided by a popularity contest among the officers, and he also had persistent problems with regular troops who disliked fighting alongside volunteer militia. John Armstrong, a member of the regular army, described the strained relationship that quickly developed because the Kentucky volunteers appeared "to be raw and unused to the gun." Not only were army regulars "disheartened at the kind of people from Kentucky," but Armstrong was convinced that half of them had no military experience, and he feared that most of the militia would turn out to be "rascals." Contending with the difficulty of organizing command of the army, Harmar effected an uneasy compromise between the different militia and army officers by creating separate battalions of Kentucky militia, Pennsylvania militia, and regular troops.[33]

St. Clair and Harmar orchestrated a two-pronged attack on the Indian villages. The first was led by Hamtramck, aimed at Ouiatenon, on the Wabash. The second, led by Harmar, was directed at Miamitown, on the Wabash-Maumee River portage. Even if all the members of the French militia and the

---

32. Samuel L. Metcalf, *A Collection of Some of the Most Interesting Narratives of Indian Warfare in the West* . . . (Lexington, Ky., 1821), 87. Ironically, it is at St. Clair's court-martial that we become fully aware of the unruly nature of his army and militia recruits. St. Clair describes at length the uncontrollable Kentucky militias that plagued Harmar's offensive actions as well as the chaotic nature of the army chain of command. See Cayton, *Frontier Indiana*, 148–154; Richard H. Kohn, *Eagle and Sword: The Federalists and the Creation of the Military Establishment in America, 1783-1802* (New York, 1975), 102–197; Wiley Sword, *President Washington's Indian War: The Struggle for the Old Northwest, 1790–1795* (Norman, Okla., 1985), 89–130.

33. Perkins, *Border Life*, 132, 136; Cayton, *Frontier Indiana*, 148–150; *Military Journal of Major Ebenezer Denny*, Historical Society of Pennsylvania, *Memoirs*, VII (Philadelphia, 1860), 344.

three hundred Kentucky militiamen had arrived on time to supplement Hamtramck's small regular force, they would have been insufficient to level "the Wea Towns" as Harmar had hoped. Hamtramck's journey began later than ordered, his force too small to fulfill the primary object of the march, which was to "divert the attention of the Miami to that quarter" and allow Harmar to march to Miamitown unnoticed and "destroy their village." Even more problematic was Hamtramck's supply shortages, which limited his ability to advance much beyond the Vermilion village, on the lower Wabash. The Piankeshaw had been aware of Hamtramck's advance and had evacuated their village, including its material goods and food stores. Finding the place empty, most of the Kentucky militia deserted and went home. To go any farther, the remaining troops would have had to march on half rations. Consequently, Hamtramck decided to return to Vincennes. Waiting for him farther up the Wabash was a combined force of six hundred warriors from the Wabash villages. Knowing where Hamtramck planned to attack, they removed their families and much of the plunder that was so attractive to the Kentuckians.[34]

Harmar left Fort Washington on September 30. With little time for training, his disorganized forces marched north into Indian lands. Swamps and wetlands hindered the march, and lack of discipline transformed it into a miserable daily struggle. The army moved slowly and had "much trouble in keeping the officers, with their commands, in their proper order, and the pack horses, etc., compact." After two weeks, Harmar was fewer than 120 miles from Fort Washington. The Indians, aware of the approaching army, quickly evacuated Miamitown. The Delaware went southwest along the Wabash to seek shelter at another Delaware village, along the White River; Shawnee families headed toward Detroit; and Miami women joined villages along the Eel River, a tributary of the Upper Wabash. When Harmar learned from a Shawnee warrior that Miamitown was abandoned, he sent Colonel John Hardin ahead with a detachment of soldiers to engage the remaining Indians. Hardin was to keep them occupied until the arrival of the main force. But by the time Hardin reached Miamitown, the Indians had set fire to the main buildings in the village and killed many of the cattle, and the warriors had gone off to hide in the adjacent forests. The Indians left a few trade goods, "some cows,

34. Harmar to Hamtramck, July 15, 1790, in Thornbrough, ed., *Outpost on the Wabash*, 237; Barnhart and Riker, *Indiana to 1816*, 285–286; James Ripley Jacobs, *The Beginning of the U.S. Army, 1783–1812* (Princeton, N.J., 1947), 67–71; William Heath, *William Wells and the Struggle for the Old Northwest* (Norman, Okla., 2015), 110–124; Cayton, *Frontier Indiana*, 148–154; Kohn, *Eagle and Sword*, 102–124; Sword, *President Washington's Indian War*, 89–130.

and large quantities of corn and vegetables." Hardin's militia halted at Miamitown and took up residence in the remaining Indian cabins, settling down to enjoy the abandoned food supply. Miamitown afforded the militia warm, dry quarters in "tolerable good log houses" while they waited for the main army. Encouraged by rumors about buried trade goods, however, the militia ignored all the rules of army discipline and ventured out into the woods in search of "plunder." When Harmar arrived, he tried to rein in the roving army and sent this message to the troops:

> The general is much mortified at the unsoldier-like behavior of many of the men in the army, who make it a practice to straggle from the camp in search of plunder. He, in the most positive terms, forbids this practice in future, and the guards will be answerable to prevent it. No party is to go beyond the line of sentinels without a commissioned officer, who, if of the militia, will apply to Colonel Hardin for his orders. The regular troops will apply to the general. All the plunder that may be hereafter collected, will be equally distributed among the army. The kettles, and every other article already taken, are to be collected by the commanding officers of battalions, and to be delivered to-morrow morning to Mr. Belli, the quartermaster, that a fair distribution may take place. The rolls are to be called at troop and retreat beating, and every man absent is to be reported. The general expects that these orders will be pointedly attended to: they are to be read to the troops this evening.[35]

Despite Harmar's call for discipline, the militia continued to search for hidden trade goods. Even the regular army associated plunder with the mission; the recently recruited Jackson Johonnet reported that, despite the "hunger, fatigue and toil" of each day, "with the idea of easy conquest, rich plunder, and fine arms in the end, we made a shift to be tolerably merry." While the troops celebrated in the deserted Indian village, the unsuspecting Harmar began planning a march to Ouiatenon, where he expected to meet Hamtramck. Understanding the indiscipline of American soldiers, the Indians took advantage of their disorder and drunkenness; while the army slept in a stupor, the Indians drove away their packhorses and cavalry mounts. The inexperienced Harmar, troubled by the loss of his horses and certain that Indians were nearby, unwisely began dividing his force into smaller units. He ordered some to search for the missing horses and others to hunt for Indians. Har-

---

35. Cayton, *Frontier Indiana*, 150–151; "Camp at the Miami Village, Oct. 18, 1790," in John B. Dillon, *A History of Indiana: From Its Earliest Exploration by Europeans to the Close of the Territorial Government, in 1816* . . . (1859; rpt. New York, 1971), 248, 250.

mar sent Lieutenant Colonel Trotter, head of the Kentucky militia, with 300 men to search the woods. They located two Indians, whom they brutally murdered and scalped. Their efforts to locate additional Indians proved futile, and they returned to camp. Trotter's failure to capture prisoners infuriated Harmar, who appointed Hardin to replace him. Hardin was ordered to take 180 men and search for Indians. "Mov[ing] off with great reluctance," the militiamen quickly began to desert. They simply "dropped out of the ranks and returned to camp." Hardin and his remaining men unknowingly headed in the direction of Little Turtle's village, walking through the woods single file, in loose formation, and directly into the trap set by Little Turtle. As they entered a meadowland, the men could see a large pile of trade goods in the distance. Little Turtle had set fire to the goods and hid 150 of his warriors in the woods behind the billowing smoke. Emboldened by greed and anxious to rescue the goods from the fire, the militia broke ranks. The Indian warriors immediately attacked from their concealed positions, emerging, retreating, and emerging again to surprise and engage the enemy in hand-to-hand combat. Hardin ordered his men to assemble and march on the Indians, but "the greatest number of the militia fled without firing a shot." Thirty men from the regular army and fewer than 100 militia confronted an organized force of 150 Indians. American casualties were high. Hardin lost almost half his men: 20 regular soldiers and 40 militiamen. Hardin returned to Miamitown in disgrace. Harmar, enraged by the behavior of the militia, declared,

> The cause of the detachment being worsted yesterday, was entirely owing to the shameful cowardly conduct of the militia who ran away, and threw down their arms, without firing scarcely a single gun. In returning to Fort Washington, if any officer or men shall presume to quit the ranks, or not to march in the form that they are ordered, the general will most assuredly order the artillery to fire on them.[36]

36. Samuel L. Metcalfe, *A Collection of Some of the Most Interesting Narratives of Indian Warfare in the West* (Lexington, Ky., 1821), 88; Dillon, *History of Indiana,* 252. Accounts vary as to what actually happened. Captain Armstrong reported that he warned Hardin of the loose formation of his troops; Hardin replied that Indians would not fight, and he scornfully rode on in front of the troops. Armstrong believed that the men were fired on from behind the fire, whereas other Indians had doubled back to simultaneously attack the troops from the rear. See James H. Perkins, *Annals of the West: Embracing a Concise Account of Principal Events Which Have Occurred in the Western States and Territories . . .* (Cincinnati, Oh., 1847), 193; Mann Butler, *A History of the Commonwealth of Kentucky* (Louisville, Ky., 1834), 193; Humphrey Marshall, *The History of Kentucky: Including an Account of the Discovery, Settlement, Progressive Improvement, Political and Military Events, and Present State of the Country,* 2 vols. (Frankfort, Ky., 1812), I, 363.

Following this crushing defeat, Harmar exacted his revenge on Miamitown. Knox had ordered the village's destruction in retaliation for the ongoing raids on settler colonists. Harmar realized that Miamitown was also a major trading center, the economic and political heart of the large Miami, Shawnee, and Delaware populations, and its destruction would punish them for failing to come to the treaty table. Harmar reduced everything to ashes: Miamitown, the nearby Delaware and Shawnee villages, all the orchards, immense fields and stores of corn, and buildings. His men were "to burn and destroy every house and wigwam in this village, together with all the corn, etc., [they] can collect." In describing the vengeful obliteration of these agrarian villages, which he referred to as the "Maumee towns," Ebenezer Denny revealed their agricultural wealth in the "pretty good gardens with some fruit trees, and vast fields of corn in almost every direction." For three long days, the army burned and looted the extensive settlements and cultivated fields of six villages at the confluence of the Maumee, St. Joseph, and St. Mary's Rivers. In the army's spree of destruction, looting became acceptable behavior. Harmar's men carted off everything they thought they could use: corn, beans, pumpkins, stacks of hay, fencing, and even parts of Indian cabins. Harmar encouraged this behavior. Taking advantage of the abundance of food stores, he transported much of the surplus to feed his hungry men. Although Harmar left no record of the destruction, it became clear to the participants that this was not a series of poor, destitute villages. Denny reported that fire "consumed and destroyed twenty thousand bushels of corn in ears," while Harmar's men had destroyed almost three hundred homes. In addition, the Miami had destroyed many of the larger homes before their departure. The army leveled an extensive agrarian landscape where Indian prosperity was evident.[37]

Harmar ordered every tree chopped down, set fire to the apple orchards, then extended the burning frenzy to the Shawnee town of Pickaway, where he ordered Colonel Hardin to "burn and destroy effectually, this afternoon, the Pickaway town, with all the corn, etc., which he can find in it and its vicinity." Every house, cornfield, garden, and orchard was razed, leaving behind charred, barren earth.[38]

Following the conflagration, Harmar moved the remaining army to a Shawnee village two miles distant from Miamitown. That evening, Harmar attempted to stop the Indians from carrying off his army's straggling horses

---

37. *Military Journal of Ebenezer Denny*, 349, 351; Dillon, *History of Indiana*, 251–252. "Wigwam" is a derogatory term, like "squaw"; these are words used to portray the Indian as uncivilized despite the visual evidence to the contrary.

38. Dillon, *History of Indiana*, 252.

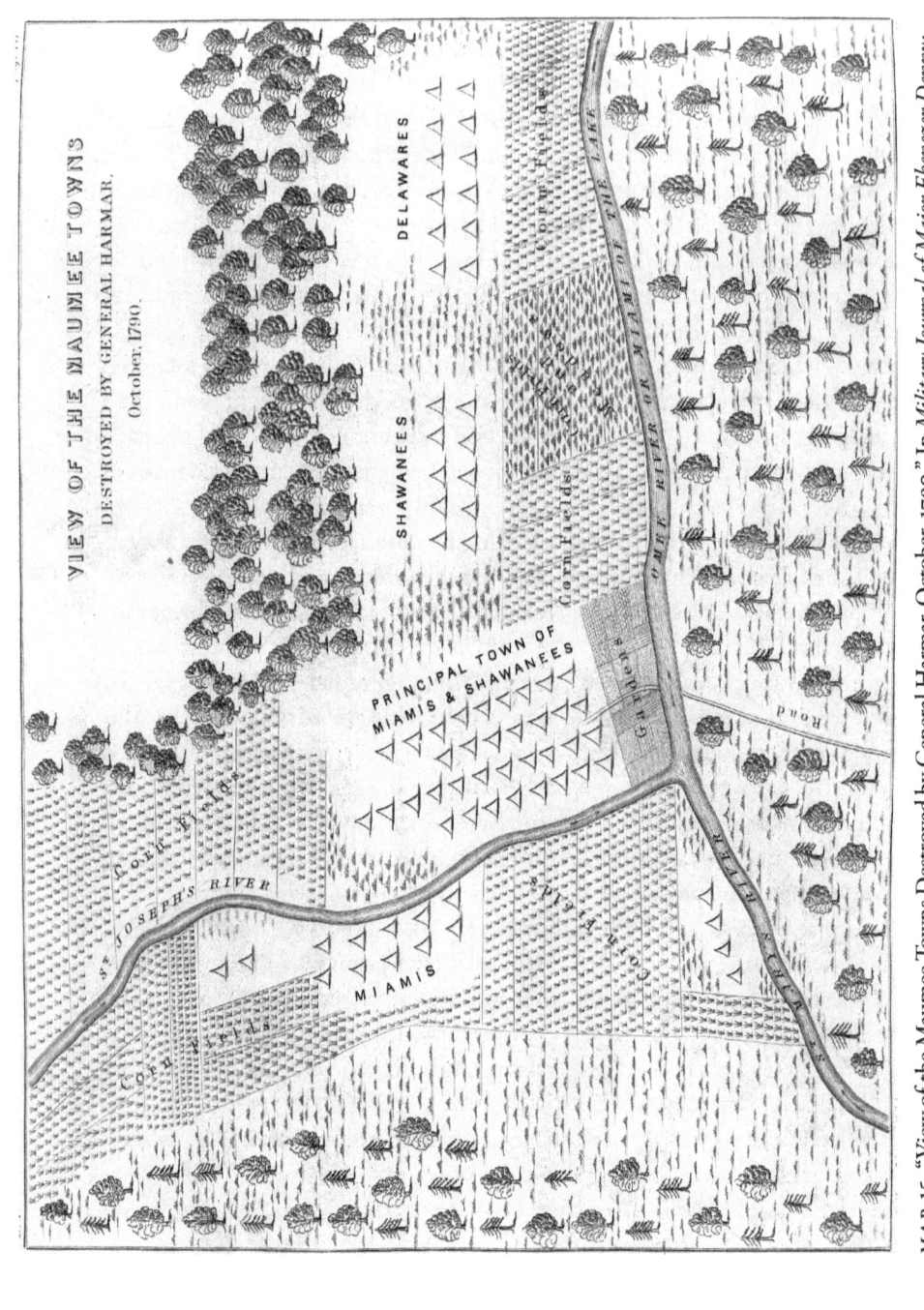

MAP 15. "View of the Maumee Towns Destroyed by General Harmar, October, 1790." In *Military Journal of Major Ebenezer Denny: An Officer in the Revolutionary and Indian Wars* (Philadelphia, 1860). The Historical Society of Pennsylvania

by setting a trap for the horse thieves. The militia managed to capture one of the Indians; they decapitated him and put his head on a pole. Marching around the camp, they claimed that Harmar owed them the bounty that was associated with capturing wolves. Harmar had created a frenzy of cruelty and destruction that ensured the Indians would seek revenge.[39]

After the destruction of the villages clustered at Miamitown, the army began its retreat to Fort Washington, but they journeyed only eight miles before making camp. Their progress was slowed by their desire to transport all the spoils from the Indian villages. Meanwhile, Harmar decided to send out detachments to find and punish the Indians that he thought were returning to Miamitown. Intending to surprise them, he planned to capture and kill the Indian families, allowing Hardin, under the command of Major John Wyllys of the regular army, to take 350 men on this proposed mission.

With Harmar dividing the larger army into smaller units, Little Turtle was able to plan a second, equally effective ambush. He positioned a small group of warriors to lie in wait along the banks of the Maumee. This time, Hardin's men did not mutiny, and seeing only a small number of Indians, they assumed that victory was possible. The army rushed headlong across the Maumee as the warriors lured them into an adjacent cornfield. Little Turtle had hidden dozens of armed men in the surrounding forest, and they rushed from the woods in a surprise attack. Little Turtle's well-disciplined warriors quickly overpowered the unsuspecting army regulars. Although Harmar's forces tried to regroup, most men simply fled the battlefield. When the fighting ended, small, terrified groups of survivors headed back to the main army. The Indians continually harassed them by firing from the woods. Harmar finally arrived at Fort Washington on November 3, 1790, in defeat. Harmar had assembled a force of 1,133 militia members, many of whom deserted. Of his U.S. Army force of 335 men, he had lost 180—more than half of his regulars. Harmar beat a hasty retreat, lost half of the horses, and left behind most of the heavy equipment. Disgracefully, he never returned to bury the dead. Harmar proclaimed the battle a major achievement because he had marched into the heart of Indian Country and destroyed four hundred acres of cornfields and burned down the Miami, Delaware, and Shawnee cabins clustered around Miamitown. But Harmar's large force was defeated by a small force of fewer than 600 to 800 Indians. Knox relieved Harmar of his command.[40]

39. *Military Journal of Ebenezer Denny*, 351.
40. Personal accounts of the expedition include the letters of Harmar to St. Clair, in Josiah Harmar Papers, Letter Book, XXIX, June 9–Dec. 29, 1790, esp. those dated Oct. 18, 24, 1790, William L. Clements Library, Ann Arbor, Mich.; "Governor St. Clair to the Sec-

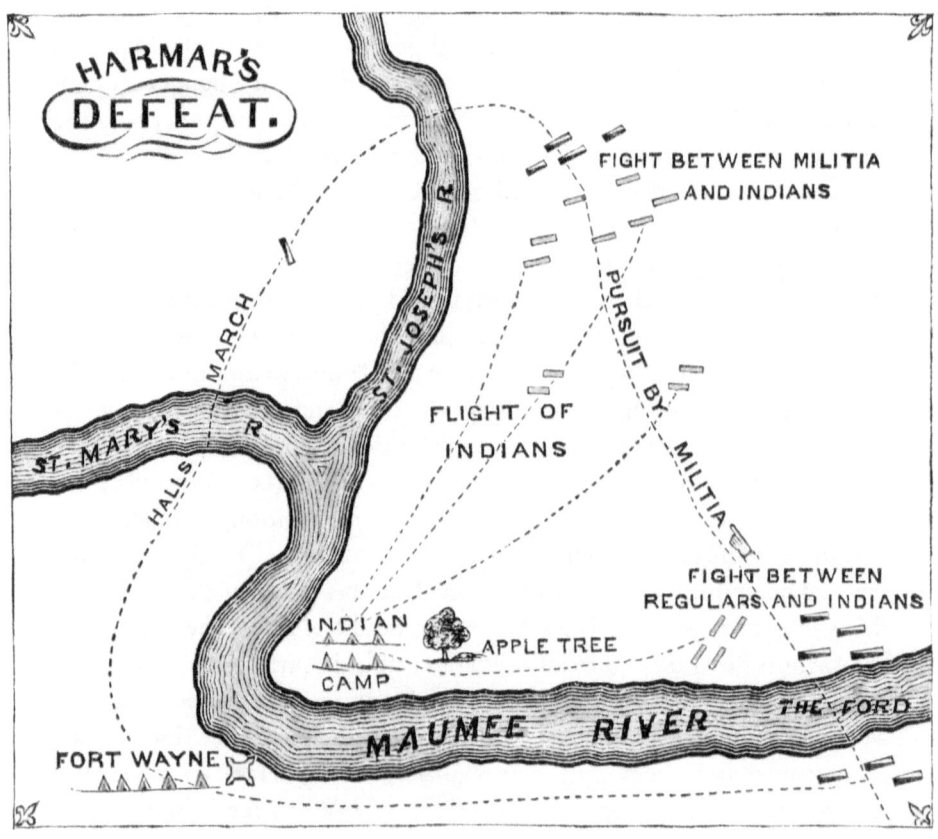

MAP 16. Map of Harmar's defeat by the Indians at Fort Wayne, Indiana. 1791. Hand-colored woodcut. Photographed by Nancy Carter, North Wind Picture Archives. Image EVNT2A-00236

The true nature of Harmar's "victory" was understood by Knox, Washington, and members of Congress. A smaller force of Indians had defeated a much larger U.S. Army. Washington railed against Harmar, claiming that he was an alcoholic whose military mistakes transformed an honorable defeat into a shameful rout. Knox had warned Harmar to "Move swiftly, strike hard,

retary of War," Oct. 29, Nov. 6, Nov. 26, 1790, in Smith, ed., *St. Clair Papers*, II, 188, 190, 192; *Military Journal of Ebenezer Denny*, 205–492; Dillon, *History of Indiana*, 245–248; Thomas Irwin, "Harmar's Campaign," *Ohio Archaeological and Historical Publications*, XIX (1910), 393–396; Cayton, *Frontier Indiana*, 149–154; Barnhart and Riker, *Indiana to 1816*, 284–287; Basil Meek, "General Harmar's Expedition," *Ohio Archaeological and Historical Publications*, XX (1911), 86–87; Jacobs, *Beginning of the U.S. Army*, 52–62.

and above all, remain sober." At a subsequent congressional hearing, Samuel Abbey, a regular army officer, testified that he watched a drunken Harmar fall out of his chair at Fort Washington. Harmar's incompetence was apparent; he had never commanded a large military force, and he was completely naive about the nature of the enemy and the type of fighting that his men faced. Henry Knox's fears proved well grounded. Harmar's Defeat did more than vex President Washington; it infuriated him. Because Harmar refused to return to the battlefield to bury his dead, he was also viciously denounced by members of Congress. Senator William Maclay of Pennsylvania echoed Washington's ire: "The ill-fortune of the affair breaks through all the coloring. ... [It] look[s] finely on paper, but were we to view the green bones and scattered fragments of our defeat on the actual field, it would leave very different ideas on our minds. This is a vile business and must be much viler." Congressional hearings eventually exonerated Harmar, but Indian victory galvanized Congress. Anxious to avenge the reputation of the nation, Congress authorized an additional $312,000 in revenues to create a new and larger army of three thousand men. No matter the cost, the United States intended to defeat the Indians. Washington appointed St. Clair to command an enlarged army and to begin planning an offensive operation against the Indians.[41]

The massacre of Pacanne's men and Moluntha's death had rallied Indians around the Miami and Shawnee. A confederacy of Indians fought to defend their Ohio River boundary line and, together, they had soundly defeated Harmar. More important, Harmar's Defeat and ongoing raids had slowed the intrusion of settler colonists on western lands. Despite these routs, the United States refused to recognize the Ohio River as the legitimate boundary with Indian lands. With the destruction of Miamitown, many Indians had simply moved downriver to the Glaize, where there was ample room and sufficient resources to feed their people and to attract additional refugee Indian villages. Warriors were drawn to the region with the news of Little Turtle's victory; many northern warriors who had participated in the battles remained at the Glaize. The Indians had drawn closer to the British-controlled fort at Detroit.

41. Fitzpatrick, ed., *Writings of George Washington,* XXXI, 156; Knox to Harmar, Aug. 24, Sept. 3, 1790, Draper MSS, 2W, 310, 324–326, Samuel Abbey interview by Benjamin Drake, Apr. 20, 1844, 4 U 169. When Anthony Wayne marched through the area in 1794, he and his men buried the bones of many who had fallen here in 1790. See Charles Cist, *The Cincinnati Miscellany,* 2 vols. (1845–1846; rpt. New York, 1971), I, 184; Michael S. Warner, "General Josiah Harmar's Campaign Reconsidered: How the Americans Lost the Battle of Kekionga," *Indiana Magazine of History,* LXXXIII (1987), 64, quoted in Randolph Chandler Downes, *Frontier Ohio, 1788–1803,* Ohio State Archaeological and Historical Society, *Collections,* III (Columbus, Oh., 1935), 25.

Not only was this site protected by the vast swampland that extended forty miles to the west from Sandusky, but animals were a plentiful food resource that allowed continuation of the fur trade.

The Indians now possessed a military force that was daily increasing in size. The Indian victory had transformed the Pan-Indian Confederacy into reality and solidified support for an Indian war. At the same time, Harmar's Defeat had left Washington and Knox resolved to seek retaliation. They also grasped that relinquishing control of the very fertile lands north of the Ohio would doom schemes for repaying the massive debts of the Revolutionary War and could bankrupt the new nation. Defeat had renewed the determination of the executive and legislative branches to conquer the Indians. The hope that a lasting peace could be achieved on the basis of negotiation became increasingly dim.

7

CAPTURING INDIAN WOMEN

Josiah Harmar's defeat enraged President Washington. The president, together with Knox, shaped a new military policy driven by humiliation and infused with revenge. Reversing his previous, half-hearted attempts to control the Kentucky militia, the president now empowered them. Washington deplored the men who were settling the west; they were ungovernable and brutal in their treatment of Indians. But Washington intended to punish the Indians for Harmar's Defeat by using the Kentucky militia to invade Indian lands along the Wabash, targeting the agrarian villages that stretched from Ouiatenon to Kethtippecanuck.[1]

Washington's invasion plan relied on strategies he had successfully employed during the Revolutionary War, when Sullivan's Expedition targeted agricultural resources and noncombatant Seneca populations, primarily women and children. General Washington had ordered Sullivan to "totally extirpate the unfriendly nations of the Indians . . . subdue their country, destroy their crops, and drive them to seek habitations where they would be less troublesome to us and our allies." Now, women and children in the Wabash River valley were the president's primary target; their cornfields, houses, and orchards were to be destroyed. Washington's measures went beyond the suffering inflicted on the Iroquois. The president of the United States ordered the Kentucky militia to capture as many Indians as possible, "particularly women and children," and to carry and deliver them "to the commanding officer at some post of the United States upon the Ohio."[2]

---

1. H[enry] Knox, "Instructions to Brigadier General Charles Scott," Mar. 9, 1791, in United States Congress, *American State Papers: Documents, Legislative and Executive, of the Congress of the United States . . .* , 38 vols. (Washington, D.C., 1832), Class II, *Indian Affairs*, 2 vols., ed. Walter Lowrie et al., I, 129 (hereafter cited as *ASPIA*).

2. Ibid., 130.

Kidnapping Indian women and children was meant "to bring the deluded Indians to a just sense of their situation." Both Washington and Knox were confident "that the probability would be highly in favor of surprising and capturing at least a considerable number of women and children." They had estimated the warrior strength of the Wabash River valley to be "from fifteen hundred to two thousand warriors"; these numbers would have equated with a population of six to eight thousand women and children.[3]

Destroying agrarian villages would undermine Indian resistance. The prosperous Wabash villages were the valley's breadbasket, producing the food that fed large populations, including warriors. Washington was convinced that, by leveling those villages, he was forcing Indian warriors to return home and hunt to ward off their family's starvation. Washington had used this strategy against the Iroquois during the Revolutionary War, and now he intended to apply it to Indians who refused to relinquish their lands. He attacked Indian villages populated primarily by women, invading lands that had not been ceded by treaty. Sullivan had devastated and reduced Iroquois women and children to starvation. He religiously followed Washington's orders to "cut off their settlements, destroy their next Year's crops, and do them every other mischief of which time and circumstances will permit." Now Kentuckians would enthusiastically execute Washington's orders. As we have seen, Kentucky attempts to invade settlements along the Wabash had repeatedly failed, but now, lavishly financed by the United States government, they would be assured of success. Knox stroked the egos of these rabid Indian haters by providing them the opportunity "of acting by themselves in an Indian expedition," which he believed would be "highly gratifying to the hardy and brave yeomanry of Kentucky." Attempts to raid Indian lands north of the Ohio had been hampered by small numbers of poorly equipped volunteers. Now, the federal government authorized an invading army of 500 to 750 men, fully armed and provisioned and "mounted on horses," and doubled the pay allotted to army recruits. Kentuckians were encouraged to incinerate Indian

---

3. Ibid.; Albert Hazen Wright, ed., *The Sullivan Expedition of 1779*, 4 vols. (Ithaca, N.Y., 1943), II, 37–38; Alexander C. Flick, "The Sullivan-Clinton Campaign in 1779," New Jersey Historical Society, *Proceedings*, XV (1930), 66–67; Barbara Graymont, *Iroquois in the American Revolution* (Syracuse, N.Y., 1972), 192; Anthony F. C. Wallace, *The Death and Rebirth of the Seneca* (New York, 1969), 142–144; John Grenier, *The First Way of War: American War Making on the Frontier, 1607–1814* (New York, 2005), 166–169; Andrew R. L. Cayton, *Frontier Indiana* (Bloomington, Ind., 1996), 155; John B. Dillon, *History of Indiana: From Its Earliest Exploration by Europeans to the Close of the Territorial Government, in 1816 . . .* (1859; rpt. New York, 1971), 217–220.

homes, cornfields, vegetable gardens, and fruit orchards and then cart the women and children off to a nearby federal fort.[4]

Washington's rampage across Iroquois farmlands had scarred Seneca memory; even today, the first president remains known among the Seneca as the Town Destroyer. Ironically, late in 1790, shortly before the fateful attack on the Wabash River villages, Cornplanter reminded federal officials of the indelible mark Washington had left on Seneca women: "When your army entered the country of the Six Nations, we called you town destroyer; and to this day, when that name is heard, our women look behind them and turn pale, and our children cling close to the necks of their mothers."[5]

Washington's strategy of holding Indian leaders hostage had encouraged the Iroquois chiefs to sign the Fort Stanwix treaty. One of Joseph Brandt's closest friends, the Mohawk chief Aaron Hill, was among these captives. Washington intended to use that same strategy against the Wabash villages, forcing them to come to the treaty table and transforming their stubborn resistance into land cessions.[6]

Knox feared that employing those same tactics in the Ohio River valley could backfire. These villages were fiercely independent, and, although most had sufficient warriors for defense, they usually chose not to engage in pitched battles. Indians learned to protect themselves by evacuating their villages and stripping their homes of material goods. Knox cautioned Washington that an attack financed and supported by the federal government could alert the villages in the region, potentially drawing assistance from Indians near and far:

> It is to be observed that the United States have not formed any treaties with the Wabash Indians.... Some of the inhabitants, of Kentucky during the year past ... made an incursion into the Wabash country, and possessing an equal aversion to all bearing the name of indians, they destroyed a number of peaceable Piankeshaws who prided themselves in their attachment to the United States. Things being thus circumstanced it is greatly to be apprehended that hostilities may be so far extended as to involve the indian tribes with whom the United States have recently made treaties.... An inquiry would arise, whether, under the existing circumstances of affairs, the

---

4. Knox, "Instructions to Scott," *ASPIA*, I, 129; Colin G. Calloway, *The American Revolution in Indian Country: Crisis and Diversity in Native American Communities* (New York, 1995), 51–53; Graymont, *Iroquois in the American Revolution*, 192–222.

5. Lisa Brooks, *The Common Pot: The Recovery of Native Space in the Northeast* (Minneapolis, 2008), 116.

6. Ibid., 126.

United States have a clear right, consistently with the principles of justice and the laws of nature to proceed to the destruction or expulsion of the savages on the Wabash.[7]

The president failed to see the wisdom of Knox's warning. As much as George Washington loathed the Kentuckians, he backed their military operations to satisfy his own desire for revenge. He was familiar with the agrarian nature of Indian villages of the Ohio River valley, having first traveled along the Ohio in 1753 on a diplomatic mission for the governor of Virginia. In 1770, Washington returned to Ohio Country to select the bounty lands earned from his service in the French and Indian War. During that trip, Washington encountered a British convoy of two bateaux and a large canoe traveling toward the Illinois Country and carrying provisions for British-held Fort Chartres. Washington secured information from two of the men about the Cumberland River, which flowed across Tennessee and Kentucky to the Ohio River. When Washington returned to Mount Vernon, he recorded additional notes about his trip, writing that he was "well pleased with my journey, as it has been the means of my obtaining a knowledge of facts-coming at the temper and disposition of the Western Inhabitants and making reflections thereon, which, otherwise, must have been as wild, incoher[en]t, and perhaps as foreign from the truth, as the inconsistencys of the reports which I had received even from those to whom most credit seemed due, generally were." Washington's will reflected his continued speculation in western lands: he had acquired 9,744 acres on the Ohio River, another 23,341 acres on the Great Kahawa, 3,051 acres in the northwestern territory, and 5,000 acres in Kentucky, including miscellaneous lands in present-day western Virginia.[8]

---

7. Henry Knox to George Washington, June 12, 1789, in W. W. Abbot et al., eds., *The Papers of George Washington: Presidential Series*, II, *Apr.-June 1787* (Charlottesville, Va., 1999), II, 490; Henry Knox, Misc. Papers, MSS C / K, Filson Historical Society, Louisville, Ky.; Temple Bodley, *History of Kentucky*, 4 vols., I, *Before the Louisiana Purchase in 1803* (Chicago, 1928), 454–455.

8. Washington left Williamsburg, Virginia, on October 31, 1753, and completed the round trip of more than one thousand miles by horse, foot, canoe, and raft in about ten weeks. He was accompanied by Christopher Gist, an explorer and surveyor employed by the Ohio Company; Jacob Van Braam, a French interpreter; four Indian traders and baggage men; and various Indian delegations and guards, including Tanacharison, known as the "Half-King." The Virginia legislature was so pleased with his mission and his report that they voted him a fifty-pound reward. *The Journal of Major George Washington* was reprinted in various colonial newspapers as far away as Boston. See Washington to William Crawford, Sept. 20, 1767, George Washington Papers, 4th Ser., General Correspondence, Manuscript Division, Library of Congress. For the full correspondence between Washing-

The Kentucky invasion bore clear evidence of Washington's knowledge of the Ohio region. He ordered Scott to attack specific villages, targeting the villages surrounding Ouiatenon. Past Kentucky invasions had failed to reach these prosperous villages. Expeditions rarely included more than fifty or sixty men, and Indian warriors easily repelled these smaller groups. Again, most villages responded to threats of attack by evacuating their homes and removing their material possessions. Without the rewards of plunder, Kentuckians proved reluctant attackers. But now the federal government fully equipped the militia and made no prohibition against plunder. In the past, the militia had randomly killed Indians traveling along the Wabash who accidentally stumbled into the militia's path. Men like Brown had repeatedly defied Hamtramck's authority, and now President Washington had reinforced the outrageous behavior of the Kentucky militia by authorizing and financing the invasion of agrarian villages. Even Congress lent its enthusiasm and financial support to the Kentucky militia, insisting that the militia be paid to fight as part of the U.S. Army.[9]

George Washington's choice to lead the Kentucky forces was a man who detested Indians and nursed a desire for revenge that eclipsed Washington's. Charles Scott's life had paralleled Washington's in interesting ways. Both men

---

ton and William Crawford and his brother Valentine Crawford, see C. W. Butterfield, *The Washington-Crawford Letters: Being the Correspondence between George Washington and William Crawford, from 1767 to 1781, concerning Western Lands* (Cincinnati, Oh., 1877); October 1770, October 1784, in Donald Jackson and Dorothy Twohig, eds., *The Diaries of George Washington*, 6 vols. (Charlottesville, Va., 1976-1979), II, 290, IV, 58; "Washington's Tour to the Ohio in 1770," *Olden Time*, I (1846), 416-433.

9. Knox, "Instructions to Scott," *ASPIA*, I, 130; John D. Barnhart and Dorothy L. Riker, *Indiana to 1816: The Colonial Period* (Indianapolis, 1971), 289-290; Dillon, *History of Indiana*, 261. The best known of these raids was the inept operation launched by George Rogers Clark against the Wabash villages, which led to the establishment of federal authority at Vincennes; see Wiley Sword, *President Washington's Indian War: The Struggle for the Old Northwest* (Norman, Okla., 1993), 31-35. Patrick Brown's raiders flouted Hamtramck's order to disband and defiantly used the army's canoes to cross the Wabash in 1788. See John Francis Hamtramck to Josiah Harmar, Aug. 31, 1788, in Gayle Thornbrough, ed., *Outpost on the Wabash, 1787-1791: Letters of Brigadier General Josiah Harmar and Major John Francis Hamtramck, and Other Letters and Documents Selected from the Harmar Papers in the William L. Clements Library*, Indiana Historical Society, *Publications*, XIX (Indianapolis, 1957), 114-116; Harvey Lewis Carter, *The Life and Times of Little Turtle: First Sagamore of the Wabash* (Urbana, Ill., 1987), 76. The third attempt took place on August 3, 1789, and was led by Major John Hardin of the Kentucky militia when he left Clarksville and headed for the Wea towns on the Wabash. They returned several days later, following the death of two men, but failed to cross the Ohio (Hamtramck to Harmar, July 29, 1789, in Thornbrough, ed., *Outpost on the Wabash*, 182; and see Knox, "Instructions to Scott," *ASPIA*, I, 129).

served in General Braddock's doomed campaign against Fort Duquesne, and both watched in horror as the Indians decimated British forces. Scott, like Washington, returned to Virginia at the end of the war, but he made for a far less successful planter. By 1785, he had relocated to Virginia's District of Kentucky. There, he became known as a hard-bitten Indian fighter.[10] William McClelland, at first a friend and then a vociferous opponent, considered him "not fit for governor." From 1790 to 1795, Scott spent more time in active service than any other senior Kentucky officer. Increasingly motivated by a desire for retribution, he was consumed by his hatred for Indians. Scott had lost two of his sons in frontier warfare. His first son, Charles Scott, Jr., was killed by Indians while he was fishing at the mouth of a creek across from Scott's cabin. His much-loved son Merritt was killed during the Harmar defeat. Merritt was a captain in Kentucky's Woodford County militia and had fought under Major John Wyllys. When most of the militia fled the battlefield, Merritt Scott stood his ground. As Merritt lay mortally wounded, his neighbor John Mosby attempted to save him, but Merritt pleaded with Mosby to save himself. Mosby hid in a nearby swamp, from which he watched the Indians tomahawk, scalp, and strip his friend's body. He shared this horrific story with Scott and later recounted it at Harmar's court of inquiry. Newspapers seized upon its sensationalist nature, and the tale became embedded in local histories of Kentucky.[11]

SCOTT'S INVASION

Knox's command "that he should take every proper arrangement to bring the deluded Indians to a just sense of their situation" further inflamed

---

10. Charles Scott was born in Cumberland County, Virginia, in 1740. He moved to what is now part of Woodford County, Kentucky, in 1785. He settled on the Kentucky River and built his cabin and a fort at what was later known as Scott's Landing, not far from Mortonsville. He was governor of Kentucky from 1808 to 1812 and died in 1820. It is unclear whether his wife moved with him to Kentucky or remained in Virginia. See Lindsey Apple, Frederick A. Johnston, and Ann Bolton Bevins, eds., *Scott County, Kentucky: A History* (Georgetown, Ky., 1993), 45; William E. Railey, *History of Woodford County, Kentucky* (1928; rpt. Frankfort, Ky., 1938), 8, 110–111, 276–277; James Ripley Jacobs, *Tarnished Warrior: Major-General James Wilkinson* (New York, 1938), 71–73; J. W. Whickcar [Whicker], "General Charles Scott and His March to Ouiatenon," *Indiana Magazine of History*, XXI (1925), 98; Thomas Marshall Green, *Spanish Conspiracy: A Review of Early Spanish Movements in the South-West* (Cincinnati, Oh., 1891), 134.

11. Lewis Collins and Richard H. Collins. *History of Kentucky* (1882; rpt. Easley, S.C., 1979), II, 706; John Shane's notebooks, I, Lyman Draper Manuscript Collection, 11 CC 184, State Historical Society of Wisconsin, Madison; Richard G. Stone, Jr., *A Brittle Sword: The Kentucky Militia, 1776–1912* (Lexington, Ky., 1977), 17–18.

Scott's desire for revenge. The secretary at war sanctioned further expeditions against the Wabash villages, authorizing the Board of War to send a second, or even a third, expedition at government expense. In early May, Scott summoned all interested Kentucky volunteers to fight "under [his] command" and ride against the Northwest Indians. With the enthusiastic support of the *Kentucky Gazette,* Scott quickly recruited experienced Indian fighters willing to attack and plunder Indian villages. Levi Todd, Scott's recruiting officer, enlisted 852 volunteers within two weeks, quickly exceeding the authorized quota of 750. Enthusiastic volunteers supplied their own horses and weapons while others were outfitted with guns and horses at government expense. Many of these men had fought alongside Harmar, and some, like the disgraced John Hardin, were eager to redeem their reputations. Hardin was given charge of the advance party.[12]

Shortly before the troops were to rendezvous at Frankfort, Scott received an unexpected visit from General Arthur St. Clair. Scott was ordered to delay his raid until John Proctor, Knox's peace envoy, returned to Fort Washington. St. Clair told Scott that his raid was merely a diversionary tactic, to keep the Indians off-balance while the general assembled his larger, 3,000- to 5,000-man army; perhaps Scott should delay until the much larger military operation in the fall. Not surprisingly, Scott's temper got the best of him, and he angrily dismissed St. Clair. Scott bluntly told the general that his orders would be scorned by the Kentucky militia; they were eager and "itching" to attack the Indians after a season of relative inactivity. Although Scott's arrogant attitude infuriated St. Clair, the general backed down from delaying the Wabash raid. Instead, St. Clair asked Scott merely to "delay" for two weeks. The Kentucky militia were necessary to the fall offensive, and the general feared alienating Scott and his men.[13]

While at Scott's home, St. Clair reminded Scott of the need to treat all captives with "humanity." He reinforced this verbal warning in a May 18 letter to Scott.

---

12. *Kentucky Gazette,* May 7, 1791; Levi Todd letter, July 5, 1791, MS 104, folder 2011, Margaret I. King Library, Special Collections, University of Kentucky, Lexington; Knox, "Instructions to Scott," *ASPIA,* I, 129; Minutes of the Board of War, Apr. 8, May 2, 1791, Charles Scott Papers, King Library; Jacobs, *Tarnished Warrior,* 112; Carter, *Life and Times of Little Turtle,* 100; Temple Bodley, *History of Kentucky,* 4 vols., I, *Before the Louisiana Purchase in 1803* (Chicago, 1928), 465.

13. Arthur St. Clair to Charles Scott, May 18, 1791, in William Henry Smith, ed., *The Life and Public Services of Arthur St. Clair: Soldier of the Revolutionary War...,* 2 vols. (Cincinnati, Oh., 1882), II, 208.

On the subject of prisoners, give me leave to call your attention to that part of your instructions which respects the treatment they are to receive.... I request you to impress the propriety of treating with great humanity such as may fall into their hands upon those under your command of all ranks and descriptions. The dignity of the United States requires it; the character of the nation demands it; the best consequences may be expected to result from it, and it is the positive orders of the President.[14]

Scott received a surplus of volunteers, Levi Todd having recruited more than 100 men over the quota. Scott headed north with an expeditionary force of 852 men, most on horseback. They not only carried weapons but were laden down with supply bags to carry the expected plunder, and they were followed by packhorses that carried sufficient food, supplies, and ammunition to sustain a month-long invasion. St. Clair supplied Scott with 500 pounds of powder, 1,000 pounds of lead, 1,500 flints, and all the tools necessary for making rafts to cross the Ohio River.[15]

Scott planned to cross the Ohio near the mouth of the Kentucky River and then march north to Ouiatenon. This was an unfamiliar route: most Kentucky raiders traveled overland to Vincennes and north along the trails that bordered the Wabash. Charles Scott was confident that this alternative route would meet Knox's demand for "surprise, rapid marches, and attacks." Scott's reputation was as an Indian fighter and not as a military planner. He had probably never considered the logistics of moving eight hundred men across a river swollen by spring rains or through an unanticipated wetland landscape. Logistically, these movements were complicated by Scott's dedication to a mounted militia, well suited to travel across Kentucky's bluegrass prairielands, less so across marshy terrain. Including mounted infantrymen had an additional incentive for Scott: they were paid more than foot soldiers, $22 rather than $3. Prestige played an equally important motivating role. As one historian has suggested, "Their service as mounted infantrymen was perceived by them to be more glamorous and better suited to their proud temperaments than serving as 'mere' infantrymen."[16]

---

14. Knox, "Instructions to Scott," *ASPIA*, I, 130; St. Clair to Scott, May 18, 1791, in Smith, ed., *Life and Public Services of Arthur St. Clair*, II, 208.

15. Levi Todd letter, July 5, 1791, MS 104, folder 2011; Harry M. Ward, *Charles Scott and the "Spirit of '76"* (Charlottesville, Va., 1988), 109.

16. St. Clair to Scott, May 18, 1791, St. Clair to Knox, May 26, 1791, in Smith, ed., *St. Clair Papers*, II, 207-209, 212-216; Paul David Nelson, "General Charles Scott, the Kentucky Mounted Volunteers, and the Northwest Indian Wars, 1784-1794," *Journal of the Early Republic*, VI (1986), 221; Stone, *Brittle Sword*, 15.

Scott's intended crossing was at Battle Creek, just five miles below the mouth of the Kentucky River (near present-day Madison, Indiana). On May 19, the militia cut down trees and began building rafts to cross the rain-swollen river. Transporting large numbers of men, horses, and supplies across the Ohio was a process beset by problems. Horses had to swim across a strong current that threatened to carry them downriver, and they resisted entering the cold, turbulent waters. Supplies became wet or were lost when rafts overturned. Rafts swept away by the current forced men to jump off and swim to the opposite shore. Most men did not carry extra clothing, and they were wet and cold before their long land journey had even begun. Normal crossings would have taken a day, but Scott's troops spent four long, exhausting days crossing the Ohio. Scott, a man of few words, provided few details about the hazards of the crossing. He later admitted, "The delay at the river was greater than I wished."[17]

The river crossing proved a minor obstacle compared to the landscape that these 852 men encountered north of the Ohio. Prairies gave way to bogs and wetlands, and the horses were quickly mired in the soft ground; travel slowed to a snail's pace. As the mounted men struggled along a narrow Indian footpath, the spring rains descended. It rained every day for a week. Gentle showers gave way to a series of severe thunderstorms. Lightning terrified the horses, and men were forced to blindfold and lead them along narrow, muddy paths. Growing expanses of muck made it impossible to ride. North of the Ohio, Indians rode small horses that were less likely to sink in the bogs or slip on soft ground. The Kentucky militia led their huge horses through quagmires, transforming them into a slow-moving army of foot soldiers. The pace slackened to that of Harmar's infantrymen. From May 23 to early June, Scott's militia traveled about 150 miles, which on Kentucky's bluegrass prairies would have been a hard two-day march. Here in the wetlands, it took three times as long to cover the same distance.

The Shawnee guides Scott hired to direct him to Ouiatenon intensified these problems. One had a wife in the Wabash villages; unknowingly, Scott had hired his own private Indian spy. The guide stalled the expedition in a maze of environmental obstacles. There were two branches of the White River, but Scott's militia was led across the swollen stream four times. Following unfamiliar pathways on dim, rainy days, they recrossed the same river at different places. In his brief description of the march, Scott recited a litany of difficulties:

---

17. "Report of Brigadier General Scott," June 28, 1791, *ASPIA*, I, 131.

By the 31st I had marched one hundred and thirty-five miles, over a country cut by four large branches of White river, and many smaller streams, with steep, muddy banks; during this march, I traversed a country alternately interspersed with the most luxuriant soil and deep clayey bogs, from one to five miles in width, rendered almost impervious by brush and briars. Rain fell in torrents every day, with frequent blasts of wind and thunder storms. These obstacles impeded my progress, wore down my horses, and destroyed my provisions.[18]

When the militia finally exited the wetlands and reached the Shawnee Prairie, they were a dispirited, bedraggled lot. Later, the *Kentucky Gazette* described the invaders as a "proud assemblage" of "first class . . . citizens, a member of Congress, members of the Senate and Assembly, Magistrates, Colonels, Majors, Captains, [and] Lawyers." But by the time these men reached Ouiatenon, they were ill and their horses unfit to ride. More than five hundred men and horses were crippled, preventing the militia from delivering the swift blow ordered by Knox. Barrels of flour were wet and riddled with bugs, and the army had to rely on skilled marksmen to supply it with much-needed meat and waterfowl. Eighteenth-century rifles were noisy affairs, and the sound of frequent gunfire made it easy to hear the approaching militia and accurately judge their distance. Scott's expedition became known as the "Blackberry Campaign" because spoiled provisions reduced the men to eating blackberries to stave off their hunger. The militia's long, drawn-out march gave Indians time to evacuate their villages.[19]

On the Shawnee Prairie, just south and east of the Wea Plains, the militia caught their first glimpse of an Indian, probably Captain Bull, a Miami leader. He had tracked the militia's single-file progress through the swamplands and was riding across the ridgeline of the high hills to the northwest. The Indian villages were still five miles distant and across the river. Scott realized that news of their arrival would spread quickly and undoubtedly feared that he would encounter vacant villages. He spurred the militia on and, as they headed toward the ridgeline of the Round Top Hills, his men fired at the lone figure on horseback. The echo of their gunshots carried across the cliffs and bluffs of the Wabash River valley, reaching the distant villages.

There were only a few scattered hunting camps on their side of the river, and Scott dispatched John Hardin and forty mounted militiamen to attack these sites. At the Kickapoo hunting camp, the Indians mounted their horses

18. Ward, *Charles Scott*, 110; "Report of Scott," *ASPIA*, I, 131.
19. *Kentucky Gazette*, July 23, 1791; Nelson, "General Charles Scott," *Journal of the Early Republic*, VI (1986), 230.

and sped south toward a point where rocks lined the river bottom and horses and riders could cross the swollen Wabash River. For eight miles, Hardin's men chased the Kickapoo; at Pine Creek, they caught and killed the six Indian men. Hardin later referred to this as the Battle of Kickapoo. The Kentuckians then marched through three vacant Wea villages. The Indians and their belongings were gone; what remained were a number of very sick people, along with women and children who were left to care for them.

Charles Scott and the rest of the militia headed north along the eastern bank of the river. From the top of Round Hill, they could see two villages in the distance, and Scott detached a troop of light cavalry, commanded by Captain McCoy, to capture the villages. At this point, most of Scott's men were unfit to travel, and the villages were five miles away, across the rising, treacherous waters of the Wabash River. Scott ordered his Shawnee guides to find a place where the river was passable. Meanwhile, Scott sighted a log house by the side of the river and detached another group of forty men to encircle it. Two Indians were barricaded inside, and both quickly met their deaths. In his letter to Knox, Scott claimed this as his first victory. The rest of the militia continued to the Wabash but were unable to cross. When Scott saw five canoes of Kickapoo fleeing their village, he ordered Colonel James Wilkinson and the first battalion across the river. The Wabash was too deep and swift-flowing, and the horses and men floundered. Wilkinson's men withdrew from the water, remained on the bank, and took aim at the escaping Kickapoo, killing all of them.

Frustrated at being unable to cross the river, Scott's Shawnee guides led Wilkinson and the militia several miles north to another crossing. The river proved impassable again; Scott dispatched two additional detachments south along the river's edge to search for another passage. The river still hampered their crossing, and, finally, several men had to swim across it. They located a canoe on the far shore — but, by now, the main village was almost abandoned. Scott's men did find an elderly woman sitting next to a white flag and brought her to the general, thinking she signified the Indian willingness to negotiate. Unfortunately, they misunderstood the message of the flag; the elderly woman was in mourning and sitting near the burial site of a relative. Undeterred by the "aged squaw['s]" lack of interest in conversing, Scott sent her away with a message that if her people "would come in and surrender, their towns should be spared."[20]

Meanwhile, Captain Hardin sent word about his attacks on the Wea vil-

---

20. John Dabney Shane, interview with John Craig, Draper MSS, 12 CC 146; "Report of Scott," *ASPIA,* I, 131–132.

lages, and Scott immediately sent Colonel Brown to assist him. Before Brown arrived, the detachments had returned to camp, accompanied by fifty-two sick prisoners.[21]

WILKINSON DESTROYS KETHTIPPECANUCK

The next day, after reviewing his troops, Scott found only 360 men fit for service. He had ordered Colonel Wilkinson to attack Kethtippecanuck, a trading village eighteen miles to the north. Washington had not ordered this assault, but plunder was a primary objective of the Kentucky militia, and this was reputed to be a prosperous trading village. Three hundred men marched on foot along a well-worn and wide roadway. They came across the "important town of Kethtipecanunck... on the west side of the Wabash." The militia encountered an almost empty village. The remaining Indians were climbing into canoes to cross the impassable Elk Creek. Wilkinson's men fired at the fleeing Indians, and once they had disappeared into the woods, his 360 men plundered the town and set it aflame.[22]

Kethtippecanuck, as discussed in Chapter 4, was indeed a prosperous village. George Imlay, who later laid out the lands of the "back settlements," described this picturesque town and adjacent gardens with a sense of awe. The well-constructed houses, with their shingle roofs, conveyed an unexpected sense of stability and permanence. William Clark, the younger brother of George Rogers Clark, was another militia member accompanying Wilkinson. He described extensive cornfields with one thousand bushels of corn, and, nearby, a "quantity of bears oil kettles carts ploughs. Salt, cattle, hogs, and so forth." Wilkinson described Kethtippecanuck as a French trading village where "many of the inhabitants... were French, and lived in a state of civilization; by the books, letters, and other documents found there," it "was in close connection with, and dependent on, Detroit."[23]

Scott justified the attack by claiming that his men had destroyed the home of a trader who sold guns to the Indians. But the more important consideration was that this trading village offered the militia access to plunder and

---

21. George Imlay provided a detailed account of the lands along the Wabash; he was a militia member. His work is entitled *A Topographical Description of the Western Territory of North America* (London, 1793), and reprinted in Harlow Lindley, ed., *Indiana as Seen by Early Travelers,* Indiana Historical Collections, III (Indianapolis, 1916), 9–16. The Michigan Pioneer and Historical Society's *Collections,* XXIV (Lansing, Mich., 1895), has a description of the expedition that was sent to the British Indian agent Alexander McKee (June 6, 1791).

22. "Report of Scott," June 28, 1791, *ASPIA,* I, 131–132.

23. Imlay, *Topographical Description of the Western Territory,* 12–16; Journal of William Clark, Draper MSS, 63 J 141, microfilm, 1949; Barnhart and Riker, *Indiana to 1816,* 290–291.

therefore guaranteed a profitable venture, regardless of the hardships. The next day, in a prolonged frenzy of destruction, Wilkinson's men set fire to the village: "a large quantity of corn, a variety of household goods, peltry, and other articles" that belonged to fur traders "were burned." Several dozen well-built homes were torched, each described as "well firnished [sic]." Gabriel Godfroy was a trader at Kethtippecanuck who lost more than £500 worth of merchandise. The plunder that the militia secured from this village was limited to what each man could carry, although they undoubtedly used the village handcarts to secure the more valuable trade goods.[24]

In his report to Knox, Scott applauded Wilkinson for "march[ing] thirty-six miles in twelve hours" and destroying "the most important settlement of the enemy in that quarter of the federal territory." Washington's orders never included this village, but Scott rationalized his mistake by making claims for the importance of the town.[25]

The militia spent one more day at Ouiatenon, where there was little to plunder in the vacant Indian houses. There was scant stored food, and the recently planted crops of early May were far from ripe. In a fit of pyromania, the militia destroyed the corn crops, houses, and storehouses in the Ouiatenon villages. Matters worsened as militia tempers frayed, and men began torturing an elderly chief that Hardin had captured at the Wea town. They turned to slowly and painfully stripping the skin from the man's body. According to a Moravian missionary, this was Wasp, a Wea leader, captured at the first hunting camp. Horrified at the militia's behavior, the missionary reported that the chief was "treated barbarously and worse than the Indians." The British trader Alexander McKee described the act as literally skinning the man alive.[26]

While his men were busy torturing the old chief, Scott waited impatiently for the Indians to come and talk to him. Scott's message, sent with the old Indian woman, received no response. He warned the Indians that, if they per-

---

24. Imlay, *Topographical Description of the Western Territory*, 12–16; Journal of William Clark, Draper MSS, 63 J 141; Barnhart and Riker, *Indiana to 1816*, 290–291.

25. Carter, *Life and Times of Little Turtle*, 101; James R. Jones III, "An Archaeological Survey of an 18th Century Wea Village Near Fort Ouiatenon, in Tippecanoe County, Indiana," *Proceedings of the Symposium on Ohio Valley Urban and Historic Archaeology*, III (Louisville, Ky., 1985), 105–116; Elizabeth J. Glenn, "Indian Fur Trade Goods," Unpublished Papers and Surveys, Ball State University, Muncie, Ind.

26. "Letter to Col. A. McKee," June 26, 1791, in Michigan Pioneer and Historical Society, *Collections*, XXIV, 273; July 8, 1791, in Eugene F. Bliss, ed., *Diary of David Zeisberger, a Moravian Missionary among the Indians of Ohio* (Cincinnati, Oh., 1885), II, 199; R. David Edmunds, "Wea Participation in the Northwest Indian Wars, 1795," *Filson Club Historical Quarterly*, XLVI (1972), 248; Sword, *President Washington's Indian War*, 141.

sisted in their attacks, "your warriors will be slaughtered, your towns and villages ransacked and destroyed, your wives and children carried into captivity, and you may be assured that those who escape the fury of our mighty chiefs, shall find no resting place on this side the great lakes." Washington and Knox had cautioned Scott to treat the Indians honorably; at the same time, they assumed that Scott would bring terror to Indian Country by capturing a "considerable number of women and children." Hardin had captured a small number of Indians, but most were "infirm," and only forty-one were women. These women were probably left behind to tend to sick family members. Meanwhile, the Indians who remained hidden in the adjacent forests made Scott's militia increasingly nervous, and they began agitating to return to the safety of Kentucky. Desertion loomed as a possibility, and Scott made preparations for a hasty departure. He dragooned the women and children into readiness for travel, and, to avoid being slowed down, left behind those Indians too sick to go along. He also left yet another threatening message proclaiming the power of the United States to vanquish and destroy the Indians.[27]

> The sovereign council of the thirteen United States have long patiently borne your depredations against their settlements on this side of the great mountains, in the hope that you would see your error, and correct it, by entering with them into the bonds of enmity and lasting peace ... at length, their patience is exhausted, and they have stretched forth the arm of power against you; their mighty sons and chief warriors have at length taken up the hatchet; they have penetrated far into your country, to meet your warriors ... but you fled before them, and declined the battle, leaving your wives and children to their mercy; they have destroyed your old town of Ouiatenon ... but again you fled before them, and that great town has been destroyed. After giving you this evidence of their power, they have stopped their hands, because they are merciful as strong. ... The United States have no desire to destroy the red people, although they have the power; but, should you decline this invitation, and pursue your unprovoked hostilities, their strength will again be exerted against you; your warriors will be slaughtered, your towns and villages ransacked and destroyed, your wives and children carried into captivity, and you may be assured that those who escape the fury of our mighty chiefs, shall find no resting place on this side the great lakes. ... Those who are carried off, will be left in the care of our

27. "Report of Scott," *ASPIA*, I, 131, and Scott, "To the Various Tribes of the Piankeshaws, and All the Nations of Red People, Lying on the Waters of the Wabash River," June 4, 1791, I, 133.

great chief and warrior, General St. Clair, near the mouth of Miami and opposite the Licking river. . . . If you wish to recover them, repair to that place by the first day of July next, determined, with true hearts, to bury the hatchet, and smoke the pipe of peace. . . . But, should you foolishly persist in your warfare, the sons of war will be let loose against you, and the hatchet will never be buried until your country is desolated, and your people humbled to the dust.[28]

The militia returned south to Fort Steuben at the Falls of the Ohio, surrounded by stealthily pursuing Indians. Often, the Indians appeared in the distance. Fearing that their women and children would be killed, they did not attack the militia. This cautious and watchful Indian presence ensured the safety of the captives. When warriors disappeared from view, Scott's men suspected that they were hidden in the woods, not far away. The women and children remained highly visible, walking on foot in the center of the troops.

When the militia arrived at Fort Steuben on June 14, Scott delivered the female prisoners to Captain Asheton, who later transported them to St. Clair at Fort Washington. Scott's expedition was a failure. No one chastised him, perhaps because he lost only a few men, but also because he blustered his way to prominence by proclaiming his troops victorious. Washington and Knox had anticipated that he would strike the Indians with lightning speed, but the wetlands north of the Ohio transformed his assault into a slow and noisy march. Most, but not all, villages were aware of the approaching militia. Indians resorted to familiar strategies and fled, leaving Scott without an enemy to fight. But one Kickapoo village was caught by surprise. Although Scott had been ordered to spare "all those who may cease to resist" and to capture as many Indians as possible, Scott ignored Washington's order. Scott and his men were out to kill Indians, not capture prisoners. At the Kickapoo town where Scott's troops were unable to cross the turbulent Wabash River, they kept up a "brisk fire" aimed at the inhabitants. His sharpshooters took aim at those who attempted to escape and killed "all the savages with which five canoes were crowded." As many as 100 men, women, and children might have died as the heavily armed militia astride their horses picked off the escaping Indians.[29]

The exhausted army that left the wetlands under Scott's command was not an imposing force: they would not have "impress[ed] the Indians with a strong conviction of the power of the United States." These men were clad in

28. Scott, "To the Various Tribes," ibid., 132–133.
29. "Report of Scott," ibid., 131, 133.

the backcountry dress of frontiersmen and were probably viewed as Kentucky raiders rather than members of the United States Army: although heavily armed, they were not in uniform nor led by uniformed generals.[30]

When the Kentuckians marched the women and children through the woods at gunpoint, they paralyzed Indian warriors who had long experienced Kentuckians' hatred; this trapped the Indians in anger, grief, and frustration. With their villages destroyed and women's cornfields set ablaze, the fate of their family members remained uncertain. Imprisonment raised questions about how Indian women were being treated. Were they abused by the army men inside the fort? Were they raped? Were they tortured? What was the fate of their young children? Would they be returned?

Scott ignored his orders to report directly to General St. Clair. Instead, Scott sent twelve men and a sergeant to deliver his account of events. Scott assured St. Clair of his success and falsely claimed that his troops had not practiced inhumanity toward the Indians. Although Scott applauded his men for not resorting to "the inveterate habit of scalping the dead," he neglected to mention that his militia had severely tortured and killed an elderly Indian leader. He had massacred escaping villagers, among them women and children, while failing to attack the villages named in the president's orders. He had returned with fewer than fifty female prisoners, far fewer than the hundreds of women that Washington and Knox had expected. Scott had even allowed his men to raid the wrong village under the pretext of ridding the area of a gun seller. When St. Clair received Scott's report, he realized the magnitude of another militia failure and immediately requested that the War Board of the District of Kentucky send a second expedition of five hundred men to lead a full-scale attack against the upper Wabash towns that Scott had been ordered to wipe out. St. Clair wanted these upper villages, closer to the Miami-Maumee portage, destroyed, to ensure the success of his upcoming fall offensive.

WILKINSON'S DESTRUCTION OF KENAPAKOMOKO

The second Kentucky invasion took place on August 7, 1791. Scott pleaded illness and was unable to lead the operation; he was replaced by Wilkinson. In his report, Scott had praised Wilkinson for his efficient attack on Kethtippecanuck. Wilkinson, who was now commissioned a general, led his smaller, five-hundred-member militia force against the upper villages of the Wabash. St. Clair's orders were site-specific, and he provided the directions,

30. Ward, *Charles Scott*, 114.

locations, and distances that Wilkinson needed to travel in order to reach targeted villages. St. Clair directed Wilkinson to begin his attack at Kenapakomoko, then march north and destroy the chain of villages leading to Miamitown. Ten or twelve leagues north of Kenapakomoko, he was to demolish the villages at the intersection of the Calumet and Wabash Rivers. Then, continuing north, he was to raze every village along the Wabash until he reached the Mississinewa River. Once there, he was to level the multiple villages clustered along the river's banks.

Wilkinson was ordered not only to destroy every village along the banks of the Wabash and Mississinewa Rivers but also to capture the women and children and burn all the houses and fields. Once his northern destructive swath was complete, Wilkinson was to circle back to the Eel River, destroy the Kickapoo villages on the prairie lands north of the Wabash, then follow the Wabash and return to Vincennes. From Vincennes, Wilkinson was to follow the road to the rapids of the Ohio.[31]

On August 1, Wilkinson left Fort Washington with 523 men and headed north toward Kenapakomoko. Almost immediately, Wilkinson's militia ran into trouble. He complained that he repeatedly lost his way because his Indian guides were "ignoran[t] of the country." Forced to follow his own allegedly better sense of direction, Wilkinson's men struggled through the "bogs" of the region. He continually whined about the muck in the wetlands, which lamed the horses and forced his men to move even more slowly than Scott's previous expedition. As he moved through the wetlands, Wilkinson began to fear that any "delay was dangerous": "My situation had now become extremely critical, the whole country to the north being in alarm, which made me greatly anxious to continue my march during the night; but I had no path to direct me, and it was impossible to keep my course, or for horseman to march through a thick swampy country in utter darkness." With daylight, Wilkinson and his men accidentally found themselves at the nexus of the Wabash and Eel Rivers, near his first targeted village of Kenapakomoko. Wilkinson later bragged that this was "the very spot for which I had aimed." The town was almost completely abandoned. Wilkinson's mounted militia charged the village and killed "six warriors . . . two squaws, and a child." They then captured thirty-two women and children at what the Americans called Snake-Fish Town and the French had referred to as L'Anguille. It was the peace village of Little Turtle's brother, Kaweahatta (the Porcupine), just east of present-day Logansport, Indiana. Noted for its exquisite setting, the village stretched along the river for several

---

31. St. Clair to James Wilkinson, July 31, 1791, in Smith, ed., *St. Clair Papers,* II, 227–228.

miles, with orchards of wild plum trees lining the riverbanks. The houses were along a series of low plateaus overlooking the winding and gently flowing Eel River. The water supply came from three sizable creeks of clear water.[32]

> The situation of the late town ... was well chosen for beauty and convenience; it stood in the bosom of a delightful surrounding country on a very rich bottom, extending east and west, on the Wabash River about two miles; the bottom about half a mile wide, bounded on the east by Tippecanoe, and westward by a beautiful rising ground, skirted and clothed with thin woods — from the upper bank you command a view of the Wabash River, which is terminated by a towering growth of wood to the south, and Tippecanoe Creek to the East — the country in the rear from the upper bank spreads into a level prairie of firm, strong land, of an excellent quality, interspersed with copses, naked groves of trees, and high mounds of earth of a regular and conical form, all of which conspire to relieve the eye, and cheer the scene with a most agreeable variety. The top of this bank, which is level with the plane of the prairie, and about two hundred feet perpendicular from the bottom in which the town stood, forms an angle about 60 [degrees], and about midway there issues from its side two living fountains, which have hitherto constantly supplied the town with water.
>
> The country between Kathtippacanunck and the Little Kickapoo town is beautiful beyond description. The numerous breaks, and intermixture of woodlands and plains, give the whole an air of the most perfect taste; for nature here, in a propitious hour as in a benignant wood, seems to have designed to prove, in beautifying, how far she excels our utmost efforts, and the most laboured improvements of art.[33]

That evening, Wilkinson camped in Kenapakomoko. Like Scott, he had captured very few women. He had taken the household of Kaweahatta, a highly revered Miami peace chief. A white captive living at the village told Wilkinson that most families had left, having packed up their household goods and buried them in the adjacent woods. The captive also described sixty village warriors who had headed north to a "French store, to purchase ammunition." On the previous day, another group of men had left for the woods to dig roots. Meanwhile, the women described for Wilkinson the cache of munitions and trade goods that were hidden nearby. They believed that the

---

32. Robert B. Whitsett, Jr., "Snake-Fish Town: The Eighteenth-Century Metropolis of Little Turtle's Eel River Miami," *Indiana History Bulletin*, XV (1938), 72; "Lieut. Colonel-Commandant Wilkinson's Report," Aug. 24, 1791, *ASPIA*, I, 133–135.

33. Imlay, *Topographical Description of the Western Territory*, 15.

ammunition and trade goods were only two miles away. Wilkinson, like most Kentuckians, greedily responded to such rumors of potential plunder. He sent Major Caldwell and a detachment of men upriver on a wild goose chase. Meanwhile, Wilkinson dispatched another group of men into the woods to search for the buried stores of household and trade goods. The general and the remaining militia then "cut up the corn, scarcely in the milk [and] burnt the cabins." Several hours elapsed, and the treasure seekers came back empty-handed. The militia was increasingly uneasy about remaining in a village to which warriors might return at any moment. General Wilkinson and his men made a hasty departure, leaving this message for the Indians:

> The arms of the United States are again exerted against you, and your towns are in flames, and your wives and children made captives; again you are cautioned to listen to the voice of reason, to sue for peace, and submit to the protection of the United States, who are willing to become your friends and fathers, but, at the same time, are determined to punish you for every injury you may offer to their children. Regard not those evil coun-sellors who, to secure to themselves the benefits of your trade, advise you to measures which involve you, your women and children, in trouble and distress. The United States wish to give you peace, because it is good in the eyes of the Great Spirit that all his children should unite and live like brothers; but, if you foolishly prefer war, their warriors are ready to meet you in battle, and will not be the first to lay down the hatchet. You may find your squaws and your children under the protection of our great chief and warrior General St. Clair, at fort Washington. To him you will make all applications for an exchange of prisoners or for peace.[34]

The futile search efforts of the two militia detachments had given Indians time to evacuate nearby villages. As the men headed north, fears of Indian retaliation increased. Wilkinson claimed that he was unable to locate the pathway leading to the northern villages. Ignoring St. Clair's orders, he turned the company around and headed south. Wilkinson retraced Scott's invasion route from the previous month, deliberately disobeying St. Clair's orders to attack the upper Wabash villages. He feared that large numbers of Potawatomi, Shawnee, and Delaware warriors were nearby, a hair-raising rumor that led Wilkinson to lament that he was "in the bosom of Ouiatanon country, one hundred and eighty miles removed from succor." He had captured the

---

34. Ja[me]s Wilkinson, "To the Indian Nations Living on the River Wabash, and Its Waters," Aug. 9, 1791, *ASPIA,* I, 135.

household of a revered Miami chief, and he feared that these women "encumbered" his travel.³⁵

When Wilkinson finally reached the villages Scott had destroyed, he found them deserted. In the interim, they had been reoccupied; Wilkinson discovered that "the corn had been replanted, and was now in high cultivation, several fields being well ploughed." These cornfields, in "high perfection, and in much greater quantity than at L'Anguille," justified Wilkinson's decision. His men set fire to the cornfields and departed, retracing Scott's route to the Falls of the Ohio.³⁶

Because Wilkinson had little interest in destroying Indians and much more in personal glory, his invasion was equally unsuccessful. Like his predecessors Scott and Harmar, he became trapped in nightmarish wetlands. The militia struggled through the bogs, probably shadowed by Indians. Travel was slow and arduous; Harmar, Scott, and Wilkinson all carped that their men were continually mired in "bog after bog, to the saddle skirts, in mud and water." Wilkinson's protests were the loudest and most self-congratulatory, claiming that, "after persevering, for eight hours, I found myself environed, on all sides, with morasses, which forbade my advancing, and, at the same time, rendered it difficult for me to extricate my little army." For Wilkinson, each day's journey produced "the most unfavorable effects." For Indians, the wetlands were the early warning system for upcoming attacks. Horses trapped in bogs slowed the invaders' advance, giving villages time to respond to warnings of the militia's approach. The security system had been perfected since Scott's attack: Wilkinson rarely caught a glimpse of the men spying on him, but he encountered empty villages. He did not kill any stray or straggling Indians. When Wilkinson retreated from his attempt to march north, he stumbled across the villages that Scott's men had previously burned. Wilkinson, like Scott, claimed that his movements were deliberate. Both men ignored the orders laid out for them and failed to admit blame. Wilkinson attributed his failure to carry out his orders on his nervous, five-hundred-man militia force. It was his men's resistance that prevented the advance north into Indian country:

---

35. Sword, *President Washington's Indian War*, 156, 158; "Wilkinson's Report," *ASPIA*, I, 134, 235; "Col. Alexander Mc Kee's Speech to the Indians," July 1, 1791, in Michigan Historical Commission, *Historical Collections: Collections and Researches Made by the Michigan Pioneer and Historical Collections*, 29 vols. (Lansing, Mich., 1886–1912), XX, ed. M. Agnes Burton, 310–311, "Queries by Capt. Hendrick, Answered by Timothy Pickering," XXIV, 274–297; Timothy Pickering to Richard Butler, July 19, 1791, Detroit Public Library; *Diary of David Zeisberger*, II, 198–217.

36. "Wilkinson's Report," *ASPIA*, I, 135.

In the course of the day, I had discovered some murmurings and discontent amongst the men, which I found, on inquiry, to proceed from reluctance to advance farther into the enemy's country; this induced me to call for a state of the horses and provisions, when, to my great mortification, 270 horses were returned lame and tired, with barely five days' provisions for the men. Under these circumstances, I was compelled to abandon my designs upon the Kickapoos of the prairies.[37]

In the end, Wilkinson praised his own narrow, redundant achievements and claimed that he had "done which could be done in my circumstances." Historians have roundly criticized Wilkinson for exaggerating his accomplishments, and Wilkinson offered proof of his own pretentiousness with bombastic claims like, "I have destroyed the chief town of the Ouiatenon nation, and made prisoners of the sons and sisters of the king." In reality, Wilkinson failed to engage any sizable number of warriors and constantly feared that large Indian forces lurked in the nearby forests.[38]

Neither Scott nor Wilkinson engaged in face-to-face combat with Indian warriors during their offensives. The Indians hid in the woods and let the environment ensnare the invaders. Indians avoided fighting, infuriating renowned Indian fighters like Scott, who claimed that his militia "have at length taken up the hatchet; they have penetrated far into your country, to meet your warriors... but you fled before them." The frustrated militia burned fields and villages. Indians learned not to defend their villages but, instead, to seek the safety of woodlands and wetlands. Historians have claimed that attacks like this "disrupted ancient cycles of planting, harvesting, fighting, hunting, and gathering." This was not true in the Wabash River valley, where early spring cornfields charred by fire were easily replanted. In fact, the ash served as fertilizer. Riverways also had stretches of cleared fields that were not annually planted, and these were used when villages moved or when women needed to plant additional fields. In addition, the cornfields the invaders so assiduously burned were just one part of a wider, more extensive Indian diet. Rivers teemed with fish, mussels, and waterfowl. In the forests and wetlands, there was a wide variety of game and plants. When crops were burned late in the season and there was no time to raise new crops, Indian men fed their households by hunting and fishing. Burning cornfields did not lead to starvation in the Ohio River valley. Hamtramck, while commander at Vincennes, wrote to St. Clair, "The Indians can never be subdued by burning their houses and

37. Ibid.
38. Dillon, *History of Indiana*, 267–271.

corn, for they make themselves perfectly comfortable on meat alone." Hamtramck understood the futility of these Kentucky militia raids and realized that, rather than subduing Indians, they infuriated and motivated them to seek revenge. Villages were numerous and connected by marriage and kin networks. The winter months were cruel for those whose crops had been burned, but Indians survived, often quite comfortably, by taking refuge with relatives. People driven away from their lands were unfortunate, but, even in these worst-case scenarios, networks of kin living amid this dense complex of villages were an insurance policy against starvation.[39]

Washington anticipated that abducting Indian women and imprisoning them for a year would disrupt the agrarian cycles of the Wabash villages. During the Revolutionary War, when Washington ordered the Sullivan Expedition to destroy Seneca homes, fields, and orchards, the Seneca were forced to flee to Canada to secure British protection. The Senecas' expulsion from their homelands had ended Iroquois attacks on frontier settlements in Pennsylvania's Wyoming Valley. Sustained attacks on Wabash Indian villages should have forced Indians off their lands and halted attacks on frontier settlements. But Wilkinson ignored St. Clair's order to destroy the Wabash villages stretching from Ouiatenon to Miamitown. Anxious about venturing too far into Indian Country, he destroyed one village and then retreated south. Scott's destruction of the Kickapoo villages and the capture of these women had the greatest impact — these were young women, who had stayed behind to care for the sick. For the Kickapoo, with limited kin in the region, winter was harsh, and next spring's planting cycles were interrupted. Had Wilkinson's forces destroyed multiple villages and captured all the women, then a famine might conceivably have afflicted the region. But even then, the plentiful supply of fish and animals would have made starvation unlikely.[40]

Raids and counterraids were part of the reciprocal violence that had char-

---

39. Elroy McKendree Avery, *A History of the United States and Its People, from Their Earliest Records to the Present Time,* 16 vols. (Cleveland, 1904–1910), VII, 97; Hamtramck to St. Clair, Dec. 2, 1790, in Smith, ed., *St. Clair Papers,* II, 197. Heidi Bohaker's work on the pictographic signatures on treaty documents provides evidence of the long-range stability of Indian villages. In instances of displacement, she shows how kin relations in other villages provided a social safety net in the western Great Lakes. See Bohaker, "Reading Anishinaabe Identities: Meaning and Metaphor in Nindoodem Pictographs," *Ethnohistory,* LVII (2010), 11–33; Bohaker, *"Nindoodemag:* The Significance of Algonquian Kinship Networks in the Eastern Great Lakes Region, 1600–1701," *William and Mary Quarterly,* LXIII (2006), 23–52.

40. Colin G. Calloway, *New Worlds for All: Indians, Europeans, and the Remaking of Early America* (Baltimore, 1997), 110–111.

acterized the Ohio River valley since the outbreak of the Revolutionary War. The Ouiatenon village attack planned by Washington and Knox dramatically escalated the level of violence. Provocatively, Indian women and children were Washington's objectives, and the recruiting of militia who were well-known Indian haters provided Indians a common cause for confederation and retaliation. Washington encouraged the behavior of those Kentuckians who believed that revenge and war, rather than magnanimity and negotiation, were the only way to treat Indians. Knox had warned Washington again and again of the Kentuckians' antipathy toward Indians. Arthur St. Clair also disliked the Kentuckians' attitude toward Indians, and he repeatedly warned the governor of Virginia that backcountry residents in Kentucky engaged in "incursions ... upon the tribes of Indians [living] in amity with the United States" and that "conduct like this is highly dishonorable to our national character ... [and] it becomes our duty to enjoin you to exert your authority to prevent any attempts of this kind in the future." St. Clair, like Hamtramck at Vincennes, found himself dismissed by both the Kentuckians and by political leaders who despised the army. These types of men scorned the idea of negotiating with Indians and the more deliberate tactics of the regular army troops, who they believed "will never produce the wished for Effects." Brutality, death, decapitation, torture, capturing women and children, and burning villages became central to carrying out an "Enterprise against the Indians from our Country." In turning to the Kentucky militia, Washington undercut the U.S. Army, the very institution he sought to strengthen. More important, the president alienated those very villages that could have become the nation's loyal allies, and he intensified and widened support for a Pan-Indian Confederacy that would seek revenge for the destruction of the Wabash villages and the capture of Indian women and children. What Washington had deemed an effective strategy among the Iroquois was disastrous in the Wabash River valley, where employing the same brutal tactics became a rallying cry that united Indians across the western Great Lakes. When the peace village of Kenapakomoko lost its women and children, the outcry of Little Turtle's brother echoed throughout villages far north of the Ohio River valley.[41]

41. R. Douglas Hurt, *The Ohio Frontier: Crucible of the Old Northwest, 1720–1830* (Bloomington, Ind., 1996), 97; William Littell, *Reprints of Littell's Political Transactions in and concerning Kentucky and Letter of George Nicholas to His Friend in Virginia also General Wilkinson's Memorial* (Louisville, Ky., 1926), 56. The intense dislike felt by many Kentuckians for Indians is echoed by other historians. Patrick Griffin contends that many of the squatters who settled in Ohio Country "harbored an intense hatred for Indians" (Griffin, "Reconsidering the Ideological Origins of Indian Removal: The Case of the Big Bottom Massacre," in Andrew R. L. Cayton and Stuart D. Hobbs, eds., *The Center of a Great Empire: The Ohio*

Financial support from President Washington, Congress, and states like Virginia and Pennsylvania played a key role in escalating militia violence. They provided militants the material resources and political credibility necessary to organize attacks. Extreme violence was not solely the result of Indian hating; it depended on the readiness of the federal government and individual states to lend material and organizational support to perpetrators. During the early years of the Republic, scorched-earth campaigns were carried out by volunteers from Kentucky but made possible by financial support from Pennsylvania and Virginia, and made larger scale by federal resources. The situation was further inflamed by the practice of repeatedly recruiting infantrymen from the same Kentucky counties. These militiamen were inclined to kill, rather than capture, Indian women. St. Clair described Kentuckians as "in the habit of retaliation . . . without attending precisely to the nations from which the injuries are received." This orientation was well understood by the federal leaders who issued those orders. Kentuckians had a reputation among Indians for vindictive raids targeting even villages that were innocent of any wrongdoing. Their militia leaders maintained the pretense of decency but also routinely looted Indian homes. Plunder rewarded militiamen and attracted impoverished — or avaricious — recruits. Indian goods sold at public auction were the profit margin that inspired many men to join the militia. The Kentucky militia continually claimed that it accidentally shot women, children, and male warriors and that its behavior was above reproach. Charles Scott lied when he reported to Washington that his men "acquitted themselves with their usual good conduct," because they had tortured and killed the elderly Wea leader by ripping the skin off his body.[42]

By the time Indians banded together to confront the imminent assault by St. Clair, many Indian warriors knew and could identify Kentucky militia-

---

Country in the Early Republic [Athens, Oh., 2005], 18). Several Kentuckians acquired nicknames that reflected their hatred of Indians. "Savage Morgan" was the sobriquet for Daniel Morgan, who was known for displaying a razor strop fashioned from Indian skin. Military historian Wiley Sword suggests that men perpetuating "unreasoning hatred of the Indian" were "all too common along the frontier" (*President Washington's Indian War*, 73). See also Dillon, *History of Indiana*, 217–220; "Representatives of the Counties Composing the District of Kentucky Now in the General Assembly of Virginia to Washington," [1790], Scott Papers; Barnhart and Riker, *Indiana to 1816*, 291.

42. Rob Harper, "State Intervention and Extreme Violence in the Revolutionary Ohio Valley," *Journal of Genocide Research*, X (2008), 233–248, esp. 234, 244; C. Gerlach, "Extremely Violent Societies: An Alternative to the Concept of Genocide," ibid., VIII (2006), 455–471; Carter, *Life and Times of Little Turtle*, 100; Ward, *Charles Scott*, 109; St. Clair to Washington, Sept. 14, 1789, in Smith, ed., *St. Clair Papers*, II, 124.

men who had fumbled through the swamplands, destroyed their villages, and seized their wives and children. The wetlands proved to be a perfect setting to spy on invaders, and, in any event, a few hundred Indians would have been foolhardy to engage 852 well-armed Kentuckians. The muck of the wetlands and the foliage of the forest gave Indian men the time and cover needed to choose their targets for revenge.

IMPRISONMENT AT FORT WASHINGTON

The capture of Kaweahatta's household raises the question of the Indian village's strategy. He was one of the most powerful men among the Miami. Did the village evacuate most of its residents and intentionally leave behind the headman's household to be captured? Did Kaweahatta recognize that the previously captured women and children needed the guidance and companionship of his household? Among the captives were Nancy, the first wife of William Wells, and their son. Wells was a white captive and cultural mediator who was free to travel to settler colonist communities and who had access to military leaders like General St. Clair and Hamtramck. Wells traveled to Fort Washington and helped secure the captives' release by organizing the merchants from Vincennes to advocate for the release of the women and children.

Most interesting of all were the names these women provided to their captors. At Fort Steuben, Captain Asheton dutifully recorded the names of the forty-one prisoners that Scott left with him, and we catch a glimpse of Indian women who chose to provide names indicative of the agrarian world in which they lived. Theirs was a world of "Short Groves" and "Bushy Groves." They lived amid the "Soft Corn" that was "Proper and Tall" and in a universe of forests filled with "Deep Moss" and "Groves" of "Green Willows." Their lakes had "Swift Waves" and were filled with "Speckled Loons," "Beaver Girls," and "Mermaids." The women were watched over by a "Clear Sky," and the "Cook Wife" made sure that the corn was "Proper and Tall" before it was harvested. In a very literal sense, these women revealed nothing about their personal lives and probably did not share their real names; instead, they provided a window into the wondrous environment in which they lived.[43]

At Fort Washington, the women and children were imprisoned for more than a year in primitive, overcrowded, and unsanitary conditions. Fort Washington had been hastily constructed of hewn timber and planks from dismantled flatboats in 1789. The fort stood two stories high, surrounded by a

---

43. Scott, "To the Various Tribes," *ASPIA,* I, 133.

TABLE 4. *List of Indian prisoners, 1791*

#	Name	Translation
1.	Mass-wockcomwoh, Queen in English	Thunderstruck
2.	Wonong-apate, her daughter, 17 years old	Speckled Loon
3.	Kenchestonoquah, 2d daughter	Swift Waves
4.	Keshequamas-anongwah, prince, 7	Clear Sky
5.	Cotohemongoquah, 3d daughter	Mermaid
6.	Keshockcotoquah, 4th do.	Cook Wife
7.	Puckcontomwoh, cousin to the queen	Crack Nuts
8.	Collobwoh, her son	
9.	Kechemataquah, warrior, about 32	Short Grove
10.	Katankellocaset, his wife	Speckled Over
11.	Nepehhequah, his child, a girl, 4	Green Willows
12.	Mekehquah, his daughter	Old Mother
13.	Wanpingivet, squaw	White Face
14.	Pegewoh, her daughter	Cat
15.	Mataquah, son to the last	Grove
16.	Nokingwahmenah, do.	Soft Corn
17.	Packocockcoset, do.	Proper and Tall
18.	Equahcong, squaw	Short Neck
19.	Cateweah	What's Here?
20.	Kenonesanc	Deep Moss
21.	Waughpochke	White Stalk
22.	Kanketoquah, squaw	
23.	Huntechelapelo	Look Yonder
24.	Pamenkishlopelo	High-Look
25.	Nepahkaquah	Green Willows
26.	Cataholoquah	Striped Huzzy
27.	Wecaupeminche	Lynn Tree
28.	Kechewanpaume	Close Look
29.	Kechemetaquah	Bushy Grove
30.	Mossoolocaset	Dear Nothing
31.	Puckcontomwoh	Crack Nuts
32.	Pakakenong	Trod Ground
33.	Wahpequagh	White Huzzy
34.	Kehenackashwoh	Gash Hand
35.	Onsiongwet, squaw	Yellow Face
36.	Wecawpeminah	Roasting Ears
37.	Mecah-cats	Eat All
38.	Pacomequah	Muddy Water

TABLE 4. *Continued*

39. Taqualanah	Grove Man
40. Packosequah	Pretty Girl
41. Machonsackquah	Beaver Girl

Source: United States Congress, *American State Papers: Documents, Legislative and Executive, of the Congress of the United States...*, 38 vols. (Washington, D.C., 1832), Class II, *Indian Affairs*, 2 vols., ed. Walter Lowrie et al., I, 129–130. Courtesy of the Library of Congress. This list of Indian prisoners was attributed to General James Scott in the *State Papers* and identified the women and children that he left at Fort Steuben. Scott captured forty-two women and children, and Wilkinson captured thirty-two prisoners. This list contains forty-one names. Because the final tally of prisoners at Fort Washington was close to one hundred, it is likely that there was no list of prisoners captured by Wilkinson, and he probably left his prisoners at Fort Washington rather than dropping them off at Fort Steuben.

---

wooden palisade that varied in height from ten to sixteen feet, with four log blockhouses situated at the corners. Along the walls were the barracks for the men. To house the captives, St. Clair constructed a ravelin, or extended lean-to, attached to the fort. Women and children lived in the interior shelter of the ravelin, adjacent to the army barracks. They were isolated from their families and communities and surrounded by American soldiers, many of them veterans of Harmar's Defeat. These men had burned the homes of their families and kin at Miamitown and were daily reminders of the violence that had swept them from their villages.[44]

There were no reports of rape at Fort Washington, but Indian women's proximity to soldiers provided men many opportunities to commit such outrages. It is not surprising to find in the journals of St. Clair's adjutant, Ebenezer Denny, Shawnee and Delaware phrases for "I love you," "I must sleep with you," and "Will you sleep with me?" Knox's orders to General Scott had stressed the need to treat Indian women with respect, warnings then forcefully repeated by St. Clair in face-to-face interviews and, later, in St. Clair's instructions. Knox had told Charles Scott, "It is the positive orders of the Presi-

---

44. Sword, *President Washington's Indian War*, 90–91; Arthur St. Clair, *Narrative of the Manner in Which the Campaign against the Indians . . . Was Conducted . . .* (Philadelphia, 1812). The destruction of agrarian villages was an ongoing legacy of Sullivan's campaign against the Iroquois during the Revolutionary War, as was violence against Indian women. See *ASPIA*, I, 130; Grenier, *First Way of War*, 197.

dent of the United States, that all such captives be treated with humanity." Though Scott reported to Knox "that the men had behaved admirably," we can't be certain that incidents of abuse, rape, or murder weren't simply going unreported.[45]

When the women are traced through Scott's and Wilkinson's reports to Knox and St. Clair, significant numbers of them appear to be missing. At least nineteen and perhaps as many as thirty-two women disappeared after being captured. In Scott's report, he informs Secretary Knox, "Colonel Hardin joined me a little before sunset, having killed six warriors, and taken fifty-two prisoners." When the militia arrived at Fort Steuben, Scott delivered forty-one, not fifty-two, prisoners. Their names were recorded by the commanding officer and became the receipt that Scott sent to Knox. Eleven women had disappeared—left behind after their capture, one hopes. After the second attack, Wilkinson reported, "Thirty-four prisoners were taken." It is not clear where Wilkinson first deposited his prisoners. In a diary kept by a Kentucky schoolmaster, the writer refers to Colonel Wilkinson's marching the Indian prisoners through town: "Augst 24th, 31 Indian prisoners were brought into geoTown from the Wabash on their way to Cincinnati all women and children but one." The date corresponds with Wilkinson's attack, outlined in the report that Wilkinson later sent to St. Clair from Frankfort, Kentucky. At some point, thirty-one of the prisoners were transported to Fort Washington, joining those from the Scott attack. When they were released a year later, only fifty-six women and children remained in captivity. One warrior, Kecheataquah, whom Scott captured, was no longer among the prisoners. Seventy-five prisoners should have been released. Their disappearance remains a mystery but suggests that incidences of escape or even murder remained unreported.[46]

The women and children who were imprisoned at Fort Washington in 1791 watched fearfully as the government began preparing for another major offensive under St. Clair. Congress had authorized a standing army of three thousand men. This much larger army was assembled and trained at Fort Wash-

---

45. *Military Journal of Ebenezer Denny: An Officer in the Revolutionary and Indian Wars* (Philadelphia, 1859), 274–277.

46. "Report of Brigadier General Scott," *ASPIA*, I, 131–132, "No. 5, List of the Indian Prisoners Taken by the Army under the Command of Brigadier General Scott, on the Wabash River, at the Ouiatanon Town and Neighboring Villages," June 1, 1791, 133, and "Lieut. Colonel-Commandant Wilkinson's Report," Aug. 24, 1791, 134; "Extracts from the Journal of Samuel Shepard," Apr. 10, 1787–Dec. 3, 1796, M-683, microfilm, Special Collections, University of Kentucky, Lexington; Paul A. W. Wallace, ed., *Thirty Thousand Miles with John Heckewelder* (Pittsburgh, 1958), 268.

ington. It strained the capacity of the fort and nearby housing and required the erection of tents on land surrounding the fort. Kentuckians had pushed Washington to consider Charles Scott for command of the army, but, following Scott's assault on Ouiatenon, Washington had new reasons for considering him "of inadequate abilities" and intemperate habits. Even before Scott began his June 1791 assault on the Wabash villages, Washington had chosen St. Clair to lead the fall offensive—the same man whom Scott had openly disparaged.[47]

ST. CLAIR'S DEFEAT

It was almost five months before army recruiters fulfilled most of their enlistment quota. By the fall, even before the army departed Fort Washington, many early enlistments were about to expire. Low military salaries, lower than those of the average laborer, stymied recruiting efforts. Most army recruits came from New Jersey, Pennsylvania, Maryland, and Virginia; they were poorly equipped and lacked discipline. St. Clair's manpower and supply situation at Fort Washington were dire. Congress's recruiting quotas were not met, and St. Clair's regulars were not even at half strength. The regulars present didn't draw favorable reviews. One veteran officer described them as "urban riffraff . . . totally unfamiliar with army methods and frontier life. The quality of his troops was not much higher than those of Harmar's campaign." According to Major Denny, St. Clair's aide, recruiting in Philadelphia's city taverns made it "utterly impossible that they could be otherwise," and he complained, "The bulk of the army was composed [of] men collected from the streets and prisons of the cities, hurried out into the enemy's country and with the officers commanding them totally unacquainted with the business in which they were engaged."[48]

---

47. Cayton, *Frontier Indiana*, 154; Robert B. Whitsett, Jr., "Snake-Fish Town: The Eighteenth-Century Metropolis of Little Turtle's Eel River Miami," *Indiana History Bulletin*, XV (1938), 72; Nelson, "General Charles Scott," *JER*, VI (1986), 236.

48. Sword, *President Washington's Indian War*, 148–150; Smith, ed., *St. Clair Papers*, II, 262; Denny, *Military Journal*, 170. Major Denny had served as an officer in the First American Regiment and remained in the army at the conclusion of the Revolutionary War. Denny kept a journal that extends from May 1781 to May 1795, which includes the victory at Yorktown and his activities under Harmar and St. Clair. He participated in the 1790 Harmar campaign and traveled to Philadelphia to deliver Knox the official report of St. Clair's defeat. He served as aide-de-camp to Major General St. Clair. See *Military Journal of Ebenezer Denny;* James H. Perkins, *Annals of the West: Embracing a Concise Account of Principal Events Which Have Occurred in the Western States and Territories* . . . (Cincinnati, Oh., 1847), 358.

The Kentucky Board of War ordered a draft of 1,150 men; many of those who actually appeared were substitutes hired by the draftees wishing to avoid service. They were as unfit and ill-armed as the army recruits. Recruiting efforts yielded 2,700 men, a number lower than the congressional authorization of 3,000 men. The army was not operational until September, partially delayed by Wilkinson's August raid against Kenapakomoko. Few men were adequately trained, and Sargent described the army as "badly clothed, badly paid and badly fed." Packsaddles did not fit the horses, guns were defective, and the boat transporting much of the gunpowder sank en route to Fort Washington. In response, St. Clair transformed the fort's interior into a factory where ammunition was manufactured and stored, an armory was built to hold weapons, and a smithy repaired weapons and equipment. Enlisted men disliked this work, and officers complained that it took them away from training.[49]

By early September, St. Clair's campaign was two months behind schedule. St. Clair lacked adequate supplies to carry out the offensive, and his quartermaster, Samuel Hogdon, and second-in-command, Major General Richard Butler, did not arrive until September 7. Restless, unruly soldiers roamed the Cincinnati streets, and their "riotous and promiscuous behavior" raised the ire of town residents. St. Clair resolved the situation by ordering most troops several miles north to Ludlow's Station. Knox wrote St. Clair, describing the president as "exceedingly anxious that the troops . . . should be assembled at fort Washington, at as early a period as possible, so that you may commence and effect your operations in due season"; St. Clair replied, "Nothing can exceed the anxiety I feel to have the operations of the campaign begun . . . a point on which . . . I have been uneasy to a great degree."[50]

Prompted by Knox's criticism, St. Clair moved the army twenty-three miles north to the Miami River, where they began construction on Fort Hamilton.

---

49. Bodley, *History of Kentucky*, I, 474; *A Journal of the Adventures of Matthew Bunn, a Native of Brookfield Massachusetts . . .* (1796; rpt. Providence, R.I., 1962), 5; *Military Journal of Ebenezer Denny*, 170; St. Clair, *Narrative of the Campaign against the Indians*, 12; "Winthrop Sargent's Diary while with General Arthur St. Clair's Expedition against the Indians," *Ohio Archaeological and Historical Society Quarterly*, XXXIII (1924), 242.

50. St. Clair to John Brown, July 18, 1791, St. Clair to Wilkinson, July 31, 1791, Wilkinson to St. Clair, Aug. 24, 1791, St. Clair to Knox, Aug. 24, 1791, Knox to George Washington, Oct. 1, 1791, all in Smith, ed., *St. Clair Papers*, II, 225, 227, 233–239, 244; *Military Journal of Ebenezer Denny*, 152–153; St. Clair letter, Aug. 11, 1791, *ASPIA*, I, 181; *Journal of the Adventures of Matthew Bunn*, 175; Kevin Patrick Cooper, "Arthur St. Clair and the Struggle for Power in the Old Northwest, 1763–1803" (Ph.D. diss., Kent State University, 2005), 174.

They built a barracks and four bastions. Supplying the troops remained problematic, desertions increased, and in early October, twenty-six disaffected militiamen abandoned their posts and returned to Kentucky. Desertions became so commonplace that St. Clair detached men to retrieve the runaways.[51]

On October 4, with the fort completed, the army headed north, cutting roads through deep forests. Hogdon had supplied the army with fifteen axes, eighteen broadaxes, twelve hammers, and twenty-four handsaws — an insignificant number for a three thousand–man army. Dull and broken axes delayed their progress. Temperatures dropped precipitously and reduced the already-insufficient forage for the army's packhorses. Indians spied on the army's movements, stole, and killed or captured isolated soldiers. With provisions low, St. Clair wrote an angry letter to Israel Ludlow, his contractor, demanding supplies and telling him that no excuse could satisfy "a starving army and a disappointed people."[52]

On October 13, St. Clair's forces began construction on a second fort. Conditions worsened, and cold winter rains drenched the weary soldiers and damaged their equipment. Tents, meant for summer weather, provided little respite from the cold. Frosts further destroyed the animals' forage, threatening the survival of the army's packhorses. St. Clair ordered daily flour allowances cut in half. He blamed his problems on negligent behavior by the quartermaster and contractor and threatened to abort the campaign. As desertions increased, St. Clair was determined to restore order to his unruly troops. On October 22, 1791, he executed two deserters in front of his men. Although officers agreed with the general's decision, these heavy-handed tactics failed to elicit the intended results and, instead, increased the troops' bitterness toward the officer corps.[53]

---

51. "Causes of the Failure of the Expedition against the Indians, in 1791, under the Command of Major General St. Clair Communicated to the House of Representatives," May 8, 1792, in United States Congress, *American State Papers: Documents, Legislative and Executive, of the Congress of the United States . . . ,* 38 vols. (Washington, D.C., 1832), Class V, *Military Affairs,* 7 vols., ed. Walter Lowrie et al., I, 36; *Military Journal of Ebenezer Denny,* 155; St. Clair to Knox, Oct. 6, 1791, in Smith, ed., *St. Clair Papers,* II, 245; "Sargent's Diary," *Ohio Arch. and Hist. Soc. Quarterly,* XXXIII (1924), 242; Frazer Ells Wilson, ed., *Journal of Capt. Daniel Bradley: An Epic of the Ohio Frontier* (Greenville, Oh., 1935), 19.

52. Sword, *President Washington's Indian War,* 150; *Military Journal of Ebenezer Denny,* 153; "Causes of the Failure," *American State Papers: Military Affairs,* I, 36, 46.

53. St. Clair to Israel Ludlow, Oct. 8, 1791, in Smith, ed., *St. Clair Papers,* II, 246. For information on the construction of fortifications and the march to the battlefield, see William H. Guthman, *March to Massacre: A History of the First Seven Years of the United*

Despite the worsening conditions, St. Clair decided not to go into winter quarters but led his army six miles north to begin his march against the Indian towns. His destination was the newly reestablished Miamitown at the Glaize. Harmar had destroyed the old Miamitown at the Maumee-Wabash portage, and Indians had relocated upriver to the Maumee River, closer to Detroit. But, still far from reaching it, the soldiers' restlessness and anger against the officers increased. The enlisted men refused to perform their duties, claiming that their enlistments had expired. They argued that their commitment had begun when they signed up for service, not when they arrived at Fort Washington. They openly defied orders, and the morning of October 29, they kept up a constant firing "round the camp, notwithstanding it is known there is a general order against it."[54]

Faced with insubordination, St. Clair moved the army deeper into Indian Country and away from their fellow soldiers at Fort Jefferson. He reasoned that when the soldiers' enlistments ended, they would be too far into enemy territory to leave their comrades. When sixty militiamen deserted and threatened to attack and plunder the approaching supply train, St. Clair ordered Major Hamtramck and his First Regiment to head south and overtake the deserters. Unfortunately, St. Clair dispatched those men "estimated as the best in the service." After reducing the army to 1,400 men, the general marched them north toward the Indian towns.[55]

Conditions deteriorated: an early snowfall and below-freezing temperatures fatigued the weary troops. On November 2, the troops marched until sunset and encamped on the banks of the Wabash River. St. Clair decided not to erect defensive works, since the men were exhausted and Miamitown was still distant. Meanwhile, the general, suffering from gout, had been carried in a litter, unable to bear the pain of riding his horse. The Second Regiment camped along the frozen river in two 350-yard lines, 70 yards apart. Artillery pieces, horses, and supplies were placed between the lines. A rectangular formation was created by placing units of riflemen along the right and left flanks

---

States Army, 1784–1791 (New York, 1974), 220–244; Sword, *President Washington's Indian War*, 155–171; Richard M. Lytle, *The Soldiers of America's First Army: 1791* (Lanham, Md., 2004), 73–85. For primary accounts of the march, consult "Sargent's Diary," *Ohio Arch. and Hist. Soc. Quarterly*, XXXIII (1924), 241–256; *Military Journal of Ebenezer Denny*, 154–162.

54. "Sargent's Diary," *Ohio Arch. and Hist. Soc. Quarterly*, XXXIII (1924), 247; Wilson, ed., *Journal of Capt. Daniel Bradley*, 26.

55. *Military Journal of Ebenezer Denny*, 161; "Sargent's Diary," *Ohio Arch. and Hist. Soc. Quarterly*, XXXIII (1924), 247–248; St. Clair to Knox, Nov. 1, 1791, in Smith, ed., *St. Clair Papers*, II, 249–251; Wilson, ed., *Journal of Capt. Daniel Bradley*, 30.

of the troops. The militia was encamped on the opposite riverbank, 300 yards away from the main body of soldiers.[56]

It was a cold, snowy day when, just north, Indian forces waited for the army. Chickasaw scouts had joined the army, but St. Clair failed to deploy them. The general remained unaware of the nearby Indians, who had decided to wait for the army's arrival near the Wabash. Miami and Shawnee had drawn warriors from the Wyandot, Odawa, Ojibwe, Potawatomi, Canadian Mohawk, Creek, Cherokee, Potomac-area Conoy and Nanticoke, and Delaware nations. Warriors were eager to fight alongside Blue Jacket, Little Turtle, and Buckongahelas, who led the alliance. This was a confederacy built largely through the hard work of Shawnee and Miami diplomats. That summer, Shawnee and Miami emissaries had crisscrossed the Ohio River, following familiar trade routes and carrying wampum belts and tobacco painted red to allied villages; then they headed into the northern Great Lakes. In the early months of the fall, as the army gathered at Fort Washington, envoys were again sent to the villages, warning that the United States was going to invade Indian Country. By the fall, a fighting force of at least a thousand men was assembled. They were joined by many French and British traders, supported and supplied by members of the British Indian Department. Whereas Washington and Knox blamed the British for Indian resistance, nearby Americans recognized that the Indians "were afraid of losing their lands," which led warriors to join the confederacy, in numbers far greater than "the British Government, with all their arts and money, were able to persuade." Britain had instructed John Simcoe, Canada's governor, to urge the Indians to make peace with the Americans; but Alexander McKee of the British Indian Department warned Lord Dorcester that Indians were so infuriated by Scott's recent attacks on the Ouiatenon villages that "little attention will now be paid to any [peace] proposals."[57]

56. *Military Journal of Ebenezer Denny*, 171.

57. Sword, *President Washington's Indian War*, 141; Michigan Pioneer and Historical Society, *Collections*, XXIV, 173, 262, 263. Pan-Indian alliances followed in the wake of Pontiac's Rebellion. For instance, during the Revolutionary War, a militant network of Shawnee and Chickamauga Cherokees initiated an alliance that drew together distant people from the Gulf Coast to the Great Lakes. In late May 1780, Mingo, Delaware, Shawnee, Potawatomi, Chippewa, Huron, and Odawa accompanied Captain Henry Bird and 150 British soldiers from Fort Detroit to Kentucky. They attacked civilian stations and captured both Ruddell's Station and Martin's Station and took numerous prisoners. See Robert M. Owens, *Red Dreams, White Nightmares: Pan-Indian Alliances in the Anglo-American Mind, 1763–1815* (Norman, Okla., 2015), 77; Colin G. Calloway, *The Victory with No Name: The Native American Defeat of the First American Army* (New York, 2015), 93–94.

When the combined force attacked St. Clair's army before dawn on November 3, Indians focused their initial offensive on the Kentucky militia, who were camped on the opposite shore of the Wabash, across the river from the main army. Ebenezer Denny vividly described the assault:

> The poor militia, who were but three hundred yards in front, had scarcely time to return a shot—they fled into our camp. . . . The enemy . . . completely surrounded the camp, killed and cut off nearly all the guards, and approached close to the lines. They advanced from one tree, log, or stump to another, under cover of the smoke of our fire. The [our] artillery and musketry made a tremendous noise [huddled together as they were], but did little execution. The Indians seemed to brave everything, and when fairly fixed around us they made no noise other than their fire [guns], which they kept up very constant and which seldom failed to tell, although scarcely heard. Our left flank, probably from the nature of the ground, gave way first; the enemy got possession of that part of the encampment, but it being pretty clear ground, they were too much exposed and were soon repulsed. [I] Was at this time with the General [St. Clair] engaged toward the right; he was on foot [he had been sick some days] and led the party himself that drove the enemy and regained our ground on the left. The battalions in the rear charged several times and forced the savages from their shelter, but they always turned with the battalions and fired upon them back; indeed they seemed not to fear anything we could do. They could skip out of reach of the bayonet and return, as they pleased. They were visible only when raised by a charge. The ground was literally covered with the dead. The wounded were taken to the centre, where it was thought most safe, and where a great many who had quit their posts unhurt, had crowded together. The General, with other officers, endeavored to rally these men, and twice they were taken out to the lines. It appeared as if the officers had been singled out; a very great proportion fell, or were wounded and obliged to retire from the lines early in the action. [Major] General [Richard] Butler was among the latter, as well as several other of the most experienced officers. The men being thus left with few officers, became fearful, despaired of success, gave up the fight, and to save themselves for the moment, abandoned entirely their duty and ground, and crowded in toward the centre of the field, and no exertions could put them in any order even for defense; [they became] perfectly ungovernable. The enemy at length got possession of the artillery, though not until the officers were all killed but one and he badly wounded, and the men [gunners] almost all cut off, and not until the pieces were spiked. As our lines were deserted the Indians contracted theirs until their shot centred

from all points, and now meeting with little opposition, took more deliberate aim and did great execution. Exposed to a cross fire, men and officers were seen falling in every direction: the distress too of the wounded made the scene such as can scarcely be conceived; a few minutes longer, and a retreat would have been impracticable. The only hope left was, that perhaps the savages would be so taken up with the camp as not to follow. Delay was death; no preparation could be made; numbers of brave men must be left a sacrifice, there was no alternative. It was past nine o'clock, when repeated orders were given to charge toward the road. The action had continued between two and three hours. Both officers and men seemed confounded, incapable of doing anything; they could not move until it was told that a retreat was intended. A few officers put themselves in front, the men followed, the enemy gave way, and perhaps not being aware of the design, we were for a few minutes left undisturbed. The stoutest and most active now took the lead, and those who were foremost in breaking the enemy's line, were soon left behind. At the moment of the retreat, one of the few horses saved had been procured for the General; he was on foot until then; I kept by him, and he delayed to see the rear. The enemy soon discovered the movement and pursued, though not more than four or five miles, and but few so far; they turned to share spoil.... By this time the remains of the army had got somewhat compact, but in the most miserable and defenseless state. The wounded who came off left their arms in the field, and one-half of the others threw theirs away on the retreat. The road for miles was covered with firelocks [flintlock guns], cartridge boxes and regimentals. How fortunate that the pursuit was discontinued; a single Indian might have followed with safety upon either flank. Such a panic had seized the men, that I believe it would not have been possible to have brought any of them to engage again.[58]

News of the defeat spread quickly across the nation. One broadside bordered the harrowing news of General St. Clair's gruesome defeat with caskets. Heavy black lines surrounded the macabre descriptions of the disastrous outcome; thirty-nine "gallant officers" massacred by bloodthirsty Indians, their names inscribed beneath each black casket. "Nine Hundred brave youthful soldiers" had lost their lives in a "Columbian Tragedy," which newspapers and broadsides described as a contest for "the future Freedom and Grandeur" of the nation. Distortion and inflammatory rhetoric decried the army's de-

58. *Military Journal of Ebenezer Denny,* 165–168. Although the army was reported to be this large, desertions had probably reduced the army to 1,200 men. See also Lieutenant Colonel William Darke's letter to President Washington describing this defeat in the Henry Knox Papers, XXX, 12, Library of the New England Historic Genealogical Society, Boston.

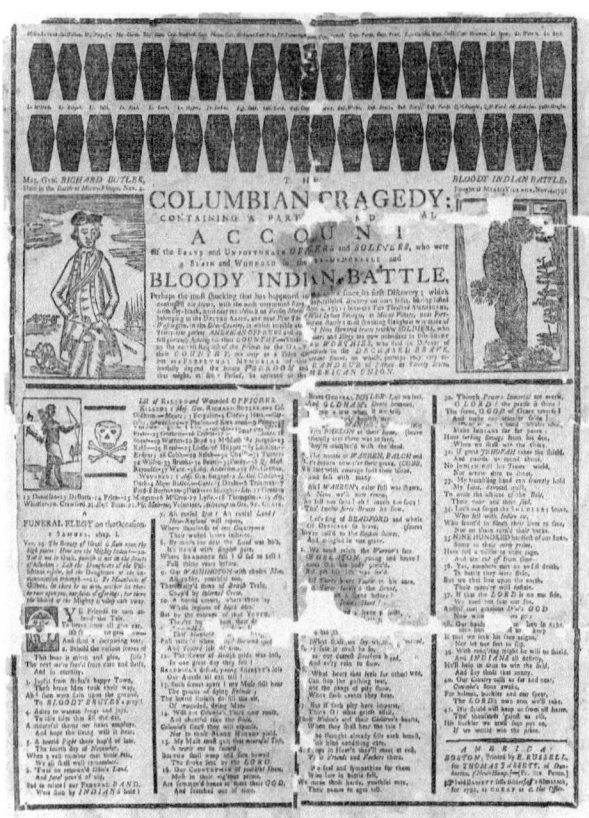

FIGURE 32. *The Columbian Tragedy* (Boston, 1791), broadside. It reads: "Containing a Par[ticular a]nd [Offici]al account of the Brave and Unfortunate Officers and Soldiers, who were Slain and Wounded in the [Ev]er-memorable and BLOODY INDIAN BATTLE, Perhaps the most shocking that has happened in [A]merica since its first Discovery; which continued Six Hours, with the most unremitted Fury [and] unparalleled Bravery on both Sides, having lasted from day-break, until near ten o'clock on Friday Morning, Nov. 4, 1791; between Two Thousand Americans, belonging to the United Army, and near Five Th[ousan]d Wild Indian Savages, at Miami-Village, near Fort-Washington, in the Ohio-Country, in which terrible an[d des]perate Battle a most shocking Slaughter was made of Thirty-nine gallant american officers and up[wards] of Nine Hundred brave youthful soldiers, who fell gloriously fighting for their Country.—These [Partic]ulars and Elegy are now published in this Sheet by the earnest Request of the Friends to the De[ceas]ed Worthies, who died in Defence of their Country, not only as a Token [of] Gratitude to the Deceased Brave, but as a Perpetual Memorial of this [imp]ortant Event, on which, perhaps may very eisentially *[sic]* depend the future Freedom and [G]randeur of Fifteen or Twenty States, that might, at some Period, be annexed to the [A]merican Union." Early American Imprints, no. 23268, John Hay Library, Brown University Library

feat by "Five T[housan]d Wild Indian Savages, at Miami-Village, near Fort-Washington, in the Ohio-Country." There were only about 1,000 Indian warriors who dealt St. Clair's depleted forces of 1,400 men this staggering defeat. In addition to the soldiers, more than 100 American women died in the Columbian Tragedy, although some sources reported their number to be as high as 250. Some were camp followers; others, women who had accompanied their husbands to the battlefield, hoping to stake a claim to the prime agricultural fields of the Indian villages.[59]

Newspapers cast the Indians as savages who had relied on brute force to defeat the vastly outnumbered Americans. In reality, it was the outnumbered Indians who relied on clever tactics to defeat the larger U.S. Army. Little Turtle led his men into a half-moon formation that rapidly surrounded the Kentucky militia, then the larger army camp. The militia ran "helter skelter" from their position into the main camp, throwing the attempt to form a front line into disorder. The women who had accompanied the army were caught in the crossfire at the start of this battle, between the soldiers trying to form a front line and the terrified militia rushing into the camp. "Some were running to and fro, wringing their hands and shrieking out their terrors; some were standing speechless, like statues of horror with ... eyes fixed upon the not very distant scene of strife." Others knelt in prayer, "calling on Heaven for protection," and some were "sobbing and groaning in each other's arms." Still others collapsed from fright and "lay as if dead upon the ground."[60]

Winthrop Sargent described the militia's conduct as "cowardly in the most shameful degree." Their actions had left the women defenseless, and most of the women died in the ensuing chaos of battle. Ebenezer Denny confirmed the panicked flight of the Kentucky militia, but he also considered the Indian warriors efficient as they "completely surrounded the camp, killed and cut off nearly all the guards," and advanced in relentless, orderly fashion.[61]

---

59. The number of Indians and the final number of men involved in fighting this battle vary by accounts. Part of the problem arises from exaggerated newspaper reports, where the number of warriors was reported to be 5,000. Little Turtle's biographer, Harvey Lewis Carter, estimates the number of Indian warriors at 1,400 men. Carter estimates that, if the hunters and scouts were excluded from the fighting, this would have reduced the number of warriors to 1,000. Carter also confirms that, in 1804, William Wells, Little Turtle's son-in-law, confirmed the size of the army as 1,400. See also Gerard T. Hopkins, *A Mission to the Indians from the Indian Committee of the Baltimore Yearly Meeting to Fort Wayne, in 1804*.... (Philadelphia, 1862); Henry Howe, *Historical Collections of Ohio* ... (Cincinnati, Oh., 1875), 228; "Sargent's Diary," *Ohio Arch. and Hist. Soc. Quarterly*, XXXIII (1924), 269.

60. "Sargent's Diary," *Ohio Arch. and Hist. Soc. Quarterly*, XXXIII (1924), 258–259.

61. *Military Journal of Ebenezer Denny*, 369.

When Lieutenant Colonel Darke attempted to break up a cluster of men who were crowding together in the center of camp, the men became so distraught that they "ran in a huddle," and the officer's efforts to get them into order proved futile. Sargent wrote that "they were huddled together in crowded parties . . . where every shot from the enemy took effect. . . . Their surviving leaders used threats and entreaties, and almost every other means that could be devised, to [bring] them to the appearance of order," but their attempts were hopeless. Denny also viewed the army as a frightened mob, incapable of fighting. He watched in horror as the Indians shot his men at close range; they killed so many that he was too overcome with emotion to describe it.[62]

It was not merely that St. Clair's army was ill prepared for battle but also that the Indians were well-prepared and highly organized. Colonel James Smith, who later wrote of his captivity among the Shawnee, described the disciplined nature of Indian warfare and claimed that it was a mistake for army officers like St. Clair to believe that Indians lacked the social organization necessary for planning and carrying out military operations and the sense of subordination needed to follow orders. "I have often heard . . . officers call the Indians undisciplined savages. . . . This is a capital mistake, as they have all the essentials of discipline. They are under good command, and punctual in obeying orders: they can act in concert, and . . . each man is to fight as though he was to gain the [victory] himself." In this well-executed battle, the Indians remained in the tactical formation devised by Little Turtle, and they focused their fire on primary targets: the army officers. Those officers' deaths furthered the disarray of the poorly disciplined army.[63]

St. Clair's army was badly trained, inadequately supplied and clothed, and moved so slowly that winter weather engulfed it before the onset of fighting. Desertions continued to be commonplace. By November 3, when the battle began, only 1,400 men remained in St. Clair's army. Little Turtle and his allies, Blue Jacket and Buckongahelas, had planned to wait for the army to splinter into smaller groups, but with dwindling numbers, they no longer had to wait. They divided their warriors into three forces and pinned down the Ameri-

---

62. Darke to Washington, Nov. 9, 1791, Knox Papers; "Sargent's Diary," *Ohio Arch. and Hist. Soc. Quarterly*, XXXIII (1924), 261.

63. *An Account of the Remarkable Occurrences in the Life and Travels of Col. James Smith . . . during His Captivity with the Indians . . .* (Lexington, Ky., 1799), rpt. as *Scoouwa: James Smith's Indian Captivity Narrative* (Columbus, Oh., 1978), 161–172; Metcalfe, *Collection of Some of the Most Interesting Narratives*, 265; "Washington's Tour to the Ohio in 1770," *Olden Time*, I (1846), 124.

cans in their own camp, which backed up to the Wabash. The U.S. Army had advanced to the Wabash by carving only a single-lane road out of the dense woods. When the men fled the battlefield, they stumbled in confusion along that stump-ridden, swampy, narrow route. Denny and Sargent were critical of the army's withdrawal. Sargent protested, "The conduct of the army after quitting the ground was in a most supreme degree disgraceful. Arms, ammunition, and accoutrements were almost all thrown away, and even the officers in some instances divested themselves of their fussees." St. Clair himself described the retreat as "a very precipitate one. It was, in fact, a flight." One story, recorded later, describes a distraught young mother, Catherine Miller, who fled the battlefield and quickened her pace by abandoning her baby. The child was later adopted by the Wyandot and raised at their Sandusky village. St. Clair lost $33,000 worth of equipment, which Sargent enumerated as "three six-pounders and three threes, brass, and two pieces of iron ordinance. Two traveling forges and four-oxteams, complete; two baggage wagons with horses; three hundred and sixteen pack-horses full-harnessed, besides those of the contractor's department; thirty-nine artillery, and a considerable number of dragoon and private riding horses" and the personal possessions and uniforms of the officers.[64]

Once the Americans retreated, the Indians returned to desecrate the bodies left on the battlefield. Several Americans, silent observers from the swamplands, described a brutality that was widely and sensationally broadcast in the nation's newspapers. Those atrocities horrified America's reading public. Soldiers described hands and legs being severed from both men and women. Helpless wounded were tossed on the army's campfires and burned alive. No distinction or mercy was shown to women. In the past, injured people left on the battlefield were often held as hostages or captives; now they were put to death. The Indians abandoned many of their long-established practices, and death and dismemberment became intentional. The battlefield conveyed a terrifying message to spectators hiding in the swamps. There were far too many bodies to burn and, instead, the Indians marked those already dead. They "crammed clay and sand into the eyes and down the throats of the dying and dead" while other Indians "fill[ed] the mouths of the slain with earth." Americans would choke to death on their greed for land if they invaded again.[65]

64. Wilson, ed., *Journal of Captain Daniel Bradley,* 31; "Sargent's Diary," *Ohio Arch. and Hist. Soc. Quarterly,* XXXIII (1924), 262, 265; *ASPIA,* I, 137; Dillon, *History of Indiana,* 280.
65. Benson J. Lossing, *The Pictorial Field-Book of the War of 1812* . . . (New York, 1868), 48n; Sword, *President Washington's Indian War,* 191; White, *Middle Ground,* 454; Samuel G. Drake, *Biography and History of the Indians of North America* . . . (New York, 1834), book V,

Indians retaliated for the repeated invasions of homelands they had steadfastly refused to cede, the destruction of their homes, the burning of women's cornfields, the devastation of their stored food supplies, the slaughter of their livestock, and the kidnapping and imprisonment of their women and children. Reiterated attacks had left the Indians resolved to drive out the Americans. Military historians who have studied St. Clair's defeat and have attempted to explain why the American army suffered this large number of fatalities generally focus on the role that Indian warriors played in achieving that victory. They look to the leadership and military skill of leaders like Little Turtle, Blue Jacket, and Buckongahelas. But at a deeper level, it was the suffering of Indian women that rallied these warriors to victory. The mutilation of bodies and other barbarities that occurred on that battlefield were a direct response to the invasion of the Wabash villages, where the militia had captured the sick and elderly, kidnapped the women and children, and skinned alive an elderly Wea warrior. The Kentucky militia had burned homes and crops, then marched women and children to a federal fort. The Indian response was similar to that at the Battle of Blue Licks in 1782, when they scattered forty dismembered bodies along the Buffalo Trace after defeating the Kentucky militia. Blue Licks was the Indian reaction to Anglo-American overhunting, meant to inspire terror in those who traveled along that pathway. Violence became a symbolic act to dissuade Americans from appropriating Indian lands and destroying their food supply.

St. Clair's defeat, or the Battle of the Wabash, was not an anonymous battle. Indian warriors had been forced to watch silently and helplessly from the woods as their wives and children were driven at gunpoint through the swamps to imprisonment at Fort Steuben. Because the Kentucky militia had camped across the river from the main army encampment, Indians recognized many of the same men who had burned their villages and captured their women and children. Militia leaders like Oldman, Brown, and Clark were targeted because they had a long history of Indian atrocities. Each of these men had been involved in the destruction of the Wabash villages and the abduction of their families.

The battle was also a personal message to St. Clair, who had failed to restrain the repeated Kentucky militia attacks on Indian villages since his appointment as territorial governor in 1790. He had issued repeated warnings to the militia but done nothing to enforce them. During his two-year tenure as territorial governor, St. Clair was involved in every U.S. offensive against the

---

54. In Perkins's *Annals of the West,* one observer described how the Indians drove stakes through a young woman's body until she died (377).

Indians, planning and supervising Harmar's 1790 attack, and following the raids on the Wabash villages, he became the architect of his own defeat. He had sanctioned Scott's first attack, then ordered the second assault by Wilkinson. Those two assaults had yielded almost one hundred captive women and children. St. Clair then moved and isolated the captives at Fort Washington, where he prohibited Indians from visiting their kin.

When Little Turtle assembled his warriors for the early morning attack on St. Clair's forces, he was joined by warriors from as far away as the Mohawk nation in Canada and Ojibwe people from the western Great Lakes; some warriors came from as far north as Green Bay, Michilimackinac, and Montreal. These warriors had long established kinship ties and alliances to the Wabash villages, with sisters or daughters who had married into those villages. What happened in the Wabash River valley threatened the existence of this interconnected Indian world. Corn was crucial to daily diets, and it was women who planted, raised, and produced a surplus to trade. In the Great Lakes, with its dense kin networks, news spread quickly during the summer months, and the kidnapping and imprisonment of women held implications for the entire region as the Americans attempted to establish sovereignty over the region.[66]

The Ohio River valley was transformed by, and in the long term dependent on, the agrarian labor of Indian women. Women's labor was central to Indian prosperity. Placing gender at the heart of this narrative suggests why kidnapping women threatened this village world and why defeated soldiers were brutally treated. The specter of an invading army drew hundreds of Indians to Miamitown and the Glaize, and an already multiethnic world became even more diverse. Knox's worst nightmare had come true: the kidnapping united Indians of many nations.

The Indians inflicted upon the army a defeat of such magnitude that it should have warned Americans away from future attacks on Indian villages. Americans failed to heed that message, but the defeat also suggests a different way of understanding U.S. history—and why targeting Indian women in the Wabash River valley had broader implications. Experience had taught Washington that the destruction of agrarian villages undermined Indian resistance.

66. Ouiatenon ranked fourth in the western Great Lakes sites for the amount of furs collected in the Great Lakes region. Only Michilimackinac, Detroit, and St. Joseph collected more furs. Ouiatenon was a widely known trading village where Indians from the Great Lakes gathered following the winter hunt. The furs exported from Wabash villages exceeded the number of pelts acquired at more distant and well-known places like Michilimackinac; thus, many distant Indian villages had kinship ties to these Wabash villages. See R. Cole Harris, *Historical Atlas of Canada*, I, *From the Beginning to 1800* (Toronto, Ont., 1987), plate 40.

During the Revolutionary War, the destruction of Seneca villages by Sullivan's militia forces led to famine and forced Seneca migration to Canada. Along the Wabash River valley, the villages were so numerous and the environment so luxuriant that refugee Indians could find welcome at nearby villages, where they had kin. Starving times did not immediately follow the U.S. invasions by Scott and Wilkinson, but, the next spring, the absence of Kickapoo women limited the kinds and quantity of crops that they could plant. In the long run, and if repeated, the capturing of women posed a threat to agrarian village life. Washington's directive was an effort to intimidate all agrarian villages; instead, it led Indians to join a confederated force against American invasion. Stuffing dirt and grass into the mouths of dead soldiers was not just a warning about future incursions onto Indian land; it was a message about abducting women and obliterating the agrarian village world they had created.

Simultaneously, the brutal images associated with the Columbian Tragedy embedded in American public consciousness the horror of confronting Indians on the western frontier. Newspapers magnified the barbaric imagery of Indians. Narratives published about the battlefield atrocities went far beyond the horrors of scalping and quickly stemmed the tide of western migration. Previously, many Americans had blamed the western turmoil on greedy settler colonists who encroached on Indian lands; now, Americans increasingly viewed the Indians as barbarians and, as the next chapter demonstrates, clamored for the creation and expansion of a standing army.[67]

67. Richard H. Kohn, *Eagle and Sword: The Federalists and the Creation of the Military Establishment in America, 1783-1802* (New York, 1975), 93.

8

AFTERMATH

*"I Foresaw, That if I Parted with My Land,
I Should Reduce the Women and Children
to Weeping"*

We tend to view the Ohio Valley as a relatively vacant landscape. When we do imagine that landscape peopled with Indians, they are generally depicted as hostile warriors whose resistance to settler intrusion resulted in defeat and, ultimately, their own demise. Although the Western Confederacy defeated both Josiah Harmar and Arthur St. Clair, it was vanquished by the finally competent American army that triumphed at Fallen Timbers in 1794. Even a resurgent early-nineteenth-century Indian confederacy led by Tecumseh and Tenskwatawa met with defeat. As important as these figures and forces were, focusing on them has caused us to miss a crucial part of the narrative: following the captivity of Indian women at Fort Washington, the loss at Fallen Timbers, and the Battle of Tippecanoe, many Indians chose a pathway of accommodation, unobtrusiveness, and avoidance of war. Still, Indians persisted and retained their distinctive identities. Today, many of their descendants live in northeast Indiana and southwest Michigan.

To understand what happened, it's best to think not just about the Indian defeat at Fallen Timbers and the failure of Tecumseh's Pan-Indian Confederacy. It's important also to reconsider two 1792 conferences — the treaty conference at Vincennes and the Pan-Indian gathering at Miamitown — and, indeed, to consider the contest between two figures at Miamitown, Captain Hendrick Aupaumut and Joseph Brandt, who embodied a more pacific, adaptive strategy that drew upon the successes of Indian women in the eighteenth-century Ohio Valley and proved highly effective in the centuries that followed.

WASHINGTON SEEKS PEACE TO PREPARE FOR WAR

St. Clair's defeat left Indians in control of the Ohio River valley and interrupted the United States' western movement. Repeated blunders and missteps by President Washington and Secretary of War Knox had encouraged Indian hostility, subjecting St. Clair to public ridicule and the president to congressional criticism. Following the Columbian Tragedy, Washington pursued a new Indian policy of pacification. Indian responses to these new overtures of peace were influenced by the Indian women who had suffered imprisonment at Fort Washington. There are no written descriptions of the harsh circumstances that these women and children endured, but we can imagine that their isolation, the loss of their families, and the destruction of their homes would have led to recurring flashbacks, nightmares, depression, anxiety, and remorse. After almost a year of living in the midst of American men who were both soldiers of a hostile power and witnesses of the carnage of St. Clair's defeat, it would not be surprising if many of these women chose to move their villages west of the Mississippi, to where Pacanne's village had relocated. Instead, almost all of these women chose to remain on their homelands and strenuously opposed any further land cessions at the Vincennes treaty negotiations, which secured their release. While the United States attempted to secure ceded lands north of the Ohio, these former hostages demanded that the Ohio River remain the boundary between Indian lands to the north and American lands to the south. North of the Ohio was to remain the Indian coast.[1]

The United States based its claims to Ohio lands on the McIntosh and Fort Harmar treaties, which Indians regarded as illegal land cessions. They were angered by the bargaining away of their homelands by the Indians who had signed those treaties, short-term residents with no valid land claims. Most easterners believed that Indians had legitimately participated in both the McIntosh and Harmar treaties and that the lands north of the Ohio and east of the Miami River belonged to the United States. The distorted news that followed St. Clair's defeat intensified negative perceptions of Indians. The *Maryland Journal* was one of the first papers in early December to spread the news about the army's defeat; it claimed that the army's straggling remnants had taken refuge at Fort Jefferson and were under siege, "cooped up and

---

1. Historian Elizabeth A. Perkins describes the country west of the Appalachian Mountains as divided into "separate Indian and Anglo-American provinces," with an "Indian coast" along the northern banks of the Ohio and a "Virginia shore" along the southern expanse. See Perkins, *Border Life: Experience and Memory in the Revolutionary Ohio River Valley* (Chapel Hill, N.C., 1998), 47.

starving." In Boston, the broadside that circulated described a "Bloody Indian Battle" and rimmed that news with a bold graphic of caskets labeled with the names of the dead officers. An eyewitness to the account publicly mourned, "This is a fatal stroke to the United States." The public was horrified by the cruelty and brutality of the Indian victory — but unaware that Indian women and children had been kidnapped and were imprisoned at Fort Washington. Newspapers and broadsides blamed the gruesome desecration of the soldiers on the barbaric nature of Indians. "Savagery" was the refrain, and such repeated and harsh condemnations led to public support for an increasingly powerful force that would crush the Indians. In the aftermath of St. Clair's defeat, public opposition to a standing army gradually softened.[2]

Washington understood that a standing army was only part of the solution. In deciding how best to defeat the Indians, he interviewed St. Clair and the officers who had fought alongside him. The president determined that defeating the Indians would require a large standing army — organized, disciplined, and led by an experienced combat general. Washington also planned to eliminate future dependence on militia forces, since each officer described the militia's cowardice and insubordination. He determined that he would need a congressional allocation of close to one million dollars to build a new army that could defeat the Indians, and such an outlay would be possible only with widespread public support.

The president also needed several years to reorganize, recruit, and intensively train a larger army. To Washington and Knox, this required a pacification policy to ensure that Indians remained quiescent. This shift from confrontation to peace was political posturing, playing it safe until a larger, well-trained army could ensure victory. This new direction in Indian policy required a new coterie of leaders and more determined restraint of the Kentucky militia. Most important, Washington had to end his experiment in hostage taking and needed a quick, face-saving means of releasing the women imprisoned at Fort Washington. This was best accomplished through Americans that the Indians would trust.

PACIFICATION POLICY AND
VINCENNES TREATY CONFERENCE

Washington's domestic blunder of capturing and imprisoning Indian women was intended to cast fear into the heart of Indian Country, but, in-

2. Lyman Draper Manuscript Collection, 4 JJ 206, 217, 223, State Historical Society of Wisconsin, Madison; William H. Guthman, *March to Massacre: A History of the First Seven Years of the United States Army, 1784–1791* (New York, 1974), 247.

stead, St. Clair's defeat cast fear into the hearts of federal leaders. Hostage taking became a presidential embarrassment. High praise for the capture of women and children by Charles Scott and James Wilkinson proved a bitter pill for the government to swallow. Washington's first attempts at establishing peace failed miserably because his appointment of Wilkinson as St. Clair's replacement provoked a horrified Indian reaction. Meanwhile, Knox instructed Wilkinson to send "confidential agents" to the hostile Indians, inviting them to gather at Fort Washington. In March 1792, Knox sent Captain Alexander Trueman to Fort Washington with his official dispatch to promote a new peace treaty. On April 3, Wilkinson dispatched Trueman and John Hardin, the recently appointed Kentucky militia commander, to confer with the multiethnic villages at the Glaize and Sandusky. Trueman ascended the Maumee while Hardin headed to Sandusky. Indians responded to these overtures of peace by killing both of them. Their deaths sent a clear message: it was Hardin who had captured the first group of women during Scott's raid on the Ouiatenon towns in 1791, and Trueman had fought alongside St. Clair. On April 6, Wilkinson dispatched two more emissaries from Fort Washington to carry his personal message of peace. Both men were captured and killed.³

Wilkinson's representatives were, needless to say, poor messengers for peace. To make his new policy credible, the president had to select his own envoys: men not associated with the Kentucky militia who could creditably foster this new direction in Indian affairs. Rufus Putnam, who lived in Ohio, was chosen to lead a new delegation to the Wabash Indians. He was a native New Englander, Revolutionary War veteran, friend of Washington's, and resident of Columbia, adjacent to Fort Washington. Putnam's most crucial attributes were his lack of connections to the Kentucky militia and his New England tendency to blame the Kentuckians for the unrest in Indian Country. Putnam also had previous experience as a mediator; he had negotiated with the Abenaki for lands along the Vermont border.⁴

---

3. Wilkinson was a member of the Continental army and entered the military a second time after moving to Kentucky in 1784. He served in the Kentucky militia and received a commission in the U.S. Army as lieutenant colonel, commandant of the Second Infantry, then was appointed commander at Fort Washington until General Anthony Wayne arrived. See United States Congress, *American State Papers: Documents, Legislative and Executive, of the Congress of the United States . . .* , 38 vols. (Washington, D.C., 1832), Class II, *Indian Affairs*, 2 vols., ed. Walter Lowrie et al., I, 227, 229–230, 235, 236 (hereafter cited as *ASPIA*); John D. Barnhart and Dorothy L. Riker, *Indiana to 1816: The Colonial Period* (Indianapolis, 1971), 294; Rowena Buell, comp., *The Memoirs of Rufus Putnam and Certain Official Papers and Correspondence* (Boston, 1903), 296.

4. For a discussion of opposition to a standing army and the sectional differences in those

During his trip to Philadelphia in 1792, Putnam was appointed the government's chief negotiator. Putnam had traveled there to request government relief for the Ohio Company, which was about to default on a large land payment due to the federal treasury. Washington asked Putnam to return to the army and head his peace commission to the Indians. Putnam reluctantly accepted his new appointment as brigadier general. He had "not the remotest wish to enter again into the Military," but as an officer of the Ohio Company, he was committed to stabilizing the Ohio River valley. The ongoing war with the Indians had halted western migration and contributed to the Ohio Company's default. Nonviolent resolution of Indian grievances appeared the only avenue for bringing peace to Ohio lands and financial stability to the Ohio Company.[5]

Shortly after Putnam's appointment, Knox had asked him to attend a council of "hostile Indians" at Miamitown in the summer of 1792. Putnam planned to meet Mahican chief Aupaumut at Fort Washington and journey with him to discuss peace with the Indians at the Glaize, the new site of the Miamitown villages. Unfortunately, Putnam's arrival at the fort was marred by a recent and deadly Indian assault on a settler village near Fort Washington, which led Putnam to change his plans. Instead, Putnam sent his speech with two Munsee captives, who read it at the conference. Hendrick went on to the Glaize, but without Putnam.[6]

Putnam planned to distance the Kentuckians from the peace process; he chose two representatives who were sympathetic to Indians—John Heckewelder and William Wells. Heckewelder was a Moravian missionary, a prominent friend of the Indians in the Ohio River valley, and one of their staunchest defenders in Philadelphia. Wells was a white captive raised at Kenapakomoko and named Apekonit (Wild Carrot) when he was adopted by the household of the Porcupine, Kaweahatta, a civil chief. At adulthood, Wells probably received the name Blacksnake. He was respected by the Indians because he had "learned their language, became a good huntsman and useful man." His adopted father "had given him his freedom . . . and . . . allowed him to go wherever he pleased." He was described by a young captive as "a prisoner at large among the Indians." His family, including his first wife and his son, were among the Indians imprisoned at Fort Washington. Wells was a skilled

---

attitudes, see Richard H. Kohn, *Eagle and Sword: The Federalists and the Creation of the Military Establishment in America, 1783-1802* (New York, 1975), 121.

5. Harvey Lewis Carter, *The Life and Times of Little Turtle: First Sagamore of the Wabash* (Urbana, Ill., 1987), 114.

6. H[enry] Knox, "Instructions to Brigadier General Rufus Putnam," May 22, 1792, *ASPIA*, I, 235.

translator and had emerged as a cultural mediator between the Indian villages of the Wabash River valley and the Americans. He carried crucial information from one Indian village to another and forwarded their messages to military commanders at the forts. William Wells was married first to an Eel River Miami woman, referred to as Nancy in English, and he later married Sweet Breeze (Manwangopath), the daughter of Little Turtle, after his first wife and son were captured. His presence would prove vital to the release of the imprisoned women and children and to events that would unfold in the Wabash River valley following the Battle of Fallen Timbers in 1794, when he became the U.S. Indian agent at Fort Wayne.[7]

Heckewelder's invitation to join the peace commission came directly from Knox, at Putnam's behest. Heckewelder was an assiduous journal writer and recorded Knox's invitation:

> Sir,
>
> I have the honor to inform you that the United States have for some time past, been making pacific overtures to the hostile Indians north west of the Ohio. It is to be expected that these overtures will soon be brought to an issue under the direction of Brigadier General Putnam of Marietta, who is specially charged with this business.
>
> He is now in this city, and will be in readiness to set out on Monday

---

7. "Narrative of John Heckewelder's Journey to the Wabash in 1792," in William Elsey Connelley, ed., *A Narrative of the Mission of the United Brethren among the Delaware and Mohegan Indians, from Its Commencement in the Year 1740, to the Close of the Year 1806* (Cleveland, 1907), 72–73; Milo Milton Quaife, ed., *The Indian Captivity of O. M. Spencer* (1917; rpt. New York, 1955), 50; William Heath, *William Wells and the Struggle for the Old Northwest* (Norman, Okla., 2015), 43, 61, 97; Carter, *Life and Times of Little Turtle*, 86. Both Delaware and Shawnee had long traditions of cultural mediators, as James H. Merrell discussed in *Into the American Woods*. In this changing Indigenous world of the eighteenth century, William Wells paved the way for many of the white children raised as Indians to walk "out of the woods" and serve as intermediaries with incoming settler communities (Merrell, *Into the American Woods: Negotiators on the Pennsylvania Frontier* [New York, 1999]). In living with the Indians, Wells acquired diplomatic and linguistic skills. Wells was prominent in the 1790s and killed by the Indians at Fort Dearborn during the War of 1812. For additional information on Wells, see Donald F. Gaff, "Three Men from Three Rivers: Navigating between Native and American Identity in the Old Northwest Territory," in Daniel P. Barr, ed., *The Boundaries between Us: Narratives and Newcomers along the Frontiers of the Old Northwest Territory, 1750–1850* (Kent, Oh., 2006), 145. One of the best known accounts of Indian captivity in the Ohio River valley was written by a young boy kidnapped near Fort Washington in 1792, who later became a minister and many years later published an account of his captivity in a Cincinnati newspaper (Quaife, ed., *Indian Captivity of O. M. Spencer*).

next; and being acquainted with you, he is extremely desirous that you should accompany him in the prosecution of this good work.

Being myself most cordially impressed with a respect for your character and love of the Indians, on the purest principles of justice and humanity, I have cheerfully acquiesced in the desire of General Putnam.

I hope sincerely it may be convenient for you to accompany, or to follow him soon, in order to execute a business which is not unpromising, and which if accomplished, will redound to the credit of the Individuals who perform it.

As to pecuniary considerations I shall arrange them satisfactorily with you.[8]

On July 2, Putnam and Heckewelder arrived at Fort Washington. Putnam lodged at the fort while Heckewelder roomed in the town with an old friend from New Jersey. The missionary, a keen observer of human behavior, described Cincinnati as a developing frontier community with the fort located along the shoreline of the river and built on two forty-foot bluffs overlooking the nine hundred inhabitants who lived below. The community was far from peaceable — indeed, it was rather tumultuous — and although the military sought to govern, "the city insists upon its rights under the constitution, and in consequence frequent quarrels ensue."[9]

Heckewelder, critical of Cincinnati's growing population, considered the town "teeming with idlers" who were openly hostile to Indians. Heckewelder believed, once laws were passed and civil order established, that these people would take flight. "Yet they hope that this place, as well as the others on the north bank of the Ohio, will perhaps in time, or soon, be purged of this wicked class, for experience teaches, that as soon as they are made subject to the law, they leave for Kentucky." No comment was more revealing of Heckewelder's perspective than his remark that these "idlers," when faced with an orderly world, would flee to Kentucky.[10]

The sense of hatred pervading this town was evident from the events that took place following the burial of an Indian leader who had died unexpectedly while visiting the imprisoned women. In an attempt to pursue Washington's new pacification policy, the army chose to honor the dead chief by burying him with military honors.

8. "Narrative of Heckewelder's Journey," in Connelley, ed., *Narrative of the Mission of the United Brethren*, 58.
9. Ibid., 70–71.
10. Ibid.

At his funeral on the 17th, by order of Gen. Putnam and Wilkinson, every military honor was shown him and three salutes fired over his grave. The majority of Indians followed his remains, one of them carrying a white flag on a long pole, which he afterwards planted at the head of the grave. The procession marched in the best order, accompanied by the most prominent gentlemen of the place. The funeral march was beaten on the drum draped in mourning. They granted him a resting place in the cemetery believing that this might be of advantage to them, among the relatives as well as among the Nation in general.[11]

Heckewelder then described the malevolence that became evident when the townspeople exhumed the Indian's body and desecrated his corpse.

Malicious people dug up the body again at night, tore down the flag and post, threw them into a mud-hole and dragged the body down along the street and stood it up there. The generals had the body buried again immediately in the morning and a flag raised. Governor Winthrop's secretary issued a proclamation offering 100 dollars reward for the discovery of the perpetrators. On the following night however the flag and proclamation were torn down, but the body remained unmolested. For the second time a new flag was raised, a guard placed near by, and nothing further happened.[12]

Early community histories offer standard narratives about the hardships of frontier settlement, but there is little to suggest either the racial hatred then apparent in Cincinnati or the fear that these Indian women and children experienced during their twelve-month imprisonment. Ironically, it was the army who protected them from the wrath of the surrounding townspeople. We know very little about their imprisonment; it is shrouded by a veil of reticence. There are no requisitions in the War Department for clothes or even for food. An offhand comment by one soldier to Heckewelder reveals that the presence of these women and children at the fort was financially onerous: the officer in charge of mustering told Heckewelder that their imprisonment had cost the government $60,000.[13]

Shortly after Putnam and Heckewelder's arrival, several merchants arrived from Vincennes accompanied by William Wells and five Indian men and one woman, who were either Wea or Piankeshaw. Heckewelder referred to them as

11. Ibid., 73–74.
12. Ibid., 73.
13. Paul A. W. Wallace, ed., *Thirty Thousand Miles with John Heckewelder* (Pittsburgh, 1958), 274.

the Wawiachteno nation. The party was escorted by an armed guard to ensure their safety. They had come to secure the release of the captives. That night, Putnam facilitated the reuniting of the families; he ordered the guards withdrawn from the stockade and allowed the visitors to meet with their relatives and friends. But Putnam wisely ordered a guard to maintain vigilance outside the fort entrance. Heckewelder was present and described the joy and tears that were shed by the reunited Indians. The next day, the Indian spokesman, perhaps the Wea or Piankeshaw chief, requested that Putnam accompany them to the Wabash to speak with the Indians. He

> believed that if he did this he [Putnam] would find opportunity of announcing to the Indians there the peaceful intentions of the United States. He added that, if they were obliged to remain here much longer, they would surely all die, and if they must die, they would rather die in their own country than be buried here on foreign soil.[14]

A formal release of the women offered Putnam an ideal opportunity to meet with the Indians from the Wabash, and he responded to their request by setting "the date for their departure 30 days hence." He simultaneously sent a message on July 23 inviting the Wabash Indian villages to a hastily arranged peace conference at Vincennes, where he promised to free the prisoners. It was not safe to release them at Fort Washington, where the angry community would have massacred them. On July 24, Putnam noted in his journal that he "sent a Speech to all the Western tribes inviting them to meet me in council at post vincent the 20th of September, assuring them that I Should bring their fri[e]nds and relations with me (meaning the Indian prisoners at Fort Washington)." Vincennes was a short, two-day journey from the Wabash villages at Ouiatenon. His message, far different in tone than previous messages to the Indians, was devoid of the threats that had continually unsettled this region.

> To Kaweahatta. The great Chief on the Eel River
> And to all the Chiefs and Warriours of the Wyach-tenos, and other Indian Tribes living on the waters of the Wabash River
> Brothers
> I am now on my way from the great Councill fire of the United States, where the great and good Chieff General Washington resides—I am coming with the wishes of his heart to You which are very good, and which I hope will make Your hearts rejoice when You hear them.

14. Paul A. W. Wallace, *The Travels of John Heckewelder in Frontier America* (Pittsburgh, 1958), 273.

Brothers

Out of love to You I am come this Way — I wish you to become a happy People, and believe nothing is wanting to make you so, but that You and the United States might once see and hear one another and remove Such obstacles, against which we hitherto have stumbled — In order to obtain this end, I have appointed the 20th Day of September for us to meet each other at Post Vincent there to consult each other in a friendly and brotherly manner, — to wipe off all Tears — to sett our hearts aright — and to establish a lasting Peace and friendship, taking one another by the hands as true brothers, and loving one another from our hearts.

Brothers,

You see something very good preparing for You — make yourselves ready and come and see what it is — I expect to meet you on the Day appointed — Your friends and relations I shall bring with me.[15]

Putnam proposed that, if the Wea, Piankeshaw, Kickapoo, and Eel River Miami would gather at Vincennes, he would reunite them with their wives and children. Putnam's opening salutation to Kaweahatta referred to him as "The great Chief on the Eel River." Kaweahatta was considered the most powerful peace chief among the Miami, and his wife and her two sisters were among the captives. Wells undoubtedly influenced the substance of Putnam's message, for he assured Putnam that Kaweahatta "is a very sensible man; that the British account him the best speaker among all the Indian nations; that he is the greatest chief, and has more influence than any other man in the Wabash country." Putnam's message acknowledged the problematic relationship between the United States and the Wabash Indian villages. He suggested that, if they would meet with him at Vincennes in "a friendly and brotherly manner," together they could create a more open and lasting pathway for "Peace and friendship."[16]

Several weeks later, the prisoners, guarded by sixty soldiers, began their journey down the Ohio River. The women were lodged in four barges, and all went well until they reached Fort Steuben. They were greeted by nine cannon shots fired in their honor, treated kindly by the fort's commander, Thomas Doyle, and guarded by soldiers as they slept that evening in tents.

Unfortunately, disembarking at the Falls of the Ohio further traumatized these women. Almost a year earlier, the Kentucky militia had crossed the falls

---

15. Buell, comp., *Memoirs of Rufus Putnam*, 307–308.
16. Ibid., 307; *ASPIA*, I, 238–240.

to plunder their Wabash villages, then kidnapped and imprisoned them in Fort Steuben's small stockade before they were transported to Fort Washington. As if that terrifying memory were not bad enough, they then experienced the difficulty of crossing the falls. The morning after their return stay at Fort Steuben, when the four flatboats were lowered over the falls, only one boat made it safely across. One of the highly damaged boats sank, and the two sick women and two soldiers on board were forced to save themselves by clinging to the roof of the boat. Low water levels grounded the other three boats, suspending them on the rocks. The water soaked the women and children, and they feared they would be imprisoned on the flatboats that night. The women had no one to calm their fears; no one spoke their language, and William Wells had left to visit his white family in Kentucky.

> The poor Indians who had to see and experience all the difficulties and dangers and were at a place where Kentucky fury raged towards them, wept aloud together. As their interpreter had gone ashore to visit his brother, I consoled them as best I could and towards evening brought them back under cover of the cannons at the fort. Here they were out of danger and Capt. Doyle took the best care of them, until at last, they were taken next day to the headquarters of Gen. Putnam on the other side of the Ohio and below the falls, where they seemed to be quite contented.[17]

It was the arduous labor of the soldiers that rescued them. The next day, the soldiers relied on strong ropes to transport the boats safely below the falls. The journey was further delayed when Putnam's boat lost its rudder; several days passed before the journey was resumed. There were now 140 people distributed among four flatboats, and when they arrived at the mouth of the Wabash, they stopped to camp and rest. Meanwhile, the soldiers demolished the boats and erected a fortified building to hold the trade goods for the treaty conference. Twenty-five soldiers were left to guard the goods, which Putnam would later distribute at the Vincennes conference. Heckewelder reported, "The Indians, who are now on their own land and soil, become quite cheerful." The women and children were traveling along well-known pathways, covering about seven or eight miles a day. Two weeks later, on September 12, when they arrived at Vincennes, their relatives were there to meet them. When the Indians gathered for the conference "saw their friends who had been prisoners, they fired off their guns for joy and sang various songs to these friends . . . after

---

17. "Narrative of John Heckewelder's Journey," in Connelley, ed., *Narrative of the Mission of the United Brethren,* 78.

a speech by Gen. Putnam [the captives] were turned over to their friends, at which they all rejoiced."[18]

The tenor of this conference reflected the women's desire for a secure peace. Putnam carefully recorded all of the Indian speeches, which became part of the official proceedings. There were 439 women and children at the conference — almost twice as many as the 247 men. This gender ratio was unusual for treaty conferences; equally unusual was the diverse population of Mascouten, Potawatomi, Kickapoo, Kaskaskia, Piankeshaw, Peoria, Mifsoutins, Weaughtenow, and Miami. Many of the warriors along the Wabash had already left for the larger Indian confederacy meeting that was to take place at the Glaize, which Putnam had declined to attend.[19]

The Vincennes treaty negotiations were unique because of Putnam's sensitivity toward the Indian women. Their release created an open discussion forum where their voices could be heard, even though only one woman spoke at the conference. Putnam noticed that those leaders who spoke during the talks lacked political authority and repeatedly adjourned for discussion with the women before responding to his questions and requests. Female participation in decision making was central to village life. For example, among the Miami, it was not unusual for women to speak at village councils. Tacumwah had held forth at council meetings on behalf of her son, Jean Baptist Richardville, who later became chief of the Miami. Miami chieftainships were hereditary, but the selection of a chief rested with the chief's sister. Succession was generally awarded to the son of a chief's sister, not his own son. When there were several sons among the sisters of a chief, then the successor was put forward publicly by his mother. Once the successor was acknowledged, he served as a type of deputy chief until the old chief died. This system provided a voice to women in the selection process and prevented young and inexperienced men from becoming chiefs. These were common practices for many communities along the Wabash. Putnam's recognition of consensual decision making and his patience in allowing that process demonstrated his respect for Native traditions and an appreciation of how peace might best be achieved.[20]

Putnam's grasp of Indigenous protocols made these proceedings far different from those of the previous treaty conferences held along the Ohio River valley. He had released the hostages without imposing conditions, then demonstrated his generosity by distributing gifts to all the Indians. Putnam trans-

18. Ibid., 80–82.
19. Wallace, ed., *Thirty Thousand Miles,* 283; Buell, comp., *Memoirs of Rufus Putnam,* 121.
20. Charles Callender, "Miami," in Bruce G. Trigger, ed., *Handbook of North American Indians,* XV, *Northeast* (Washington, D.C., 1978), 110–121.

ported sufficient goods to supply seven hundred Indians with "a blanket, stroud, or breech-clouts, leggings, and a shirt to each, besides thirty hats and thirty coats for chiefs, knives, looking glasses, and some other small articles" as well as "medals, arm, and wrist bands, and other jewels." Clothing and ornaments were gifted to both men and women. Additionally, the chiefs who signed the treaty received "twenty sets of silver ornaments" as well as "nose and ear jewels." The outcome of this council, Putnam understood, was shaped by the women whose hard work had been destroyed by the Kentucky militia. They had endured a year-long imprisonment, and Putnam referred to these women as "queens"; although the terminology seems strange, his use of it acknowledged women as respected members of their villages. Putnam even identified one woman who rose to speak as the Queen of the Wea. This term appears throughout the treaty conference notes, and it was she who stepped forward to shake Putnam's hand, greeting him in a forceful, rather than retiring, way. Although we do not know her name, she was prominently positioned as the second speaker after John Baptist de Coigne, chief of the Kaskaskia, whom Indians had chosen as their primary speaker. Speaking order indicated social importance, suggesting that the Queen of the Wea's prestige was considerable.[21]

To ensure that his overtures of peace were understood by all participants, Putnam employed multiple interpreters to translate the speeches. Each man—William Wells, Rene Colder, Captain Meyet, and Jean Baptiste Constant—spoke several languages, and each speech was translated into the multiple languages of this diverse audience. Indigenous cultural references framed Putnam's speeches: he wished to "have this dark Cloud removed and dispersed" and to "take each other by the hand anew." His words described pathways of peace; he did not threaten further retribution, which had characterized previous addresses to the Indians. He took individual responsibility for past governmental actions and incorporated traditional peace rhetoric, telling his audience, "I shall always speak to You from my Heart, not from my Lip's only—Speak also from Your Heart—Tell me the cause of Your Uneasiness, and I will endeavor to remove it."[22]

The conference opened with the calumet ceremony, followed by the formal exchange of greetings. Putnam asked the Indians to discuss their terms and return the next day with an answer for him. This opening council lasted only a short time, the "Women and Children being hungry," and Indians wished to deliberate among themselves how best to secure peace with the Americans.

21. Buell, comp., *Memoirs of Rufus Putnam*, 341.
22. Ibid., 337.

Putnam understood and respected the deliberative, consensual nature of Indigenous decision making. He was neither angered by the brevity of the initial meeting nor troubled by the Indian desire to discuss alternatives among themselves before addressing him. Putnam even suggested that they close the first day's proceedings with a dram and told them, "You are very right in postponing the Answer till to-morrow; and if You want more time, You shall have it." The first day's meeting adjourned at two o'clock. The next morning, at ten o'clock, the meeting was rekindled with the smoking of the peace pipe, which was then offered to "evry person present" by the Kaskaskia chief, de Coigne. He requested Putnam carry this same pipe to George Washington. As the peace pipe circulated through the gathering, a Wea chief stood and told Putnam that they had chosen de Coigne to speak for all of them because, although he was "Young, he is the best Speaker."[23]

When de Coigne rose to talk, he opened with repeated references to the women attending the council. He asked General Putnam to present the pipe to General Washington on behalf of all the people in attendance, both men and women: "We all, together with our Queens, present you with this Pipe, which has never been stained.... We all have one heart.... We wish you to conceal nothing; to speak truth and make the hearts of our women and children glad."[24]

Like most treaty conferences, this Vincennes meeting was also framed by the issue of land. De Coigne warned against further U.S. encroachments on their homelands. He cited the Indians' experience with other foreign nations to show that Europeans had lived with and traded among them for many generations, and he described Indians' continuing sovereignty over their homelands. He told Putnam, "The French English and Spaniards never took any lands from us. We expect the same from you." Indian lands were given to them by the Master of Life, and they could be taken away from Indians only by the one who bestowed them. He described Indian lands as resting on an interlocking network of villages surrounded by sufficient land to sustain their individual households. He made repeated efforts to identify Indians at the conference as a sedentary people and rejected all images of Indians as nomadic. He told Putnam that, if Indians lost their lands, they "would regret the loss of our beds. The Author of life created us on these lands; and we wish to live and die on them.—No person can take them from us but he who gave them to us." De Coigne then moved the negotiations to one of the most important points of the conference: whether or not Indians would consider sharing their

23. Ibid., 339–341.
24. Ibid., 341.

lands. His statement was clear and direct. "You are many and so are we. Were we on the same land we might quarrel. It is best that the white People live in their own Country and we in our's. . . .We desire of you to remain on the other side of the river Ohio."²⁵

Each orator reinforced this message. They identified the Ohio River as the boundary line between the United States and Indian people. A civil chief from Kenapakomoko, Gawiahaetle delivered the crucial speech of the conference. He described the kidnapping of women and children from his village as disturbing "my bed." He thanked Putnam for returning the women of his household and assured him, "All darkness is removed." Once again, the central part of his speech focused on the Ohio River valley as the boundary line: "We think it is best for you to live Yonder, with your faces towards us, and we live here with our faces towards you. When we want to go to see you we can go thither; and when you want to come and see us you can come hither." The Wabash River valley Indians demanded that the Ohio River remain the border for Indian lands, which they considered essential for maintaining a safe distance from the Kentuckians. Further encroachment would not only jeopardize the peace but make daily life impossible to sustain. The irrational and arbitrary borders drawn by previous treaties threatened the subsistence patterns of large numbers of Indian villages. Each speaker viewed his people and their lands as intertwined and maintained that villages needed sufficient land to support their families. Speakers identified women as being "aggrieved" by the cession of Indian lands in the previous treaties. One Potawatomi chief from the Wabash River valley told Putnam that he had rebuffed all previous attempts to secure control over the lands of his village: "When I received the message that a great Chief would arrive here from the United States; And that he wished to speak to us, I expected the business would be of another nature, not that I find it to be. I did not expect that we would spend our time in speaking of Land, as I find the case to be — I have often been asked by the British to sell them Land, but Merchandize never tempted me. I foresaw, that if I parted with my land, I should reduce the Women and Children to weeping."²⁶

The speakers at this conference repeatedly linked women to the land, invoking the extreme grief, or "weeping," associated with land loss. Following the last Indian speaker, Putnam rose to respond. He raised the issue of the Ohio as a natural boundary, with lands south of the river as belonging to the United States and north of the river to the Indians. Putnam was concerned for his own interests — as well as those of the Ohio Company. The company's

25. Ibid., 342–343.
26. Ibid., 346–351.

lands were north of the Ohio, and Putnam asked the chiefs to clarify their perceptions of this border: could "White People" remain in their country, or should they remove "on the other side of the Ohio?" Putnam asked the Indians to consider this "dark Cloud" that had arisen in their discussions and left it to them to decide the fate of U.S. settlements and forts that had been erected on the Indian side of the Ohio River. Did peace require these spaces to be abandoned, or were there advantages if these new settlements remained? Putnam reminded them of the long-term presence of Frenchmen living among them and asked Indians whether they had granted the French lands near their villages.[27]

The Ohio River boundary was crucial to Rufus Putnam and to the future of Ohio Company lands. Putnam owned lands in Columbia and had moved his family here, north of the Ohio. The Indians adjourned to discuss his questions about existing American settlements and about the French. They promised to provide him an answer by two o'clock that afternoon. When they returned, de Coigne delivered their answer: "It is not our intention that any persons settled on this side the Ohio, should move away — Our request is that no other settlement shall be made." The other chiefs then rose, reinforced de Coigne's statement, and detailed the lands they had given to the French.[28]

The council lasted two days, and Putnam read the treaty articles, telling the gathering, "The White People commit to writing what they transact, that the paper may speak when they are dead. Your custom is to record by Belts. We shall do it both ways." Thirty-one chiefs signed the six-article agreement, whose primary intent was to establish "Peace and Friendship" between the United States and the Wabash and Illinois Indians. Knox had instructed Putnam to assure Indians *"in the strongest and most explicit terms"* that the United States renounced "all claims to any Indian land which shall not have been ceded by fair treaties, made with the Indian Nations." Knox's instructions were reflected in the fourth article of the treaty, which eventually proved a stumbling block for Senate ratification:

> The United States solemnly guaranty to the Wabash, and Illinois nations, or tribes of Indians, all the lands to which they have a just claim; and no part shall ever be taken from them, but by a fair purchase, and to their satisfaction. That the lands originally belonged to the Indians; it is theirs, and theirs only. That they have a right to sell and a right to refuse to sell. And that the United States will protect them in their said just rights.[29]

27. Ibid., 351–355.
28. Ibid., 355–356.
29. Francis Paul Prucha, *American Indian Treaties: The History of a Political Anomaly*

When the conference ended, Putnam had won a reprieve for the Ohio Company settlements north of the river: they were allowed to remain. Indians simultaneously delivered a clear message: there were to be no additional land cessions north of the Ohio. In return, the Indians were to return all captives and stop stealing "Negroes and Horses from the people of Kentucke"; they were permitted to sell their lands "by a fair purchase and to their satisfaction," with the "right to Sell and a right to refuse to Sell" resting with the Indians.[30]

At the conference, Putnam had established a reservoir of goodwill with Indian villages along the Wabash and defused discontent with the United States. While the treaty reaffirmed the Ohio River as the boundary between Indian and American lands, the existing settlements north of the Ohio were to remain. The Indians refused to accept additional settlements, which was more than problematic for the Ohio Company; it meant certain bankruptcy. After the conference ended, Putnam developed severe ague and a high fever that delayed his return to his family. It also left him unable to accompany the Indians to Philadelphia. Putnam remained at Vincennes, and in early October, Major Hamtramck and John Heckewelder led ten of the chiefs and a delegation of sixteen Indians, including several women, to Philadelphia. Putnam's illness left him too weak to reach his family in Marietta until December 18.

Although the treaty was sent to the president, it was not ratified by the Senate. When Putnam recovered his health, he journeyed to Philadelphia to provide a detailed report of the council meeting to Knox. On February 18, 1793, Putnam resigned his peace commission. Despite his best efforts, the U.S. Senate refused to ratify the peace accords that he had so carefully crafted with the Wabash Indians at the Vincennes treaty council. The fourth article was a sticking point, since the Senate wished to have an amendment that would "guard, in the ratification, the exclusive pre-emption of the United States to the land of the said Indians." The Indians were never informed of the Senate's action. Knox dismissed this by explaining to the president that most of the principal chiefs who had signed the treaty were now dead from smallpox.[31]

Even before the Vincennes treaty conference, ongoing violence had led many Indians to move west of the Mississippi. After the Vincennes confer-

---

(Berkeley, Calif., 1994), 14; see also "A Journal of the Proceedings at a Council Held with the Indians of the Wabash and Illinois, at Post Vincents, by Brigadier General Putnam," in Buell, ed., *Memoirs of Rufus Putnam,* 359–361; R. David Edmunds, "'Nothing Has Been Effected': The Vincennes Treaty of 1792," *Indiana Magazine of History,* LXXIV (1978), 23–35. The treaty is in *ASPIA,* I, 338; it also appears in Buell, comp., *Memoirs of Rufus Putnam,* 363–366.

30. Buell, comp., *Memoirs of Rufus Putnam,* 364–365.

31. Prucha, *American Indian Treaties,* 91; Knox to Washington, Jan. 2, 1794, *ASPIA,* I, 470.

ence, the Kickapoo left the Wabash River valley. They traveled the western pathway forged by Pacanne, who had secured lands in Spanish territory. Pacanne had lived at Vincennes, served as an intermediary for Clark with villages along the Wabash, and then welcomed and worked with General Harmar. Hamtramck considered Pacanne "a good Indian" and also employed him as an emissary to other Indian villages. But during Harmar's tenure, the 1789 ruthless slaughter of nine of Pacanne's men led him to retreat from supporting the Americans. Pacanne negotiated with British and Spanish officials to obtain new lands for his Miami village west of the Mississippi. He was a principal chief at Miamitown, and when Jean Baptiste Richardville assumed a similar role at the end of 1779, Pacanne led his Miami followers to new homelands across the Mississippi. He secured lands adjacent to the Quapaw from the Spanish and donned his British medal to meet with Joseph Valliere, then in charge of the Arkansas Post. Pacanne had led thirty-two members of his family and nine additional men to live in the west. He was welcomed by the Spanish, traded his British medal for a Spanish one, and initially settled his immediate family outside the French community of Ste. Geneviève. Pacanne continued to seek lands in the lower Arkansas River valley, where they could escape the violence engulfing the Ohio region. Like the lands of the Wabash and Ohio River valleys, the lower Arkansas abounded in natural resources.[32]

Pacanne's movement to the west was deliberate and well planned, and it established a pathway that other villages would follow. When Kickapoo villages suffered repeated invasions, their smaller villages were especially harmed by their lack of kin networks in the region, and the kidnapping of their women exacerbated the impact on their food supply. Although they were excellent hunters, their cornfields were not planted the next spring. Following the release of their women and children that fall, they went west to join established Kickapoo villages across the Mississippi, near St. Louis or along the Missouri. Kickapoo warriors later returned to Prophet's Town to fight alongside Tecumseh.[33]

---

32. Hamtramck to Harmar, Aug. 12, 1788, in Gayle Thornbrough, ed., *Outpost on the Wabash, 1787–1791* (Indianapolis, 1957), 108; Carter, *Life and Times of Little Turtle*, 75; Joseph Valliere to Esteban Miró, Jan. 12, 1790, *Spain in the Mississippi River Valley, 1765–1794*, in Lawrence Kinkaid, ed., *Annual Report of the American Historical Association for the Year 1945*, III, part 2 (Washington, D.C., 1945), 292–295; Kathleen DuVal, *The Native Ground: Indians and Colonists in the Heart of the Continent* (Philadelphia, 2006), 161–162; Richard White, *The Middle Ground: Indians, Empires, and Republics in the Great Lakes Region, 1650–1815* (New York, 1991), 427–429.

33. "Lieut. Colonel-Commandant Wilkinson's Report," Aug. 24, 1791, *ASPIA*, I, 133–135; A. M. Gibson, *The Kickapoo: Lords of the Middle Border* (Norman, Okla., 1963), 46–47.

AUPAUMUT AND BRANDT AT THE
GLAIZE CONFERENCE OF 1792

At the conclusion of the Vincennes treaty conference, most Indians chose to remain along the Wabash. Several villages also sent representatives to the Indians' meeting at the Glaize, which took place ten days after the Vincennes conference. In August 1792, almost one thousand Indians gathered at the Glaize. The Miami and Shawnee controlled the gathering, inviting villages from the Ohio as well as distant Great Lakes and Southeast communities. Sauk and Fox arrived from the north and west; Six Nations Iroquois, from the Buffalo Creek Reservation in upstate New York; the Seneca allied with Cornplanter, Canadian Iroquois, Creeks, and Cherokee, from the south; and Odawa, Wyandot, Potawatomi, and a few Wea, from the Wabash River valley. Alexander McKee, the British Indian agent, reported on the meeting to the new lieutenant governor of Upper Canada, John Simcoe. Simcoe had received orders from London to negotiate a peaceful resolution between the United States and the Indians, despite his previous support for Indian resistance. Canadian officials had provided Little Turtle and Blue Jacket with the military supplies that helped to defeat both Harmar and St. Clair. When Little Turtle sought additional military aid, Great Britain denied his request, fearing that continued financial support would jeopardize peace with the United States. The decision rested with London rather than with Canadian officials. Simcoe was left straddling a precarious fence: although he sympathized with Indians, he sought to maintain the profitable trade in furs, even as he realized that incoming American settlement would thwart that trade. Simcoe intensely disliked Americans and was confident that their radical experiment in republican government was doomed. He "long[ed] to renew the conflict against the republic."[34]

Meanwhile, Indian warriors began arriving at the Glaize during the summer months, although the ten days of formal discussions did not begin until October 9, 1792. The Miami invited the United States to send representatives to the council and, in early 1792, Washington and Knox began seeking Indians who could make the case that the United States was desirous of peace. Knox first approached Joseph Brandt, the well-known Mohawk diplomat and chief, enticed him to Philadelphia, and offered him a handsome reward if he would speak to the Indians gathering at the Glaize. Brandt was Washington's first choice as a spokesperson, having been born in a Seneca wintering village along the Ohio. Brandt's emergence as an Iroquois leader during the Revolutionary

---

34. Alan Taylor, *The Civil War of 1812: American Citizens, British Subjects, Irish Rebels, and Indian Allies* (New York, 2010), 27–35, 53.

War had made him Washington's fiercest opponent. He later emerged as an Iroquois diplomat, visiting with the president in Philadelphia as well as with British officials in London. Brandt was initially involved in the creation of the Indian confederacy, and Washington knew that he favored accepting the Muskingum River as a revised border to United States territory. But he had been displaced as a leader of the confederacy by the Miami when he openly endorsed moving the boundary line with the United States.[35]

Washington and Knox asked Brandt to assure the Ohio Valley Indians that the United States desired only those lands ceded through a "fair treaty." Brandt returned to his home in Niagara and, realizing the hypocrisy of the U.S. position, declined Washington's commission. Both Knox and Washington were committed to the boundary line of the 1789 Treaty of Fort Harmar, which ceded lands stretching farther west, to the Little Miami River. Rather than travel to the Glaize, Brandt remained at home. He was unwell and unable, he said, to continue his journey.

Following Brandt's refusal, Knox engaged Captain Hendrick Aupaumut to address the Indians gathered at the Glaize. In July, after visiting with Putnam at Fort Washington, Aupaumut arrived at the confederacy meeting as the United States emissary to the "Western Indians." He was a well-recognized military warrior from the American Revolution. The displacement of his Mahican people and his fluency in speaking an Algonquian language made him a welcome participant. The Mahican were long-standing allies of the Shawnee, Delaware, and Miami, who had previously invited Aupaumut's village to move west to their lands.[36]

No women spoke at the Glaize, but several orators, particularly Aupaumut, echoed the sentiments of the speakers at Vincennes. Aupaumut favored peace and raised the land issues addressed at the Vincennes treaty conference, including how treaties created arbitrary boundaries that threatened the subsistence practices of Indian villages. He blamed the unrest prevailing in the Ohio River

---

35. Jon Parmenter, "After the Mourning Wars: The Iroquois as Allies in Colonial North American Campaigns, 1676–1760," *William and Mary Quarterly*, 3d Ser., LXIV (2007), 67–68; Jon W. Parmenter, "The Iroquois and the Native American Struggle for the Ohio Valley, 1754–1794," in David Curtis Skaggs and Larry L. Nelson, eds., *The Sixty Years' War for the Great Lakes, 1754–1814* (East Lansing, Mich., 2001), 105–124. Brandt's mother was Mohawk; she returned to her home village at Canajoharie following his father's death.

36. "A Narrative of an Embassy to the Western Indians from the Original Manuscript of Hendrick Aupaumut," in Historical Society of Pennsylvania, *Memoirs*, II (Philadelphia, 1827), 61; also in Alan Taylor, "Captain Hendrick Aupaumut: The Dilemmas of an Intercultural Broker," *Ethnohistory*, XLIII (1996), 443.

valley on previous treaties, claiming that forced land cessions deprived Indians of crucial resources: "They told me that by the transactions of the big knifes, at the treaty [of] McIntosh 6 years ago was the beginning of the displeasure of the Indians — that the big knifes did wrong the Indians in taking unlawfully of their best hunting grounds. Further they upon my querie tell me that if the big knifes [are] willing to restore the hunting grounds to the Indians, they would have peace immediately."[37]

Aupaumut drew on a vision of the Ohio River valley as nurtured and sustained by women's agrarianism, in which village boundaries were defined by rivers and streams rather than delineated by arbitrary treaty lines. For Aupaumut, the Ohio River valley had no geopolitical structure but was defined by where one lived and where the land possessed sufficient environmental resources to sustain daily life. He depicted the Ohio River valley as a landscape shaped by the ongoing migration and movement of Indians, hoping that it would eventually accommodate his Mahican people. The Mahican had been pushed west from along the Atlantic coast, and his people had kinship ties to the different villages clustered around the Glaize. Like other Indians at the conference, he had come hoping to share the lands of the Miami, Shawnee, and Delaware.

Aupaumut's speeches reinforced the evolving sense that all Indians were part of an interrelated world. Aupaumut identified the Delaware, or Wenaumeau, as his grandfathers and the Shawnee, or Weshauwonnow, as his younger brothers. He considered the Miami, or Wemaumeew, and the Ottawa, or Odawa, as his grandchildren. The Wyandot were his uncles. Aupaumut's Indian world, like that of so many others in the Ohio River valley, was defined by a web of kinship that held diverse people together.

As a respected sachem, Aupaumut drew on the diplomatic roles that were familiar to Algonquian-speaking people, explaining his behavior as continuing the traditions of his ancestors: "It was the business of our fathers to go around the towns of these nations to renew the agreements between them, and tell them many things which they discover among the white people in the east." Aupaumut's presence encouraged several Indian communities at the Miamitown conference to clear and broaden the pathway of communication between themselves and the United States, and he repeatedly received requests from other Indian leaders to record their words and to forward their

---

37. Lisa Brooks, *The Common Pot: The Recovery of Native Space in the Northeast* (Minneapolis, 2008), 132; Colin G. Calloway, *The Victory with No Name: The Native American Defeat of the First American Army* (New York, 2014), 145.

speeches to government officials in Philadelphia. They were well aware of the larger venues where Aupaumut's words had credibility and of his function as an ambassador and cultural mediator with the federal government.[38]

Aupaumut blamed the recent unrest on the McIntosh treaty of 1785, which had deprived the Shawnee and Delaware of access to their hunting lands. The treaty had established artificial borders and barriers that isolated Indians from access to environmental resources and were thus detrimental to their health, even threatening their survival. The United States found that many New England Indians were willing to cede lands when their hunting and planting grounds were confirmed, and Aupaumut thought that perhaps Indians in the Ohio might do the same.[39]

Aupaumut also held white outcasts and outlaws responsible for creating unrest in the Ohio River valley. He railed against the Kentuckians — the "Big Knifes of Kentucky" — who illegally claimed possession of Indian lands, and he blamed the destruction of the Wabash villages and the kidnapping of women and children on white backwoodsmen. Such abuses had sent shockwaves through the Indian communities of the Ohio region and Great Lakes. To Aupaumut,

> the reason the Big knifes are so bad, is . . . because they have run away from their own country of different States because they were very mischievous, such as thieves and robbers and murderers — and their laws are so strict these people could not live out there without being often punished; therefore they run off [to] this contry *[sic]* and become lawless. They have lived such a distance from the United States, that in these several years the Law could not reached them because they would run in the woods, and no body could find them. But at length the people of the United States settle among them, and the Law now binds them; and if they would endeavor to run in the woods as usual, you would then have [a] chance to knock their heads and they know this.[40]

From Aupaumut's perspective, the Big Knives were intent on reducing Indians to slavery. He condemned the immorality rampant among the Kentucky militia and described these Big Knives as "cruel people [that] have kindled the bad fire, and so raised the evil smoke." He blamed extended warfare on provocations by intruding Kentuckians who settled illegally in the

---

38. Aupaumut, "Narrative of an Embassy," 77–78.
39. Brooks, *Common Pot*, 132.
40. Aupaumut, "Narrative of an Embassy," 128.

Ohio backcountry. He denounced "the inhuman practices of your people on the frontiers, who ought to have set good examples." At the same time, Aupaumut also believed that the newcomers who legitimately settled on public lands would restore order to Indian communities. He described his vision of a resettled Ohio River valley where Indian villages remained the neighbors of newly established settler communities. American farms would be added to the existing pattern of agrarian villages clustered along the tributaries of the Ohio River valley. He shared the agrarian orientation of the women who had attended the Vincennes conference, but his vision for the future differed from that laid out at the treaty conference. Whereas Aupaumut imagined a more integrated landscape of Indians and colonist settlers, the Indians at Vincennes believed the Ohio River was a border that would curtail future encroachment. Although Indians were to be north of the Ohio and Americans south of the river, there were already exceptions, since the Vincennes meeting accepted the existing settlements north of the Ohio. For Indians like Aupaumut, it was the Kentuckians who were problematic rather than the Ohio Company settlers, whom he considered orderly and peaceable.[41]

Aupaumut spoke on behalf of peace with the United States, as did Red Jacket and his Seneca people. Whereas Red Jacket was rebuffed and warned to speak from his heart and not his mouth, Aupaumut was well received. Despite his stance against majority sentiment at the conference, he helped persuade many of the Indians to meet at the rapids of the Maumee in the spring of 1793 to participate in peace talks with the United States.

Aupaumut proved a more viable spokesperson for the United States than Brandt because he did not share Brandt's belief in the need for a political confederacy. Instead, Aupaumut's views resonated with Indians who viewed kinship as the only social structure needed in the Ohio River valley. Aupaumut had adopted many Anglo-American behaviors but retained his unique identity as Mahican. He was known for his Christian piety, his sobriety, and his zeal in adopting New England modes of agricultural production. The agrarian skills of Aupaumut's villages were compatible with the agrarian orientation of many of the villages in the Ohio River valley. New England observers re-

41. Taylor, "Captain Hendrick Aupaumut," *Ethnohistory,* XLIII (1996), 433, 435–436, 439, 442. Aupaumut spoke at the confederacy meeting at the Glaize because he intended to "use the federal government to weaken the Iroquois and the state of New York, the two most proximate and historically menacing threats to Mohican independence . . . [and] to maximize the autonomy and influence of his people, whose shrunken numbers and tenuous position among the Oneidas and New Yorkers precluded military resistance" (Brooks, *Common Pot,* 76–77).

ported, "The sachem Hendrick Aupaumut has a good field of wheat, Indian corn, potatoes, and grass, and we had the pleasure of meeting him in the road driving his ox team."[42]

Despite Aupaumut's invocation of shared agrarian practices with the Ohio villages, militant warriors assembled at Miamitown railed against American proposals to "civilize" them. Aupaumut's futile attempt to resolve Indian grievances would have found greater resonance among women at the Vincennes conference. Instead, this was a conference dominated by male warriors who had no intention of learning to plow their fields. Aupaumut, in his written report of the conference, described the Indians' bellicose mood. They did not believe that the United States could control the increasingly hostile Big Knives of Kentucky. Aupaumut created a permanent record of the sentiments that transpired at the Miamitown meeting. He summarized his speeches and recorded those made by other speakers at the conference. He also described the pro-British, pugnacious speeches and included them in his report to Timothy Pickering, who then forwarded this information to both Knox and Washington.

Aupaumut's letters to Pickering detail Indian grievances; they are explanations that parallel the village voices — especially the women's — that were raised at Vincennes. Aupaumut blamed the unrest that prevailed in the Ohio River valley on previously negotiated treaties that had forced land cessions and deprived Indians of crucial resources. As the contest over Indian loyalties played out along the Glaize, Aupaumut spoke repeatedly on behalf of peace with the United States. Joseph Brandt looked toward the British to secure the same end. Both men wished to master the tangled politics of the Ohio Country frontier, but each intended to do so from different positions and perspectives. Brandt was increasingly mistrusted, whereas Aupaumut came to be regarded as a long-standing friend who spoke in the language of kinship and regarded his audience as members of his kin network — his grandfathers, uncles, and grandchildren.[43]

In the contest between Aupaumut and Brandt, it was Aupaumut whose speeches were better received by the Indians assembled at the Glaize. Brandt might have been Washington's first choice as a spokesman, but his vision of a political confederacy did not resonate with the assembled warriors. Brandt had pushed for the creation of a confederacy that would transform the Ohio River valley into a political space, one that was hierarchically structured and that incorporated all the villages within the Ohio River valley. In *The Com-*

---

42. Taylor, "Captain Hendrick Aupaumut," *Ethnohistory*, XLIII (1996), 436.
43. Aupaumut, "Narrative of an Embassy," 76–77, 129, 131; Brooks, *Common Pot*, 132.

mon Pot, Lisa Brooks argues that Brandt drew on the structure of the Iroquois Confederacy, which demanded that all Indians be formally incorporated into a complex kinship structure, one following the patterns of responsibility and authority associated with the longhouse. What Brandt proposed was a realignment of the Indian villages of the Ohio River valley with a political structure resembling the Iroquois League. This perspective tended to promote the idea of the nation-state rather than recognize the interrelatedness and interdependence of the village structure that had long characterized the Ohio region.[44]

The Indian confederacy that actually did take shape at the Glaize rejected the Iroquois model but nonetheless changed the traditional decision-making process followed by most Ohio River valley villages. Warriors no longer deferred to their village councils and the consensual decision making inherent in village governance. Warrior authority was traditionally limited to military issues, but everyday conflicts, kidnappings, and raids brought the young warriors to the forefront of village life, enhancing their power. Harmar's Defeat, followed by that of St. Clair, created new sources of power for these young men whose interests focused on warfare rather than peace.[45]

During the 1780s and 1790s, warriors engaged in an ongoing and ever-widening range of conflicts. They traversed long distances and joined with people who would not have been customary allies. Large numbers of Shawnee warriors moved from their villages south of the Ohio into Creek villages, whose primary purpose was warfare. It was these warriors that dominated the meeting and rejected Aupaumut's plea for peaceful coexistence.

In addition, the Glaize was dominated by the militant Delaware and their allies rather the Miami-related villages that had dominated the confederacy at the former Miamitown. At the Glaize, Shawnee and Delaware villages also included militant Cherokee and Creek. This volatile mix of young men were convinced that British aid was forthcoming, and they veered toward war.

The Miamitown conference failed to include female speakers, and thus there were few advocates for peace. When Molly Brandt, Joseph's sister and the widow of William Johnson, greeted Aupaumut on his way to Miamitown, she warned him that the Indians gathering at Miamitown were exclud-

---

44. Brooks, *Common Pot,* 138–139.

45. R. David Edmunds insightfully describes the dramatic changes that took place among the Shawnee during the American Revolution, when the traditional spatial divisions among the Shawnee disintegrated as large numbers of Shawnee migrated to live among the Creeks in Alabama and almost one thousand fled west to Missouri. Internal divisions also threatened the bifurcated political leadership of peace and civil chiefs, and, increasingly, war chiefs refused to relinquish control. See Edmunds, "Forgotten Allies: The Loyal Shawnees and the War of 1812," in Skaggs and Nelson, eds., *Sixty Years' War,* 338–339.

ing women. She was further dismayed by the lack of women in Aupaumut's party. Among the Iroquois, women exercised considerable influence, not only in civil matters but in political decision making. Aupaumut recorded in his journal, "The old Wm. Johnson's widow (Captn. Brandt's sister . . .) . . . said, here is another thing looks much strange. If these Indians were upon good business, they would certainly follow the customs of all nations. They would have some women with them, but now they have none." Female voices heard at the Vincennes conference were absent here.[46]

Nevertheless, women were present but not consulted. Joseph Brandt had sent Sally Ainse, or Sally Hands, a prominent female trader, to supply goods to the Indians. She did not speak, despite her negotiating ability and her position as a well-known cultural mediator and translator at treaty sessions. Her early life among the Shawnee and throughout the Pennsylvania backcountry proved invaluable in negotiating the diverse village landscape of the Ohio River valley. Between 1775 and 1785, she had been identified as an independent trader in the account books of Detroit merchants like John Askin, William Macomb, Montague Tremblay, and Angus Mackintosh. Sally, like Joseph Brandt, would probably have encouraged a pathway of peace. Later on, when Sally asserted a legitimate claim to lands along the Thames in Canada, one of the most powerful men at this 1792 confederacy meeting subsequently invalidated her land claim. That man was Alexander McKee, the British Indian agent who had been raised and lived among the Shawnee. McKee opposed Brandt's peace initiative, and Sally was a Brandt supporter.[47]

46. Taylor, "Captain Hendrick Aupaumut," *Ethnohistory*, XLIII (1996), 446; Aupaumut, "Narrative of an Embassy," 112–113; Timothy Pickering to Knox, Aug. 10, 1791, item 114, Timothy Pickering Papers, microfilm, LX, Massachusetts Historical Society, Boston.

47. Sally Ainse, or Sally Montour, functioned as both a trader and cultural broker. She followed closely in the footsteps of her husband, Andrew Montour. The types of roles these mediators played among Indians is discussed at length in James H. Merrell's "'Cast of His Countenance': Reading Andrew Montour," in Ronald Hoffman, Mechal Sobel, and Fredrika J. Teute, eds., *Through a Glass Darkly: Reflections on Personal Identity in Early America* (Chapel Hill, N.C., 1997), 13–39. For additional references to cultural brokers, see Nancy L. Hagedorn, "'Faithful, Knowing, and Prudent': Andrew Montour as Interpreter and Cultural Broker, 1740–1772," in Margaret Connell Szasz, ed., *Between Indian and White Worlds: The Cultural Broker* (Norman, Okla., 1994), 44–60. Andrew Montour's mother, Madame Montour, was a well-known fur trader and cultural broker; see Jon Parmenter, "Isabel Montour: Cultural Broker on the Frontiers of New York and Pennsylvania," in Ian K. Steele and Nancy Rhoden, eds., *The Human Tradition in Colonial America* (Wilmington, Del., 1999), 141–159. One of the most influential outsiders at the conference, McKee would sway decision making by promising that Indians could expect to receive substantial military supplies from the British.

Coocoochee, a female mystic and medicine woman, lived at the Glaize but was not present at the conference, even though warriors often consulted her spiritual powers. She would have advocated armed resistance, since she "believed that these aggressive newcomers would not be satisfied until they had crowded the Indians northward to perish in the Great Ice Lake, or pushed them westward until those who escaped their rifle fire would drown in the Great Western Sea."[48]

Women's voices were absent, but as Coocoochee demonstrates, women were not uniformly advocates for peace. However, there were other cautionary voices like Red Jacket, who warned warriors that their successes against Harmar and St. Clair had made them overly proud and unwilling to extend their hand in peace. Such warnings were rare voices because there was no one at the conference to advocate for Washington's new peace policy. Three American treaty commissioners, Benjamin Lincoln, Timothy Pickering, and Beverley Randolph, were sent to speak with the Indians at the Glaize. They never arrived because they were denied the right to travel to the Glaize by the British at Detroit. The three commissioners disembarked on the Canadian side and remained stranded on the shore of Lake Erie for two weeks. They tried to obtain passage to the mouth of the Maumee, but they failed and eventually returned home.[49]

THE ARMY OF THE EMPIRE AND THE BATTLE OF FALLEN TIMBERS

In 1792 and 1793, there remained a substantial number of Indian villages in the Ohio River valley that favored peace with the United States. Perhaps the more militant villages could have been won over had the U.S. agreed

---

48. Helen Hornbeck Tanner, "Coocoochee: Mohawk Medicine Woman," in Rebecca Kugel and Lucy Eldersveld Murphy, eds., *Native Women's History in Eastern North America before 1900: A Guide to Research and Writing* (Lincoln, Neb., 2007), 147.

49. Gregory Evans Dowd, *A Spirited Resistance: The North American Indian Struggle for Unity, 1745–1815* (Baltimore, 1992); Tanner, "Coocoochee," in Kugel and Murphy, eds., *Native Women's History,* 147, 154. Spirituality led many warriors to rely on ancient practices and reinstitutionalized older practices that would eventually contribute to their defeat at the Battle of Fallen Timbers. In 1794, Wayne encountered 1,300 warriors who had fasted for three days before the anticipated battle; the fast began on August 15, in preparation for a battle the next day. When Wayne did not arrive, the warriors fasted a second day; on the third day, they arose to go in search of food. Wayne had the good fortune to strike a reduced force of half-starved warriors, with a large number of warriors absent from the battlefield because they were scouring the adjacent forests for game. See Council, Oct. 7, 1792, in E. A. Cruikshank, ed., *The Correspondence of Lieut. Governor John Graves Simcoe,* 5 vols. (Toronto, Ont., 1923–1931), I, 227.

to maintain the Ohio River as the permanent border with Indian Country. The U.S. could have ensured the continuance of this Indian village world with an army strong enough to interrupt the raids from Kentucky and to maintain peace in the river valley. Despite its move toward pacification, the United States was readying itself for war by building a military force capable of defeating the Indians, removing them from their homelands, and opening Ohio lands for American settlement. Alexander Hamilton had tied the sale of public lands to reduction of the national debt, and the profits of land companies and speculators were linked to securing Indian lands. On March 5, before the summer conferences at Vincennes and the Glaize, Congress had appropriated one million dollars for an enlarged standing army with 291 officers and 4,272 men. Washington and Knox replaced the regimental structure with a more flexible fighting force divided into four 1,280-man sublegions led by brigadier generals. This new army shifted the burden of frontier warfare from volunteer militia forces to a professional military. The Army of the Empire became Washington's hammer of Indian destruction rather than the means of protecting Indian lands and ensuring them a place in U.S. society. Before Rufus Putnam brokered peace with the Indians and Aupaumut advocated for peaceful ties to the new nation, Congress provided President Washington with sufficient funds to destroy Indian Country. It was then the president's task to transform a disorganized volunteer force into a standing army, large and disciplined enough to overwhelm Indian forces.[50]

Washington chose Anthony Wayne to head the new army, despite intense lobbying by Charles Scott and James Wilkinson. Although not Washington's favorite, because he was "addicted to the bottle," Wayne was the Cabinet's final choice. Jefferson described Wayne as "brave and nothing else." Most Cabinet members knew Wayne for his nighttime bayonet charge against the British bastion at Stony Point; such tactics would serve him well in the Ohio River valley. In April, Wayne's name was sent to Congress for appointment to command the new army and, by mid-June 1792, Wayne had taken up residence at Pittsburgh. All new recruits were sent to him to begin their training, and for the next two years, Wayne molded his men into a well-disciplined strike force. In 1793, when war broke out between Great Britain and France, popular support for a war against Indians gained momentum. In December,

---

50. Journal of the commissioners, with speeches, July 14, 30, 31, Aug. 1, 12–14, 16, 1793, *ASPIA*, I, 344, 351–352, 355, 356, and "Letter to General Knox," Aug. 23, 1793, 359; Andrew R. L. Cayton, *Frontier Indiana* (Bloomington, 1996), 161. Wayne began drilling his troops in the fall of 1792, and the Battle of Fallen Timbers took place in fall 1794; see Richard M. Lytle, *The Soldiers of America's First Army: 1791* (Lanham, Md., 2004), 51–52.

newspapers revealed that Britain had been supplying the Indians and encouraging them to go to war with the United States. Suddenly, the public began to see war with the Indians as part of the continuing struggle against Britain.[51]

When Wayne relocated to Fort Washington in 1794, he moved the army north along the Miami River toward the Maumee and built Fort Recovery on the site of St. Clair's defeat. In January, Wayne's forces repulsed two days of assaults by several hundred Indians. At the end of July, Wayne moved north to occupy the Indian villages at the confluence of the Auglaize and Maumee Rivers, where he constructed Fort Defiance. Here, at the site of the former Miamitown, which Wayne referred to as the "grand emporium of the hostile Indians of the West," he described the luxuriant landscape. "The very extensive and highly cultivated fields and gardens, show the work of many hands. The margins of those beautiful rivers, the Miamies of the lake, and Au Glaize, appear like one continued village for a number of miles, both above and below this place; nor have I ever before beheld such immense fields of corn, in any other part of America, from Canada to Florida." As the troops advanced along the Maumee, they came across abandoned houses replete with "delightful gardens" overflowing with produce and enjoyed the ripening fruit of peach, apple, and plum orchards. That night, when the army camped at Roche de Bout, near the Wolf Rapids, they began building another fort. Lieutenant William Clark, who had accompanied Scott on his Ouiatenon expedition, recorded in his journal the breathtaking beauty of his surroundings. He described a small island dotted with dark clusters and cedar and rocks that jutted from the river's surface and described it as "one of the most beautiful landscapes ever painted." One Kentuckian thought the Maumee resembled "a flooded meadow." They were only a short distance from the battlefield where, on August 20, 1794, the United States Army defeated the Indians at the Battle of Fallen Timbers. For the next three days, Americans burned and pillaged the Indian towns at the Glaize and carted away wagonloads of corn from the fields along the banks of the rivers. His destruction of the agrarian villages and burning of their fields ravaged much of the Indian food supply. The western half, along the Wabash and its tributaries, remained intact. Charles Scott had led the Kentucky militia through the Wabash River valley to join Wayne's forces at the Battle of Fallen Timbers, traveling through a landscape that was extraordinarily productive. Corn and vegetables garnished from Indian fields fed Scott's militia and the entire 5,000-member U.S. Army. When Scott camped at the mouth of the Maumee and Auglaize Rivers, his men feasted on "corn, beans, cucumbers, potatoes and all kinds of vegetables."

51. Kohn, *Eagle and Sword,* 125.

One soldier recorded that, all along the route, they continued to harvest "the finest beans and corn I ever seen and musk melons." "The whole Army has been supplied, Man and horse for 5 days in the most plentiful manner."[52]

GREENVILLE AND ACCOMMODATION VERSUS TECUMSEH AND TENSKWATAWA

Villages along the Glaize were destroyed, but the next spring, Indians returned; many villages were reestablished, and women replanted the cornfields. Almost a year after the battle, when treaty negotiations took place at Greenville, the Indians' land cessions recalled those at the Treaty of Fort Harmar. Most of the lands west of the Miami River remained in Indian hands. The signing of the Greenville treaty gave Americans an unchallenged presence in the Ohio River valley and simultaneously left in place much of the agrarian and sedentary Indian world along the Wabash.

The Indians who intended to remain in the midst of the incoming Americans made repeated requests for additional agrarian assistance at the Greenville treaty conference. The federal government supplied agricultural implements to those Indians who wanted help in establishing farmsteads. Several villages received agricultural goods and assistance instead of annuities. Aupaumut moved into the region and offered his agrarian assistance to his fellow Indians. The Delaware village on the White River received their annuities at Fort Wayne in June 1804, which went for the labor to construct fences and build houses. The Delaware had requested that the government "send suitable men amongst them, to instruct them in building houses, making fences, etc., instead of giving them their yearly annuities in goods." Eventually, the Delaware profited from these forms of agricultural assistance and positioned themselves as controlling a tract of land that extended east from the Vincennes Tract to the Ohio Boundary, representing themselves as the owners of Miami lands.[53]

At the time of the Indian Confederacy and the Battle of Fallen Timbers, Tenskwatawa was just seventeen years old, and his reactions reflected the dis-

---

52. "Copy of a Letter from Major General Wayne to the Secretary of War, Dated Head Quarters, Grand Glaize," Aug. 14, 1794, *ASPIA*, I, 490; "Journal of the Campaign of Charles Scott," MSS A, S425, Filson Historical Society, Louisville, Ky.; William Heath, *William Wells and the Struggle for the Old Northwest* (Norman, Okla., 2015), 298; Sword, *President Washington's Indian War*, 295; Reginald E. McGrane, "William Clark's Journal of General Wayne's Campaign," *Mississippi Valley Historical Review*, I (1914), 427; "General Wayne's Campaign in 1794 and 1795: Captain John Cook's Journal," *American Historical Record*, II (1873), 316.

53. Carter, *Life and Times of Little Turtle*, 100–101, 107; Heath, *William Wells*, 298.

content long expressed by young warriors. He spoke directly to fears that changing gender roles would force men to farm. Those fears bordered on becoming reality. Following the defeat at the Battle of Fallen Timbers, many headmen and chiefs, especially those who signed the treaty, came to believe that radical changes were required in Indian lifestyles. Black Hoof, for example, believed that Indians faced extinction if men did not learn to farm and raise livestock. At his Wapakoneta village, he secured the assistance of the Quakers, who taught Indian men how to plow their fields. Black Hoof also convinced the Philadelphia Quakers to send a missionary to the Miami to teach them how to farm. In March 1804, the Quakers opened a demonstration farm on lands that Little Turtle made available to Philip Dennis at the Forks of the Wabash. His farm became known as "Little Turtle's Farm School." By fall, Dennis left—not surprising, since only Indian women were interested in his work.[54]

In the Wabash River valley, there was little reason to change a system that had worked so effectively for so long and that fed large numbers of Indians. Men helped clear agricultural fields, but they shunned planting, cultivating, or harvesting crops. The Treaty of Greenville drove a cultural and material wedge into the villages along the tributary branches of the Ohio. Miami headmen and chiefs, such as Little Turtle, Black Hoof, and Five Medals, publicly supported this gender transformation, although each leader failed to take up the plow. These men were disparaged as "annuity chiefs" because they redistributed annuity funds to their own villages and acquiesced to white ways. Resistant warriors like Tecumseh lacked access to annuity funds and dismissed these chiefs as assimilationists. Tenskwatawa's village struggled on the edge of poverty, and he condemned the annuity chiefs for their wealth. He accused them of diverting funds for their private gain, although this was not true. Most annuity chiefs lived in log cabins or timber-frame houses constructed for them by the government. Often, they dressed in American-style clothing and embraced the lifestyles of their incoming neighbors. Others, like Aupaumut, were paid by the federal government to teach the Delaware white ways of farming. Tenskwatawa loudly denounced these "white" lifestyle changes. The emulation of white values and the continuing call for Indian men to turn to agricultural labor transformed such men into vulnerable targets. These headmen have also been disparaged by historians, who have frequently accepted the Prophet's charges that "the straw dogs" against whom he railed were no longer "genuine" Indians. Very little has been written about

---

54. Cruikshank, ed., *Correspondence of Lieut. Governor Simcoe,* 277; Carter, *Life and Times of Little Turtle,* 198–199.

them. Only Harvey Carter's *Life and Times of Little Turtle* stands in contradistinction to the myriad articles on Tenskwatawa and Tecumseh. There is little doubt that the annuity chiefs represented a departure from the traditional lifestyles envisioned by Tenskwatawa—changes that came in exchange for material assistance by the government and the help of missionaries. But these leaders also believed that these changes would allow their people to remain on their lands.[55]

Tecumseh, faced with a lack of support from the villages surrounding Fort Wayne, decided to relocate his village from Greenville to the heart of the Wabash River valley. This move was encouraged by his Potawatomi supporters in the west, especially the war leader Main Poc, who believed that communication with western Indians would draw new followers to his village. Tenskwatawa chose lands at the intersection of the Tippecanoe and Wabash Rivers, moving into the rich agricultural lands that were so highly prized by the women who had attended the 1792 Vincennes peace council. This choice was far from accidental. Tenskwatawa founded Prophet's Town at the site of Kethtippecanuck, near the two villages where the Kentucky militia had kidnapped Indian women. This site was also surrounded by agrarian villages and appeared capable of feeding Tenskwatawa's growing number of young male followers. Within a very short period of time, Prophet's Town grew from fewer than a hundred people to more than a thousand supporters.[56]

Prophet's Town did not solidify Indian Country but, instead, intensified social turmoil; it created an Indian civil war in the Ohio River valley. Followers at Prophet's Town rejected "any Indian adoption of American agricultural methods and gender roles." Although these changes in gender roles were simultaneously resisted by men in the accommodationist villages, the Prophet made it appear that this issue distinguished his followers from those of leaders like Black Hoof. The annuity chiefs failed to dramatically change gender roles, but Tenskwatawa castigated them anyway for wanting to make "women of the Indians." Most Indian villages experienced limited success in teaching Indian men to farm. Culturally constructed dialogues about gender differences distorted the reality of the circumstances. Tenskwatawa's rhetoric fueled factionalism and led the government to funnel treaty annuity funds to places like Wapakoneta, Black Hoof's village, while denying Prophet's Town financial support.[57]

Historians often neglect the extent to which the Ohio River valley re-

---

55. Stephen Warren, *The Shawnees and Their Neighbors, 1795–1870* (Urbana, Ill., 2005), 28.
56. Ibid., 31.
57. Ibid., 34.

mained an agrarian village world dominated by Indian women's agricultural labor and peaceful enough to allow coexistence to emerge as a viable goal. Instead, when looking at the period following the Battle of Fallen Timbers, many historians focus on Indian dissatisfaction with the Greenville treaty and resentment over the land cessions. Tecumseh, the Prophet, and the emergence of the Pan-Indian Confederacy continue to be the historical focus. But Wabash villages remained agrarian and were actively engaged in the fur trade, even as the teachings of the Prophet threatened to undermine this way of life.

When Tecumseh's male followers gathered at Prophet's Town, the warriors turned to the forests as their source of food. Increased reliance on hunting and the depletion of animal life in adjacent forests disrupted subsistence patterns in the Wabash River valley. When the villages clustered near Ouiatenon faced increased demands from Tenskwatawa's warriors for corn, Indian women turned a deaf ear to their requests. Many of the Prophet's "traditional" views about female behavior were a denigration of their engagement in the fur trade, even though their commercial activities were crucial for the survival and prosperity of villages along the Wabash. The Prophet criticized women for their lavish dress and their emphasis on accommodation rather than resistance. Ironically, Tenskwatawa borrowed an emphasis on monogamy from white society, undermining the matrifocal households of many agrarian villages in this river valley. Monogamy restricted the yields of agrarian households, which had produced larger harvests because they consisted of an Indian couple as well as the wife's sisters and other widowed relatives. Many of these households were polygamist, and headmen often married their wives' sisters. Most late-eighteenth and early-nineteenth-century households had many more women than men, and this was especially true along the Wabash. At Kenapakomoko, the women of Kaweahatta's household had included his wife, her two sisters, and their daughters. The women's work in these households produced substantial harvests, and it was these women who attended the Vincennes treaty conference and resisted sending their harvest surpluses to Prophet's Town. Equally problematic was Tenskwatawa's condemnation of the Indian women who married white men. He accused them of confusing the boundaries of genuine Indian communities. In a valley where the fur trade remained a viable source of income, intermarriage to fur traders was commonplace and prudent. Also, in a world where the male population had been reduced by warfare, intermarriage was likely on the rise rather than the decline. Tenskwatawa criticized the flexibility and shrewdness of Indian women, but they had long upheld the prosperity of agrarian villages.

Tenskwatawa, Tecumseh, and the Battle of Tippecanoe are much celebrated and have been extensively analyzed as a part of the growing Indian resistance movement of the early 1800s. They have been lauded for uniting Indians in the Ohio River valley. Tecumseh's sustained popularity is evident from the large number of biographies published about him. Unfortunately, this continued attention to Indian resistance has left us with an inaccurate portrait of this region and has led many historians to conclude that Indians were resistant to change. Little has been done to examine how many Indians acclimated to this shifting world of incoming Americans and how they survived the military defeat at the Battle of Fallen Timbers. Large numbers of Indians dismissed the teachings of the Prophet, shunned the confederacy, and remained in the Wabash River valley.[58]

Too frequently, the Pan-Indian Confederacy is portrayed as representative of the larger body of sentiment that emerged among Indians after the Battle of Fallen Timbers. But, as R. David Edmunds has demonstrated, "over half of the Shawnee nation . . . already were living west of the Mississippi, and most of the Shawnee still in the east . . . remained neutral or supported the Americans. Only a handful of Shawnee warriors opposed William Henry Harrison at Tippecanoe; and, in October 1813, at the Battle of the Thames, more Shawnee warriors served in Harrison's army than fought with Tecumseh." Tenskwatawa might have spoken vociferously — but he did not speak for the majority of Indian people in the region.[59]

The Ohio River valley was a bounteous landscape, and it was Indian women who produced most of that bounty. They cultivated a variety of crops, including traditional favorites like squash, corn, and beans, and introduced new foodstuffs, such as potatoes. They planted orchards of Old World fruit that spread rapidly through the river valley. John Heckewelder described the Indian-created town at Schoenbrunn (Welhik-Tuppeck, "the beautiful spring"), on what is now the Tuscarawas branch of the Muskingum River, near New Philadelphia, Ohio. There, the Indians had constructed sixty log dwelling-houses, laid out intersecting streets, and established a distinctive agrarian landscape with "large fields under good rail fences, well pailed gardens, and fine fruit trees; besides herds of cattle, horses, and hogs."[60]

---

58. Ibid. Dowd examines Tenskwatawa's rise to prominence in *A Spirited Resistance* and shows the highly effective role that Tenskwatawa played in galvanizing a nativistic movement that focused on halting additional land cessions (143–144). See also Adam Joseph Jortner, *The Gods of Prophetstown: The Battle of Tippecanoe and the Holy War for the American Frontier* (New York, 2012).

59. Edmunds, "Forgotten Allies," in Skaggs and Nelson, eds., *Sixty Years' War,* 338.

60. "Narrative of John Heckewelder's Journey," in Connelley, ed., *Narrative of the Mission of the United Brethren,* 157; Paul A. W. Wallace, *The Travels of John Heckewelder in Frontier America* (Pittsburgh, 1958), 101.

An uneasy accommodation existed between Indians and incoming Americans. Women's agrarian work acquired more importance as a strategy of persistence, and Indians became gradually invisible to outsiders by retreating to areas where white settlers had little interest in establishing farms. Indian women harvested food from smaller fields and increasingly from adjacent wetlands while men continued to bring in pelts. The fur trade endured in the Wabash region until the late nineteenth century and provided an ongoing, although diminished, source of income. Persistence required a variety of tactics. The agrarian village world of women had a long history; it existed before contact and remained viable over two centuries of contact with Europeans. But the fragmentation of these communities, the aftereffect of plundering by Kentuckians and expansionary annexation by the United States, erased much of this world. Many villages moved west, but those that persisted relied on women's agrarian strategies and quietly removed themselves from public view. The revitalization of Indian life in the twenty-first-century Ohio River valley is the result of persistence in the face of destruction. Both the Miami and the Pokagon Potawatomi, who lived and persevered along the Wabash, have focused on cultural restoration, often made possible by casino monies.

The emphasis on conflict, from the fur trade wars in the sixteenth century to the Pan-Indian Confederacy of the early nineteenth century, has led many historians to consider warfare and decline as interrelated. Early national leaders, like Washington and Knox, believed that Indian populations were already in steep decline and considered Indigenous demise as irreversible. In their view, warfare and the failure to adapt to a changing world had drastically reduced Indian population levels.

Mythmaking associated with the acquisition and settlement of Indian lands problematizes our understanding of the Ohio River valley: the association of plow agriculture with civilized behavior, the beliefs that Americans brought agriculture to a wilderness landscape and that settlement was a peaceable process. Closer examination of the Ohio River valley provides a better understanding of the agrarian orientation of Indian villages, their high levels of productivity, and the ways in which violence became embedded in the acquisition of Indian lands during the Early Republic. This reexamination also reveals the rampaging that devastated these Indian villages and killed many innocent Indian women and children. It would fault a colonial settler process built, not on peaceful expansion, but rather on brutality and rapine. The conquest of Indian lands did not begin in the trans-Mississippi west but on the eastern seaboard, from where it continued into the heart of the Midwest, in the Old Northwest Territory. Scholars and raconteurs have downplayed the aggression associated with settler colonialism because of an intransigent belief that Indian victims were murderous, backward, and doomed. Anglo-Americans have come to believe their own rhetoric rather than understand that Ohio Valley Indians deployed violence in defense of their villages, their families, their homelands, and their way of life. Americans justified their brutality because of their greed for Indian land and fostered a western frontier where carnage was endemic to settlement.

American arrival changed the dynamics of Indian persistence. The newcomers cleared forestlands and drained the southern tier of wetlands along the Ohio but avoided the marshlands of the northern Wabash River valley, which stretched into present-day southwest Michigan. These undesirable farmlands lacked navigable waterways and deterred incoming Americans. Indian villages migrated north and settled adjacent to the wetlands and swamplands. Native people were skilled in securing subsistence from a variety of resources. Men continued to trap, and women processed those furs; they harvested plants from the wetlands and grew corn along the river bottoms. The marshes and swamplands of the Great Lakes basin became a haven for Native villages intent on persistence. The lost world of the Ohio River valley was not entirely lost, after all.

INDEX

Page numbers in italics refer to illustrations.

Abbey, Samuel, 241
Abenaki Indians, 19, 47, 288
Accau-Hennepin exploration, *80. See also* Hennepin, Louis
Adams, John Quincy, 192
Adoption, kinship and, 83–84, 109, 181, 190, 203, 281, 289
Agriculture, Ohio Valley: women's role in, 4–6, 13, 27–29, 319; women's three-crop system of, 6, 27, 33, 47; corn as staple crop in, 27, 29; maize cultivation history and, 27, 28, 29, 31, 33, 59, 59n; high Indian crop yields in, 28–29, 31, 33, 35, 37, 42, 65; tillage and, 28, 31–32n, 39, 61, 139, 141, 308, 315, 319; seed selection and, 29; levee ridge system and, 30; village staples and, 35–37, 35n; low crop yields and, 52, 97, 317; Indian women's invisible labor in, 65, 65n, 319; starvation and, 264; styles of, 307, 316; American arrival and persistence in, 320. *See also individual plants*
Ainse, Sally (Sally Hands), 152; Thames River land of, 151n, 310; at Glaize conference, 310; Andrew Montour and, 310n
Alabama, 6, 95, 138, 309
Alanantowamiowee. *See* Buffalo Trace (Alanantowamiowee)
Albany, N.Y., 91; beaver market in, 10, 70, 84, 90, 95–96, 103–104, *203;* English goods and, 85; Wabash peltry and, 144; silver values at, 203
Alcohol, 2, 39; applejack, 61; brandy, 86, 101, 102n, 112–114, 123–125, 124n; wine, 101; controls on, 123–124; calumet ceremony and, 124, 162–163; rum, 124, 125, 151; wintering season and, 162; at Ouiatenon, 170
Alcoholism, 61, 162, 163, 232, 240, 241, 312

Algonquian language, 8–9, 39, 70, 73–74, 128, 132n, 304, 305
Algonquians: Illinois Confederacy, 10, 16, 126; Cree Indians, 39; Fox Indians, 57, 76, *225,* 303; Menominee Indians, 73, 76, *225;* Sauk (Sac) Indians, 76
Allegheny River, 16–17, 21, *21,* 63, 91, 126
Allen, Benjamin, 190
Alligator gar, 24, *25*
Allouez, Claude, 75, 76, *80,* 81
American Indian Holocaust and Survival (Thornton), 126n
Amphibians, 24–25
Animals: extinction and, 164; ecology and overhunting of, 215–216; spiritual essence of, 216. *See also* Amphibians; Birds; Fish; Mollusks; Reptiles
Anne (queen of England), 108, *196*
Annuities (funds), 314, 315
"Annuity chiefs," 315–316
Apekonit (Wild Carrot). *See* Wells, William (Wild Carrot)
Appalachian Mountains: and landscape of transAppalachian west, 4, 6, 19n; chaos to the west of, 4, 219, 286n; landscape of, 6, *21, 23,* 46; foothills landscape and, 17, 19; as riverine, *23,* 46; food supply in, 35, 46; seasonal changes in, 46; Indians' moving to, 96; British to the west of, 134, 212
Apples, 139, 157, 313; in Grand Island area, 13–14, 14n, 55; sweet *pommes d'api,* 13; pits, trading of, 14–15; Ohio River cultivation of, 14, 14n, 15, 15n, 63n; Johnny Appleseed myth and, 61, 61n, 62–63, 63n
Aquipaquetin (chief), 83
Arapaho Indians, 187

321

Archaeology: women's food production seen in, 7, 27, 28, 65–66; village life changes seen in, 7, 51–52, 118, 203; early cultivation seen in, 27–28, 39; Ohio River valley plants in, 39; pre-contact villages and sedentism seen in, 51–52, 58, 65; distinctive villages seen in, 118, 140, 142; of trade entrepôts and Kethtippecanuck, 140–143; Wabash glass bead evidence in, 142, 171; of cloth trade, 165; impact of Wabash fur trade seen in, 165; silver found in, 194; museum silver and, 197

Arkansas, *25*

Arkansas River, 10, *80*, 113, 302

Arkansas River valley, 302

Armstrong, John, 233, 236n

Army of the Empire, 12, 312–313

Arthur, Gabriel, 92n

Asheton, Joseph, 257, 267

Askin, John, 151, 152, 310

Assiniboine Indians, 73

Atihipe-Catouy (village), 119

Audubon, John James, 24n, 26, 51

Auglaize River, 5, 20, *21*, *93*, 94, *135*, 313

Aupaumut, Hendrick: Brandt and, 285, 301–309; Putnam and, 289; as Mahican sachem, 289, 304–308; as speaker at Glaize meeting, 289, 304, 306, 307n, 308; reputation of, 304; translation skills of, 304; as diplomat, 304–306, 307, 308; Ohio River valley influence and, 305, 307; multi-tribe kinship of, 305–308; on Kentuckian "Big Knifes," 305–307; agrarian orientation of, 307–308; Pickering letters of, 308; on Molly Brandt, 309–310; Greenville treaty support of, 314; as annuity chief, 315

Bankruptcy, 85n, 87, 88n, 164, 242, 301

Barr, Juliana, 82n

Bateaux (boat), 97, 246

Battle of Blue Licks, 216, 282

Battle Creek (Ind.), 251

Battle of Fallen Timbers (1794): Wayne's victory at, 62, 64, 311n, 312n, 313, 314; Indian defeat at, 285, 311n, 313, 318; militia at, 313; troops' eating crops at, 313–314; Scott at, 313–314

Battle of Kickapoo, 252–253

Battle of the Thames, 318

Battle of Tippecanoe, 285; Harrison and, 19, 19n, 318; Indian resistance and, 317–318

Battle of the Wabash (St. Clair's defeat), 10, 11, 271–277, *278*, 279–283, 286

Battles. *See* Violence; *individual battles*

Batts, Thomas, 92n

Beads: clothing and, 6, 171, 178, *184*; glass, 76, 166, 171, 173, 202; archaeology of, 142, 171; colors of, 171, 173; cutwork and, 181, *184, 185*

Beal Horticultural Gardens, 39

Beaubien, Charles, 153–155, 161

Beaver: Albany market in, 10, 70, 84, 90, 95–96, 103–104, 120, *203;* Great Black Swamp as source of, 20, 94; Green Bay access to, 68, 69; winter prime coat, 69, 85, 87, 91, 104, 187; in New France trade, 72, 79, 88, 91–99, 120, 165; in peltry trade, 85, 88n, 92, 104, 187; summer coat, 87; Company of the Farm and, 87, 88, 88n, 103, 106, 169; high volumes of, 87, 95, 103; prices of, 87, 90, 92, 94, 103, 105; London market and, 90, 120; at Lake of the Woods, 91; in Philadelphia market, 95; Biloxi trade in, 96; women's pelt work and, 98; processing pelts of, 98–99; Montreal market in, 103; Odawa and, 104; illegal trade in, 120; Canada and, 120; Cuillerier and, 152; extinction of, 164; silver exchange for, *203*

Beaver Wars (fur trade wars), 69, 70n

Bégon de la Picardière, Michel, 167, 168, 168n

Bellerive, Louis Groston de Saint-Ange et de, 131, 131n, 133

Bienville, Jean-Baptiste Le Moyne de: as Louisiana governor, 113, 131; Chickasaw attack orders of, 117, 123n

Biggs, William, 143, 208–209

Bird, Henry, 275n

Birds: waterfowl, 19, 20, 47, 92, 143, 252, 263; fowl, 20n, 51, 68, 143; Audubon and, 24n, 26, 51; in Ohio River valley area, 31, 51; eagles, 51, 209, 227; passenger pigeons, 94

Birzer, Bradley J., 153

Bison (buffalo): and grasslands supporting, 19, 20, 48–49, 137, 138, 143, 215–216; Buffalo Trace, 24n, 48, 138, 282; salt licks and, 24, 48n, 141, 215–216; in Illinois, 48–51; wallows and, 48, 57; seasonal hunts of, 49–51; robes from, 50, 56, 137, 187, 216; women's processing of, 50; in wetlands, 57

"Blackberry Campaign," 250–257, 263

Blackhawk (Sauk), 34

Black Hoof, *191*, 210, 315, 316

322 *Index*

Blacksmith (smithy), 272
Blacksnake. *See* Wells, William (Wild Carrot)
Blanket. *See* Cloth
Bleury, sieur de. *See* Sabrevois, Jacques-Charles de, sieur de Bleury
Blue Jacket, 11, 210, 230, 275, 280, 282, 303
Blue Licks, 216, 282
Board of Trade, 157
Boats: canoes, 19, 19n, 137, 151, 246, 246n, 247n, 253–254, 257; flatboats, 23, 144, 269, 295; bateaux, 97, 246; pirogues, 97–98; keelboats, 98; barques, 137; *canots de maître,* 158n, 167
Bohaker, Heidi, 264n
Boisbriand, Pierre Dugué, sieur de, 109, 113–114
Bonnecamps, Joseph Pierre, 120
Born to Die (Cook), 126n
Boston, 198, 225, 232, 246, *278,* 287
Boudinot, Elias, 226–227
Boundaries: streams as, 22; Ohio River as, 119, 224, 228, 241, 286, 299–301, 307; Mississippi River as western, 217; in McIntosh Treaty, 228; arbitrary, 304; Muskingum River as, 304; Little Miami River as, 304; Ohio Boundary as, 314
Bouquet, Henry, 131, 131n
Bourassa family, 152
Bow-e-ting. *See* Sault Ste. Marie
Bowman, John, 214, 214n
Bowman, Joseph, 200
Braddock, Edward, 2, 158n, 248
Brandão, José António, 72
Brandt, Joseph, 245; *Common Pot* and, 121, 309; as Mohawk chief Thayeadanega, 190, *192;* Saga Yeath Qua Pieth Tow and, *196;* Aupaumut and, 285; asked to speak at Glaize, 303; as Iroquois diplomat, 303–344; kin family of, 304n, 308–309, 310; sister of, 309–310
Brandt, Molly, 309–310
Bressani, François-Joseph, 43
Britain: in Canada, 130n; Indian land and, 133; Indian policy of, 157; and Whitehall's replacement of Versailles, 159; and defiance of Treaty of Paris, 160; and fur trade profits, 160
Brown, Colonel, 254
Brown, Patrick, 222–223, 247, 247n
Brownstown, 218
Brulé, Etienne, 74, 75n
Buckongahelas, 275, 280, 282
Buffalo. *See* Bison (buffalo)

Buffalo Bird Woman (Maxidiac), 59n
Buffalo Creek Reservation, 303
Buffalo Trace (Alanantowamiowee), 24n, 48, 138, 141, 215–216, 282
Buffalo wallow, 48, 57
"Building of the *Griffin*" (engraving), *79*
Butler, John, 130n
Butler, Richard, 217, 272, 276

Caddo nation, 82n
Cadillac, Antoine Laumet de la Mothe, sieur de, 12; Detroit and, 102, 105–107, 107n, 108, 128; alliance vision of, 107–108, 128; as mediator, 107; as Louisiana governor, 108
Cahokia, 117, 159, 211, 221
Calumet (peace pipe), 218, 257, 298; of La Salle, 81, 82; symbology of, 81, 82, 82n, 83; of Hennepin, 81, 82, 82n, 83; Marquette and, 82; decoration on, 82, 82n; of Harmar, 221; as gift, 221
Calumet ceremony: Indian women in, 70, 82n, 83; symbology of, 81, 83; brings peace, 83; fall feast and, 124–125, 162; alcohol and, 124, 125, 162–163; Piankeshaw and, 125; Vincennes conference and, 297, 298
Calumet River, 259
Canada, *116;* cornfields in, 5, 313; Jesuits and Champlain in, 71; Hennepin in, *79;* Vaudreuil in, 102n, 168n; province divisions and, 113, 117, 303; trade links and, 113, 137, 168n; British posts in, 130, 134, 270; Croghan on French in, 139–140; British in, 156, 275; governors of, 156, 170, 275, 303; Seneca in, 224, 243, 264, 284; Simcoe and, 275, 303; Mohawk nation in, 283. *See also* New France; *individual cities*
Canadian Northwest, 159, 164
Cannehous, Jean, 144
Canoe: of buckeye wood, 19, 19n; of elm bark, 54; peltry flotillas and, 75, 85–88, 91; military use of, 86, 247n, 253–254, 257; goods moved by, 91, 151, 246; deepwater, 97; alcohol and, 124; *canots de maître,* 158n, 167; travel by, 246n
Canots de maître, 158n, 167
Captain Bull, 252
Captain Johnny (chief), 149, 217, 220
Carolina, 20, 96, 104, 111, 128, 167
Carte de la découverte faite l'an 1673 dans l'Amerique septentrionale (Marquette), *78*

Carte de la Nouvelle France ou se voit le cours des Grandes Rivieres de S. Laurens et de Mississipi (van Keulen), *116*

Cartier, Jacques, 33

"Ca-Ta-He-Cas-Sa—Black Hoof, Principal Chief of the Shawanoes," *191*

Catholicism: missionary priests and, 14–15n, 71, 120, 159; Dongan and, 85n; kin networks and, 153, 159; British attitude on, 159; Quebec Act and, 159; godmothers and, 159. *See also* Jesuits

Cayuga Indians, 136, 224

Céloron de Blainville, Pierre-Joseph, 120

Champlain, Samuel de, 33, 71, 74, 75n, *80*

Chapman, John (Johnny Appleseed), 61, 61n, 63; myth of, 62, 63n

Cherokee Indians, 275n; displacement of, 9; in Ohio River valley, 19, 47, 224, *225;* women and, 65n; intermarriage and, 99; trading by, 146; wintering camp of, 146; clothing of, 175; silver ornaments worn by, *207;* treaty cessions and, 211, 218; location of, *225;* St. Clair and, 275; Pan-Indian alliances and, 275; at Glaize conference, 303, 309. *See also* Chickamauga Indians

Cherokee portrait (Hodges), *207*

Chevalier family, 103n

Chicagou (chief), 123n

Chickamauga Indians, 224, 275n

Chickasaw Indians, 117, 122, 123n, 131n, 275

Chickasaw Wars, 122, 123n

Chillicothe, 214, 214n, 220

Chippewa Indians, 174, 181, 227; clothing of, *184, 185*

Chippewa River, *111*

Chouteau family, 103n

Christie, John, 129

Cincinnati (Losantiville), 50, 227, 231, 272; Ohio River at, 46n; as Fort Washington, 148; Indian prisoners and, 270; fort at, 291; racism in, 291–292. *See also* Fort Washington

Clairmont, Piere, 140, 144

Clans: Shawnee, 58n; Miami, 69, 95n, 153, 154; intermarriage and, 83, 84, 100; membership in, 174, 202

Clark, George Rogers: Fort Vincennes and, 2, 211–213, 215, 219; Kaskaskia and, 2, 212; in Ohio Country, 217, 220; Pacanne and, 221, 302; raids by, 247n; family of, 254

Clark, William, 141, 254, 313

Cloth: women's involvement in, 6, 128, 152, 163, *195;* silk as, 6, 128, 169, 175, 177–178, 181, *183–184,* 184, *185,* 202; as trade goods, 7, 43, 96, 99, 101–102, 173, 175, *189,* 214; dyes for, 27, 43–44, 44n, *45,* 190; blue, 56, 167, 169, 173, 176, 179, 190; red, 56, 103, 167, 169, 173, 176, 179, 190; British trade in, 85, 90, 95, 104, 169n; English, as superior, 85, 90, 167, 168n; strouds as, 103, 168n, 169n, 171, 176, 181, 200, 211, 214, 297; evolution of, 104, 165–171, 173–181, 184, 186–188, 192–198, 200–*201;* Indian demand for, 104, 128, 160, 163; Detroit demand for, 128, 175; calico as, 128, 169, 171, 175–176, 181, 190, 211; peltry traded for, 163, 175, 187; white-striped, 167; British, as cheaper, 167, 168; French, as expensive, 168; escarlatine blankets for, 168, 169; invoices for, 170–171, *172;* white, 173; Ohio River valley and, 175

Clothing and dress, 193n; styles of, 6, 138, 163, 171, 174–175, *178, 184;* bead ornaments for, 6, 171, 178, *184;* ribbonwork on, 6, 169, *179,* 181, 184, *184–185,* 188, 202; Potawatomi, 55–56; Nicolet and embroidered, 74; French and English cloth as, 85, 167, 168, 168n, 169; waterproof, 98, 100n; winter camp and, 98, 190; leggings as, 100n, 174, 176–177, *184,* 214; moccasins as, 100n, *186, 187;* cross-dressing and, 100n; silver ornaments for, 128, 152, *192,* 202, *204–208;* copper for, 166; earrings and, 166, *192, 196, 201, 207, 208;* color and, 167, 169n, 173, 175, 211; Pennsylvania and, 169; tools and, 170; made by women, 170–171, 174–175, 181, *184–187, 194, 207, 208;* archaeology of, 171; cutwork design in, 171, 174, *182, 187, 202;* as ceremonial, 174, 177; in museums, 175, 202; nonverbal language and, 175–176, 193; identity and stature in, 175–176, 178–179, 190, 192–193, 202, 315; shirts and brooches in, *177–179,* 190, *192,* 195n, *197,* 200, 204, *206–207;* as "Indian fashion," 178–179; trade silver and, *179, 195, 196, 199–201,* 202, 297; coats in, *180, 191, 205;* hoods as, 181, *185;* skirts as, *182;* trade blankets as, *182;* ring brooches on, *182, 192;* wearing blankets as, *183;* quilled robe as, 187; visual language of, 190, *192;* shells and, 193, *196, 197;* burial styles and, *195. See also* Cutwork; Embroidery; Silver

324 *Index*

Coigne, Jean Baptiste de, 221, 297, 298, 300
Colbert, Jean-Baptiste, 91, 103n
Colden, Cadwallader, 168n
Colder, Rene, 297
Collins, Josiah, 200
Color: symbolism in, 44, 171, 173, 275; wampum belts and, 217, 275. *See also* Dyes
Columbia City, Ind., 149
Columbian Tragedy, 277, 279, 284, 286, 287; broadside account of, *278*
Common Pot, The (Brooks), 121, 309
"Compact colony" policy, 91, 106
Company of the Farm, 87, 88, 88n, 103, 106, 169
Confederacy, Indian, 224, 241, 314; northwestern, 4, 10; Illinois, 10, 16, 126; Pan-Indian, 242, 265, 275, 285, 317–319; Tecumseh and, 285; Tenskwatawa and, 285; Western, 285; at Glaize, 296, 303–304, 307, 307n, 308–310; at Miamitown, 309
Congés trade permits, 79, 81, 86, 109, 114
Congress (U.S.), 12; army and, 11; Indian delegation to, 192, 193n; and Clark's mission to Ohio Country, 217; McIntosh treaty disputes and, 218, 224; and Kentucky militia's mission to Ohio River valley, 219, 247, 252; and Harmar's mission, 221, 240–241; Indian land sales and, 223, 224, 228; land grant to Ohio Company by, 224; peace conference treaties and, 229; settlers' Indian reports and, 231; and support for new army, 241, 271, 287, 312; military violence and, 266, 271, 287; nonratification of Vincennes treaty by, 301
Connecticut, 133–134
Connecticut Western Reserve, 224, 226
Conoy Indians, 224, 275
Constant, Jean Baptiste, 297
Constitution (U.S.), 4, 291
Continental army, 288n
Coocoochee (mystic), 311
Corn and cornfields: Washington and destruction of, 1, 243, 245, 255, 263; in Canada, 5, 313; Sabrevois on Indian women's work in, 5, 16, 55–59; as women's focus, 5, 6, 15–16, 28–29, 55–59; snow melts and, 5–6, 22, 46; Wayne's leveling of, 5, 313; women's cropping of, 6, 13, 27–29, 139; violence and evidence of, 11; types of, 13, 29–30, 36; Indian, 13, 30, 33–34, 34n, 59, 68, 139, 308; expanse of, 19; boundaries and, 22, 29; food supply from, 26; as Ohio River valley staple, 27, 29–31, 35, 47, 49, 318; maize and, 27, 28, 29, 31, 33, 59n; plow tillage and, 28, 31–32n, 39; types of, 29; seed types and, 29; oral knowledge base and, 29; climatic adaptation of, 29; color and, 29–30; higher yields in women's, 31, 35, 35n; consumption of, by Soto's army, 32; Cartier on, 33; Champlain and, 33; in Illinois, 33–34; size of, 33–34, 34n, 237; women's harvesting of, 34, 49–50, 52; hybridization of, 34n; as supplement, 37, 49, 52; cooking of, 41, 143; migration and, 52; of Potawatomi, 55–56; of Hurons, 59, 59n; at Green Bay, 68; starvation and, 83, 97, 209; Wabash River harvest of, 98; expansion of, 123; women's river-bottom, 133, 139; Kethtippecanuck and, 141, 147, 254; beaver trading for, 187; Hardin's destruction of, 235, 237; Harmar's destruction of, 237, 239; Wilkinson's burning of, 255, 262; Kentuckians' burning of, 258, 261, 264; replanting and, 262, 263, 314, 320; retaliation and, 282–283; burning of, at the Glaize, 313–314; Indian women's ignoring of demand for, 317; American arrival and persistence in, 320. *See also* Women, Indian
Cornplanter, 245, 303
Coureurs de bois, 84, 86, 104, 106, 134; as illegal traders, 79, 90, 96, 100, 105; kinship marriage and, 96, 100, 103, 109–110, 144; Odawa trading and, 105
Coustan, Jean, 144
Cramoisy, Sébastien, 71
Cree Indians, 39
Creek Indians, 47, 275; in Alabama, 90, 309n; Shawnee and, 95, 309, 309n; French and, 117; Wea and, 118; at Glaize conference, 303
Croghan, George, 51, 132–136, 211; Irish background of, 132n; journals of, 132n, 134n, 137, 140; trip from Ouiatenon to Vincennes, 138, 138n; criticism of French by, 139–140, 157
Cronon, William, 68n
Crops: women's corn, beans, and squash, 6, 27, 33, 47; of Miami Indians, 13, 20, 29, 30; wheat, 15; on Mississippi River, 19, 29–30, 34, 34n, 35–36; harvests of, 26; as staple, 27, 29, 33, 35, 36; women's higher yield of, 28–29, 31, 33, 35, 37, 42, 65; of Lake Ontario, 33, 35; of Huron Indians, 35, 36, 56, 59; winter storage of, 42; low yields of, 52, 97, 317; at Ouiatenon,

Index 325

59, 255; absent women and, 284; of Maumee River, 313. *See also* Corn and cornfields; Fruit; Plants; Vegetables and vegetable gardens
Cruikshank, Robert, 201–202
Cuillerier, Marie-Angelique, 152
Cultural mediators, 100, 100n, 107, 267, 288, 290, 290n, 306; Ainse as, 152, 310, 310n
Cumberland Gap, 126
Cumberland River, 17, 20, *21,* 91, *111,* 246
Cutwork: on specialized clothing, 171, 174, *183, 187;* on Miami clothing, 181, *182,* 184, *186,* 202; of Chippewa, *184, 185*
Cuyahoga (village), 93
Cuyahoga River, 93

Darke, William, 277n, 280
Darnaud (d'Arnaud), Nicolas-Marie Renaud Davenne, sieur de Desmeloises, 124n, 125
D'Artaguiette, Pierre, 117, 123n
Dauphin de La Forêst, François, 16n
Deaf Man (Miami), 166
"De Gannes Memoir," 35n, 68n
De La Balme, Augustin Mottin, 136n, 211, 211n
Delaware (language), 132n
Delaware Indians (Lenni-Lenape): women's planting of fruit crops for, 15; location of, 19, 47, 209, *225;* peace and, 131n, 227; language of, 132; clothing of, 176; migration west by, 209; Stanwix treaty and, 217; as refugees at Miamitown, 224; at White River, 234, 314; and Harmar's destruction of Maumee towns, *238;* as cultural mediators, 290n, 310n; Aupaumut kinship with, 305; as Wenaumeau, 305; annuities for, 314; land controlled by, 314; farming taught to, 315
Deliette, Pierre-Charles, sieur, 41–42, 42n, 43, 49–50; "Memoir concerning Illinois Country," 35n, 67, 68n
DeMaille, Ray, 82n
Dennis, Philip, 315
Denny, Ebenezer: and description of Harmar's attacks, 237, *238; Military Journal* of, *238;* and description of St. Clair's army, 269–271, 271n, 276, 277, 277n, 279–281; military service of, 271n, 281; on Kentucky militia, 279
Denonville, Jacques-René de Brisay, 85–87, 105, 107
DePeyster, Arent S., 151n, 211–212
De Tonti (Tonty), Henri, 16n, 35n, 67, 86, 91

Detroit, *115, 135,* 136; Sabrevois at, 5, 13n, 14n, 52–55; as trading center, 10, 23, 97–98, 103–108, 128, 144, 150–151; Straits of, 55–56, 105, 107n, 108, 128; villages near, 55–57, 128; wintering at, 101; intermarriage at, 102; French-controlled trade at, 104, 127; founding of, 105–107, 107n, 108, 128, 146; Indian village relocation to, 106–107; violence and, 106–107, 107n, 128; trade ban and, 109; smallpox at, 126; silversmiths at, 128, 198; demography at, 128; supply and demand at, 128; ransoms at, 129, 130; traders at, 144, 146–147, 151–152, 198; population of, 146, 151; merchants at, 148n, 152, 310; kin network at, 153; Lernoult at, 153–155, 155n, 156–157; Gladwin at, 157, 158n; Gage's regulation of trade at, 159; weapon expenditures at, 171; European goods at, *172;* DePeyster at, 211; Clark and, 213; Wyandot near, 218; Shawnee at, 234; British-controlled, 241, 275n, 311; swampland and, 242; trading villages' dependence on, 254; high fur volume of, 283n. *See also* Fort Detroit
Detroit River: islands in, 13–14, 54, 55n, 128; straits and, 55–56, 105, 107n, 108, 128; fort built at, 55, 105, 107n
Diamond, David H., 63n
Disease: measles, 119, 125, 127; Fort Miami outbreak and, 124–125; French immunity to, 125, 127; epidemics and, 126–127, 126n, 127n; smallpox, 126, 126n, 127, 301; malnutrition as, 127; mortality rates and, 127, 127n; villages' recovery from, 209; ague, 301
District of Kentucky (Va.), 2, 2n, 248, 258. *See also* Kentucky
Doctrine of discovery, 4, 218n
Dongan, Thomas, 84, 85, 85n
Doolittle, William, 28
Dorcester, Lord, 275
Dubuisson, Jacques-Charles Renaud, 101, 114; Fort Miami and, 95n, *111,* 124, 129, 136, 136n, 279; as Detroit commander, 108
Duff, Mr., 230
Duluth (Dulhut), Daniel Greysolon, sieur, *80,* 107n
Dumay, Jacque, 144
Durantaye, Olivier Morel de La, 86–87, 107
DuVal, Kathleen, 82n
Duverger, Jacques-François Forget, 54

Dyes, 27, 190; black, 43; yellows, 43; orange, 43, 45; reds, 43–44, 44n, 169, 169n; blues, 56, 169, 169n, 173; vermilion and, 56, 101–102, 169, 211

Edmunds, R. David, 309n, 318
Eel River, *115,* 234, 259, 260
Eel River Miami, 234, 290, 293, 294
Elk Creek, 254
Embarras River, *115,* 135
Embroidery: of Indian women, 6, 43, 171, 173–174, 179; madder red and, 43; on Nicolet's clothing, 74; seeds in, 171; on shirts, 177; on blouses, *178, 179;* on moccasins, 179, *186, 187;* on coats, 180; on leggings, *184;* on hoods, *185;* on shawls, *194,* 208
Erie Indians, 14n
Etherington, George, 129
Ewing, George, 164

Fallam, Robert, 92n
Falls of Powhatan, 36
Falls of the Ohio, *21, 22–24, 23,* 24n, *115, 135;* militia at, 1, 257, 294–295; Audubon at, 26; bison at, 48; Harmar at, 220. *See also* Ohio River
Ferguson, Captain, 222
Filson, John, 134, 221n
Firearms, 163; pistols, 74; exchanges and, 163; expenditures for, 170, 171, *172,* 173; rifles, 200, 214, 252, 274, 276, 311; cannons, 223, 294, 295; shots from, 236, 252, 254; Kentucky volunteers and, 249, 250, 272
Fire Lands, 224, 226
First American Regiment, 219, 271
Fish: alligator gar, 24, *25;* blue sucker, 24; hatcheries, 24; herring, 24; in Ohio River valley, 24–27, 67; paddlefish, 24, 25; sturgeon, 24, 25, 54, 55n, 67–68, 68n; catfish, 25, 26; eels, 25–26; brill, 67; muskellunge, 94
Five Medals (chief), 315
Five Nations, 71, 87, 114. *See also* Cayuga Indians; Iroquois Indians; Mohawk Indians; Oneida Indians; Seneca Indians
Forestland, 8, 17, 26, 33, 59; food plants in, 6, 39, 43, 46, 47, 263; hunting in, 6, 19, 121, 263, 311n, 317; forested plains and, 19, 19n; clearing of, 19, 63, 320; dye sources in, 44; village sites and, 52, 139; Indian trails in, 53; Black Swamp as, 92, 94; burning of, 215, 263; Indian names reflecting world of, 267; subsistence patterns in, 317
Forks of the Wabash, 315
Forsythe fur-trading company, 198
Fort Albany, 105
Fort Chambly, 14n
Fort Crèvecoeur, 16n, 69, *111*
Fort Dearborn, 290n
Fort de Chartres, 52, 109, *110, 111,* 123n, 246; Bellerive at, 131, 131n, 133
Fort Defiance, 313
Fort Detroit, 53, 136, 242; villages bordering, 55–56, 128; Indian prisoners at, 129; British control of, 130, 130n; Pan-Indian alliance at, 275n. *See also* Fort Pontchartrain
Fort Duquesne, 2, 248, *111;* renamed Fort Pitt, 131n
Fort Frontenac, 77, 105, 107n, *111*
Fort Hamilton, 273
Fort Harmar, 227–228, 228n, 286; treaty of, 304, 314
Fort Kaministiquia, *111,* 159
Fort Knox (Vincennes), 220–221
Fort La Tourette, *111*
Fort Le Boeuf, *111,* 129
Fort McIntosh, treaty at. *See* Treaty of Fort McIntosh (1785)
Fort Miami (Fort Saint Philippe des Miami), *111;* Great Black Swamp and, 93; Dubuisson and, 95n, 124, 129, 136–139, 279; alcohol and, 124; Pontiac's Rebellion at, 129, 136; name changes of, 136n; Little Turtle and, 137, 137n; Columbian Tragedy and, 277, *278,* 279, 279n
Fort Michilimackinac, 87, *110, 111,* 129. *See also* Michilimackinac (post)
Fort Niagara, 52, 53, *111,* 130, 152
Fort Nipigon, *111*
Fort Orange, 84
Fort Orleans, 131n
Fort Ouiatenon, *111;* Indians' building of first fort at, 57–58, 112; garrison at, 109, 130n; archaeology of villages near, 118–119; Indians' control of, 129–130, 132, 137, 140; Butler's rangers at, 130n; Pontiac and Croghan at, 132; British abandonment of, 132, 137; prosperous agrarian villages near, 133; trade domination by, 134
Fort Pimiteoui, 16n, 109

Index 327

Fort Pitt, 17; smallpox blankets from, 126n; siege at, 129, 131; Bouquet's command of, 131n; renaming of, from Fort Duquesne, 131n; Croghan at, 132; Stirling at, 133; treaty line near, 211, 212

Fort Pontchartrain, 93, 107, 109, *110, 111,* 151

Fort Presque Isle, *111,* 129

Fort Recovery, 313

Forts: French, in Illinois Country, 16n, 35n, 52–53, 105, 109, 131, 246; Ohio River valley, 109, *111,* 118; early French, 110, *110, 111;* near Wabash River, *110–111;* Kickapoo and, 114, 118; British, 129–130

Fort St. Joseph, 109, *110, 111,* 129, 131n, 159

Fort St. Louis, 95, 105, *111*

Fort St. Louis II (Fort Pimiteoui), 16n

Fort Saint-Louis Le Rocher, 16n, 35n

Fort Sandoské, *93, 111*

Fort Sandusky, *93,* 128, 129, 209

Fort Stanwix, 217, 217n, 228; and treaty line, 211, 212

Fort Steuben: Indian prisoners and, 1, 257, 267, 267n, *268–269,* 270, 294–295, 282; Pacanne and Harmar at, 220; militia at, 257; Doyle's command of, 294, 295

Fort Venango, 129

Fort Vincennes, *111,* 114, 117, 131n, 138; Clark and, 2, 211–213, 215, 219

Fort Washington, 249; captive Indians at, 2, 11, 257, 267–272, 283–287, 290n, 295; Cincinnati and, 46n, 50, 148, 227, 231, 270, 272, 291–292; Harmar sieges and, 221, 232, 234–241; Wilkinson and, 259–261, 288n; prisoner name list at, 267, 267n, *268–269;* Wells at, 267, 291–292; Kaweahatta prisoners at, 267, 267n; conditions at, 269–270, 271; prisoners left at, 269; St. Clair's recruitments at, 271–272, 274–275; Columbian Tragedy and, 277, *278,* 279, 279n; peace councils at, 288, 289, 291–293; Trueman and Hardin peace message at, 288; Heckewelder's description of, 291; cost of imprisonment at, 292; Wawiachteno nation at, 292–293; Indian prisoners of, taken to Vincennes, 293–294; Wayne's relocation at, 313

Fort Wayne, 92; Harmar's Defeat at, 2–4, 136n, 239, *240,* 240–241, 242; annuities paid at, 314

Fox Indians, 57, 76, 107, *225,* 303

Fox River, 69, *111*

Fox Wars, 107

France, king of, 71, 76. *See also* New France; *individual rulers*

Frankfort, Ky., 249, 270

Fraser, Alexander, 132

French and Indian War. *See* Seven Years' War (French and Indian War)

Frontenac et de Palluau, Louis de Buade, comte de, 68, 86–88, 88n, 105, 107n

Fruit, 6, 47, 52, 68, 237, 318; apples, 13–15, 36, 61–64, 63n, 139, 157, 313; peaches, 14–15, 63–64, 139, 157, 313; pits of, for trading, 14, 15, 187; persimmons, 15, 46; grapes, 15, 46; wild plum, 15, 139, 313; melons, 36, 63, 157; berries, 46, 63, 157; pawpaws, 46; pears, 63, 157; mulberries, 139

Fur trade: Atlantic-based, 6; women's influence on, 6; peltry types in, 6, 20, 92; in New Orleans, 10; canoes used in, 19, 19n, 75, 151, 246, 246n, 247n, 253–254, 257; flatboats used in, 23, 144, 269, 295; bison robes in, 50, 56, 137, 187, 216; at Montreal, 69, 75, 87, 104; Ohio River valley shift of, 70, 319; Albany expansion of, 70, 90, 103, 104, 110; Dutch and, 70, 84, 85, 90–91, 92n; English in Great Lakes for, 84–85, 104, 115; beaver in, 85, 92, 104; Frontenac and expansion of, 86–87; prices in, 87, 90, 92, 94, 103, 105; western, closure of by king's ban, 88, 90, 109, 110; Indians and British markets in, 88, 90; Indian population distribution change and, 90; Indian trade of, in ban years, 92, *110;* storage presses for, 97; bateaux used in, 97, 246; pirogues used in, 97–98; Wabash centers and, 97, 319; keelboats used in, 98; tools to process, 99; British goods in, 103, 104, 158n; Indians as, 104; Odawa as middlemen of, 104, 105; Detroit's reopening for, 104; backcountry posts and, 111; Indian women's peltry in, 119; liquor in, 123; trading communities and, 128, 140–146; women's transformation of, 138–139; archaeology of horse trails and, 139, 139n; stereotypes and, 155, 162, 170, 209; *canots de maître* used in, 158n, 167; intermarriage and, 158; Gage's regulation of, 159; British monopolization of, 159, 160; and change in Indian demand, 160; silver incorporated into, 160; alcoholism blamed on, 162; dishonest merchants and, 164; social function of, 166, 166n, 221; profit from, 170; invoice details on, 170–171; cloth bought by,

328 *Index*

170; Great Lakes and Ohio Valley in, 209; volume of, in Great Lakes, 283n
Fur trade wars, 9, 70n, 319; Beaver Wars and, 69

Gage, Thomas, 130n, 152, 154, 154n, 156–157, 158n, 159
Gage's Light Infantry (80th Foot), 130n, 136
Gamelin, Antoine, 229–230
Gamelin, Pierre, 229
Gender roles: Indian women and, 5, 27, 28, 31, 44, 65, 82n, 283; Potawatomi and, 56; Odawa, 57; terms used for, 64; in diplomacy, 82, 296; warriors' resistance to change in, 309; Tenskwatawa on, 315, 316; Black Hoof on, 315; American, 316; annuity chiefs and, 316; men's entrapment in, 320; fur processing and, 320
George II (king of England), *206*
George III (king of England), 129, *206*
Georgian Bay, 14, 35
Gift giving: to women interpreters, 99; firming of alliances by, 112; symbolic and ceremonial, 112, 113, 193, 218, 296; treaties sealed by, 164, 211, 219, 221; social function of, 166, 166n, 221; intertribal trade and, 187; women and, 187; women's clothing and, 195n; silver and clothing for, 198, 297; cost of items for, 210; at peace conference, 296–297
Gist, Christopher, 246n
Gladwin, Henry, 157, 158n
Glaize: Maumee River near, 9, 48, 134, 198, 313–314; village locations at, 9, *225*, 309, 314; bison and game at, 48, 57; fur trade at, 134; silver trade and, 198; Miamitown and, 241, 274, 283; Trueman and Hardin at, 288; Coocoochee at, 311; Wayne's burning and pillaging of, 313, 314
Glaize conference (1792), 296, 312; Aupaumut at, 289, 304–306, 307n, 308; Indian confederacy at, 296, 303–304, 307, 307n, 308–310; Indians attending, 303, 309–310; time of, 303; Miami control at, 303; Shawnee control at, 303; Cherokee at, 303, 309; McKee's report on, 303; Brandt as speaker at, 303; women's silence at, 304, 310, 311; Vincennes land issue and, 304, 307; Miamitown conference and, 305, 309; Red Jacket as speaker at, 307, 311; agrarian issues at, 308; warriors at, 309; commissioners' barring from, 311; location of, 313–314

Glass, as trade goods: beads, 76, 166, 171, 173, 181, *184, 185,* 202; bottle, 142, *197;* looking glasses, 211, 297
Godfroy, Francis (chief), 145–146, *145*
Godfroy, Gabriel (trader), 145, 255
Gold medals, 194, *206.* See also Medals
Goldsmiths, 194
Gordon, Francis, 129
Goulet, Louis, 101
Grand Island, 13–14, 55
Grand Medicine Society. See Midewiwin (Grand Medicine Society)
Grand Portage, Mn., *111*
Grasslands: 17, 47, 121, 139, 213; bluegrass and, 19, 24, 34, 215, 250–251; bison herds and hunting on, 19, 20, 48–49, 137, 138, 143, 215–216; on plains, 24, 49
Great Black Swamp, 93; as fur source, 6, 20; size of, 20, 92; river borders of, 20, 22, 57, 92, 94–95; wintering camps at, 20, 26, 146; Miamitown near, 57; creation of, 92; name origin of, 92; fish in, 94; wildlife in, 94; Ohio River valley's division by, 115
Great Lakes: waterway navigation of, 121; winds and storms in, 122; silver as most desired trade commodity in, 128, 160, 184, 188, 193–194, 197–198, 201–202; American arrival and persistence in, 320. *See also individual lakes and rivers*
Great Miami River, 93, 226
Great Peace of Montreal, 9, 90
Green Bay: Perrot at, 33, 76, 76n; Indian women at, 66; multiethnic population changes at, 66, 68, 68n, 69, 74–75, 77, 96, 100; trading center at, 66, 68–69, 73, 77, 91; fishing at, 68; Indian cornfields at, 68, 68n, 73, 75; lush environment near, 68; as *la Baye des Puans,* 69, 74; Indian villages encircling, 69; beaver and, 69; trade closed at, 70, 87–88; Iroquois and, 71, 73; Indian migration to, 73; precontact culture at, 73–75; Nicolet at, 73–75; Allouez at, 76; La Salle and, 77, 81–82; *Griffin* voyage to, 77, *79;* kin networks at, 83–84, 96, 127, 159; Sioux feared at, 87; disease and, 127; Gage's regulation of trade at, 159; European trade goods in, 172–173; warriors from, 283
Green River, 20, 21
Greverat, Garret (silversmith), 198
Griffin, Patrick, 265n

Index 329

Griffin (Le Griffon) (ship), 77, 79
Groseilliers, Médard Chouart Des, 75, 84, 91
Guns, Germs, and Steel (Diamond), 126n

Haldimand, Frederick, 210, 211
Hamilton, Alexander, 312
Hamilton, Henry, 212–213; Pacanne portrait by, 160, *161*, 200
Hamtramck, John Francis, 227, 235, 263–264; and construction of Fort Knox, 221, 222; Harmar and, 221, 223, 230–231; Pacanne and, 222–223, 302; Kentucky raiders and, 222, 230; men's defiance of, 222, 247, 247n, 265; American peace and, 223; St. Clair and, 229, 267, 274; village attacks led by, 233–234; Philadelphia delegation led by, 301
Hands, Sally. *See* Ainse, Sally (Sally Hands)
Hardin, John, 236n; Harmar's dispatch of, 234; Miamitown and, 234–235; attacks on, by Little Turtle, 236, 239; Pickaway's burning by, 237; Wea raids and, 247n, 253, 255; reputation of, 249; attack on Kickapoo by, 252–253; torture by, 254–256; prisoners of, 256, 270, 288; peace talks and, 288; death of, 288
Harmar, Josiah: defeat of, 2–4, 232–239, 240, 240–243, 269, 309; Kekionga and, 136, 136n; forts built by, 219, 220; First American Regiment and, 219, 271n; at Vincennes, 219, 220, 221; gift giving by, 219, 221; at Miamitown, 220; Pacanne and, 220–222; Hamtramck and, 221, 223, 230, 231; calumet given to, 221; at Illinois Country, 221; at Kaskaskia, 221; at Fort Washington, 221, 232, 234, 236; disregard of Hamtramck by, 231; Miamitown attacks by, 231, 233; reorganization of militia and troops by, 231, 232–233, 233n, 234n, 239; alcoholism and, 232, 240, 241; as officer, 232, 233, 235, 239, 241; and attacks by Little Turtle, 236, 239, 240; vengeance on Miamitown by, 237, *238*, 239; looting and, 237; Maumee towns destroyed by, *238*; casualties and, 239; map of battle area of, *240*; exoneration of, 241; Denny's service with, 271n
Harmar's Defeat, 2–4, 232–239, *240*, 240–243, 269, 309
Harrison, William Henry, 19, 19n, 318
Hay, Henry, 147–148, 148n, 149; journal of, 150, 155
Hay, Jehu, 147, 148n

Headmen, 58n, 99, 154, 160, 188, 267, 315–317. *See also individual headmen*
Heckewelder, John: salt licks described by, 48; as Moravian missionary, 169, 289, 291; on Indian dress and body ornamentation, 169, 176, 179, 181, 289; as Putnam's peace delegate, 289, 290; invitation of, to peace commission, 290; at Fort Washington, 291; criticism of Cincinnati "idlers" by, 291; on Indian body desecration, 292; on cost of Indian imprisonment, 292; on Wawiachteno nation, 292–293; on prisoner release, 293; on Indians at Vincennes, 295–296; as leader of delegation to Philadelphia, 301; on Ohio River valley and Indian-created town, 318
Hendrick (Mohawk), 193, 193n
Hennepin, Louis, *79, 80*, 84; calumet of, 81, 82, 82n, 83; Sioux capture of, 82–83, 87
Hidatsa Indians, 29, 187
Hill, Aaron (chief), 245
Ho Chunk Indians, *225*
Hodges, William, 207
Holmes, Robert, 129, 130n, 136
Households, Indian: matrifocal, 6, 7n, 70, 70n, 117, 122, 128, 150, 170, 317; feeding of, 22, 26–27, 34, 37, 39, 50–52, 59–60; women's control of, 65–66, 96, 100, 101n, 207; clans and, 69, 100; illegal traders' marrying into, 88, 89, 100, 102, 104, 109–110, 135; kinship and, 89, 96, 99, 101, 110; surplus food for, 97; trade activity organized by, 97–101; cultural mediators and, 100; as patrilineal, 100, 102; legal French traders' marrying into, 102, 114, 150, 158; wintering camps and, 124; property ownership in, 153; matrifocal trading and, 170; trade cloth made in, 170–171, 175, 181, 202; monogamy and, 317
House of Ewing, 164
Hudson Bay, 68n
Hudson River valley, 72–73
Hudson's Bay Company, 100, 167
Hundred Associates fur company, 74
Hunters: Indian men as, 6, 52, 97, 140; daily kills by, 20n; of bison and buffalo, 49, 216; near Detroit, 54–55; as trappers, 98–99, 140, 142, 162, 164, 320; winter ice pond traps and, 98; of fish and fresh meat, 147; steel traps and, 163; environmental extinction and, 164
Huron Confederacy, 35

Huron Indians: Wendat, 14; corn agriculture of, 14, 14n, 59, 59n; staple crop of, 35, 36, 56, 59; clothing of, 56, *206;* villages of, near Detroit, 56; populations of, 59; encouragement of English trade by, 85; beaver trade of, 85; Tsawanhonhi, *206;* treaty line cessions and, 211. *See also* Tobacco Huron

Hurt, R. Douglas, 224n

Hutchins, Thomas, 51, 63, 157; *Plan of the Rapids,* 23

Identity: and Indian names' reflection of natural world, 22, 267; cross-dressing and, 100n; clothing as symbols of, 175–179, 190, 192–193, 202, 315

Illinois Confederacy, 10, 16, 126

Illinois Country, *225;* Indians in, 16, 85, 91, 117–118, 122, 143; French forts in, 16n, 35n, 52–53, 105, 109, 131, 246; alligator gar and, 24, *25;* corn varieties in, 34; Deliette's exploration of, 35n, 41–42, 42n, 43, 49–50, 67, 68n; bison in, 48–51; French control in, 52–53, 131; Duverger in, 54; fur traders in, 85, 91, 109, 122, 170, 181, 210–211; frontier at, 105, 264; Boisbriand in, 109, 113–114; Vincennes and, 117; Croghan's opening of, 132, 132n; Biggs's capture in, 143; British in, 210–211, 246; Harmar in, 221

Illinois District, 109

Illinois Indians, 34, 41, 69, 48n, 76–77, 95, 107, 110, 123n; Deliette's description of, 49, 50, 67; women's roles as, 50; migration of, 73; La Salle and, 83; fur trade and, 86, 90, 103, 104; epidemic disease and, 126, 209; Fraser captured by, 132; peace treaty and, 300

Illinois River, 16, *21, 115,* 118; corn cultivation on, 33–34; French explorers on, *80;* French forts on, 109, *111;* traders on, 109

Imlay, George, 254; *Topographical Description of the Western Territory of North America,* 254n

Indiana. *See* Kethtippecanuck; Winter, George; *individual cities*

Indiana Chute, 23

"Indian Burial, Kee-Waw-Nay Village, 1837" (Winter), *195*

Indian Country, 1; Ohio River border of, 4, 5, 213, 224, 228, 312; fish in, 67; Great Lakes as part of, 130; Harmar's destruction of, 239; Scott's attack on, 256, 264; St. Clair in, 274; U.S. invasion of, 275, 287–288, 312; Prophet's Town unrest in, 316

Indian Department, 148n, 198, 275

Indian Removal, 99, 162

Inman, Henry, 204

Intermarriage, 317; kinship and trade in, 36, 69, 83, 203; as social linkage system, 84; Colbert's encouragement of, 91, 103n; Cherokee and, 99; Indian women in clans and, 100; of Indian women to French traders, 102; children of, 103n, 127, 158; disease and, 127; women's facilitation of, 207

Into the American Woods (Merrell), 290n

Iroquois Confederacy, 309

Iroquois Indians: Algonquian push from Ohio River valley by, 9, 14; location of, 16, 47, *225;* fruit trees of, 63; Beaver Wars and, 69, 70n; fur trade share of, 70n, 71–72; assaults by, 71n, 72, 72n, 86–88, 108; "internationalism" of, 71n, 73; migration by, 73; decline of, in western trade, 108; English warriors' supply by, 108; as British allies, 108; epidemics and, 126; as conquered nation, 217, 217n; land cessions and, 217; at peace conference, 227; in Canada, 303; League, 309. *See also* Five Nations; Mingo Indians; Six Nations

Jack-in-the-pulpit (Indian turnip), 39, *40*

Jackson, Andrew, 192

James, duke of York (James II of England), 85n

Jamet, John, 129

Jay, John, 219

Jefferson, Thomas, 65, 312; *Notes on the State of Virginia,* 64

Jenkins, Edward, 130, 130n

Jesuit Relations, 71, 72

Jesuits, 43, 81, 117, 166; in Great Lakes, 14, 72, 75; in Ohio River valley, 14, 14n, 71–72n, 113; Perrot as, 33, 76, 76n; historiography and, 71–72; *Relations* narratives of, 71, 71n, 72; Five Nations and, 71; on "custom of the country," 96; on intermarriage, 99. *See also* Marquette, Jacques; Roman Catholic Church

Johnny Appleseed. *See* Chapman, John (Johnny Appleseed)

Johnson, Sir William, 134, 154n, 193, 193n, 211; death of, 156; Molly Brandt as widow of, 309–310

Johnson v. McIntosh, 218n

Index 331

Johonnet, Jackson, 232, 235
Joliet, Louis, 77, 77n, *80*, 81, 120
Josselyn, John, 30
Journal of Major George Washington, 246n
Juchereau de Saint-Denis, Louis, 138

Kanawha River, 19, 20, 21
Kankakee River, 20, *21, 115,* 135
Kankakee Swamp, 16n, 120
Kaskaskia: Clark's seizure of, 2, 212; missionaries at, 48n; Boisbriand at, 109, 113–114; trade goods from, 117; Vincennes and, 117n; French at, 133; fictive kin networks at, 159; British loss of, 210; Harmar at, 221; Pacanne at, 222
Kaskaskia Indians, 296; Coigne and, 221, 297, 298, 300
Kaskaskia River, *21, 80, 110, 111, 212*
Kaweahatta (the Porcupine): as Little Turtle's brother, 2, 259, 265; captured household of, 260, 267, 317; as powerful peace chief, 260, 290, 293, 294; captive Wells, and, 289; Putnam's peace message to, 293–294
Kecoughtan (village), 36
Kee-Waw-Nay Village, *195*
Kekionga. *See* Miamitown
Kenapakomoko (Kenapacomaqua), 1, *135;* Kaweahatta from, 2, 259–260, 265, 267, 289–290, 293–294, 317; and women's domination, 57, 317; Wilkinson's capture of women and children from, 258–261, 265, 272; Kaweahatta at, 260, 267, 289, 317; Wells's upbringing in, 289; Gawiahaetle as civil chief of, 299; and women's production of large harvests, 317
Kentuckians. *See* Kentucky militia
Kentucky, 211; governor of, 2–3n, 248; grasslands of, 17, 19–20, 47, 138, 213; bluegrass and, 19, 24, 215, 250–251; bison in, 24n, 48, 141, 215–216; alligator gar and, 24, *25;* Cumberland River in, 91, 246; salt flats in, 141; plunder in, 212, 213; squatters in, 213; frontier of, 214, 215; fur traders in, 216; Washington's land in, 246; Scott's attack on villages in, 247–248; dislike for Indians in, 265n, 266n
Kentucky Board of War, 1, 272
Kentucky Gazette, 1, 249, 252
Kentucky invasions, 247; led by Scott, 248–249, 253–258, 263, 264, 266; Wilkinson's replacement of Scott in, 258–263, 264, 266, 275, 284
Kentucky militia: led by Scott, 1, 247–248, 313;

Wea attack by, 1, 230; terrorizing of Wabash and Ohio River valley towns by, 1, 4–5, 11, 141, 145, 214; recruits for, 3; violent reputation of, 215, 233, 266, 306–307; defeat of, at Blue Licks, 216, 282; led by Logan, 217; Hamtramck and, 222; attack on Wabash villages by, 230, 243, 247, 247n, 282; Harmar's reorganization of, 232–234, 233n, 234n; St. Clair's description of, 232n, 234n; as haters of Indians, 233, 249, 251, 263, 265, 282; insubordinate members of, 233–234, 234n; deserters from, 234; as led by Trotter, 236; Shawnee village destroyed by, 237, 239; Washington's empowerment of, 243, 265–266; as part of U.S. Army, 247; Kethtippecanuck's plunder by, 254, 255, 316; Wilkinson's attack and burning of, 255, 288n; Indians' defeat of, 276–277, *278,* 279–282; and new policy of Indian restraint, 287–288; Hardin's command of, 288; Ohio River valley villages' plunder by, 294–295, 297; as squatters, 306–307
Kentucky River, 2n, 17, 20, *21,* 23
Kethtippecanuck: archaeology of, 7, 130, 140–142; Scott's destruction of, 7; as dominant trading center, 97, 128, 134, *135,* 140, 141, 254; on Wabash River, 119, 134; as precontact village, 135, 141; traders' move to, 140, 142–145; Indians' migration to, 140; Americans' burning of, 141, 143; cornfields at, 141, 147, 254, 255; Indian women's provision of food to, 142–144; Biggs's ransom at, 143; permission to trade and, 144; peltry from, 144; Godfroy at, *145,* 145–146, 255; Kentucky militia's plunder of, 254–255, 316; Wilkinson's burning of, 255; founding of Prophet's Town at, 316–317
Kickapoo Indians: in Ohio River valley, 9, 20, *225;* location of, 20, *225;* Miami and, 69, 70; trading by, 70, 91, 143, 208–209; migration of, to Green Bay, 73, 76; resettlement of, in Wabash River valley, 88, 90, 118, 135; French fort and, 114, 118; three principal groups of, 118; Prairie bands of, 118, 263; salt and, 141; prisoners of, 143; identity in clothing of, 175, 202; goods' distribution and, 208–209; "Beggar's Dance" of, 209; Eel River Miami as, 234, 290, 293, 294; Hardin's battle with, 253; Scott's destruction of villages of, 257, 264, 284; Wilkinson's attack on, 259–260, 284; kin

of, 264; agrarian life of, 284; Putnam's reuniting of families of, 294; at treaty conferences, 296. *See also* Vermilion Indians

Kidnapping. *See* Prisoners, Indian

King William's War, 108

Kinship network: women's building of, 8, 88–89, 89n, 97, 110, 152, 159; New France's expansion and, 76, 81; French traders' intermarriage and, 83, 88–89, 89n, 99, 104, 110, 144, 156–158; at Green Bay, 83–84, 96, 127, 159; political protocol of, 89n; at Ohio River valley, 152, 153, 264; of Tacumwah, 152–156; in Detroit, 153; English marriage into, 158; Indians in, 158, 283, 283n, 305; Catholic, fictive, 159; godmothers and, 159; and prevention of starvation, 264; lack of, 302; of Aupaumut, 305–308; Brandt and, 308–309; Iroquois Confederacy on, 309

Kinzie, John, 147, 148–149, 198

Knox, Henry, 220–223, 230; as Secretary of War, 1, 137, 217n, 219, 286; assault on Ouiatenon towns and, 1; treaty negotiation and, 217n; Hamtramck's letters and, 231; Miamitown's destruction by, 237; Harmar's campaign and, *238*, 239, 240–241, 242, 243, 244, 271n; military policy of, 243, 303; Wabash village captives and, 244; Ohio River valley tactics of, 245–247; Scott's Ohio attacks and, 245, 248, 250, 252–253, 257, 258; and warning to Washington, 246; peace envoy Proctor and, 249; Scott's battle reports to, 253, 255, 256; plan of, for Ouiatenon attack, 265; humane treatment by, 265, 270, 271n; letters of, to St. Clair, 272; Indian resistance and, 275, 283, 286; Indian peace treaty and, 286–288, 289, 290, 300; Putnam and, 301; Brandt treaty and, 303–304; Pickering and, 308; standing army reorganization by, 312; belief of, in Indian demise, 319

La Barre, Joseph-Antoine, 107n

Lac Frontenac, *110, 111*

Lac Illinois, *110, 111*

Lacrosse, 56, 57, 129

La Demoiselle (chief), 221, 221n

Ladouceur, Nicolas, Sieur, 114

Lafertie (silversmith), 198

Lake Champlain, 73, *110, 111*

Lake Erie, 33, 55, 93; bison at, 53; French explorers and, 53, *80*; weather and, 54; French forts on, 71, *111*; Indians' control of access to, 114; location of, *115, 225*; Ainse land and, 151n

Lake Huron, 93, 109, *212*; corn as staple crop at, 35; French explorers on, *80*; trader expedition attacked on, 85; Detroit outpost at, 107n; French forts near, *111*

Lake Michigan, 74, 77, 112, *115, 135*, 137, 232; on Marquette's map, *78*; French explorers on, *80*, 82; Miami Indians and, 90, 232; traders at, 109; regulated posts at, 159

Lake Nipigon, *111*

Lake Nipissing, 74, 75n, *110, 111*

Lake of the Woods, 91

Lake Ontario (Frontenac), 33, 35, 72, *80, 111*, 130n

Lake Pimiteoui, 69

Lake St. Clair, 93

Lake Superior, *80, 111*

Lamoureux fils (trader), 140, 144

Land, forced removal and, 99, 162, 164

Land cessions, 4, 211, 216, 245; after Seven Years' War, 130, 130n; Treaty of Fort McIntosh and, 217, 217n, 218, 224, 228, 286, 305–306; at Fort Harmar conference, 228; paying for, 228; as illegal, 286; Indian women's refusal of, 286; Indian women's aggrievement by, 299; end of, 300–301, 318n; forced, 305, 308; Glaize and, 314; Tenskwatawa and nativist movement's halting of, 318n

Landscape: Indian names and identity in, 22, 121; riverine, 122; Ohio land divisions and, 226. *See also* Appalachian Mountains; Wetland landscape

Land speculation, 11, 133, 223, 312; George Washington and, 4, 5, 132n, 224, 246; Great Black Swamp as, 92; Croghan and, 132n; in Indiana, 164; cost per acre and, 224, 224n, 225; Ohio Company and, 224, *226*, 231, 246n, 289, 299–301, 307; "Miami Purchase" and, 227; violent Indian wars and, 231, 284, 289; Delaware land control as, 314

Language, 75n, 76n; American vs. French references in agrarian record, 64; visual Indian dress as, 82n, 100, 175, 190, 193, 193n; explorers and, 120, 289, 295; Miamitown's diversity of, 146; trading and, 146, 190; Cuillerier as interpreter of, 152; epithet use and, 155; translation and, 297; Aupaumut's skills at, 304; of kinship, 308

Index 333

—Indian: Algonquian, 8–9, 39, 70, 73–74, 128, 132n, 304, 305; Miami-Illinois, 22; Mohegan, 37; Cree, 39; dialects of, 58, 118; Miami, 114, 118; Delaware, 132n; Iroquoian, 132n; Mohawk, 132n
L'Anguille. *See* Snake-Fish Town (L'Anguille)
La Pointe, *111*
La Potherie, Bacqueville de (Claude-Charles le Roy), 68
L'Arbre Croche, 129
Larrivé, Joseph, 101
La Salle, René-Robert Cavelier, sieur de, 42n, 149; New France explored by, 16n, 77, *80,* 81–83, 120; Ohio River and, 16n, 53n; at Wabash River, 16n; bison recorded by, 48; Green Bay and, 77, 81–82; Frontenac and, 77, 86; *Griffin (Le Griffon)* of, 77, *79;* calumet peace pipe used by, 81, 82; and stealing of seed corn to avoid starvation, 83
Lasell, Antoine, 144
Lavasseur, Michel, 198
Lawson, John, 99
Leavelle, Tracy Neal, 82n
Le Baril (village), 93
Lee, Arthur, 217
Le Gris (chief), 144, 149, 150, 220, 232
Le Gris ("Les gros") (village), 58, 93, *135,* 147
Lenni-Lenape. *See* Delaware Indians (Lenni-Lenape)
Lernoult, Robert, 153–155, 155n, 156–157
Leslie, William, 129
Lewis, James Otto, 205
Licking River, 20, *21,* 190, 227, 257
Life and Times of Little Turtle, The (Carter), 279n, 316
Lincoln, Benjamin, 311
Little Egg (chief), 144
Little Miami River, 17, 96, 131; wintering camps at, 20; location of, *21,* 114, 115, *135;* wetlands and, 22; Miami settlements and, 94; English traders at, 115; trading west of, 117; settlers along, 149, *226;* land cessions to, 304
Little Turtle, 2, 11; Mahican mother of, 15; Fort Miami and, 137, 137n; Lasell and, 144; Miamitown and, 147, 149, 150, 154; family of, 153, 259, 265, 290; Tacumwah and, 153; as war chief, 210–211, 220, 232, 236, 239, 241, 275, 279–283; Sweet Breeze and, 267, 290; defeated of St. Clair's army by, 275, 279, 279n, 280–283, 303; biography of, 279, 279n, 316; William Wells and, 279n; British aid to, 303; Quaker farming and, 315; treaties and, 315; Farm School of, 315
Little Wabash River, 60, 115
Logan, Benjamin, 214n, 217
Logansport, Ind., 259
Long, John, 184, 186
Louis XIV (France), 88, 108, 168. *See also* France, king of
Louis XV (France), 102n. *See also* France, king of
Louisiana, *116;* Fort de Chartres in, 52, 109, 123n, 131–132n, 132, 133; governors of, 108, 113, 131n; trade and, 117; Chickasaws attacked in, 123n; Spain's rule in western, 133; French-Canadian settlers in, 138; Mobile in, 138
Louvigny, Louis La Porte, sieur de, 87
Lower Arkansas River valley, 302
Lower Louisiana (la Basse-Louisiane), 113, 123
Lower Mississippi valley, 16
Lower Shawnee (village), 93
Lower Shawneetown, 95
Lower Wabash River, 2, 26, 138, 213, 220–221, 229, 234
Lower Wea (village), 135
Ludlow, Israel, 273
Ludlow's Station, 272
Lunn, Jean, 120n
Lusson, Simon François Daumont, sieur de St., 76, 81
Luxury goods trade, 142, 160, 169, 178, 210

McCauslin, John, 143
McClelland, William, 2, 248
McCoy, Captain, 253
McGary, Hugh, 215
McGill Company, 201
McKee, Alexander, 254n, 255, 275, 303, 310, 310n
McKenney, Thomas Lorraine, 192, 193n
Mackintosh, Angus, 310
Maclay, William, 241
Macomb, William, 310
Madder: red ("haut a the caugh"), 43–44; rose, 44
Madison, James, 192
Madison, Ind., 251
Madisonville, Oh., 50

Mahican Indians, 153, 289, 304–305, 307. *See also* Aupaumut, Hendrick
Mahican Johns, *93*
Maillou, Amable, 198
Main Poc (Potawatomi), 316
Maisonville, Alexis, 152, 154n, 156
Maisonville, Toop, 140, 144
Maize, 27, 28, 29, 31, 33, 59, 59n. *See also* Corn and cornfields
Mandan Indians, 187
Manette / Monette (Indian), 152
Many Tender Ties (Van Kirk), 100n
Maple sugar, 97, 142, 143
Marietta, Oh., 228n, 290, 301
Marquette, Jacques, 75, 77, 77n, *80,* 82, 120; *Carte de la découverte faite l'an 1673, 78*
Marrero, Karen L., 153n
Marriage: illegal traders and, 88; "in the manner of the country," 88, 96n, 110; trade access directly through women's kinship and, 88–89, 89n; women married out for, 89, 110; "in the custom of the country" (*à la façon du pays*), 96, 96n, 102
Martin, Hugh, 44, 44n
Martin's Station, 275n
Maryland, 95, 96, 138, 271
Maryland Journal, 286
Mascouten Indians, 9, 88, 90; Weas and, 69, 73, 76, 162, 163; migration of, to Green Bay, 73; trading by, 91; Vincennes post and, 114; location of, 118, *225;* women of, 296
"Mas-saw in Fulton County" (Winter), *208*
Matrifocal household. *See* Households, Indian
Maumee River, 5, *21,* 47; Glaize near, 9, 48, 57, 134, 198, 313–314; Great Black Swamp bordered by, 20, 22, 57, 92, 93, 94–95; fur trade and, 20, 98, 101, 105, 113; buffalo herds and, 48; villages on, 58; Appleseed myth and, 62, 64; orchards along, 64; Miami-controlled, 70, 88, 90, 94, 107, 114, 152; portage and, *80,* 96, 114–115, *115;* watershed at, 94; Shawnee along, 105, 224; marshes along, 114, 147; traders' use of, 134, 137; headwaters on, 136n; Harmar attacks and, 233, 237, *238,* 239, 274; portage of, with Miami, 258; peace talks at, 288, 307, 311; Wayne's forces at, 312–313; crops on, 313; beauty of, 313. *See also* Miami-Wabash portage
Maumee River valley, 6
Maumee-Wabash portage: Miami population at, 52, 90, 94, 107; control of, 52, 70, 88, 152, 156; villages at, 57, 274; trading and, 88, 98, 101; crucial location of, 109, 113, 114–115, *115,* 137; Dubuisson's fort at, 114–115; old village at, 136
Mauss, Marcel, 166n
Maxidiac. *See* Buffalo Bird Woman (Maxidiac)
Medals, 194, *197, 206,* 297; of Pacanne, 302
Medicine, Beatrice, 82n
"Memoir concerning Illinois Country" (Deliette), 35n, 67, 68n
Menominee Indians, 73, 76, 225
Merrell, James H., 100n, 310n; *Into the American Woods,* 290n
Merrior, Abel, 85
Metal trade goods: agricultural tools, 31; kettles, 76, 104, 141–142, 160, 165–167, 211, 214, 254; fur-processing tools, 99; and French introduction of metals, 104; cloth's replacement by, 104, 167; repurposing of, 165–166, 202; copper, 166, 175, 211; gold, 194, 206. *See also* Silver
Meyet, Captain, 297
Miami Indians (Wemaumeew): peace villages of, 1–2, 2n, 232, 259, 265; civil chiefs of, 2n, 58n, 289, 299, 309n; war chiefs of, 2n, 58n, 153, 211, 309n; crops of, 13, 20, 29, 30; women's roles in, 29, 57, 154n; diet of, 42n; and village populations, 58n, 69; clans of, 69, 95n, 153, 154; as fur trade middlemen, 70, 88, 187; St. Joseph and, 95n; Dubuisson and, 95n; totems of, 95n; Pacanakoma of, 101; Marguerite Ouabankikoué of, 101–102, 102n; Roy family and, 101–102; relocation of, to Miamitown, 107; English traders and, 117; villages of, near Ouiatenon, 119; river origin myth of, 121; river routes of, 122; alcohol and, 124, 124n, 125; disease and death of, 124, 124n; Darnaud at, 124n, 125; wintering camps of, 146; Tacumwah of, 152–157, 153n, 160, 296; Tacumwah's son as chief of, 153, 153n, 154, 296, 302; as patrilineal, 154n; chiefs chosen by women in, 154n; Pacanne portrait and, *161;* the Son as chief of, *205;* treaty line cessions and, 211; Treaty of Fort Stanwix and, 217; La Demoiselle as chief of, 221, 221n; attacks by, 231; Harmar's destruction of towns of, *238;* Captain Bull of, 252; Aupaumut's kinship with, 305; cultural restoration of, 319. *See also* Eel

Index 335

River Miami; Kaweahatta (the Porcupine); Kethtippecanuck; Le Gris
— clothing and cutwork of, 57, 181, 184, 202; in Pacanne portrait, *161;* linen shirt with silver, *178;* skirt, silver, and cutwork, *182;* moccasins of, with cutwork and beads, *186;* and the Son, with silver armbands, *205*
"Miami Purchase," 227
Miami River, 16n, 20, 217
Miami River valley, 6
Miamitown, 277, *278,* 279, 279n; Sabrevois at, 57; as largest trading village, 57, 128, 134, 137, 140, 146–147, 150, 224; location of, 57, *135,* 140, 147, *225;* women's corn at, 57; garrison at, 109; Ladouceur at, 114; ruins of, 134; portage at, *135;* as precontact village, 135; Vincennes's arrival at, 136; first French fort at, 136; as Kekionga, 136; importance of, 137, 146; population of, 137, 146, 224; coalition at, 137n; Le Gris and, 144, 149–150, 220, 232; formal culture at, 146–147; food source at, 147; Little Turtle and, 147, 149, 150, 154; traders at, 147, 150; Hay family at, 147–148, 148n, 149–150, 155; alcohol at, 148, 149; holiday celebration at, 148–149; Indian communications and, 150; French traders' kin links in, 150; peace desired at, 220; Indian refugees in, 224; and attacks on squatters, 231; Harmar's destruction of, 274; Wayne at, 313
Miami-Wabash portage, 52, 57, 70, 88, 90, 94, *115,* 152; as fur trade route, 98, 101, 137; importance of, 107–109, 113, 137; Croghan on, 134n, 137; Miami-controlled, 136, 156; Gage on, 156; St. Clair's offensive at, 258; old Miamitown at, 274
Michigan, *21, 135;* Indians in, 9, 285; French forts in, 16n; La Salle in, 77, 82; traders in, 137; persistence in, 320
Michilimackinac (post): Jesuits at, 14, 75; La Salle's visit to, 77; illegal trade at, 85; British incursion at, 85; Durantaye's command of, 86–87, 107; Louvigny's command of, 87; Louis XIV's closure of, 88; trade resumes at, 90; as beginning of Pontiac's Rebellion, 129–130; traders at, 151–152; fictive kin networks at, 159; Gage's regulation of trade at, 159; trade profit at, 170, 283n; high fur volume at, 283n; Little Turtle's warriors and, 283. *See also* Fort Michilimackinac

Middle Chute, 23
Middle ground: Franco-colonial, 9–10, 69, 69n, 165; fictive kin and, 159
Middle Ground, The (White), 9, 20n, 69, 69n, 89n, 123n
Midewiwin (Grand Medicine Society), 173, 174
Migration, Indian: to Green Bay, 69, 73; to Ohio River valley, 70, 121, 305; Iroquois, 73; Indian land sales and, 231, 284, 289; to Canada, 284
Military Journal of Ebenezer Denny, 238, 269, 271n, 276–277, 279–280
Miller, Catherine, 281
Mingo Indians, 218, 224, *225,* 275n
Ministry of marine (*ministère de la marine*), 52, 60, 120; communications and, 53n; beaver trade and, 79, 90–91, 106; minister of, 88, 90, 106, 119
Missionaries, Moravian, 136n, 169, 255, 289
Mississinewa, Ind., *135,* 145, 205
Mississinewa River, 60, *115, 135,* 145, 259
Mississippi, 117, 123n
Mississippi River, 10, 16, 77, 109, 126, 119–120; crops and, 19, 29–30, 34, 34n, 35–36; Ohio River at, *21,* 21; trade and, 23, 137, 164, 187, 217, 318; fish and, 25–26, *25,* 67, 68n; on Marquette's map, *78;* French explorers and, *80;* French forts and, *111;* villages and, 302
Mississippi Valley, 16, 113, 117
Missouri, 29, 132n, 309n
Missouri River, 10, 77; cornfields and, 59n; French explorers and, *80;* explorers and, 131n; Kickapoo villages at, 302
Mobile, Ala., 138
Moccasins, 174; waterproof, women's production of, 98, 100n; repair of, by women, 171; Miami cutwork on, 184, 186, *186, 187,* 202
Mohawk Indians, 73; language of, 132n; clothing of, 186, 190, 192; moccasin work of, 186; Joseph Brandt as Chief Thayeadanega of, 190, *192;* Hendrick as, 193, 193n; as refugees in Miami lands, 224; hostage chiefs of, 245; and Little Turtle's attack, 283; Brandt's mother as, 304n; Canajoharie village and, 304n
Mohawk River, 151
Mohegan Indians, 37
Mollusks: mussels, freshwater, 26, 59, 94, 142, 263; shell mounds from, 26; clams, 31; shellfish, 52; wampum and, 52, 179, 217, 221, 275; shell ornaments from, 193, *196,* 197

Moluntha (chief), 217–218, 229, 241
Monongahela River, 17, 20, *21,* 21, 126
Monroe, James, 192
Montour, Andrew, 100n, 151, 310n
Montour, Madame, 100n, 310n
Montour, Sally. *See* Ainse, Sally (Sally Hands)
Montreal, *110, 111;* fur trade onset and, 69, 75; French explorers at, *80;* beaver trade and, 86, 87, 92, 108; Odawa at, 86; peltry supply at, 87–88; peace at, 90; silversmiths at, 193, 198, 200–202. *See also* Great Peace of Montreal
Moravian Indians, 63–64, 151, 151n; missionaries and, 94, 136n, 169, 176, 255, 289, 291
Morgan, Daniel (Savage Morgan), 215
Morgan, George, *197,* 197
Mosby, John, 248
Mt. Pleasant, Jane, 28
Munsee Indians, 289
Museums, silver and fur trade clothing in, 175, 197, 202
Muskingum River, 19, *21;* Great Black Swamp near, 20, 93, 94; watershed of, 94; smallpox at, 126n; Ohio Company land and, *226;* Fort Harmar at, 228n; as border, 304; Tuscarawas branch of, 318
Myaamia (Miami), origin myth, 121–122
Mythmaking, Indian land and, 60, 61, 61n, 62–63, 63n

Nan-matches-sin-a-wa, 145–146, *145*
"Nan-Matches-Sin-A-Wa, 1839, Chief Godfroy's Home" (Winter), *145*
Nanticoke Indians, 224, *225,* 275
Natchez, Miss., 216
Needham, James, 92n
Neutral Indians, 14
Newberry Library, 35n
New France, *116;* Sabrevois at, 13n; ministry of marine and, 52, 53n, 60, 79, 90–91, 106, 120; closure of western trade in, 70, 100–101, 103; Iroquois aggression and, 71n, 72, 72n, 86–88; French forts in, 72, *111;* policies of, 72; voyages west begun in, 74, 79; Hundred Associates fur company of, 74; Nicolet and, 75n; Perrot at, 76n; travel and exploration at, 77, 79, *80;* beaver and trade in, 79, 88, 91–99, 120, 165; *congés* trade permits in, 79, 81, 86, 109; *coureurs de bois* and, 79, 103; explorers in, *80;* kinship in, 81; calumet ceremony and, 81; Company of the Farm in, 87–88, 88n, 103, 106; minister of marine and, 88, 90, 106, 119; "compact colony" policy in, 91, 106; Versailles's control in, 91, 106, 122, 168; cultural mediators of, 100, 290n, 310n; French population of, 103n; Detroit and, 105, 106, 107n, 128; westward expansion of, 106, 109; Illinois as ally of, 107; portage controlled by, 109; Vincennes and, 113; illegal traders in, 120; climate and riverine landscape of, 122; French maps of, 122; liquor trade control in, 123–124; Cadillac's policy and allies in, 128; French power and Indians in, 165; preference for cheaper cloth in, 167–168; officials in, 168, 168n, 194; Governor Ramezay and, 194

New Orleans, 132; fur trade in, 10, 57, 96–97, 113–114, 216; port in, 52–53; route to Montreal from, 57, 109; French center in, 104; Great Lakes route to, 113, 117
New York, 193; Governor Dongan and, 84, 85, 85n; trading in, 84, 96, 108, 120; Indian land and, 132n, 225, 303; silversmiths in, 198; treaty line and, 211; Iroquois in, 303, 307n
Niagara, 130, 186, 304. *See also* Fort Niagara
Niagara River, 130n
"Nicholas Vincent Tsawanhonhi" (Chatfield), *206*
Nicolet (Nicollet), Jean, sieur de Belleborne, 73–75, 75n
Nicolet, Madeleine Euphrosine, 75n
Nicollet, Joseph, 174
Nipissing Indians, 73, 76
Northern Department, 134, 154n, 211
Northwestern Indian confederacy (Northwest Confederation), 4, 10, 11
Northwest Ohio, 92
Northwest Ordinance, 224
Northwest Territory, 227, 246, 319
Notes on the State of Virginia (Jefferson), 64–65
Nouvel, Henry, 14
Nuts, 6, 15, 19, 47; acorns, 39, 41n, 68; hickory, 39; walnuts, 41

Odawa Indians: location of, 56, *225;* as Ottawa, 56, 85, 136, 217; gender roles of, 57; encouragement of English trade by, 84, 85; wintering camp of, 146; Sally Ainse and, 151; Walpole Island and, 181; treaty line cessions and, 211; at

Index 337

1788 peace conference, 227; at Glaize conference, 303; Aupaumut's kinship with, 305
Ogoula Tchetoka (village), 123n
Ohio Boundary, 314
Ohio Company: Putnam and, 224, 226, 231, 289, 299–301, 307; and land division in Ohio, *226*; Symmes and, 226; Gist and, 246n
Ohio Country: Croghan in, 132n; Clark sent to, 217; land divisions in, *226;* Washington's bounty lands in, 246; squatters in, 265n, 266n; Columbian Tragedy at, *278;* politics of, 308. *See also* Ohio River valley
Ohio/Mississippi confluence, 126
Ohio River (<*8AB8SKIG8*>), 121, *226,* 227; drainage area of, 16, 22; as "River of Ohio," *18, 23,* 63; tributaries of, *21,* 119, 120, 122; river system of, *21,* 21–24, 26; village siting at, 22; Falls of, 22–24, *115;* flood season travel on, 22n, 46n; expeditions down, 23; rapids chutes on, 23, *23;* Indian and Virginia shores of, 24, 286n; fish species in, 24–26; mussels in, 26; La Salle's misidentification of, 53n; French forts on, *111;* portage of the Maumee and Wabash Rivers and, *115;* length of, 119–120; trade routes and, 120; importance of, 120; challenges for, 122; as Indian lands border, 286. *See also* Grasslands; Great Black Swamp; Wetlands; Wildlife
Ohio River valley: as agrarian, 4–6, 28, 41, 41n, 61, 119, 134, 317, 319; Indian Country in, 5, 286n; transformation of, by Indian women, 5, 15, 36, 60–61, 283, 317, 318, 319; Indian resistance in, 12n; Sabrevois's description of, 16, 57–60; landscape of, 16, 318; forests in, 19, 19n, 41n, 121; grasslands in, 19, 20, 21, 24, 121, 143; hunting in, 20, 20n, 94; river system in, 20, *21,* 121, 126; corn as staple crop in, 27, 36; birds in, 31; Indian population in, 58n, 96, 110, 121, *225;* Johnny Appleseed myth and reality of, 60–61, 61n, 62–63, 63n; Indian migration to, 70, 121, 305; Great Black Swamp and, 93, 115, 121; Shawnee in, 95; trade in, 96, 103–105, 108, 110, 124, 128; *coureurs de bois* in, 103; forts in, 109, *111,* 118; French in, *110,* 112, 117, 121, 128; portages in, 114–*115;* Black Swamp as geographical division of, 115, 121; Wabash Valley as borderland for, 117; explorers in, 120–121; land tenure and migration in, 121; disease in, 124, 126–127; Quebec control of, 133; trade dominance in, 134; prosperous fur trade in, 134, 162, 317; tribal locations north of, *225;* Indian control of, 285; Perkins on Indian provinces of, 286n; Kentucky militia's plunder of, 294–295, 297; kinship as social structure of, 307; Pan-Indian Confederacy and, 317; revitalization of, 319; persistence in, 320

Ohio Valley, 28, *110,* 122; women's role in agriculture of, 4–6, 13, 27–29, 319; Indian names' symbolizing of identity in, 22, 121; Miami totems in, 95n; first map of, 120
Ojibwe Indians, 76, 193; migration of, to Green Bay, 73; wintering camps of, 146; clothing of, 173, 174, 181, 184, *185;* at Lake Superior, 181; Walpole Island and, 181; intertribal trade and, 187, 209; treaty line cessions and, 211, 217, 218; location of, *225,* 232; St. Clair surrounded by, 275; Little Turtle joined by, 283
Old Northwest Territory, 61, 62, 319
O'Neal, Antoine, 198
Oneida Indians, 307n
Onontio ("father"), 89n
Opechancanough, 36
Oral tradition, 29, 43
Orchards, 6, 13–15, 139, 260, 265, 318; destruction of, by soldiers, 1, 63, 237, 243, 245, 264; settlers' taking of Indians', 62, 64
Oswego (post), 128
Ottawa Indians, 56, 85, 136, 217; Sally Ainse and, 151; Aupaumut and, 305. *See also* Odawa Indians
Ottawa River, 80
Otter, 20, 94, 95, 99, 221
Ouabankikoué, Marguerite (Miami), 101–102, 102n
Ouiatenon: terrorizing of, by Kentucky militia, 1–5, 11, 141, 145, 255; agriculture of, 5, 59, 264; women's fields in, 5, 58; population at, 5, 9, 57–58, 88, 112, 114, 118, 128, 137, 146; buffalo and bison at, 19, 48, 137, 143; grass prairies at, 19, 20, 21, 58, 137, 139, 143; Wea Indians and, 48, 59, 112, 118, 171; Indian fort at, 57–58, 112, 118–119; ethnic villages and, 58–60, 118, 317; warriors in, 58; environment at, 60; traders in, 91, 102, 103, 105; Indian households at, 101–102; Ouabankikoué household at, 101–102; garrison in, 109; stockade outpost at, 112; Vincennes's new stockade at, 113, 118; location of, *115, 135,* 137, 138, *225;* trade goods from,

338 *Index*

117, 137, *172;* peltry from, 117; women's high fur volume at, 118–119, 283n; archaeology of villages in, 118, 140, 142; disease at, 125; prosperity of, 128, 134, 137; traders left, 140; marriage and kin networks at, 158; Gage's regulation of trade at, 159; alcohol at, 170; Native dress styles at, 171, 178; trade goods invoices at, 172–173; Harmar and violence at, 220, 223, 235; peace policy and, 229; Hamtramck and attack on, 233; Washington's attack plans and, 243, 247, 264–265; Scott's assault on, 250–252, 255–257, 263, 271, 275, 313; crops' destruction at, 255; Wilkinson's march to, 262–264; women's capture at, 288; beauty of, 313; food demand at, 317. *See also* Fort Ouiatenon

Ouiatenon (village), 57–58, 59, 134

Ouiatenon Indians, 10, 22, 122, 157, 214; Harmar's arrival and, 220; Pacanne and, 223; peace and, 229, 275. *See also* Wea Indians

Owl (village), *93*

Pacanakoma (Miami), 101

Pacanne: Tacumwah and, 153–154; portrait of (as "Pecan"), *161;* silver worn by, 160, *161,* 200; as headman, 160; Harmar and, 220–222; Clark and, 221, 222, 302; new village of, 221; murdered men of, 222, 223; Kaskaskia and, 222; moved west, 223, 302; medals of, 302; in Arkansas River valley, 302

Pacanne dit Roy, 153

Page, Jacques, 198

Pan-Indian Confederacy, 242, 265, 275, 285, 317–319

Pan-Indian world, dress and identity, 176, 202–203, 207

Pantonne, Etienne, 144

Patoka River, 60, *135*

Patrilineal society, 7, 100, 154n

Paully, Christopher, 129

Payette, Diaum, 144

Pays d'en haut (Upper Country), 106

Peace: calumet pipe as symbol of, 81–82, 82n, 83, 124–125, 162, 218, 297; Fort Harmar conference on, 227; U.S. and, 311–312

Peace village, 1–2, 2n, 232, 259, 265

"Pecan, a Native American Chief of the Miami Tribe" (Hamilton), *161*

Peltry:
— sources of: Great Black Swamp, 6, 10, 20, 92, 94–95; Ohio River valley, 8, 10–11, 20n, 162, 164, 283n; Kanawha River area, 19; Ohio River shores, 20, 320; Indian women near Ouiatenon, 119; Rocky Mountains and Canadian Northwest, 164; Wabash River valley, 165
— types of: muskrat, 20, 94, 95; otter, 20, 92, 94, 95, 99, 221; mink, 20, 92, 95, 96; buffalo, 50, 56, 137, 187, 216; raccoon, 54, 92, 94, 95, 96, 150; coyote, 92; fox, 92, 95; marten, 92, 94; possum, 92; elk, 94; skunk, 94, 95; bear, 95; bison, 95; deer, 95, 163, 164; wildcat, 95; wolf, 95. *See also* Beaver
— processing of, 60, 98–99, 123, 170, 320

Pennsylvania, 53, 133; traders in, 9, 95, 96, 108, 132n, 167, 310; settlers in, 61, 61n, 96, 132n; Sally Ainse in, 151; cloth trade and, 167, 169, 181; treaty line and, 211; Indian scalp bounty in, 215; land divisions in, *226;* army recruits from, 232, 271; militia from, 233, 266; Senator Maclay of, 241; Seneca in, 264; Iroquois attacks in, 264. *See also* Philadelphia

Peoria, Ill., 109

Peoria Indians, 144, 221, 296

Pepicokes (village), 58

Perkins, Elizabeth, 286n

Perrot, Nicolas, 33, 76, 76n

Petun Indians, 76, 107

Philadelphia: beaver market, 91, 95–96, 104; Shawnee trade and 110; cloth market at, 169; silver market and, 197–198; land speculators in, 225; army recruiting in taverns of, 271; Denny at, 271n; Putnam and, 289, 301; Brandt in, 303–304; Aupaumut speeches and, 305; Quakers and Black Hoof in, 315. *See also* Pennsylvania

Piankeshaw Indians, 20, 111, *225,* 245; calumet ceremony and, 125; at Vincennes, 138; Young Tobacco and, 212; La Demoiselle and, 221, 221n

Piankeshaw village, 58

Pickaway (town), 237

Pickawillany, 93, 221n

Pickering, Timothy, 308, 311

Pilgrims, corn found by, 30, 33

Pipe Creek, 60

"Plan of the Rapids, in the River Ohio, A" (Hutchins), *23*

Plants: cornfields, 4–5, 34, 59n, *238;* wild, 6, 32, 35, 55, 65, 237, 313–314, 318; Indian corn, 13,

Index 339

30, 33–34, 34n, 59, 68, 139, 308; maize, 27, 28, 29, 31, 33, 59, 59n; dyes from, 27, 43–44, 44n, *45,* 190; sunflowers, 27, 39; roots, edible, 31, *38, 39,* 39n, *40,* 41–43, *45,* 47, 142; tobacco, 36, 73, 138, 209, 211; tuckahoe ("Indian bread"), 37, *38,* 39, 39n, 41; ferns, 37, 39; jack-in-the-pulpit, 39, *40;* in marshes, 39; macopin, 41–42, 42n; tubers, 42, 142; Keeshikeehaukee, Poak-shikwileearkee, Waukeepaaneekee, and Waukpeeseepina, 42n; puccoon (poccoon), 43, *45;* wild rice, 68. *See also* Fruit; Vegetables and vegetable gardens

Platte River, 131n

Plowing and tillage, 28, 31–32n, 39, 61, 139, 141, 308, 315, 319

Point Pelee, 54

Pokagon Potawatomi, 319

Policy: of Versailles, on French settlement, 52, 91; French imperial, 72; Colbert's "compact colony," 91, 106; of *coureurs de bois,* 103; and Cadillac's creation of Detroit, 106; Versailles and New France, 111; on French and riverine landscape, 122; for Cadillac's Indian village, 128; anti-French ideas and, 157; Knox and treaty negotiation, 217n; Pacanne's men and new peace, 222; and land cession, 228, 229, 230, 286; humiliation-based, via military, 243, 303; Washington's new peace and, 286, 287–288, 291, 311; Washington's, and Indian women prisoners' response, 286

Pontchartrain, Louis Phélypeaux, comte de, 88, 91

Pontiac (chief), 132

Pontiac's Rebellion, 7, 136–137, 152–155, 158; violence toward British forts in, 129–130; Detroit's siege during, 130, 158n; Bouquet's role in, 131n; Croghan and, 132, 132n; as French inspiration, 156, 157; honoring Indigenous exchange and, 159; Pan-Indian alliances following, 275n

Population: of Ouiatenon, 5, 9, 57–58, 88, 112–114, 118, 128, 137, 146; of Ohio River valley, 8, 58n, 96, 110, 121; of Miami Indians, 52, 58n, 69, 90, 94, 107; of Huron Indians, 59; multiethnic, in Green Bay, 66, 68, 68n, 69, 74–75, 77, 96, 100; of Wabash River valley, 90, 94, 117; of Wabash villages, 122; of Miamitown, 137, 146, 224; of Detroit, 146, 151; male, reduction of through warfare, 317; Indian, steep decline in, 319

Porcupine, the. *See* Kaweahatta (the Porcupine)

Porcupine quills, 6, 43, 171, 174, 179, 187

Portage, 109, 114–115, *115,* 135. *See also individual portages and rivers*

Portage River, 94

Post St. Vincent. *See* Vincennes (post)

Potawatomi Indians, 84; Ohio River and, 47; Detroit village of, 55–56; appearance of, 55–56; wintering camp of, 146; clothing of, *177, 179, 183;* intertribal trade and, 187; Indian burial and, *195;* location of, *225;* at early peace conference, 227; Walpole Island and, 181; at Glaize conference, 303; and support of Tecumseh, 316; cultural restoration of, 319. *See also* Pokagon Potawatomi

Poteaux-en-terre (houses), 7

Potomac Bay, 224

Potomac River, 36, 95

Potomac River valley, 36, 37

Powhatan (chief), 36

Powhatan Indians, 36, 72

Prairie du Rocher, 211, 221

Prejudice: women and, 4, 156; British, toward French traders, 154–156, 160; religious, 159; derogatory terms and, 237n, 266n; Kentuckians', toward Indians, 265n, 266n

Presque Island (Isle), 53, *111,* 129

Price, George, 129

Price, Robert, 63n

Prisoners, Indian: women and children as, 217, 244, 257, 261, 267, 271; Washington's empowerment of Kentuckians to capture, 243–248; from Wabash villages, 244; at federal forts, 245, 246, 257, 258, 270–271; Scott's invasion and, 248; humane treatment of, 249–250; after Battle of Kickapoo, 253; Scott's treatment of, 253, 258, 270; illness and, 254; Wilkinson on women as, 256–261, 264, 267n, 267–271, 288; Kickapoo as, 264; women as, 264, 270–271, 293; Scott's list of Indians as, 267, 267n, *268–269;* missing women as, 270; marched by Wilkinson, 270; at geoTown, 270; release of, 270, 293–295; ransoms for, 288

Prisoners of war: as Vincennes's slaves, 113; Chickasaws' taking of French, 123n; killing of, 123n, 129, 236, 257, 266, 270; Pontiac's Rebel-

340 *Index*

lion and, 129–130, 275n; Wilkinson's taking of, 263, 270
Proctor, John, 249
Prophet's Town: Kickapoo with Tecumseh at, 302; founding and growth of, 316; gender roles in, 316; financial support for, 316
Puccoon (poccoon) (*Batschia canescens*), 43, *45*
Putnam, Rufus: Ohio Company investment of, 224, 226, 231, 289, 299–301, 307; Kentuckians and, 231, 288–289; Vincennes conference and, 285, 286, 296–304, 317; and Wabash Indian delegation, 288, 293, 294; career of, 288n, 289; at "hostile Indians" council, 289, 301; Heckewelder and Wells as delegates of, 289; as chief negotiator, 289; Aupaumut and, 289, 304; at Fort Washington, 289, 291; as head of peace commission, 290; pacification policy and, 291, 289; illness of, 301
Pyatt, Mr. (trader), 144

Quakers, 192, 315
Quapaw Indians, 33, 302
Quebec, *110, 111;* traders and, 69, 85, 87; French presence and fall of, 133; Ohio River valley Indian ties with, 134; English cloth sent to, 168–169; silversmiths in, 193, 194; Hamtramck's birth in, 221
Quebec Act (1774), 159
Quebec City, *80, 110*
Queen Anne's War, 108
Quilling society, 187

Raccoon Creek, 60
Radisson, Pierre Esprit, 75, *80*, 84, 91
Rafert, Stewart, 58n
Rainbeare, Henri, 144
Ramezay, Claude de, 194
Randolph, Beverley, 311
Rangers, 130n
Ranvoyzé, François, 198
Rasles, Sebastian, 48, 48n
Red Jacket, 307, 311
Reed, Joseph, 215
Regiments, 312; Royal American Regiment (60th Foot), 130, 130n, 131n; 80th Foot, 130n, 136; Highland Scots, 131, 132; 78th Highlanders, 132; First American, 219, 271n, 274; Second Regiment, 274

Reptiles: alligator snapping turtle, 24, 25; turtle, 26
Reservations: Iroquois, 63; forced removal to, 99, 162; Buffalo Creek, 303
Revolutionary War: Clark's capture of Vincennes in, 2, 213; Clark's seizure of Kaskaskia in, 2, 212; Scott's service in, 2; Washington's service in, 3–4, 243, 244, 264; army size and, 11; famine during, 63, 244, 264, 269n, 284; French officers in, 136–137n; and Biggs's capture by Indians, 143, 208–209; Gage's service in, 158n; Indians' fighting in, 160; Pan-Indian movement's beginning at, 202, 275; Indian population and, 209; Indian trade good prices in, 210; Hamtramck in, 221; debts of, 223, 242, 312; veteran land rewards after, 224–225; Denny's service in, 271n; Rufus Putnam as mediator after, 288; Brandt as Iroquois leader in, 303
Ribbonwork, 6, 169, 179, 181, 184, *184–185*, 188, 202
Richard, Jean, 102, 102n
Richardville, Jean Baptiste (Joseph) (Pinšiwa), 153n, 154, 296, 302
Richardville, Joseph Drouet de, 153n, 154–156; battle report of, 123; Tacumwah and, 152–153; son of, 296. *See also* Chickasaw Indians
Ridgway, Robert, 17
Riopelle, Dominique, 198
"River of Ohio" (Gordon), *18*
Robertson, William, 148n
Roche de Bout, *135,* 313
Rock River, 34
Roman Catholic Church: missions of, 14; Jesuits and, 14, 14n, 33, 43, 71n, 76, 76n; priest explorers from, 14–15, 33, 54, 71, 77, 120, 159; fictive kin network and, 159; and Quebec Act's permission of practice, 159
Romney, George, 192
Rooseboom, Johannes, 85
Roots, edible, 31, *38,* 39, 39n, *40,* 41–43, *45,* 47; tubers and, 42, 142; storage of, 61. *See also* Dyes
Roy, Narcisse, 200–201
Roy, Pierre, 101–102, 102n
Royal American Regiment (60th Foot), 130, 130n, 131n
Ruddell's Station, 275n

Index 341

Sabrevois, Jacques-Charles de, sieur de Bleury: as Detroit commandant, 5, 13, 13n, 14n, 52–54; on Indian women's cornfield work, 5, 16, 55–59; Montreal death of, 14n; overview of Ohio River valley by, 47, 52–60, 119

Sabrevois, Jacques-Charles de (son), 14n

Sagard, Gabriel, 33

"Saga Yeath Qua Pieth Tow, King of the Maquas" (Verelst), *196*

St. Clair, Arthur: defeat of, 10, 11, 271–277, *278,* 279–283, 286; defeat of, by Blue Jacket, 11, 210, 230, 275, 280, 282, 286, 303; as Northwest Territory governor, 227, 282–283; at Fort Harmar conference, 227–229; court-martial of, 232n, 234n; as army commander, 241; and disagreement with Scott over Wabash raid, 249; humanitarian treatment and, 249–250; Denny on army of, 269–271, 271n; Sargent on army of, 272, 279–281; Little Turtle's defeat of, 275, 279, 279n, 280–283, 303; Buckongahelas's defeat of, 275, 280, 282; Denny's description of attack on, 276, 277, 277n, 279–281; broadside depicting defeat of, 277, *278*, 279; organized Indian warfare and, 280, 282; equipment lost by, 281; militia attacks on villages and, 282; and movement of captives to Fort Washington, 283; and Indian control over Ohio River valley, 285

Ste. Geneviève, 221, 302

St. Ignace, 14, *111*

St. Joseph (post), 88, 90, 283n. *See also* Fort St. Joseph

St. Joseph des Miamis (post), 90

St. Joseph River, 20, 93, 122, 238

St. Lawrence Bay, 73

St. Lawrence–Great Lakes Basin, 20, 72

St. Lawrence River, 55, 68n, 75n, *110, 111, 116;* trade goods and canoes on, 20, 87, 158n; trade routes on, 73; French explorers on, *80;* control of, 122

St. Lawrence River valley, 91, 106

St. Louis, 118, 133, 302; trading at, 135, 138, 144–145, 167, 187; Spanish governor at, 211, 221

St. Marys River, *21, 115, 135,* 136, *240;* Great Black Swamp at, 20, 93; Maumee towns destroyed at, 238

St. Philip, 211

Salmonie River, 60, *115,* 135

Salt, 39, 141, 142, 215, 216, 254

Salt licks, buffalo and, 24, 48n, 141, 215, 216

Sandusky Bay, 54

Sandusky River, *21,* 105; Great Black Swamp near, 20, 22, 53, 92, 93; hazardous travel at, 54; French traders at, 96

Sandusky River valley, 6

Sandusky watershed, 94

Sargent, Winthrop, 272, 279–281

Sauk (Sac) Indians, 34, 76, *225,* 227, 303

Sault Ste. Marie, *111;* as Bow-e-ting, 76

Savagery: of Indians, 75, 215, 278; of Daniel Morgan, 215, 266n; of Kentuckians, 215; public reaction to, 287

Scalps: Clark's taking of, from British-allied Indians, 213; bounty on, 215; Kentuckians' taking of, 215, 217, 230, 236; as taking spirit, 216; Virginians' taking of, 218, 230; Brown's boast of taking, 222, 223; from Pacanne's peaceful men, 222; of Merritt Scott, 248; Scott's humane attitude on, 258; published horrors of, 284

Schindler, Joseph, 201

Schlösser, Francis, 129

Schoenbrunn (town), 64, 318

Schoolcraft, Henry, 193

Scioto River, *21,* 22, 93, *135,* 224, 226–227; Great Black Swamp and, 20, 53–54, 94–95; smallpox at, 126n

Scott, Charles C.: career of, 1–3n, 247–248, 248n, 312, 313; Levi Todd and, 2, 214n, 249, 250; family of, killed by Indians, 2, 248–249; reputation of, 2, 258, 262, 266, 271, 288; death of, 3n; Ouiatenon expedition of, 7, 247, 250–252, 313; Kentucky invasions and, 248–249, 253–258, 262, 264, 266, 275; St. Clair and, 249–250, 258; "Blackberry Campaign" and, 250–257, 263; Shawnee guides of, 251, 253; sending of Hardin to attack hunting camps, 252–254, 256; sending of Wilkinson to camps, 253; captive women's treatment by, 253, 256–258, 260, 264, 267n, 267–270, 288; Colonel Brown and, 254; failed expedition of, 257; Indian prisoner list attributed to, 267n, *268–269*

Scott, Charles, Jr., 248

Scott, Merritt, 248

Scott's Landing, 2, 248n

Secretary of War. *See* Knox, Henry

Senat, Antoine, 117

Seneca Indians, 4, 9, 131; wintering camps of, 20, 146, 303; apple orchards of, 63; and Sullivan Expedition's destruction of orchards, 63, 243–245, 264, 269n, 284; trade and, 85, 125, 146; disease and, 125; peace and, 131n, 307; expulsion to Canada of, 224, 243, 264, 284; as noncombatants, 243; Cornplanter and, 245, 303; and naming of Washington as Town Destroyer, 245, 264, 284; women of, affected by Washington, 245; in Pennsylvania, 264; Glaize peace conference and, 303, 307; Red Jacket as, 307
Seran, François, 101
Seven Ranges, 224, 226
Seven Years' War (French and Indian War), 7; Ohio River valley during, 9, 126n, 128, 168; smallpox blankets in, 126n; British victory in, 130, 130n, 131; French at end of, 136, 168; Tacumwah during, 152; Gage's service during, 158n; cloth trade and, 168; trade expansion after, 169–170; Indians' move west after, 209
Shannon, Timothy, 190
Shawnee Indians (Weshauwonnow): location of, 20, 47–48, 91, 95, 225; language of, 37; plant dyes and, 43; clan headmen of, 58n; fur trade and, 90, 91, 95, 105; Viele's wintering with, 91; epidemics and, 126; peace and, 131n, 307; chief Captain Johnny of, 149, 217, 220; adoption by, 190; wintering camp of, 190; move of, to west, 209; treaty line cessions and, 211; attacks on, by militia, 214, 214n, 217, 220; Treaty of Fort Stanwix and, 217; chief Moluntha of, 217–218, 241; as refugees at Miamitown, 224; and Hardin's destruction of Pickaway town, 237; and Harmar's destruction of Maumee towns, *238;* Smith as captive of, 280; as cultural mediators, 290n, 310n; Aupaumut's kinship with, 305; Edmunds on changes in, 309n, 318; Sally Ainse and, 310, at Tippecanoe, 318. *See also* Black Hoof; Tenskwatawa
— clothing of, 176, 190; linen shirt, with pierced brooches, *177;* Shawnee coat, embroidered, *180;* silver armbands, pierced silver, and earrings on the Prophet, *204*
Shawnee Prairie, 252
Shepard, Samuel, 200, 214
Sieur de Vincennes Identified (Roy), 101, 123n
Silver (trade): archaeology of, 7, 194, 197; as most desired commodity, 128, 161, 184, 188, 193–194, 197–198, 201–202; transformation of women's clothing by, 128, *195,* 197; in trading, 152, 160, 169; as ornament, 152, 160, 177–*179, 182,* 188, *192, 196,* 195–198, 200–202, 204–*208;* earrings as, 160, *161, 195, 192, 196, 201, 204,* 206–*208;* Pacanne's clothing and, 160, *161;* Beaubien and, 160; as brooches, 160, 176, 177–*179,* 184, 190, *192,* 194–*195,* 197–198, *199–200;* symbolism of, 163; on pipe tomahawks, 166; in museums, 175, 197, 202; identity and, 176, 178–179, 202; on blouses, *177, 178, 179;* as buckles, 179; replacement of shell ornamentation by, 193, *196;* melting of coins to make, 193–194, 197; male bodies' embellishment by, *195;* order for, by George Morgan, 197, *197;* as rings, *197;* Spanish goods and, 198; Albany values for, *203;* as medals, *206,* 302
Silversmiths, 128, 193–194, 198, 200–202
Simcoe, John, 275, 303
Simpson, George, 100
Sioux Indians, 82–83, 87
Sirropp, The (chief), 144
Six Nations, 211, 245, 303. *See also* Iroquois Indians
Slavery: L'île aux Esclaves and, 55; prisoners and, 113; Indians as, 113, 306; Vincennes and, 113; females in, 151, 152; trader competition and, 151; in kin networks, 152
Smallpox. *See* Disease
Smith, James, 280
Smith, John, 39n, 43
Snake-Fish Town (L'Anguille), 259–260, 262
"Son, a Miami Chief, The" (Lewis), *205*
Soto, Hernando de, 32
Spain: archaeology and, 7; trading and, 7, 15, 95, 132–135, 143–145, 167, 202; Council of the Indies and, 53; St. Louis and, 132n, 133, 211, 221; army of, 132n, 133; Miamitown and, 147; Indian land and, 157, 302; silver ornaments made in, 198; Harmar and, 220–221; Pacanne and, 302
Spencer, O. M., 195n, 290n
Spirited Resistance, A (Dowd), 318n
Spirituality, and fasting, 311n
Squatters, 133, 265n; militia as, 2; Johnny Appleseed as, 61, 61n, 62; silver plundered by, 198, 222; on Indian land, 209, 213–214, 231; Indians' raid on, 220, 231
Starved Rock, 16n, 35n

Stereotypes, Indian, 8, 75, 155, 162, 170, 209, 278
Sterling, James, 151–152
Sterling (Stirling), Thomas, 132n
Stevens, Scott Manning, 71n, 73
Straits of Detroit, 55–56, 105, 107n, 108, 128
Straits of Mackinac (Michilimackinac), 85, 109
Stroud (blanket), 171, 176, 200, 211, 214, 297; as trade staple, 103, 181; from England, 168n, 169, 169n
Sturgeon. *See* Fish
Sturgeon River (*mameewa siipiiwi*), 136
Sugar River, 60
Sullivan, Daniel, 218, 230
Sullivan Expedition, 63, 243–245, 264, 269n, 284
Supreme Court (U.S.), 218n
Sweet Breeze (Manwangopath), 290
Sword, Wiley, 266n
Symmes, Cleves, 226, 227
Symmes Purchase, 224, 226

Tacumwah (Miami): as Richardville's wife, 152–153, 155; as kin network trader, 152–157, 160; children of, 153, 153n, 154; as sibling of Pacanne and Little Turtle, 153, 155; Mahican mother of, 153; Beaubien and, 153, 154, 160; Hay's description of, 155; as speaker at councils, 296
Tadoussac, 73, 75
Tanacharison (Half-King), 246n
Tanner, Helen Hornbeck, 14n
Tea, 150, 151, 169, 210
Teaontorai, *93*
Tecumseh, 207; followers of, 141, 317; Pan-Indian Confederacy and, 242, 265, 275, 285, 317–319; Battle of Tippecanoe and, 285; at Prophet's Town, 302, 317; annuities and, 315–316; resistance movement and, 315, 317–318; and moving of village from Greenville, 316; at Battle of the Thames, 318; popularity of, 318
Tennessee, 24, 25, 91, 95, *111*, 211, 224, 246
Tennessee River, *111*, 211
Tenskwatawa: followers of, 141, 316, 317; Indian confederacy and, 202, 207, 285, 314–315, 317; as Prophet, *204*, 315; annuities and, 315–316; founding of Prophet's Town by, 316–317; popularity of, 316, 318; rhetoric of, 316, 317, 318; women criticized by, 317; nativist resistance movement and, 317–318, 318n; intermarriage criticized by, 317
"Tens-Kwau-Ta-Waw, the Prophet" (Inman), *204*
Thames River (Canada), 151n, 310
"Thayeadanega, Joseph Brant, the Mohawk Chief" (Romney), *192*
Tionontati Indians, 14n, 225
"Tippecanoe and Tyler Too," 19n
Tippecanoe Creek, 260
Tippecanoe River, 20, *21*, 60, *115*, *135*, 140, 260, 316
Tobacco, 36, 73, 138, 209, 211, 275
Tobacco Huron, 36, 76. *See also* Huron Indians
Todd, Levi, 2, 214n, 249, 250
Tool and utensil trade, 99. *See also* Metal trade goods
Topographical Description of the Western Territory of North America, A (Imlay), 254, 254n
Totem, 95n
Trabue, Daniel, 213, 215
Trade goods, *197*, 202, 203; in New England, 52; as luxury, 142, 160, 169, 178, 210; social function of, 166, 166n, 187, 221; changes in types of, 166–167; increases in, 167; most desirable, 167; in early western Great Lakes, 172–173. *See also individual types of trade goods*
Traders: colonial, 9, 92n, 95, 97, 167, 197; Viele as, 90–91, 92n; French, 103n; at Michilimackinac rebellion, 129; unlicensed, 134
Trans-Appalachian west, 4, 6
Trans-Mississippi west, 12, 164, 319
Treaties: Indian lands secured with, 4, 229; Indians' payment for land in, 4, 217n, 228; land cessions and, 4, 228; erasure of Indian titles in, 164; Indian village stability and, 264n; American commissioners and, 311. *See also individual treaties*
Treaty of Fort Harmar (1789), 228, 286, 304, 314
Treaty of Fort McIntosh (1785): conference and, 217, 217n, 228; revocation of, 218, 224, 228; St. Clair at, 228; U.S. land claims in Ohio based on, 286; Aupaumut and, 305–306; Shawnee and Delaware land lost in, 306; borders and, 306
Treaty of Fort Stanwix (1768), 211; treaty line for, 212
Treaty of Fort Stanwix (1784), 216–217, 217n, 228, 245

Treaty of Greenville (1795), 146–147, 166, 314, 317; annuities and, 315–316
Treaty of Mississinewa (1826), 205
Treaty of Paris (1763), 131n, 160
Treaty of Vincennes (1792), 285, 286–287, 296–304, 316, 317
Trees, 92; apple, 1, 6, 13–15, 62–64, 139, 313; peach, 15, 63, 139, 313; forests of, 17, 19n; hickory, 17, 39, 43, 44, 94; maple, 17, 44, 97, 142; oak, 17, 39, 41n, 94; tulip, 17, 44; walnut, 17, 41, 43, 44; dyes from, 44; orchards of, 237, 243–245, 260, 265, 318. *See also* Nuts
Tremblay, Montague, 151, 310
Trois Rivières, *110, 111*
Trotter, James, 236
Trowbridge, C. C., 26, 42n
Trueman, Alexander, 288
Tsawanhonhi (chief), 206
Tubers. *See* Plants
Tuckahoe. *See* Plants
Tupelo, Miss., 117, 123n
Tuscarawaras River, 93

U.S. Army, 11, 241, 258, 313; recruits and, 232, 233, 249, 266, 271–272, 287; pay and, 244; federal financing for, 312
U.S. Military District, 224, 226
Upper Country. *See* Pays d'en haut (Upper Country)
Upper Louisiana (la Haute-Louisiane), 113, 123n
Upper Maumee River, 9
Upper Sandusky, 126
Upper Wabash River, 211, 234, 258, 261
Upper Wea (village), 135

Van Braam, Jacob, 246n
Vaudreuil, Philippe de Rigaud, marquis de: on Fort Miami, 95n; as governor of Canada, 95n, 108, 112, 136n, 167–168, 168n; and renaming of Fort Miami, 136n
Vegetables and vegetable gardens: militia's destruction of, 1, 235, 244–245; squash, 6; beans, 6, 27, 32, 46, 139; corn, 6, 28–29, 32, 34, 34n, 35; in Illinois Country, 34; pumpkins, 34, 36; Indian women's provision of, 34–36, 42, 55, 64, 139, 142, 147; fields of, 34–36; village size and storage of, 35, 36; onions, 42; as dye sources, 44; at Detroit, 55; feeding army on, 313–314

Véniard, Étienne de, 131n
Vermilion (pigment), 56, 101–102, 169, 211
Vermilion (village), *135,* 234
Vermilion Indians, 118, 135
Vermilion River, 60, 117, 118, *135,* 229
Versailles (French government): Ohio River valley control and, 16, 52–53, 76, 120, 122; French empire expansion and, 76; "possession" ceremony and, 76, 81; LaSalle and, 77; British trade incursion and, 85–86; and Denonville's blame of Iroquois, 86; Frontenac's Iroquois warning and, 86, 88; fur trade ban by, 90, 127; and French settlement policy, 91, 111–112; peltry increase and, 105; Cadillac on allies at, 105, 106, 108, 128; profitability of New France and, 106; British competition and, 109; imperialism of, 127–128; Whitehall and, 159; Gage and trade for, 159; plea for English cloth and, 168
Viele, Arnout, 90–91, 92n
"View of the Maumee Towns Destroyed by General Harmar, October, 1790" (Denny), *238*
Vincennes (peace conference), 303, 317; and Ohio River as treaty boundary line, 224, 228, 241, 299–300, 301, 304; signing and ratification of treaty at, 285, 286–287, 296–304, 316, 317; Indian women prisoners' release at, 292–293, 295–296, 299, 301; Fort Steuben prisoners at, 294; Indian speeches at, 296; Putnam's gift giving at, 296–297; interpreters at, 297; calumet ceremonies at, 297, 298; Coigne as speaker at, 298–299, 300; land issues' framing at, 298–299, 300; Gawiahaetle at, 299; women's link to land at, 299, 316; Ohio Company lands and, 299, 300, 301; Putnam's staying at, 301; tribes' moving west after, 302
Vincennes (post), 2, 97, 227; location of, *115, 135,* 138; domination of Ohio River valley trade by, 117, 134; as Post St. Vincent, 135, 293, 294; agrarian description of, 138; Buffalo Trace adjacent to, 138; Juchereau trading post at, 138; Virginians at, 218; U.S. government presence at, 219; Harmar at, 219, 220, 221; description of, 220; Harmar's building of Fort Knox at, 220–221; Hamtramck and, 222, 223; Kentucky raider killings at, 222, 223; Pacanne at, 302. *See also* Fort Vincennes

Vincennes, François-Marie Bissot de (son), 102, 122; Ouiatenon post of, 112, 113; funds from Boisbriand to, 113; Indian world definition and, 113–114; family of, 113, 117n; capture of, 117; death of, 117, 123n, 131n

Vincennes, Jean-Baptiste Bissot, sieur de: death of, 95n, 109; Montreal family of, 102, 112, 117; as post namesake, 114; arrival of, in Miamitown, 136

Violence: kidnapping and, 4; military and, 11; in Ohio River valley, 11, 217, 220, 231, 264–265, 301–302; Jesuits and, 71; Frenchmen and, 84, 107, 108; by militia, 212, 216, 266–267; Indian control of, 218, 220; "Enterprise against the Indians" and, 265; financial aid and, 266; at Miamitown, 269; toward Indian women, in Sullivan's campaign, 269n; body desecration as, 281, 282, 287, 292–293; as symbolic act to dissuade taking land, 282, 320; as symbolic act about agrarian life, 282, 319; Columbian Tragedy as, 284; and defense of Indian land, 320. *See also* Prisoners; Savagery; Scalps

Virginia, 133, 211–212, *226*, 286n; Washington and, 3, 246, 246n, 248; traders and, 9, 20; Ohio River south bank and, 24; descriptions of, 36–37; Indians of, 36, 43, 64, 72; Jefferson on, 64; traders from, 167, 169; governor of, 265; military violence and, 266; military recruits from, 271

Virginia Military District, 224, 226

Virginians, 212, 218

Voyage to Virginia, A (Norwood), 39, 41

Voyageurs, 123, 158n

Wabash Indians: Washington's violent actions and, 3–4; agrarian villages of, 4; intertribal trade and, 88, 97, 117; marriage and, 96; as cultural mediators, 100; as British allies, 103, 211; Chickasaws' killing in, 117; archaeology of villages and, 118; village populations and, 122; Brown's plunder of, 122; Kentuckians attacked, 230, 264; attacks by, 231; treaties and, 245; raids on villages of, 247n; high fur volume from, 283n; Putnam delegation and, 288, 293, 294, 301

Wabash River, *21*; settlers along, 2, 96; villages raided on, 2, 211, 213, 220–221, 229, 234, 258, 261; militia raids and, 3–4; agriculture along, 4–6, 22, 139; Miami land and, 8, 10, 52, 57, 70, 88; La Salle at, 16n; as fur trade route, 20, 113; mussels and shell mounds in, 26, 138; bison along, 48, 138; Maumee portage at, 52, 57, 70, 88, *115*; as Ouabanchi, 53n; tributaries of, 60; French explorers and, *80*; fur trade importance of, 88, 91, 96–103, 109, 112–113; harvests and, 98; forts near, *110–111*; Wea village on, 118; Miami origin myth and, 121–122; and villages' domination of Ohio River valley trade, 134, 138; grasslands along, 139; wild horses along, 139; archaeology of Native dress at, 171; upper, 211, 234, 258, 261; Imlay's description of, 254; Wilkinson and, 259. *See also* Lower Wabash River; Upper Wabash River

Wabash River valley, 101; as agrarian, 4, 5, 6, 123; lower part of, 17; forests in, 17; villages along, 52, 88, 125, *135*; Indian population in, 90, 94, 117; foot trails in, 97; seasonal activities and, 98; importance of, 113; French trade and, 113, 117; Chickasaw wars and, 122–123; female labor in, 123; wetland peltry in, 123; disease in, 125–126; Indian rebellion in, 131; and villages' domination of trade, 134, 135, 144; migrating traders in, 144; charred fields regrown in, 263; American arrival and persistence in, 320

Waketomica (village), 93

Walpole Island, 181

Wampum, 52, 221; as war belt, 179; color symbolism and, 217, 275

Wapakoneta (village), 315, 316

War of 1812, 160, 188, 290n

Washington, George: village attacks ordered by, 1, 2–5, 243, 246, 247, 265–266; career of, 2, 3–4, 8, 11–12, 248; discipline and ethics of, 3; land speculation by, 4, 5, 19, 132n, 224, 246, 246n; women and children's imprisonment by, 11, 243; leadership of, 12n; Army of the Empire and, 12, 312–313; Sullivan Expedition destruction ordered by, 63, 243–245, 264, 269n, 284; Ouiatenon villages and, 137, 265; Indian war unwanted by, 219; Indian peace and, 230, 286–287; Putnam's letters to, 231; enraged by Harmar, 240, 241, 243; Wabash River valley demise and, 243, 319; as Town Destroyer, 245, 264, 284; in Ohio Country for bounty lands, 246, 246n; Ohio region knowledge of, 246, 247; *Journal of Major George Washington*, 246, 246n; increased violence level and, 265; Iroquois strategy and,

346 *Index*

265; Darke's letter to, 277n, 280; new peace policy of, 286, 287–288, 291, 311; Brandt treaty and, 303, 304; in Philadelphia, 304; Pickering and, 308; standing army organization and, 312, 232n, 234n

Wasp (Wea), 255

Wayne, Anthony, 5, 241n, 288n; Fallen Timbers victory of, 62, 64, 311n, 312n, 313; career of, 312–313

Wea Creek, 118

Wea Indians, 135; Kentucky militia attack on, 1, 230; homelands of, 9; location of, 20, *225*; trading by, 20, 91, 111; bison and, 48, 59, 143; Ouiatenon villages and, 48, 59, 112, 118, 171; at Green Bay, 69, 73; as traders, 70; Wabash River valley villages of, 70, 88, 90; migration of, to Green Bay, 73; French control and, 76, 111, 112; routes of, 111; Vincennes and, 122, 123n; disease and death of, 124–125; at calumet ceremony, 125; winter camps and, 125; attacks by, 130, 140; salt and, 141; imported goods and, 142; prisoners of, 143–144; chief Little Egg of, 144; Mascouten peace with, 162; glass beads from dress of, 171; Hardin raids and, 247n; Queen of, 297; at Glaize conference, 330

Weapons: knives, 98–99, 215; tomahawks, 129, 130, 166, 202, 209, 213, 217, 248; Deaf Man's pipe tomahawk, 166; armory for, 272; smithy repairs for, 272; bayonets, 276, 312; swords, 305, 306. *See also* Firearms

Welhik-Tuppeck (Schoenbrunn), 64, 318

Wells, William (Wild Carrot): as captive adopted by Porcupine, 267, 289, 290n; as cultural mediator, 267, 290, 294; at Fort Washington, 267, 291–292; Indian captive releases and, 267, 292, 294; Sweet Breeze and, 267, 289, 290; as son-in-law of Little Turtle, 279n, 290; Indian names of, 289; as Putnam's peace delegate, 289; as translator, 290, 290n, 295, 297; wives of, 290; as Indian agent, 290; freedom for captive white children and, 290n; death of, 290n

Wemaumeew Indians. *See* Miami Indians (Wemaumeew)

Wendat Indians, 14

We-saw (chief), 188, *189*

Weshauwonnow Indians. *See* Shawnee Indians (Weshauwonnow)

Western Confederacy, 285

Wetland landscape, 6, 10, 17, 22, 30, 121–122, 188; precontact, 24; explorer descriptions of, 47, 54, 60; armies slowed by, 250–253, 257, 259, 262–263, 267

Wetlands: edible plants in, 4, 6, 22, 30–31, 37, 39, 41–43, 47, 60; Ohio River and, 5, 22, 24; peltry from 10, 92, 123, 163, 165; forests in, 17; village siting in, 36, 37, 60, 188; dye sources in, 43; wildlife at, 47, 57, 137, 263; Miamitown and, 57, 137; bison in, 57; medicinal plants in, 60; rivers and, 60; women's fur processing in, 60, 123, 320; basket reeds from, 97; soggy soil of, 139; landscapes of, 188; American arrival and persistence in, 320. *See also* Great Black Swamp

"Wewissa" (Winter), *189*

White River, *21*, 26, 60, *115*, 135; Delaware at, 234, 314; branches of, 251–252

Wigwam, as derogatory term, 237n

Wild Cat Creek, 60

Wildlife. *See* Amphibians; Animals; Birds; Fish; Mollusks; Reptiles

Wilkinson, James: Kethtippecanuck's destruction by, 254, 258–263, 272; applauded by Scott, 255; failure of, 262–263; prisoners of, 267n, *268–269;* Indian disappearances and, 270; peace messengers of, 288; military career of, 288n

William of Orange (William III of England), 84, 85n, 108

Williams, Roger, 35n

Williamsburg, Va., 246n

Winnebago Indians, 73, 76

Winter, George, 42n; "Nan-Matches-Sin-A-Wa, 1839, Chief Godfroy's Home," 145, *145, 146;* stylistic Indian dress in art of, 188, *189*, 193, 200; "'Wewissa,' or Wesaw," *189;* untitled [Indian women on a hilltop], *194;* "Indian Burial, Kee-Waw-Nay Village, 1837," *195;* "Mas-saw in Fulton County," *208*

Wintering camp: river locations of, 20, 26, 190; Kickapoo and, 20, 264; Miami Indians and, 20, 124, 155; Seneca and, 20, 146, 303; Shawnee and, 20, 190; in Black Swamp, 20, 26, 146, 146; in Ohio forestlands, 26; women's roles in, 33, 34, 42, 46, 98–99; peltry processing in, 98, 99, 140; at Detroit, 101; disease outbreaks and, 125; Kethtippecanuck and, 140; Cherokee and, 146; Odawa and, 146; Ojibwe and, 146; Potawatomi and, 146; Miamitown New Year celebration and, 148–150; French traders in Indian households and, 150; Sally Ainse and, 151; Tacumwah and, 153, 155; alcohol and, 162; Brandt's birth in, 303

Witgen, Michael, 89n

Women, Indian: kidnapping of, 1, 3, 264, 287, 302; agricultural role of, 4–6, 13, 27–29, 319; Ohio River valley's transformation by, 4, 5, 16, 27, 64–65, 68, 138–139, 207, 283; agrarian role of, 4–6, 13–15, 27, 32, 35, 52, 57, 70, 284, 302; gender roles and, 5, 27, 28, 44, 57, 64–65, 82, 283, 296, 315–316; high-yield cornfields planted by, 5, 15, 27–29, 34–35, 35n, 36, 64, 139; Sabrevois's praise of, 5, 13, 16, 55–59; trade control and, 6, 70, 101, 170; matrifocal households of, 6, 7n, 70, 70n, 101, 101n, 117, 170, 317; cloth trade expansion by, 6, 128, 152, 163, *195;* fur trade role of, 6, 70, 97–99, 119, 151–152; three-crop system of, 6, 27, 33, 47; fruit tree planting by, 6, 14–15, 62–63; archaeology and, 7, 65–66; changing of architecture by, 7; invisible labor of, 8, 64–65, 65n, 66, 283, 319; animals raised by, 15–16; diverse skills of, 15–16; wheat crops and, 15; Ohio growing season and, 26; animal death and, 27; maize cultivation by, 27, 28, 29, 59; higher crop yields planted by, 28–29, 31, 33, 35, 37, 42, 65; plowing and, 28, 31–32n, 39, 61, 139, 141, 308, 315, 319; wetlands roles of, 33, 34, 42, 46, 98–99; vegetables provided by, 34–36, 42, 55, 64–65, 139, 142, 147; corn as staple Huron crop and, 35; intermarriage and, 36, 69, 83–84, 99–102, 103n, 127, 158, 203, 207, 317; in Virginia, 37, 65; cooking by, 37; seasonal camp work of, 49; bison hunting and, 49–50; Illinois Indians and, 50; in Detroit's Potawatomi villages, 55–56; as erased, ignored, or forgotten, 63, 64, 65, 138–139; census records of acreage planted by, 63; language deceptions and women in agrarian record, 64; household decision making by, 66; peltry processed by, 66, 207; in calumet ceremony, 70, 82n, 83; corn saved underground by, 83; food supply controlled by, 83, 207; as interpreters, 99; in Wabash area, 117, 122, 128, 170; village buildings of, 139; food bartering by, 147; chiefs chosen by, 153n; social gifts made by, 166, 187; and Heckewelder's description of ornamentation, 169; clothing made by, 170–171, 174–175, 181, 184–*187,* 194, *207, 208;* Kickapoo absence of, 284; at peace conferences, 309–310. *See also* Clothing and dress

Wood, William, 29

Woodford County, Ky., 2, 2n, 248, 248n

Wyandot Indians: as Wendat, 14; location of, 20, *225;* fruit orchards of, 64; smallpox epidemic and, 126; Fort Sandusky burned by, 129, 209; treaty line cessions and, 211, 228; at Brownstown, 218; at early peace conference, 227, 228; Miller baby adoption by, 281; at Glaize conference, 303; Aupaumut kinship and, 305

Wyllys, John, 239, 248

Wyoming Valley, 264

Young Tobacco (Piankeshaw), 212

Zeisberger, David, 94, 136n, 176

www.ingramcontent.com/pod-product-compliance
Lightning Source LLC
Chambersburg PA
CBHW031425230426
43668CB00007B/440